LOGICAL FICTIONS IN MEDIEVAL LITERATURE AND PHILOSOPHY

In the twelfth and thirteenth centuries, new ways of storytelling and inventing fictions appeared in the French-speaking areas of Europe. This new art still influences our global culture of fiction. Virginie Greene explores the relationship between fiction and the development of neo-Aristotelian logic during this period through a close examination of seminal literary and philosophical texts by major medieval authors, such as Anselm of Canterbury, Abelard, and Chrétien de Troyes. This study of Old French logical fictions encourages a broader theoretical reflection about fiction as a universal human trait and a defining element of the history of Western philosophy and literature. Additional close readings of classical Greek philosophers Plato and Aristotle, and modern analytic philosophy including the work of Bertrand Russell and Rudolf Carnap, demonstrate peculiar traits of Western rationalism and expose its ambivalent relationship to fiction.

VIRGINIE GREENE is Professor of French in the Department of Romance Languages and Literatures at Harvard University. She is author of *Cent vues de John Harvard* (2011), co-author of *Thinking Through Chrétien de Troyes* (2011), translator of *Le débat sur le* Roman de la Rose (2006), and editor of *The Medieval Author in Medieval French Literature* (2006).

This series of critical books seeks to cover the whole area of literature written in the major medieval languages – the main European vernaculars, and medieval Latin and Greek – during the period *c.*1100–1500. Its chief aim is to publish and stimulate fresh scholarship and criticism on medieval literature, special emphasis being placed on understanding major works of poetry, prose, and drama in relation to the contemporary culture and learning which fostered them.

LOGICAL FICTIONS IN MEDIEVAL LITERATURE AND PHILOSOPHY

VIRGINIE GREENE

CAMBRIDGE
UNIVERSITY PRESS

CAMBRIDGE
UNIVERSITY PRESS

University Printing House, Cambridge CB2 8BS, United Kingdom

Cambridge University Press is part of the University of Cambridge.

It furthers the University's mission by disseminating knowledge in the pursuit of
education, learning and research at the highest international levels of excellence.

www.cambridge.org
Information on this title: www.cambridge.org/9781107068742

© Virginie Greene 2014

First published 2014

Printed in the United Kingdom by Clays, St Ives plc

A catalogue record for this publication is available from the British Library

Library of Congress Cataloguing in Publication data
Greene, Virginie Elisabeth, 1959–
Logical fictions in medieval literature and philosophy / Virginie Greene.
pages   cm – (Cambridge studies in medieval literature ; 93)
ISBN 978-1-107-06874-2 (hardback)
1. French literature – To 1500 – History and criticism.   2. Latin literature – History
and criticism.   3. Literature – Philosophy.   4. Philosophy, Medieval.   5. Logic in
literature.   6. Dialectic in literature.   I. Title.
PQ151.G74   2014
840.9′001–dc23
2014018780

ISBN 978-1-107-06874-2 Hardback

To Matilda, Irit, and Zrinka.

Contents

Tables

Acknowledgments

I am not good at explaining what I am doing. To those who, nonetheless, have listened to the explanation I attempted, and often failed to provide, I owe much, as well as to those who helped me on specific issues or encouraged me in various ways. I thank Ron Akehurst, Catherine Brown, Gennaro Chierchia, Daniel Donoghue, Noah Guynn, Daniel Heller-Roazen, Anna Klosowska, Simone Marchesi, John Marenbon, Hugo Moreno, Laure Murat, Nick Nesbitt, Steve Nichols, Michael Puett, James Simpson, Daniel Smail, Vance Smith, Jacob Vance, Nicholas Watson, John Woods, Michel Zink, and Jan Ziolkowski. I owe much to the pioneer works of Gene Vance, but I cannot thank him any more.

A special thank to my fellow "girls of Chrétien," Sarah Kay, Sharon Kinoshita, Peggy McCracken, and Zrinka Stahuljak: working with them on another book project helped me not to abandon this one. I thank Sarah Kay also for the generous intellectual and professional support she has given me for many years. I thank my colleagues and students in the Department of Romance Languages and Literatures at Harvard for their individual and collective energy, good humor, and pleasant company. I thank in particular Janet Beizer, Tom Conley, Verena Conley, Mary Gaylord, Alice Jardine, Christie McDonald, and Susan Suleiman for their support and advice. I thank my research assistants, Michael McLaughlin and Stefanie Goyette, who checked, ordered, and formatted my chapters and bibliography. I thank Stefanie for her heroic help at the last hour, and for having greatly contributed to the improvement of my English and the clarification of my argument. I thank the two anonymous readers of the manuscript for the crucial feedback they provided me. I thank Linda Bree and Anna Bond from Cambridge University Press for their care and professionalism. I thank Roberto Rey Agudo for his hospitality, and Beatriz Rey Kleiman for playing with me. I thank Alan Greene, my husband, for his presence, companionship, and *conseil*.

Friendship is one of the issues I address in this book. I have dedicated it to Matilda Bruckner, Irit Kleiman, and Zrinka Stahuljak, who read and read again, and provided comments, corrections, advice, support, comfort, and attention – *vraies amies sans qui écrire n'aurait ni rime ni raison.*

Introduction

> "It seems to me that I have done you full justice in the matter," I
> remarked with some coldness, for I was repelled by the egotism which
> I had more than once observed to be a strong factor in my friend's
> singular character.
> "No, it is not selfishness or conceit," said he, answering, as was his
> wont, my thoughts rather than my words. "If I claim full justice for my
> art, it is because it is an impersonal thing – a thing beyond myself.
> Crime is common. Logic is rare. Therefore it is upon the logic rather
> than upon the crime that you should dwell. You have degraded what
> should have been a course of lectures into a series of tales."
>
> Arthur Conan Doyle, *The Adventure of the Copper Beeches*

Sherlock Holmes solves crimes and detects criminals because he is enamored
of logic – says he. The reason why Dr. Watson writes down reports of
Holmes's detecting is less obvious, but it is not because he is enamored of
fiction. Watson claims to report the truth, nothing but the truth. However,
for Holmes, Watson's narratives are "a series of tales," not because they are
untrue, but because they are entertaining instead of instructive. Holmes
associates lecture with logic, and tale with crime. He views logic as an
"impersonal thing" whereas he would probably qualify crime as a personal
matter of anecdotal relevance – a crime is just an opportunity for him to
exercise and display his art. No doubt, he considers himself the thinker or
the brain, Watson being the writer or the heart, but Watson has the last word
and the upper hand, at the price of representing himself as an idiot, which he
does cleverly.

Although it can be argued that Holmes's method is clinical and empirical
rather than strictly logical,[1] numerous modern logicians have chosen
Sherlock Holmes as their favorite example of a fiction. Holmes first
appeared as a substitute for Hamlet or Pickwick in John Woods's 1969
article "Fictionality and the Logic of Relations." The article begins with two
questions: "It is true, is it not, that Sherlock Holmes lived in Baker Street,

and false or anyhow not true that he lived in Bleeker Street? And is it not the
case that Hamlet slew Polonius, but that he did not kill Rosencrantz?"[2]
After this initial bow to tradition, Hamlet disappears and Sherlock remains
the exemplary fictional person that Woods uses to reopen the controversy
over nonexistent objects initiated by Bertrand Russell in 1905.[3]

Literary scholars are generally not interested in what analytic philosophers have to say about fiction. Conversely, analytic philosophers do not
include literary criticism in their discussion of fiction. This may be changing
as our disciplines evolve.[4] It still remains difficult to address the relation
between logic and fiction from the perspective of a non-logician or a non-
analytical philosopher. However, I believe it is important to try.

The controversy over the status of nonexistent objects mentioned above
belongs to a tradition of intellectual quarrels going back at least to Plato.
Whether they focus on the nature of things, predication, universals, the
Trinity, or nonexistent objects, to outsiders such quarrels sound like
"much ado about nothing" ("nothing" being one of their pet topics).
This impression comes mostly from the use of an abstract, technical
vocabulary and sophisticated modes of argumentation acquired through
training and exercise. This said, dismissing the "Great Quarrels About
Nothing" as futile games would be even worse than throwing the baby out
with the bath water: it would be throwing out the bathtub and the
bathroom with the baby and the bath water. This is because the quarrels
question fundamental modes of thinking allowing us to delineate things,
to assert and deny, to assess truth-value, and, ultimately, to structure
and share our experience of the world. And they do so in a fashion that
blends reasoning with emotion, abstraction with drama, and logic with
affect. Otherwise, there would be no quarrel.

Before explaining the purpose of this book, I must clarify my use of the
following terms: dialectic, logic, and philosophy. They are closely related
and share a common origin in ancient Greek thought and vocabulary. In
their Latin and modern English forms, they continue to speak "ancient
Greek" and to signal a relation to this tradition, whether those who use
them know ancient Greek or not. I will use "dialectic" in its ancient and
medieval sense (not in its Hegelian sense), to designate a way of arguing
based on analysis, deduction, and contradiction, the art of arguing in such a
fashion, or, more specifically, the third art of the trivium, within the
medieval classification of disciplines.[5] I will use "logic" to refer to a way of
reasoning (by which I mean to connect thoughts and ideas consciously), the
study of such a way of reasoning, or a discipline founded by Aristotle. I will
use "philosophy" to signify an aspiration to understand applied relentlessly

to all things, an intellectual and ethical tradition rooted in ancient Greece, or a mode of writing related to this tradition.

The purpose of this book is to address problems traditionally ascribed to logic from a literary perspective. Since the study of literature is always rooted in places and times and entwined with languages, my literary perspective comes with a historical timeline (the Middle Ages, and, specifically, the twelfth and thirteenth centuries), a geography (Northern France and the Anglo Norman territories), and specific languages (Latin and Old French). The revival of logic in the Middle Ages coincides with the emergence of Old French literature, in the same geographical area and at about the same time (the late eleventh century).[6] These two trends were not just running on parallel courses within the greater context of the "twelfth-century Renaissance."[7] Literature and logic intersected in various ways, as many scholars have pointed out.[8] I am convinced by the general thrust of their arguments and grateful for their pioneering work, which has brought to the fore a nexus of related problems treated in the literary as well as in the philosophical corpus: contradiction, reasoning, truth, human versus animal, contingency and necessity, reference, signification, knowledge. Not all Old French literary texts display a logical turn of mind, but a sufficient number of them do to justify scholarly interest in this direction. It also happens that some of the texts studied from this perspective, such as Chrétien de Troyes's romances, Marie de France's lais and fables, and Guillaume de Lorris and Jean de Meun's *Roman de la Rose*, are amongst the best known in the Old French corpus.

Although inspired by this type of studies, my book will not aim primarily at providing a better understanding of Old French literature by relating it to a larger intellectual context. My main goal is to reflect on the nature of fiction through a small corpus of philosophical and literary texts. I have to confess this sounds rather philosophical (in the first meaning of "philosophy" I defined above), although I do not situate myself within philosophy as a tradition (in the second meaning of the term), and do not write philosophy (in the third meaning of the term). My main mode of thinking and writing derives mostly from the commentary and close reading techniques literary critics have practiced from the 1950s until today.

This book project began as a study of ambivalence in twelfth- and thirteenth-century Old French romances, but evolved in unexpected directions when I decided to read some of Aristotle's logical and metaphysical texts in order to understand how the principle of non-contradiction came into existence. This move led me to consider the fictions operating in philosophical texts related to the Aristotelian tradition. I believe this aspect of my work may be the most original, and, therefore, the most problematic and tentative. Reading logic into fiction may or may not interest scholars, but it does not touch any sensitive nerve; reading fiction into logic does. Sherlock Holmes would say that it degrades "what should have been a course of lectures into a series of tales." To which it could be replied that a tale results from an operation of the mind as complex and sophisticated as logical reasoning. I would even argue (if Holmes would agree to continue listening to me) that logic and fiction are sisters born from the habit of guessing what our senses cannot perceive.[9] From pragmatic strategies, they may evolve into arts of creative thinking. We all speculate, induce, deduce, and fantasize. We are not all logicians, poets, or storytellers. Through my work on the most elaborate products of ancient traditions of thought, I hope to raise a number of questions and provoke investigations that I am myself unable to ask or undertake for they belong to anthropologists, psychologists, and philosophers rather than to literary critics. Such questions or investigations would have as objects thought processes belonging to all, and not only to a small group of exceptional minds. I recognize that my own investigation is limited to such a small group. However, with all due respect and admiration for the authors I study, I allow myself to consider them as normal humans, not immune from the common twists and turns, limitations and blind spots of human minds.

The corpus of texts I study is small and eclectic. It includes philosophical works from classical Greece and Rome, the Middle Ages, and the twentieth century. The literary corpus is limited to the Middle Ages. I tend to dwell on the texts or passages of texts that have caught my attention and imagination, and to stay with them for a long time. I wish though I could have included a few more texts, such as Boethius's *Consolation of Philosophy* and his treatise *On the Trinity*, Thomas Aquinas's comments on Aristotle's *Metaphysics* IV, Greek tragedies (in particular Euripides's *Bacchae*), and further medieval literary works. But, at some point, I had to transform my "series of tales" into a book, and stop adding primary sources.

Outline

This book is divided into three main sections, organized thematically, not chronologically. A certain sense of history may emerge within the sections, for I have tried to follow threads of thoughts through time, but I have not attempted to construe a history of logic and fiction in ancient and medieval times.

In Part I, titled "Logical fables," I study twelfth- and thirteenth-century literary and philosophical texts by Abelard, Anselm of Canterbury, Marie de France, Chrétien de Troyes and the anonymous authors of the *Roman de Renart*. I compare their ways of addressing our grasp of things, whether these authors use logic or fiction to do so. Thinking and talking about a particular thing is one of the most banal operations we accomplish every day, usually without thinking about it. However, our sense of reality as well as our imagination depends on our ways of identifying and sorting out particulars.[10] My main point in the three chapters of this section is to show that the creation of fictional particulars plays a role as important as the creation of generic categories in our apprehension of the world and its content.

In Chapter 1, "Abelard's donkey: the nonexistent particular," I look at the way Abelard considers imagination and fiction as cognitive tools, essential to the life of the mind, albeit in a subaltern position with regard to higher modes of understanding.[11] Thus Abelard allows fiction to stand as a mental space of semiotic and ontological experimentation. In this chapter, I create a neologism: the noun *adstraction*. If we understand *abstraction* as pulling (*trahere*) general ideas from (*ab*) real or fictional particulars, then adstraction is the operation of pulling the general toward (*ad*) a fictional particular. An adstraction is also the result of such an operation, in the same way that fiction is both an operation and its result. I examine adstractions created in the late twelfth century, such as the knight and the lion in Chrétien de Troyes's *Yvain* and some animal characters in the *Roman de Renart*, suggesting a family resemblance between the theory and the practice of fiction in Northern France at this time.

In Chapter 2, "The literate animal: naming and reference," I move from the cognitive aspect of fiction in Abelard to a semantic inquiry based on Anselm of Canterbury's dialog *On the Grammarian*, and Marie de France's fable, "The Lion and the Peasant." Animals are again at the forefront, for they support logical and fictional reflection on categories, reference, and naming, while at the same time provoking questions on the "human" as a category, a predicate, a subject, or a substance. I refrain from creating any further neologisms in this chapter, but manage to picture Rudolf Carnap as a character in an animal fable, with all due respect.

Chapter 3, "The fox and the unicorn: naming and existence," starts with the quarrel concerning nonexistent objects between Bertrand Russell and Alexius Meinong in the early 1900s. I comment on the use of the unicorn as an example in texts focusing on reference, meaning, and naming by Russell, Carnap, and Kripke. Then, using Kripke and Donnellan's idea that fictions have "historical trails" leading to "blocks" demonstrating their nonexistence, I follow the historical trail of the unicorn, through ancient treatises on animals, early translations of the Jewish Bible (the Septuagint and the Vulgate), and medieval bestiaries. I want to say from the start that I have not uncovered new evidence proving that unicorns exist (or have existed, or could exist), except as fictions. But my historical inquiry shows that at no point did someone deliberately decide to invent an imaginary animal species. The unicorn is an offspring of science and exegesis, not of poiesis and mimesis. I compare the history of the unicorn with the history of Renard the fox, the fictional hero of a large corpus of medieval tales, the Old French *Roman de Renart*. Although it is impossible to attribute the invention of Renard to a single author or group of authors, his stories bring to the fore the notion of fiction as human creation. I study closely a pseudo-Genesis of Renard present in a thirteenth-century rewriting of the *Roman*. This shrewd text distinguishes Belief from belief, Truth from truth, and Scripture from scripture, giving fiction its own house in the city of men. I end this chapter by returning to the debate on nonexistent objects in order to sketch a theory of fiction as a mode of thinking closely related to Western rationalism.

Part II, titled "Figures of contradiction," examines the foundational fiction upon which Aristotle built his theory of negation. The texts studied include Aristotle's *Metaphysics* (Book iv), Anselm of Canterbury's *Proslogion*, and Guillaume de Lorris and Jean de Meun's *Roman de la Rose*. The fiction in question is the figure of an opponent appearing in various debates, whether philosophical, theological, or ethical. The opponent is set up to prove that his negative or contradictory position is impossible. However, through his presence in texts that deny his existence, the opponent acquires a life of his own, installing ambivalence at the heart of the principle of non-contradiction.

Chapter 4, "The opponent," focuses on Aristotle's *Metaphysics* iv and the demonstration of the principle of non-contradiction as the foundation of logic and rationality. What interests me most in this text is the staging of an opponent, named "*ho amphisbētōn*," who does not say anything but is indispensable to demonstrating the principle through refutation. This staging results in the contradictory gesture of rejecting the contradictor while giving him shape and function. Besides being a logical and rhetorical accessory, Amphisbeton represents the opponents (sophists, poets, and madmen) Aristotle found in himself or his world and had to overcome in order to anchor his philosophy in rationality. It is not until the early twentieth century that Amphisbeton's silent speech will find a name,

Ambivalenz, coined by the Swiss psychiatrist Eugen Bleuler to describe one of the symptoms of schizophrenia.[12] This postponement did not prevent Amphisbeton from reappearing in various figures in Western philosophy. My next two chapters examine three of such figures in medieval texts.

"The fool who says no to God" (Chapter 5) refers to the biblical character who appears in three psalms, and is defined in Psalm 13:1 as "the fool" (Insipiens) who "said in his heart that there is no God." In the Bible, saying that there is no God is closely (if quite illogically) related to saying "No" to God's commands. In this chapter, I return to Anselm of Canterbury and focus on his *Proslogion*, often referred to as Anselm's "ontological argument" establishing the logical necessity of God's existence. Like Amphisbeton, Insipiens has a limited role to play in the argument. But, unlike Amphisbeton, he has something to say, if only to himself: "There is no God." This does not contradict the principle of non-contradiction, but *does* contradict the Christian principle that God is both the warrant of and the exception to the principle of non-contradiction. God is the only thing that necessarily exists.[13] Anselm, like Aristotle, struggles to demonstrate how something he views as unthinkable can nonetheless be thought of, or presented as a thought, if only for the sake of refutation. The inner sophist to be tamed has become an inner miscreant, whom Anselm attempts to trap in a position that I view as the logical space for fiction: that which cannot be thought to exist, but nonetheless can be thought.

"The man who says no to reason" (Chapter 6) refers actually to two characters in Guillaume de Lorris and Jean de Meun's *Roman de la Rose*: an allegorical figure named False Seeming, and the Lover, hero and narrator of the quest for the rose. Through his speech False Seeming presents himself as the true heir of the Liar invented by Greek logicians, and a loquacious opponent to reason, Aristotle, and God. But, the most important avatar of the opponent in the *Rose* is the Lover, for, in his dispute with Reason, he reclaims for the rational animal the right to be a fool at certain times and in certain circumstances. Reason herself admits that following or loving her may involve paradoxes and emotions as well as reasoning and judgment. Since the Lover is a first person narrator, the logical tradition that created the opponent finds itself wedded to the tradition of courtly lyric poetry and its songs about loving, feeling, and singing in the first person singular. The opponent becomes at once a paradoxical "I" (attached to two persons, Guillaume de Lorris and Jean de Meun), a plausible self that is able to reason, argue, complain, hope, and despair, and a subject representing contingency in a fictional mode.[14]

In Part III, titled "Fathers, sons, and friends," I examine some of the fictions and phantasms embedded in the philosophical tradition associated with the principle of non-contradiction. This tradition, which can be called rationalism, tends to repress or deny ambivalent affect. At the same time, like any other field of human interest and activity, rationalism fosters emotions and passions, creates circles of initiated, traces lines of exclusion, and composes its own romances. Current visions of friendship as an ideal are still influenced by the fear that the friend may turn into an opponent undermining rationality, a heretic threatening the authority of the institution holding the keys to salvation (or promotion), or a woman turning reasoning and friendship into childish games. See what Phyllis did to Aristotle?

In "Aristotle or the founding son" (Chapter 7), I present the first logician as the first philosopher to have viewed himself as part of a history. Our vision of Greek philosophy is still deeply influenced by Aristotle's invention of this history. Socrates' death gave it an ambivalent turn from the beginning, as a patricide that was impossible to forget or to acknowledge. The custom of using Socrates as an example of a man or every man starts with Aristotle. I understand this custom as the transformation of a threatening ghost into a tutelary spirit, which generation after generation of apprentice philosophers can gently tease out and tame. By setting himself within a temporal, generational frame instead of among a circle of immortal divine men, Aristotle accepted mortality as a price to pay for inscribing philosophy in human history.

In "Abelard or the fatherless son" (Chapter 8), I look at the period of Anselm of Canterbury and Abelard, when logic once again attracted minds and souls. Given what is known of Abelard's life through his autobiographical writings and other documents, it is easy to view him as a real (not a fictional) Amphisbeton or Insipiens – an opponent in all respects, arrogant and irascible, and ambivalent toward his masters and peers. However, a different picture can be drawn from his logical and theological works. As a logician, Abelard was a conciliator who tried to find a third way in the quarrel between vocalists (or the first nominalists) and realists. As a philosopher, he attempted to reconcile Aristotle, Plato, and Christ. He failed on both fronts, perhaps because of the uncompromising "desire for authenticity" that led him to question authorities and view language as deeply flawed.[15] His quest for truth *and* orthodoxy took place in a culture of heightened suspicion among the literate. Abelard inherited the quarrel between Anselm of Canterbury and Roscelin of Compiègne on the Trinity, and repeated the pattern of provocation, denunciation, betrayal, and insults that led Roscelin in 1093 and Abelard in 1121 to be tried in Soissons and recant their teachings or writings. This painful story of fatherless sons, enemy brothers, and rebellious disciples has positive aspects: it (painstakingly) rooted the philosophical tradition in a Christian ground and developed a culture of debate and criticism whose heirs are the scholars of today. Moreover, the notion of the self that was developed throughout the debates of this time (in particular the debate on the three persons of the Trinity) opened a path toward the first person experiments and the fictional subject of the *Rose*, a century later.

The ninth and last chapter, "The dialectics of friendship," is a response to Jacques Derrida's *Politics of Friendship*, as well as a way to bring together several of the threads of thought I followed in the preceding chapters. The constitution of philosophy as a patrilineal genealogy or a society of disputing brothers comes with two side effects: the erection of friendship as an ideal associated to philosophy and philosophers, and the exclusion of women from both philosophy and friendship. In *Politics of Friendship*, Derrida recognizes the problem, which is to his credit, but does not do more than open the question of friendship in the feminine – in parentheses and footnotes. In this chapter I study the constitution of the philosophical discourse on friendship in relation to the principle of non-contradiction and ambivalence, in texts by Plato, Aristotle, and Cicero. In these texts friendship tends to become a virtue practiced by great men, who are celebrated after their death by other great men – their friends. That type of friendship is immune to ambivalence and instability: the friend cannot be an enemy. In the twelfth century, the Cistercian Aelred of Rievaulx, rewriting Cicero's treatise on friendship for the cloister, reintegrates ambivalence and instability within the scope of friendship between sinners seeking salvation. In all these texts, including Aelred's treatise, friendship is gendered in the masculine. In *Yvain or the Knight with the Lion*, Chrétien de Troyes presents in a mock dialectical debate the self as ambivalent, not fully aware of its affects, able to love and hate the same object at the same time. The ideal male friends of the story (Yvain and Gauvain) get close enough to kill one another, while less than ideal friendships across genders and species still provide fictional models of friendship that work. The romance does not create a counter-discourse of friendship (something like a Consolation of Literature for women), but loosens things up a bit. That, after all, is what fiction is best at doing to philosophy.

PART I

Logical fables

CHAPTER I

Abelard's donkey: the nonexistent particular

Introduction

What is the contrary of a lion? Some may say a mouse; some may say a snail. What is the contradictory of a lion? Aristotle may say a non-lion.[1] Then we may say that the contradictory of the contrary of a lion is a non-mouse or a non-snail. Does a non-mouse or a non-snail attacking a lion have more chance to win than a mouse or a snail attacking a non-lion? And what if a non-mouse or a non-snail allies with a non-lion to attack a non-fox?

> *Li limaçon porte l'ensaingne,*
> *Bien les conduit par la champaingne.*
> *Renart regarde devant soi,*
> *Et a veü devant le roi;*
> *Et vit Tardif qui les chaele,*
> *Et vit l'enseigne qui ventele;*   (*Roman de Renart*, ll. 1553–8)[2]

> The snail carries the banner,
> He leads them right through the plain.
> Renard looks ahead
> And sees the king in the front line
> And sees Slow urging them to fight,
> His banner floating in the wind.

No one needs to have studied dialectic in the schools of Laon, Chartres, or Paris to invent such a scene. However, its comic effect relies on the juxtaposition of contraries (slow / fast, fierce / meek, big / small, aggressive / defensive, one / many), and the construction of a contradictory sequence of action, which seems to undo itself as it builds up. A lordly wolf and a noble sheep go to the fray side by side: "*Qui dont veïst dant Ysengrin / Et le mouton sire Belin*" [You should have seen Lord Ysengrin / And the sheep Sir Belin] (ll. 1539–40). Next, in martial order, appear a bear, a cat, a rat, a rooster, a hen, a horse, a dog, a cricket, a ferret, and a boar, each one named and some titled. Noah's ark gets stranded at

Roncevaux. A mad singer of tales takes Aesop for Homer. Genre, genus, and gender (what is a hen doing in the host and a rooster in the roster?) overlap in outmost confusion. At last comes *"Bruiant li tors touz esragiez"* [Bruyant the bull, full of rage] and *"Brichemer touz eslessiez"* [Brichemer [the stag] at full speed] (ll. 1551–2), standing in for a whole charging cavalry, cavaliers and mounts fused together. These unstoppable, hybrid alpha-males are led by a lonely snail, and the mighty charge all of a sudden turns into a slow-motion choreography of Achilles and the tortoise. No need for Slow to exert himself: they'll never catch up. The wind gently imparts the last blow to Verisimilitude, Truthfulness, and Consistency. This is the wind of Imagination blowing into the flag of Intellection. Unsurprisingly, the resulting action is a non-fight, since Renard escapes once more into his stronghold of Maupertuis, while the following narrative effectively provokes an enjoyable feeling of bafflement.

Fiction can be enjoyable in various ways. One of its ways is to distort our sense of reality while playing with the mental tools we absentmindedly employ to mind our serious, real business, our struggling-to-be-in-the-world-and-decipher-its-user-manual. We grasp the fact we have to struggle as a human universal; we understand "our sense of reality" as historically and culturally determined. As charming as he can be, *Tardis li limaçons* does not unsettle my sense of reality as much as does the brutal killer rabbit of *Monty Python and the Holy Grail*. *Tardis* makes me laugh because I am a professor of medieval literature. He also helps me to think historically about "my sense of reality" and the fictions that can unsettle or consolidate it, at the same time that he helps me to think about fiction as a human universal.

In this chapter I will examine Abelard's thoughts about imagination and the status of its products in the soul. This will be a little dry for a while, but the appearance of Browny the Donkey in Abelard's commentary of Porphyry's *Isagoge* will bring comic relief while introducing my own theory about fiction as a mental process of creating imaginary particulars. I will then return to the *Roman de Renart* and a chivalric romance involving animals: Chrétien de Troyes's *Yvain or The Knight with the Lion*, in order to underscore their way of imagining particulars. I will also use Bernard de Clairvaux's astute criticism of chivalric fictions to compare his understanding of imagination with Abelard's theory and Chrétien's practice.

The texts cited in this chapter belong to the twelfth century or the first half of the thirteenth century, and were all composed in Northern France, in Latin or Old French. Abelard's commentary of Porphyry's introduction to logic (known as the *Isagoge*), is dated from between 1117 and 1120, and his treatise *De intellectibus* from about 1123–6.[3] Bernard de Clairvaux wrote his

De laude novae militiae, or *In Praise of the New Knighthood*, around 1128.[4] Chrétien de Troyes's *Yvain* dates from the late 1170s.[5] The collection of tales known as the *Roman de Renart* was composed between 1170 and 1250 by about twenty authors, of whom three only are known by name.[6] Whether these texts are rooted in learned Latin writings or in popular vernacular oral tales, they reflect a common spirit of inquiry, debate, and innovation. They also share an abstract or idealistic side, able to carry readers far away from everyday life, while they foster a concrete grasp of things and incite readers to look anew at their here and now. The minds who named twenty-four sorts of syllogisms with names such as Barbara, Festino, or Bamalip belong to the same culture as the minds who invented the Arthurian realm of fiction and its heroes, Arthur, Gawain, or Lancelot.

Abelard and the quarrel of the universals

The discussion concerning the relationship between words and things that is known as "the quarrel of the universals" began with Aristotle and may appear particularly technical and obscure to the reader who is not a specialist in medieval philosophy. In his account of the quarrel, Alain de Libera stresses its importance in a short formula: "*L'histoire des universaux est une histoire du logos*" [The history of universals is a history of the *logos*].[7] It should therefore be of interest to anyone concerned with the relation between words, thoughts, and things.

Abelard's position in the quarrel can be described as a middle way between the nominalism of Roscelin, holding that universals are words, and the realism of Guillaume de Champeaux, holding that universals are things (to make it simple). Abelard's concept of "status" may not have solved the issue, but it led to a new way of considering nonexistent things and beings, such as talking animals and fictional knights. It is that side effect of Abelard's reflection on universals and particulars that will be my main focus here.

We are usually so immersed in things and words that their relationship rarely concerns us in our daily lives. There are two things standing within my close field of vision, to the right of the computer.[8] One consists of a square base supporting a long cylindrical stem crowned with a pyramidal contraption containing two glass bulbs, one of which presently produces a soft yellow light: a desk lamp. The second object consists of a round, flat, red dish morphing into a cylindrical, red vessel, out of which a disorderly mass of green stuff sticks out: a potted plant. I am usually unconcerned by these things, except when the former refuses to light up and the latter turns from green to yellow. So far I have never had trouble identifying them. I never water the lamp or attempt to switch on the plant. I never talk to them. I never pet them. There is no need for me to question their lampness or plantness.

Abelard confronted the question of "thingness" as an important issue for a student or master of dialectic in the first decades of the twelfth century. It came with the corpus of texts that constituted logic, a corpus to be learned, taught, and expanded by glosses. Aristotle had bequeathed a contradictory understanding of universals to future logicians and metaphysicians. Acccording to Libera, this has to do with the vexed relationship between Aristotle and Plato. In sum, Aristotle contradicts himself by stating that universals (such as genus and species) are and are not things, exist and do not exist.[9] Porphyry, aware of this issue, put it on hold from the very beginning of his introduction to Aristotle's *Categories*, addressed to a certain Chrysaorius:

> I shall attempt, in making you a concise exposition, to rehearse, briefly and as in the manner of an introduction, what the older masters say, avoiding deeper inquiries and aiming suitably at the more simple. For example, about genera and species – whether they subsist, whether they actually depend on bare thoughts alone, whether if they actually subsist they are bodies or incorporeal and whether they are separable or are in perceptible items and subsist about them – these matters I shall decline to discuss, such a subject being very deep and demanding another and a larger investigation.[10]

Many readers, such as Boethius, took Porphyry's dodging as a challenge. The debate about the universals turned into a productive philosophical work aimed toward building a consistent set of logical principles, proposing a consistent, rational account of reality, and salvaging Aristotle's legacy for later times.

Abelard addressed the debate in various parts of his logical works. He did not find "a" or "the" solution, but, through fighting the opposing positions of Roscelin and Guillaume de Champeaux, he elaborated an original argument that allows him to avoid equally undesirable theses: (1) Universals are words; (2) Universals are things. Between Roscelin's "sparse ontology" containing only "primary substances and wholes,"[11] that is, natural individuals (this dog and that dog, but no "dog") and whole artifacts (this house and that house, but no "house" and no walls), and Guillaume's crowded universe full of things, parts of things, sorts of things, and thingnesses, Abelard opted for a universe or an ontology in which things and non-things can at least cohabit, if not coexist, on different levels.[12] A universal is not a thing, but it is not a mere word (*flatus vocis*) either; it is a *sermo* (a word bearing meaning)[13] that has an ontological motivation (it has to do with reality) described by Abelard as "*status*," the state of being something.[14] A state is not a thing, it does not exist as things exist, but nonetheless it bears on things. No one will ever meet his majesty The Dog in all its dogginess whether in this world or in the next, but if we understand what we mean when we call a certain individual "dog" instead of "snail," it is because dogs are dogs by virtue of being dog. This sounds tautological, but it is not. By making a distinction between "dog" and "being dog," Abelard expands his ontology and universe without doubling them in a platonic fashion. Only things exist truly in this world, but they exist both in actuality and in potentiality. The way things are depends on their natural possibilities and their individual powers.[15]

In a similar fashion, Abelard sees time as a whole made of parts (years, days, hours, instants) but, unlike a house or any other concrete whole, time is a whole that does not exist altogether. As Peter King points out, for Abelard "only the present exists," while past and future are "fictitious substances" to which we attribute "fictitious properties."[16] Abelard expands on Augustine's reflections on time in Book 11 of the *Confessions*: "*praeteritum enim iam non est et futurum nondum est*" [For the past now has no existence, and the future is not yet].[17] If only the present exists in our human experience, the world of present things is what it is because a number of non-things intervene in and on it: past, future, causes, relations, and events. Last, human language is both a thing in the world (in each of its physical manifestations) and another non-thing. Or, more exactly, language produces meaningful propositions (*dicta*), which are "no real things at all" or "absolutely nothing" and do not denote real things but say something that may be true or false about the state of things.[18]

Thinking with fiction: Socrates and Browny the donkey

The main effect of Abelard's view on things and non-things is to avoid the reification of everything that can be thought and the multiplication of realms of reality. As Peter King puts it, using his own real world as a reference:

> There is no more need for a realm of special entities, propositions, to account for the fact that sentences say things than there is for a realm of promises that are embodied when somebody makes one, or timeless platonic resolutions waiting for a committee to pass them.[19]

A second effect of Abelard's view bears on the status of fiction. Abelard's relation to literature is far from obvious. It has been argued that his training in logic left little space for literature in his earlier education and that Heloise may have been for him at the least a guide in classical literature and perhaps a model as a writer.[20] There is no doubt he was a talented prose writer and a productive poet, both in Latin and the vernacular.[21] But he left no *Ars poetica*.[22] From his scattered remarks, it seems that Abelard held a rather conservative and traditional clerical view on literature in general. Literature of any kind should aim primarily toward spiritual education and edification, and Christians should not waste their time with idle *poetica figmenta*.[23] This seems at odds with the practice of writing love poems. Moreover, in his logical and ontological discussion of non-things, Abelard repeatedly mentions fictions. These discrete mentions do not constitute a theory of fiction by any means, but they do open up a field in which fiction can be located as an object of thought.

In his commentary on Porphyry's *Isagoge*, Abelard criticizes different realist positions on the universals. I will now look at a number of examples Abelard uses to illustrate his points. To demonstrate the absurdity of stating that a universal is a single thing which can be found in many individual things, Abelard resorts to Socrates, the traditional example of "a man" or "every man" or "man" since Aristotle.[24] But his argument requires a second example sufficiently individualized and different from Socrates to make their confusion (logically due to the fact that, if two individual things belong to the same universal conceived as a single thing, they would end being the same individual thing) absurd. If "animal" is a real thing, then Socrates and any single animal are the same individual. Enter Browny the donkey.

> *Vere rationalitas et irrationalitas in eodem individuo sunt, quia in Socrate. Sed quod in Socrate simul sint, inde convincitur quod simul sunt in Socrate et Burnello. Sed Socrates et Burnellus sunt Socrates. Et vere Socrates et Burnellus sunt Socrates, quia Socrates est Socrates et Burnellus, quia scilicet Socrates est Socrates et Socrates est Burnellus.* (Geyer, pp. 11–12)[25]

> Rationality and irrationality are truly in the same individual because they are in Socrates. Now the fact that they are together in Socrates is proved on the grounds that they are together in Socrates and Browny. But Socrates and Browny are [identical with] Socrates. Socrates and Browny really *are* Socrates, because Socrates is Socrates and Browny – that is, because Socrates is Socrates and Socrates is Browny. (Spade, p. 31)[26]

The whole argument (this is just the beginning) turns out to make sense, although, at first, this reader felt that she too was Browny, and was very much tempted to bray. Eileen Sweeney explains Abelard's reasoning through a metaphor:

Abelard's *reductio ad absurdum* essentially collapses the Porphyrian tree as one would an umbrella. When that common trunk connecting all the branches is taken to be a thing, all the branches become identical to the trunk and, hence, each other. Thus since animal, the genus, includes the rational as well as the irrational animal, the same thing, animal, is both rational and irrational, and Socrates and the ass become identical.[27]

While collapsing the realist tree, Abelard nonetheless sets up in the imagination of the reader a small puppet theater in which Socrates meets Browny, dances with Browny, and becomes Browny.[28] Socrates connotes a philosophical lineage going straight from Socrates to Abelard and from Athens to the Montagne Sainte-Geneviève, while Browny calls up the more humble and immediate whiff of the stables next door. Abelard never went to Athens, but probably rode on a few donkeys in his life. Whatever the ontological position of the philosopher using it is, Browny does not stand for the ideal Donkey in a platonizing sense. He clearly does not refer to any real, specific donkey either, whether or not it happened that Abelard owned or knew a donkey named Browny. However, "Browny" calls attention to the fact that some animals are apt to receive proper names and to be individualized in that way. Browny has potential as a would-be fictional character. He is in fact the hero of Nigel Longchamp's *Speculum stultorum*, or *The Mirror of Fools*, a Latin poem written around 1180.[29] The abbot's horse in Umberto Eco's *The Name of the Rose* is also named Brunellus, because, according to William of Baskerville, "when [Buridan] wants to use a horse in one of his logical examples, he always calls it Brunellus."[30]

From a purely logical or argumentative perspective, Socrates and Browny could have been called "this man" and "this donkey" or "a specific man" and "a specific donkey" or simply X and Y, where X belongs to the species of rational animal (i.e., man) and Y to a species of irrational animals (i.e., non-man). Socrates and Browny did not need to meet; the Socrates and Browny of Abelard's *Glosses on Porphyry* did not need to come into textual existence. Like any other *poetica figmenta*, they are unnecessary, but, once they are here, irrepressible. In the course of his *reductio ad absurdum*, Abelard uses the name "Burnellus" no fewer than twenty times in fifteen lines, giving the donkey a short lead over the philosopher ("Socrates" is named nineteen times). Logic set aside, the resulting text could be called an ode to asininity demonstrating that in the fantasyland of Realism (a land described by Quine as an "overpopulated universe," "a slum of possibles," and "a breeding ground of disorderly elements")[31] Browny takes over Socrates as the animal takes over the man and the genus takes over the species.

Imagination serving the intellect: Hercules's lion

In the *Roman de Renart*, Bernard the donkey is *arceprestres*, archpriest, "*Qui mout fu preudons et de pes*" [Who was very wise and a man of peace] (*Renart*, l. 2063, p. 784). He confesses other animals, exhorts them to fight the Saracens (i.e., an army of elephants, camels, tigers, snakes, and scorpions), and conducts Renard's funerals.[32] He is such a good priest and cleric that king Noble considers promoting him to a bishopric:

> *Je vos vodrai mout hennorer,*
> *Se Diex me donne retorner*
> *Que, par la foi que je vos doi,*
> *Evesques serez de la loi:*
> *Le don vos en otroi ici.*   (ll. 2077–81. pp. 784–6)

> I would like to honor you greatly,
> If God grants me to come back;
> By the faith I owe you,
> You will be a bishop in our Church:
> This I grant you here and now.

This promise will never be fulfilled in the *Roman de Renart* as we have it, but it brings back again the donkey and the philosopher, who both "could be a bishop." Abelard explains what "possible" means in the following terms:

> *"Possibile" quidem et "contingens" idem prorsus sonant. Nam "contingens" hoc loco <non> quod actu contingit accipimus, sed quod contingere potest, si etiam numquam contingat, dummodo natura rei non repugnaret ad hoc ut contingat, sed patiatur contingere; ut, cum dicimus: "Socratem possibile est esse episcopum", etsi numquam sit, tamen verum est, cum natura ipsius episcopo non repugnet.*[33]

> "Possible" and "contingent" mean the same thing. For we do not here take "contingent" for what actually happens, but for what can happen, even if it should never happen, so long as the nature of the thing is not incompatible with its happening but instead permits it to happen. For example, when we say "It is possible for Socrates to be a bishop," this is true even though he never is one, since his nature is not incompatible with it.

In Abelard's ontology, Socrates (or any competent man – i.e., human male) has nothing in his nature incompatible with a bishopric. He could be a bishop. Browny could not. He is male, which pleads in his favor but is not enough. His nature as an irrational animal does not allow him even to envision this possibility, and no one should encourage him to entertain such a notion. In the realm of the *Roman de Renart*, it is a fact that a donkey is an archpriest, and a lion the king. Therefore, Bernard should rightly aspire to a bishopric and Noble should rightly promise one to him, since it is as possible for Bernard to become a bishop in his own realm as it is for Socrates to become one in the realm of philosophical examples, which is as fictional as the realm of the *Roman de Renart*. But how does a fictional realm stand with regard to a non-fictional one in Abelard's thoughts?

In his *Glosses on Porphyry*, Abelard moves from refuting his adversaries' positions to laying out his own position on the universals, a position based on the notion of *status*, "which is not a thing," Abelard insists.[34] This done, he shifts from the question of the "signification of the universals" to their "understanding" (*intellectus*), that is from a logical and grammatical analysis to a psychological, or cognitive, study.[35] If we live in a world where only particular things exist, but according to certain states of being or *status*, how do we grasp and understand both things and their states of being? Abelard starts with the Aristotelian's assumption that "all human knowledge begin[s] with sense perception."[36] This prevents us from a true, complete intelligence of reality[37]:

> *quia homines, qui per sensus tantum res cognoscunt, vix aut nunquam ad hujusmodi simplicem intelligentiam conscendunt et ne pure rerum naturas concipiant, accidentium exterior sensualitas impedit. Deus vero cui omnia per se patent, quae condidit, quique ea antequam sint, novit, singulos status in se ipsis distinguit nec ei sensus impedimento est, qui [solam] solus veram habet intelligentiam.* (Geyer, p. 23)

> For men, who know things only through the senses, scarcely ever – or perhaps never – rise to this kind of simple intelligence. The external sensuousness of accidents prevents men from conceiving the nature of things purely. But God to whom all the things he created are plain through themselves and who knew them before they existed, distinguishes the single *status* in themselves. Sensation is not an obstacle for him who alone has true intelligence. (Spade, p. 45)

Once the philosopher has properly deplored the cognitive limitation imposed by the human condition and piously acknowledged the divine privilege of intelligence, he can develop a theory "which also emphasizes the intellect's active power to penetrate the structure of particular things and to think about them in different ways."[38]

Let us now focus on the role images and imagination play in Abelard's thought. It could be argued that mental images are the psychological counterpart of the *status* theory. We sense things; we imagine their state of being. From both operations may come understanding, if we make the effort to understand:

Sicut autem sensus non est res sentita, in quam dirigitur, sic nec intellectus forma est rei quam concipit, sed intellectus actio quaedam est animae, unde intelligens dicitur, forma vero in quam dirigitur, res imaginaria quaedam est et ficta, quam sibi, quando vult et qualem vult, animus conficit, quales sunt illae imaginariae civitates quae in somno videntur vel forma illa componendae fabricae quam artifex concipit instar et exemplar rei formandae, quam neque substantiam neque accidens appellare possumus. (Geyer, p. 20)

Now just as the sense is not the thing sensed, to which it is directed, so the understanding is not the form of the thing it conceives. Instead an "understanding" is a certain action of the soul on the basis of which the soul is said to be in a state of understanding. But the form to which it is directed is a kind of imaginary and made-up thing, which the mind contrives for itself whenever it wants and however it wants. The imaginary cities seen in a dream are like this, or the form of a building that will be made, which the architect conceives as a model and exemplar of the thing to be formed. We cannot call this either a substance or an accident. (Spade, p. 43)

In this passage, imagination appears as a convenient and versatile mental tool capable of producing forms that are neither substances nor accidents but allow the mind to "be in a state of understanding" independently of the sensory activities. Or as Lucia Urbani Ulivi comments: "On the whole, imagination is an additional instrument given to the intellect, unbinding it from the sole moment of the sensation; it appears to be a more constant presence in the soul than the senses."[39] Imagination is at work when we dream, remember, invent, plan, conceive, and abstract. It is what allows us to understand a universal name through conceiving "*confusam imaginem multorum*" (Geyer, p. 21) [a common and confused image of many things] (Spade, p. 44). That is to say, in fact, an image based on nothing, as Kevin Guilfoy points out: "Universals are not subject to sense, not because they are insensible, but because they do not exist."[40] They do not exist but they make what exists significant. In the same way, imagination makes sense out of *res ficta*, fictional things, that can either summon up a universal in all its nonexistence or a particular thing in its absence. For Eileen Sweeney, Abelard's arguments "bring abstractions and fictions much closer to each other and further from things than they are for Boethius."[41]

There is another passage in the *Glosses on Porphyry* where Abelard shows how abstraction and fiction are close for him. Once more, an animal comes to the fore:

Sic enim ad omnium leonum naturam demonstrandam una potest pictura fieri nullius eorum quod proprium est, repraesentans et rursus ad quemlibet eorum distinguendum alia commodari, quae aliquid eius proprium denotet, ut si pingatur claudicans vel curtata vel telo Herculis sauciata. (Geyer, p. 22)

> In this way, to indicate the nature of all lions one picture can be made that is proper to none of the lions it represents. Again, another picture can be applied to distinguish any one of them, a picture that denotes something proper to it. For example, if the lion is painted as limping, maimed or wounded by Hercules's spear. (Spade, pp. 44–5)

What the word "lion" evokes in Abelard's mind is of a different imaginary class than what the word "donkey" evokes. Browny is probably made up of many individual donkeys that Abelard saw, heard, smelled, and touched. It is less likely that Abelard had such a direct encounter with a lion, although royal and aristocratic menageries existed in the twelfth century.[42] The fact that he mentions "Hercules's spear" when he tries to individualize a lion suggests a bookish and fictitious encounter with lions. This distinction does not matter for his theory, but does matter for mine. If only individual things exist but can be what they are only because a number of non-things such as time, causality, possibility, universals, etc. intervene despite their nonexistence, then imagination is the only mental faculty that can turn things and non-things into a livable, sensible, and, in some measure, understandable reality. Abelard does not celebrate imagination: he presents it as a servant, like sense, of *intellectus*, understanding. Like Browny, imagination is a humble, familiar presence, carrying on all sorts of things we may need or enjoy and that can make of us better or worse persons, depending on what we make of them.[43]

Adstraction

When Abelard wants to illustrate the work imagination does, he puts on the same level: a donkey named Browny, Socrates, the lion maimed by Hercules, a chimera, a centaur, a siren, a goat-stag.[44] They may not refer to real, existing things, but they can still have a role to play in our thoughts. Abelard clearly separates the truth-value of any mental representation from its content:

> *Si autem deceptum dicat eum qui de futuro statu quasi iam de existenti providendo cogitat, ipse potius, qui deceptum dicendum putat, decipitur. Non enim qui futurum providet, decipitur, nisi iam ita credat esse, sicut providet. Neque enim conceptio non existentis rei deceptum facit, sed fides adhibita. Etsi enim cogitem corvum rationalem nec tamen ita credam, deceptus non sum.* (Geyer, p. 26)

> Now if someone calls a person "deceived" who in his planning thinks about a future *status* as if about what already exists, rather he himself is deceived who thinks such a person should be called "deceived." For one who plans the

future is not deceived unless he believes the situation to be already as he
plans. Neither does the conception of a nonexistent thing make one
"deceived," but rather the belief added to it. For even if I think of a rational
crow, yet if I do not believe in it I am not deceived. (Spade, pp. 49–50)

As long as one does not believe that a rational crow exists or has ever existed,
there is no harm done in thinking, listening, telling, or reading about it.
Tiecelin, the well-spoken crow in the *Roman de Renart*, can justify stealing a
cheese in octosyllabic couplets.[45] If I listen to Tiecelin while not believing in
his existence, I also may not agree with his justification of theft. The interest
of such non-things as rational animals, pagan demigods, and Arthurian
knights is that they can be significant without having any existential weight
or authority. Anything they are reported to have said or done is subject to
evaluation, discussion, and doubt, because they are inhabitants of a realm of
signification that is not exhausted by a referential analysis.

   According to Jean Jolivet, Abelard opposes a semantic based on signification to his master Roscelin's semantic, which is based on reference.[46]
Abelard conceives the relation between things and words as a complex
system, views language as a human convention and invention, and does
not expect signs to give an exact transposition of the natural world.[47] This
disjunction allows fiction to stand not as a degraded reflection of reality
but as a space of semiotic and ontological experimentation, as just one
possible set of non-things among many. Reflecting on twelfth-century
romances, Matilda Bruckner observes: "Romance fictions thus allow a
kind of free space for experiments – in forms and ideas – that may function
as a way to redirect and change the society it mirrors."[48] In this space,
"a chimera" does not exist any more than "the lion." But if I can imagine
"a chimera," I can abstract "the chimera." And if I can abstract "the lion,"
I can imagine "a lion" as inexistent as a chimera or the chimera. The great
gift of fiction to the human mind is the nonexistent particular, this
maimed lion that Abelard could see limping in his mind's eye, whether
or not he had seen any lion. Such an act of the imagination, I call
"adstraction."[49] Abelard's first act of the imagination concerning
the lion is an abstraction: "*Sic enim ad omnium leonum naturam demonstrandam una potest pictura fieri nullius eorum quod proprium est*"
(Geyer, p. 22) [to indicate the nature of all lions one picture can be
made that is proper to none of the lions it represents] (Spade, pp. 44–5).
If we understand this operation as pulling (*trahere*) the general from (*ab*)
real or fictional particulars, then adstraction is the operation of pulling the
general toward (*ad*) a fictional particular. Abelard describes this second act
of his imagination in the following sentences: "*repraesentans et rursus ad*

quemlibet eorum distinguendum alia commodari, quae aliquid eius proprium denotet, ut si pingatur claudicans vel curtata vel telo Herculis sauciata" (Geyer, p. 22) [Again, another picture can be applied to distinguish any one of them, a picture that denotes something proper to it. For example, if the lion is painted as limping, maimed or wounded by Hercules's spear] (Spade, pp. 44–5).

It has been observed that this is not the way imagination works and that it is impossible to imagine without particularizing.[50] For modern commentators objecting to Abelard's description of the process, there would be no reason to distinguish adstraction from abstraction. What led me to neologize is the sudden thought of a coat of arms bearing a lion. When Abelard reflects about the abstract image of a lion "proper to none of the lions it represents," he might have a shield and not an illustration in mind. Michel Pastoureau dates the apparition of heraldry in northwestern Europe from the second quarter of the twelfth century.[51] This means that it was during Abelard's lifetime that individuals and groups started to use consistently certain patterns of forms, figures, and colors to identify themselves on the battlefield, since nosepieces and chain mail hoods they wore hid their faces and made them otherwise unidentifiable. If heraldry does not rely on a process of abstraction, what does? Abelard could conceive an abstract, general image of the lion. He chose the lion because it was the most commonly abstracted animal in his day. But when he evokes the Nemean lion, he reflects on a different process of the imagination, the construction of an imaginary substance by adstraction of accidents added to an abstract, generic support. The same process is used to compose stories.

Painted lions and thoughtful knights

In 1129, not long after Abelard wrote his commentary on Porphyry's *Isagoge* and his treatise *On Intellections*, Bernard de Clairvaux lashed out eloquently against the secular knights of his time while praising the recently created order of the Templar:[52]

> *Quis ergo, o milites, hic tam stupendus error, quis furor hic tam non ferendus, tantis sumptibus ac laboribus militare, stipendiis vero nullis, nisi aut mortis, aut criminis?*
>
> *Operitis equos sericis, et pendulos nescio quos panniculos loricis superinduitis; depingitis hastas, clypeos et sellas; frena et calcaria auro et argento gemmisque circumornatis, et cum tanta pompa pudendo furore et impudenti stupore ad mortem properatis. Militaria sunt haec insignia, an muliebria potius ornamenta?*[53]

> What then, O knights, is this astounding error and what this unbearable
> madness: spending so much and working so hard for no other profit than
> death or crime?
>   You cover your horses with silk, and hang upon your cuirass I know not
> what sort of rags; you paint your spears, shields, and saddles; you adorn bits
> and spurs with gold, silver, and precious stones, and then in all this pomp
> you rush to your death with shameful madness and shameless stupidity. Are
> these military insignia or rather womanish trappings?

Knights, as portrayed by Bernard (who knew them well for, like Abelard,
he was the son and brother of some), are inclined to show off. Banners,
saddles, and shields adorned with gold, red, silver, azure, lions, eagles, or
unicorns look wonderful on the battlefield. Bernard's anger is probably
commensurate with his fascination as a child or youth for the *ornamenta* of
knighthood. He can envision the symbolic and political potential of
knighthood, once reined in for God's service. Current, secular knights
waste their symbolic power in ostentation, that is, effeminacy. The new
knights ought ostensibly to get rid of ostentation without getting rid of its
symbolism: "*Ita denique miro quodam ac singulari modo cernuntur et agnis
mitiores, et leonibus ferociores*" [Thus in an amazing and unique manner
they appear gentler than lambs, yet fiercer than lions] (*Eloge*, p. 72). The
Templar knights do not wear lions on their shields, which would turn
them into women; they are lions in their hearts, that is, real men.[54]
Bernard can imagine (that is, abstract or adstract) a lion as well as
Abelard, and move between genders, genera, and species as swiftly as the
narrators of his time. He is sketching both the ideal knight and the
decadent knight with the talent for vivid evocation that is his signature,
although he loathes the secular entertainers who seem to be a necessary
counterpart to painted knights: "*Mimos et magos et fabulatores, scurrilesque
cantilenas, atque ludorum spectacula, tamquam vanitates et insanias falsas
respuunt et abominantur*" [As for jesters, magicians, and storytellers, gaudy
songs, games, and shows, they (the Templar knights) reject and abhor
them as so many vanities and insane falsities] (*Eloge*, p. 70). Bernard will
not buy Abelard's statement: "if I do not believe in it I am not deceived"
(Spade, p. 50) [*nec tamen ita credam, deceptus non sum*] (Geyer, p. 26). For
Bernard, if you do not listen to it, you are not deceived. Fictions deceive
not by leading people to believe that nonexistent things exist but by
distracting their mind with sensual, worldly musings. As opposed as
Bernard de Clairvaux and Abelard can be in their assessments of moral
life, they both acknowledge the "working" of the imagination, and they
know well one of its predominant forms: chivalry, that is, an aggressive,

competitive culture with a vivid imagination and a keen understanding of the power of signs.

Let's do a little bit of adstraction. If you were a knight riding through the forest of Brocéliande, and if you encountered a lion fighting a dragon, what would you do? Personally, I would gallop away and let them take care of each other. That is not what Chrétien de Troyes decided Yvain was to do, even though, in the imaginary realm of courtly romances Chrétien helped to design, knights are supposed to rescue damsels, not dragons or lions, in distress:

> *Et quant il parvint chele part,*
> *vit.i. lion en.i. essart*
> *Et.i. serpent qui le tenoit*
> *Par le keue, si li ardoit,*
> *Toutes les rains de flambe ardant.*
> *N'ala mie mout regardant*
> *Mesire Yvains chele merveille.*
> *A lui meïsmes se conseille*
> *Auquel des deuz il aidera.[55]*

> And when he arrived at the spot,
> He saw a lion in a clearing
> And a serpent holding it
> By the tail while burning
> Its rump with a blazing flame.
> Sir Yvain did not waste much time
> Staring at this wonder.
> He asks himself
> Which one he will help.

Yvain decides to intervene because he recognizes in this scene a "*merveille*," a wonder, that needs to be analyzed and interpreted before its full signification can be grasped. Yvain bases his action upon reflection, although he cannot take too much time reflecting: a lion is on fire. On the other hand, Yvain is just recovering from a bout of madness, caused by his inability to make a choice and assume its consequences. He has tried to avoid choosing between being a husband and being a knight, with the result that he has lost both his wife and the companionship of knights. The fight between a lion and a dragon gives him an opportunity to make a choice and live with it. Since he better make a good choice this time, it deserves a reflective pause:

> *Lors dist c'au lyon secorra,*
> *Qu'a enuious et a felon*
> *Ne doit on faire se mal non.*
> *Et li serpens est enuious,*

Si li saut par la goule fus,
Tant est de felonnie plains.
Che se pense Mesire Yvains
Qu'il l'ochirra premierement.   (ll. 3356–63)

Then he thinks that he will help the lion,
Because one ought only to harm
An evil and mean creature.
The serpent is evil
And so full of malice
That fire comes through its mouth.
My lord Yvain decides
That, first, he will kill it.

Yvain's reasoning is based on a syllogism:
   Major premise: All evil creatures must be killed
   Minor premise: This serpent is an evil creature
   Conclusion: This serpent must be killed.[56]
Would a real knight of the twelfth century use a syllogism? Would a
twelfth-century courtly audience recognize a syllogism? For one thing,
some syllogisms are like prose: as Molière's *bourgeois gentilhomme*, we
practice them without knowing we do. However, in this case, since the
author insists on the thought process of his hero, it is likely that he (the
author) knows something about syllogisms, which he should if he went
through the trivium. Another reason why the language of the schools
(scholastic Latin) could be translated into Old French romances is that
medieval logic does not use a formalized language like modern logic, but a
"metalanguage" describing the rules and laws of logic in common Latin.[57]
Moreover, syllogism meets common sense (sometimes), and many
unschooled members of the audience could have agreed on the soundness
of Yvain's reasoning from a practical perspective. If you encounter two
dangers, take care of the greater one first. A dragon spitting fire is
obviously more dangerous than a lion who is not spitting fire. Finally,
bestiaries and their peculiar form of biblical exegesis give a clear answer to
such dilemmas: lions are good; dragons are bad. Yvain's inference that the
dragon spits fire because it is full of malice demonstrates his bookishness.[58]
Whether he uses syllogism, common sense, or Christian exegesis, Yvain
proves that he is now back in a world that is not just wild. A mad man
inhabits a wild world. A sensible, rational man inhabits a meaningful
world. The process of adstraction Chrétien uses to write this passage
brings together the three types of reasoning mentioned above within a
specific man confronting a specific dilemma.

This is fine and good for the dragon, but what about the lion? Yvain decides at first to help it for a contingent reason: the adversary of the lion being an obviously evil beast, it makes sense to fight it, which entails rescuing the lion. This does not mean that the lion ought to be rescued. While he is both attacking the dragon and avoiding being torched, Yvain continues to think about the issue:

> *Se li lions aprés l'assaut,*
> *De la bataille ne li faut.*
> *Mais quoi qu'il en aviegne aprés,*
> *Aidier li vaurra il adés,*
> *Que pités l'en semont et prie*
> *Qu'il faiche secours et aÿe*
> *A la beste gentil et franche.* (ll. 3369–75)

> If the lion attacks him afterward
> He will not refuse the fight.
> But whatever may come out of it,
> He wants to help him now,
> For pity urges and begs him
> To help and rescue
> The noble and generous beast.

Yvain is aware that the lion is "the mightiest of beasts," hence a dangerous animal.[59] But he cannot help feeling pity for it and attributing to it the virtue of nobility. Thus he humanizes the lion even before the lion acts humanely. Yvain's sympathy for the lion is presented as an intuition, an internal urge. Killing the dragon is justified by reasoning; helping the lion is justified by feeling. We can observe in this passage a move from a logical argument toward a psychological one, similar to the move made by Abelard in his glosses on Porphyry's *Isagoge*. Whether his thought process is logical or psychological, Yvain resolves the problem of universals by thinking about universals (e.g., the *status* of lions and dragons, as Abelard would say) and attacking or defending particulars. Thinking does not prevent him from acting; it helps him to act rationally, as much as a human being can act rationally.

It may seem odd to see rationality at stake in a fight involving a lion, a dragon, and a knight. This is all idle *poetica figmenta, vanitates et insania falsa* that may lead us to believe in the existence of inexistent things, or to avoid the pain of living in the existent world by knowingly escaping to an imaginary one, or to think with simplified categories. The problem with that argument against fiction is that it can apply to abstraction as well. After all, who is more imaginative, escapist, or simplistic: Homer or

Plato? Abelard or Chrétien? Bernard paints a vivid portrait of the colorful, vain, vacuous knights that a true Christian knight should *not* be. To define a new knightly identity and propose for those new knights practical rules of behavior and principles of moral life, Bernard has to imagine "the knight." So does Chrétien, with a difference. "The knight," once fictionalized into a knight named Yvain, cannot be taken for a universal in any realist perspective. He has to be taken as a particular "non-knight," deprived of existence but full of meaning. Still, his meaning is not given at once and unequivocally. It has to be understood through a process of reflection, indicated (but not entirely laid out) by Yvain's own thought process.[60] Thus the fiction signals its own working within the narrative. This is not something that all fictions – thought, told, or written – do, or do all the time. Chrétien does it at times, with subtlety. The passage I analyzed above is one such occurrence. *The Roman de Renart* does it constantly, in a rougher way, through the conceit of speaking and thinking animals. Both *Yvain* and the *Roman de Renart* call attention to universals such as "man" and "animal" by endowing their heroes (humans and animals) with qualities that may fit or not their genera and species.

Conclusion

It cannot be claimed that Chrétien de Troyes or the authors of the *Roman de Renart* owe their creativity to Abelard's inventive answer to the quarrel of the universals. But it can be suggested that the inventiveness of twelfth-century dialecticians and the creativity of twelfth-century vernacular authors have in common a desire to conceptualize the particular without abstracting it.

The last decades of the eleventh century and the first decades of the twelfth century saw a shift from rhetoric to dialectic within clerical Latin culture. Marcia Colish talks about a "revival in speculative thought that culminates in Anselm of Canterbury."[61] For Stephen Jaeger, "eleventh- and early twelfth-century school life was a literary-poetic as opposed to an analytical-philosophical culture of learning... Its dominant arts were grammar and rhetoric, not logic."[62] To say that logic came to dominate clerical culture throughout the twelfth century is not to say that a new model entirely supplanted an old one, although twelfth-century logicians may have liked to think that way for their own discipline, nor that there is no relation between rhetoric and dialectic. However, thanks to Mary Carruthers' detailed description of the arts of memory and the craft of thought, that is, various mental techniques used by Western monks from early Christianity through the twelfth century, we can see what a different activity "thought" became with Anselm, Abelard, and their followers. It is striking that memory does not play any significant role in Abelard's cognitive theory. The five faculties of the soul that Abelard lists at the beginning of his *Tractatus de intellectibus* are: *sensus, imaginatio, existimatio, scientia, ratio*.[63] Carruthers reminds her readers that the five traditional parts of rhetoric are "Invention, Disposition, Style, Memory, Delivery."[64] She also states that she has "chosen to deal with meditation primarily as a rhetorical process and product" and not as a psychological process, since she views modern psychological analysis as too focused on "the individual and personal" to be useful for understanding medieval monastic culture, which was centered on the communal or "civic" being.[65] Her choice makes sense. However, to understand the new techniques of the mind contemporary with the revival of logic, the development of towns and courts, the advent of the knight, the invention of heraldry, and the translation of written culture from Latin into the vernacular, we may need to resort to "psychology" or rather its ancestor, the "psycho-logic" doctrine that Alain de Libera attributes to Aristotle in parallel to his ontology.[66] We may need to see the development of Old French narrative fictions in relation to logic and psycho-logic as well as to rhetoric and oral performance. We may need to reevaluate fiction as an act of the mind as fundamental as abstraction and having something to do with logic. We may need to revise our conceptual schemes with regard to our grasp of medieval reality, in order to make more sense out of our documents and monuments, texts and images. A conceptual scheme, as Quine describes it, is the most basic act of the mind: "We adopt, at least insofar as we are reasonable, the simplest conceptual scheme into which the disordered fragments of raw experience can be fitted and arranged."[67] We abstract to overcome fragmentation and we adstract in order to get back the thrill of raw experience. Insofar as we are reasonable – and alive.

In this chapter, I addressed the cognitive and ontological side of fiction, following the lead offered by Abelard in his reflection on the universals and the faculties of the human soul. Chrétien de Troyes's *Yvain* and the anonymous *Roman de Renart*, if not directly influenced by Abelard and the development of dialectic in the twelfth century, display a turn of mind germane to this development. The presence of animals in both Abelard's works and in the two romances is not mere coincidence.

"Animal" is the category of beings that raises most dramatically questions about our perception of our place in the world, and our way of referring to the world. In the next chapter, I will focus on the semantics of fiction, through texts using the categories "human" and "animal" to explore and question the relation between names and things.

CHAPTER 2

The literate animal: naming and reference

Introduction

Logic was in the air in the late eleventh century, but in a way that still remains mysterious for scholars. Historians of medieval philosophy agree that a "revival in speculative thought" occurred, culminating in Anselm of Canterbury.[1] Who were the agents of this revival? How were they related? What were the major trends or schools? No definitive answer has been given to these questions. It may not even be appropriate to talk about eleventh-century "thought," "trends," or "schools of thought" for lack of records, continuity, and distinct figures of philosophers.[2] One of the first complete books of medieval logic that has been preserved is Garland the Computist's *Dialectica*. Scholars cannot agree on a precise identification of the author, or a precise date or place for the work.[3] More recently, Yukio Iwakuma has associated Garland with the first nominalists, whom he prefers to call "vocalists," and particularly to Roscelin, Abelard's first master.[4] Whether we choose to term it nominalism or vocalism, the logic that appears in Garland's *Dialectica* is clearly separated from theology and philosophy. For Martin Tweedale, "this 'nominalism' amounts simply to the refusal to think of logic as being about anything but words, and of itself has no ontological implication."[5] If this position has no ontological implications, it still has epistemological effects, for it makes possible the development of an almost purely formal type of speculation (even if it does not use symbols) in an intellectual context that seems at first sight hostile to rational speculations.

Another important aspect of eleventh-century intellectual history is the recurrence of theological debates on issues such as the Trinity, the Eucharist, and the Incarnation, which require discussing the relation between faith and reason, and the usefulness of logic applied to theological matters.[6] Peter Damian's anti-dialectic stance ultimately meets with Garland's pro-dialectic one: both try to isolate dialectic in a self-contained space, thus avoiding the risk of contaminating faith – or dialectic.[7] But as Alain de

33

Libera points out, eleventh-century anti-dialecticians did not resist the temptation to "use dialectic against those who use it, and thus to turn it against
itself."[8] Thus Lanfranc and Peter Damian contributed to the revival of logic as
much as their opponent, Berengar of Tours.[9]

Anselm of Canterbury's barn

De grammatico *or Anselm's introduction to Aristotelian dialectic*

Anselm of Canterbury (1033–1109) managed to be both an original logician
and a creative theologian.[10] Anselm, aware the two arts he practiced could
be in conflict, was keen to draw clear lines between his different written
works and bring them to public attention:

> *Tres tractatus pertinentes ad studium sacræ scripturæ quondam feci diversis
> temporibus, consimiles in hoc quia facti sunt per interrogationem et responsio-
> nem, et persona interrogantis nomine notatur "discipuli," respondentis vero
> nomine "magistri." Quartum enim quem simili modo edidi, non inutilem ut
> puto introducendis ad dialecticam, cuius initium est De grammatico: quoniam
> ad diversum ab his tribus studium pertinet, istis nolo conumerare.*[11]

> Over a period of time I have written three treatises which pertain to the study
> of Sacred Scripture; they are alike in employing the style of question and
> answer, the person asking being designated the Student and the one respond-
> ing the Teacher. I wrote a fourth in this same mode, not without its utility,
> I think, as an introduction to dialectic, called *De grammatico* (*On the
> Grammarian*), but since it pertains to a different inquiry than the three
> just mentioned, I do not number it among them.[12]

Modern scholars view Anselm's introduction to dialectic as fundamental in
the history of Western logic and semantics. Alain de Libera calls it "the
medieval beginning of theories of signification and reference."[13]

De grammatico is a dialogue in the tradition of Augustine's *De magistro*,
featuring a vivid, although unequal, exchange between master and student.[14]
The master leads while displaying his dialectical mastery, but the student is
pugnacious, resilient, and astute. Both student and teacher are struggling with
the ambiguities of natural language (in their case, Latin) and the ambiguities of
one of the rare logical texts passed from the Greeks to the Latin world available
at their time: Aristotle's *On Categories*. The title *De grammatico* comes from
the example Aristotle gives to illustrate the linguistic phenomenon he calls
paronymy: "When things get their name from something, with a difference of
ending, they are called paronymous. Thus for example, the grammarian gets
his name from grammar, the brave get theirs from bravery" (*Categories*, 1a,

p. 3).[15] The student, who has carefully read Aristotle's discussion on subject and predicate that follows this definition, is puzzled by the contradiction it creates and initiates the dialogue with a request for clarification: "*Discipulus. De 'grammatico' peto ut me certum facias utrum sit substantia an qualitas*" (p. 145) [Student: I would like you to clear up for me the question as to whether *literate* is substance or quality] (p. 124). "Grammaticus" can be taken as an adjective or a noun in Latin, which makes the confusion even greater, thus necessitating a correct use of syllogisms and analogies. Both student and master have to exercise their ability to distinguish between different levels of understanding and to reflect on the relation between words and things.[16]

Humans, animals . . . is there a difference?

During the discussion, three different groups are called to the fore: animals, humans, and literates (or grammarians, depending on how one translates "grammaticus").[17] Thus the teacher explains that some of the propositions held by the student lead to viewing "literate" as a substance:

> M: *Nihil horum si bene meministi quæ iam diximus, aufert grammatico substantiam, quia secundum aliquid grammaticus non est in subiecto, et est genus et species, et dicitur in eo quod quid; quia est et homo qui species est, et animal quod est genus, et hæc dicuntur in eo quod quid.* (p. 155)

> T. None of your points, if you bear in mind what has been said, deprives *literate* of its substantial aspect. For insofar as something *literate* is not incidental to a subject, not only is it both genus and species, but it is also predicated in respect of quiddity; this is because such a being is both a man, i.e., a species, and an animal, i.e., a genus, and these are predicated in respect of quiddity. (p. 136)

A logical and simple way to envision the relation between these three groups is to see them as Russian dolls containing one another, from the larger one (animals) to the smaller one (literates). All literates are humans, all humans are animals, therefore all literates are animals. Conversely, not all animals are humans (but some are), not all humans are literates (but some are), therefore not all animals are literates (but some are). In *De grammatico*, the student and the teacher come upon another classification, which sets apart the categories "man" and "animal":

M. *Definitio hominis est definitio animalis?*
D. *Minime. Si enim "animal rationale mortale," quæ est definitio hominis, esset definitio animalis: cuicumque conveniret "animal," conveniret "rationale mortale," quod falsum est.*
M. *Non est igitur esse hominis esse animalis.*

(pp. 152–3)

T. Is the definition of man also the definition of animal?
S. Not at all; for if *rational animal*, the definition of *man*, were likewise the
    definition of *animal*, then to whatsoever "animal" was applicable, "rational
    mortal" would also apply; but this is not so.
T. Hence, being a man is not being an animal.

                                             (p. 133)

It is logically problematic to hold at once "all humans are animals" and
"being a man is not being an animal." However, in common thinking and
natural language both are perfectly compatible. We use the term "animal" at
times to mean a general group of beings sharing common traits by opposition to other groups such as minerals and plants. In this perspective, yes,
we are animals. But at times we use "animals" to mean "all living creatures
but us."[18] "You are a beast!" means that you are not an animal and should
not behave like one. Interestingly, "literate" does not function in the same
way in common language and thought. I have never heard literates claiming
that they were not humans, or insulting each other by saying: "You are a
human" or "you behave just like a human." This means that "literate" never
functions as the opposite of "human," as "animal" does, but introduces the
idea that some humans (the illiterates) are closer to animals than others (the
literates).[19]

    More important for my purpose is that the idea of a "literate animal"
creeps through the dialogue, as another passage shows:

M. *Ponamus quod sit aliquod animal rationale – non tamen homo – quod ita sciat*
    grammaticam sicut homo.
D. *Facile est hoc fingere.*
M. *Est igitur aliquis non-homo sciens grammaticam.*
D. *Ita sequitur.*

                                            (pp. 157–8)

T. Let it be supposed that there is some rational animal – other than man – which
    has the learning constituting literacy in the same way as does man.
S. That is easily supposed.
T. There is thus some non-man having the learning constituting literacy.
S. So it follows.

                                           (p. 139)

"*Facile est hoc fingere*" does not mean that both student and teacher conceive
a non-human rational animal as existent or even possibly existent, but that
they can easily imagine it or create a fiction of it. Does this mean they are
mentally ready for the adstraction that, a few decades later, will produce
Bernard the donkey, archpriest, and the camel who comes to Noble's court
as papal legate and honorable jurist?[20] I think so, for *De grammatico* lacks

neither humor nor fantasy. It invites the reader to practice a rigorous analysis of terms and propositions, move nimbly between categories, and reconsider fundamental questions such as: "What is the difference between man and animal?" *De grammatico* may not lead to a radical questioning of the domination of man over animals, but opens up a fictional space in which the paradoxical relation between man and animal can be exposed and left unresolved.[21]

Doing semantics in a barn

Anselm does not treat proper names as a special problem but they too creep in the dialogue through the traditional slip from "man" to "Socrates." Just after locating "literate" in relation to the genus "animal" and the species "man," the teacher adds:

> *Est etiam individuus sicut homo et animal, quia quemadmodum quidam homo et quoddam animal, ita quidam grammaticus est individuus. Socrates enim et animal et homo est et grammaticus.* (p. 155)

> But it also occurs individually, as in the cases of a man or an animal, for a given *literate* is individual in the same way as are a given man and a given animal. For instance, Socrates is not only an animal and a man, but also a *literate*. (p. 136)

"Socrates" comes at the intersection of the three defining groups as an example of the individuals that may fulfill the conditions expressed by "animal," "man," and "literate." "Socrates" is certainly not alone in this sub-group and more needs to be done to get to the point at which the proper name coincides exactly with a sub-group containing one and only one element.[22] The teacher's addition highlights one of the difficulties Aristotle's logical works contain: the status of the particular with regard to syllogisms. Jonathan Barnes explains that the Aristotelian model of syllogisms is based on the assumption that only general terms can be predicates or subjects: "all," "some," and "none" cannot be associated with a particular term such as "Socrates," "my cat," or "this woman." But, as Barnes notes, "Aristotle's followers and commentators – and also Aristotle himself – sometimes introduce singular sentences into syllogisms. They do so with no embarrassment."[23] This explains why the most famous syllogism is generally memorized as: "All men are mortal / Socrates is a man / Socrates is mortal" whereas it should be "All men are mortals / All philosophers are men / All philosophers are mortal." As we have seen in the preceding chapter, "Socrates" became shorthand in the philosophical tradition for "every man" or "every philosopher" instead of functioning as a normal proper name.

When Anselm introduces "Socrates" in *De grammatico* he insists on indi-
viduation and does not take "Socrates" as "every man" but as "a man." This
seems to be part of his effort to make the theory of predication much closer to
his experience of common language usage than the fragments of ancient logic
he has received. If we (non-philosophers) predicate at all, we do so more often
about particulars than about generals. We actually learn to predicate (at an early
age) through pointing and naming particular things.[24] To disentangle the
semantic problems he addresses, Anselm draws a subtle distinction between
signification and appellation, which allows him to explain that the term
grammaticus may, at times, call to mind a substance (a man) which it does
not signify, and, at times, signify a quality (literacy) without calling a particular
substance to mind. According to Peter King, Anselm's use of the concept of
"appellation" is pragmatic rather than semantic since it depends greatly on the
context of the utterance, as the teacher's example shows:[25]

M. *Si est in domo aliqua albus equus te nesciente inclusus, et aliquis tibi dicit: in hac
    domo est album sive albus: an scis per hoc ibi esse equum?*
D. *Non. Sive enim dicat album albedinem, sive in quo est albedo: nullius certæ rei
    mente concipio essentiam nisi huius coloris.*
    [. . .]
M. *Quid si vides stantes iuxta se invicem album equum et nigrum bovem, et dicit tibi
    aliquis de equo: percute illum, non monstrans aliquo signo de quo dicat: an scis
    quod de equo dicat?*
D. *Non.*
M. *Si vero nescienti tibi et interroganti: quem? respondet: album: intelligis de quo
    dicit?*
D. *Equum intelligo per nomen albi.*
                                                                        (p. 160)

T. Suppose that, unknown to you, a *white* horse were to be enclosed within some
    dwelling or other, and someone told you, "There's a *white* in this building";
    would that inform you that the horse is inside?
S. No; for whether they speak of a *white*, or of whiteness, or of that within which
    the whiteness is enclosed, no definite thing is brought to my mind apart from
    the essence of this colour.
    [. . .]
T. Suppose you were confronted with a *white* horse and a black bull standing
    together, and someone issued the order, "Give it a thwack!," thereby meaning
    the horse, but without giving any indication as to which he intended; would
    you then know that he was referring to the horse?
S. No.
T. But suppose, while still in ignorance, you were to ask "Which?", and they were
    to reply, "The white!", would you then gather his reference?
S: I would gather from the name *white* that he meant the horse.
                                                                        (pp. 141–2)

The logical point is to demonstrate that "white" is able in certain contexts to "appellate" a specific individual, group of individuals, or category of individuals, but does not do this constantly and independently of context. To make this point, Anselm moves away from the stock of examples he inherited from the logical tradition – e.g., "Socrates is white," "Callias is musical," – and, as Abelard does with Browny, introduces a whiff of daily life in his semantics.

Logically speaking, this does not change the argument. Textually speaking, something happens which is reflected in translations and comments. Peter King's account of *De grammatico* is clear and sober. However, when he paraphrases the passage involving a white horse and a black bull, he adds details that are not in the original Latin:

> Anselm offers examples: "man" appellates man, "brave" appellates humans (the brave ones), "white" appellates the white horse of the two animals in the stable (a white horse and a black ox) . . . Anselm draws the distinction in *De Grammatico* 14 (S 1: 161) with the examples of barn animals mentioned in the discussion above. If someone is given a stick and told to hit the animal, he will not know which is meant. (King, "Anselm's Philosophy of Language," p. 93)

The Latin equivalent of "barn" or "stable" is not in Anselm's text, which uses the term "*domo*," literally "house" or "home." Indeed, since a horse and a bull are "barn animals," they ought to stay in a barn, not in a house. This maneuver resembles what readers of fiction do: they fill the story in to make it work for them. The logician John Woods explains the "filling in" process in the following terms: "part and parcel of what it is to understand a work of fiction involves the reader's ability to fill the story in, in various places, with sentences that do not occur in the story or logically follow from those that do, but which somehow need to be true for the story to make full and proper sense."[26] In my jargon, King abstracts a barn where stands a vague structure belonging to the general category of "houses." He also abstracts a stick from the imperative "*Percute illum.*" Anselm does not say in what way the animal must be hit. The phrase "If someone is given a stick" adds an accessory and an episode into the story, and perhaps some danger as well. Can you imagine the effect of hitting a mean, black bull with a stick?

The translators of the 1998 Oxford edition of Anselm's major works, Brian Davies and Gillian Rosemary Evans, are no more aiming toward a creative translation than Peter King is aiming toward a creative commentary. However, they too felt it awkward putting a horse in a house, and proposed for "*aliqua domo*" the translation "some dwelling or other." They do not go as far as "some barn or stable" but are moving in this direction.

More boldly, they translate *"percute illum"* by "give it a thwack," moving from the literate toward the colloquial registrar. It is quite natural to do so, for if the master, the student, Anselm, you, or I were in a barn, in the presence of a horse and a bull, and told to exercise a certain amount of violence against one of them, the order would certainly not be given in polished Latin, but in a non-polished vernacular dialect. Anselm may have thought of an expression in his native Aostian dialect or in the Norman dialect talked in the villages around Le Bec, equivalent to modern English "give it a thwack." The phrase *"percute illum"* representing whatever Anselm had in mind reins in the fictional kernel and helps to fit it into the language of dialectic. Or, perhaps, Anselm had no idea what Latin terms would be appropriate for a barn conversation.

There is no doubt that *De grammatico* is a text for logicians rather than for literary scholars.[27] I stole it to show how Anselm uses his power of adstraction while he pushes logic a step further from the text he debates. It is important to note that for Anselm the most immediate materials at hand for staging a credible exchange involving appellatives are interactions between humans and barn animals. This was part of Anselm's daily life, daily language, and imagination, even if he did not have to take care of animals, just as cars are features of our internal landscape, even if we are not mechanics.

Naming animals is summoning individuals

Animals were a material help, a material problem, and a constant presence in human dwellings of Anselm's times. So it should not be surprising to find them involved in the philosophical conundrums that Anselm addresses in *De grammatico*. The question of categories and universals is an abstract, technical way to tackle the question "What is it to be human?" No serious consideration of this question can avoid the question "What is it to be animal?" and the consideration that "human" and "animal" are interdependent concepts, at times synonymous, at times correlated, at times contrary, and at times contradictory. The question of predication is an abstract, technical way to tackle the question "What is language?" Again, a serious consideration of that question ought to bring animals on the stage. Is language something that differentiates humans from animals or not? If animals could speak, what would they say to us? Could they be called human then?[28]

Last, the question of appellatives, or the way certain linguistic expressions, used in certain ways and contexts, have the power to call individuals to mind, tends to be discussed with human and animal examples, as we see in *De grammatico*, rather than with inanimate objects or plants, because we are more likely to individualize a man, a woman, a horse, or a bull than a table, a carrot, or a stone. There are no logical reasons to make a distinction between a man, a book, a stone, or a horse, as particulars or individuals. But if we take proper names as the highest index of individualization, we can see that there are only two categories of beings or items which are susceptible to receiving a proper name: animals and places. By animals, I mean living beings, including humans and any thing that may be assimilated to a living being, even if it is not living (when a boat is named, she becomes assimilated to a living being). By places, I mean portions of space or any thing that becomes a marker for a portion of space (when a pile of rocks is named, it becomes a place). Names of places and names of animals share common traits but have also distinctive characters due to the fact that life and space are not itemized in the same fashion and do not produce the same type of individuals. This is a distinction that storytellers discover intuitively when they invent names for the animals and places they tell about. Moreover, storytellers may decide to give a proper name or title to their stories, changing them either into a kind of being belonging to some genus or species, or into a kind of place on the large, ever-changing map of imaginary realms.[29]

Anselm does not develop his theory of the appellatives in the direction of the proper name, although, given the type of animals chosen in his horse-and-bull example, the denominatives "white" and "black" can be understood as proper names. The sentence "*in hac domo est album sive albus*" [there's *white* in this building] takes a different spin if "*Albus*" [White] is the name of a horse, in the same fashion as, for Abelard, "*Brunellus*" [Browny] is the name of a donkey, or, in the *Roman de Renart*, "*Blanche*" [White], "*Rousse*" [Red or Rusty], and "*Noire*" [Black] are the proper names of hens.[30]

Anselm is mostly preoccupied by the way grammatical categories relate to logico-ontological categories. The confusion between substance and quality that the word *grammaticus* creates opens up a range of related issues including the naming of and referring to an individual as individual. Anselm, with his barn example, gets close to acknowledge that individualizing and categorizing are not the same operations, and do not produce the same result. If one wants to act upon a given situation (e.g., to hit the right individual and not the wrong one), one would be better served by using individualization than categorization. If one wants to solve a problem (e.g., to calculate the correct size of a barn for a given number of barn animals, or to study quadrupeds), one would be better advised to use categorization, and avoid individualization. This does not mean that individualization belongs to "intuitive" or "pre-conscious" thoughts, below the rational radar. It means that Aristotelian logic is poorly equipped to understand it, or even to describe it, as a thought process. Categorizing produces items, not individuals. In order to obtain individuals, one needs to create a narrative out of a situation. This narrative can be minimal: "There is a horse in the barn" is enough to summon a horse. "Horses are animals," "horses have four feet," "horses can be white," "horses are not literate," etc. cannot deliver any equine individual. In *De grammatico*, Anselm went as close as he possibly could to thinking of the individual and the process of individualization in a logical fashion (not in an ethical, legal, or theological fashion). In her *Fables*, Marie de France went further than the dialecticians of her time on this path of thought, using, like Anselm, the paradoxical difference between human and animal to stage naming in action.

Marie de France's menagerie

Marie's fables and Aesopian wisdom

"Marie de France" is one of the most famous authorial names in Old French literature, although her identification with any historical figure remains elusive. The texts attributed to her have been dated from the last quarter of the twelfth century and the early thirteenth century. She seems to have been connected to the court of England, and perhaps to Henry II.[31] Her collection of fables, known as the *Ysopet*, contains 102 fables. The relation of Marie de France to Aesop is analogous to the relation of Anselm to Aristotle. Neither Anselm nor Marie had access to Greek texts. Both worked within a long tradition of rewriting, translation, and commentaries, pegged onto the shadowy figure projected by a Greek author name. Both left their mark on the tradition they appropriated. For Harriet Spiegel (editor and translator of the fables), "Marie did more than put these fables into verse; she made them her own."[32]

    The prologue to the fables starts with literates and literacy:

> *Cil ki seivent de lettruüre,*
> *Devreient bien mettre cure*
> *Es bons livres e escriz*
> *E as [es]samples e as diz*
> *Ke li philosophe troverent*
> *E escristrent e remembrerent.*   (ll. 1–6)[33]

> Those who are literates
> Should study carefully
> Good books and writings,
> And the examples and sayings
> That philosophers found,
> Wrote down, and recorded.

When Marie mentions "those who are literates," she may not have had in mind the same *grammatici* that Anselm had in mind when he tried to figure out what or whom this term may call to mind. For one thing, she writes about a century later than Anselm, and things have changed in the intellectual landscape. For another, she writes in Anglo-Norman and not in Latin, in verse and not in prose, animal fables and not logical treatises. That said, she does not shy away from locating herself and her readers within a philosophical tradition, and not only once in her prologue to the fables – which after all derive from the respectable Greco-Latin written tradition – but twice, since she also mentions *li philosophe* [philosophers] in the prologue to her collection of lais – which derive from a tradition of oral, vernacular narratives. After explaining that ancient texts were written obscurely in order to give posterity interpretative work to do, she adds:

> *Li philosophe le saveient,*
> *par els meismes l'entendeient,*
> *cum plus trespassereient li tens,*
> *plus serreient sutil de sens*
> *e plus se savreient guarder*
> *de ceo qu'i ert, a trespasser.*   (ll. 17–22)[34]

> Philosophers knew this;
> by themselves, they understood
> that with the passing of time,
> they will become more subtle
> and will know better how to keep themselves
> from what is to be avoided.

Marie practices what she describes as the custom of the ancient philosophers: this obscure passage has provoked many subtle glosses and interpretations.[35]

In both prologues, Marie describes interpretive practices that seem at first sight more appropriate to philosophy than to fables and lais. In *De grammatico*, Anselm struggles valiantly to "*gloser la letre / e de lur sen le surplus metre*" (Marie de France, "Prologue," *Lais*, ll. 15–16) [gloss the letter / and to add meaning from [his] own understanding], the text he glosses and expands being Aristotle's *On Categories*. Is there a real need to invest as much mental energy into fables and lais? Are they as difficult and obscure to understand as Aristotle's logical treatises? Apparently Marie thought so.[36] On this, she is in agreement with Leslie Kurke, whose recent book locates Aesop, as emblem of a form of *sophia*, at the root of both prose philosophy and prose history.[37] A study of Marie's fable titled "The Lion and the Peasant" [*Del leün e del vilein*], in comparison with two earlier versions by other authors, will demonstrate the level of subtlety Marie applied to her interpretive rewriting, and will focus on issues related to naming, reference, and individualization.[38]

A fable on fables: the lion disputing with a man

"The Lion and the Peasant" derives from a group of Aesopian fables in which a man and a lion dispute the superiority of their respective species. This is a translation of Aphtonius's Greek version:

> "The Lion and the Man Disputing"
> A story about a lion and a man, urging us to be honest and to refrain from boasting.
> A man and a lion were arguing. The man proclaimed the superiority of the human race, while the lion argued on behalf of his own kind. As they were contending with one another as to who was superior, the man produced as evidence the statue of a lion being defeated by a man. The lion retorted, "And if there were also sculptors among us lions, you would see more people being conquered by lions than lions by people!"
> One who deals with others honestly will win the victory.[39]

The lion's remark throws a new light on animal fables: if they were written by non-human animals, they would be quite different from the so-called animal fables we know. So can we trust the fables? Can we trust any representation? On the other hand, well... too bad for lions. Since only humans make sculptures and fables, they have some ground to boast about their superiority, at least with regard to the ability to represent. This fable, while saying that boasting is bad, justifies human boasting by demonstrating the unique human ability to represent and invent. But if we take the cue of the moral at the end and understand that the lion represents another man, are we convinced that victories can be achieved through restricting our own power of representation to fit our own biases? Does the lion represent the "honest" man, who is able to realize how biased is his own vision of things? Does the lion win the dispute? If so, what does it add to the fable that the lion represents the wisest, winning side of the dispute? Is it necessary to step outside humanity and adopt a non-human perspective in order to assess a most human trait (taking our own inflated vision of ourselves for the truth about ourselves)? Can we step outside our humanity and leave out our biases in order to show them for what they are?

Ademar de Chabannes (989–1034), a historian of Aquitaine, is the author of a collection of sixty-three Latin fables, including a version of *The Lion and the Man*:

Homo et Leo, cum inter se quaererent quis eorum esset superior, et quaererent huius altercationis testimonium, uenerunt ad monumentum, ubi erat pictum quomodo ab Homine suffocabatur Leo; hanc ostendit Homo picturam in testimonium. Cui Leo : Hoc ab homine pictum est; nam si Leo pingeret, nosset quomodo suffocasset Hominem. Sed ego dabo tibi uerum testimonium. Induxit Leo Hominem in amphitheatrum, et ostendit illi uera fide quo[modo] Homo a Leone suffocatur. Hinc dixit : Colorum non sunt opus testimonia, sed ueritate facta. Mendacium colore compositum a ueritate actorum parari, ubi est certa probatio.[40]

"The Lion and the Man Disputing"

A man and a lion were arguing about who was best, with each one seeking evidence in support of his claim. They came to a tombstone on which a man was shown in the act of strangling a lion, and the man offered this picture as evidence. The lion then replied, "It was a man who painted this; if a lion had painted it, you would instead see a lion strangling a man. But let's look at some real evidence instead." The lion then brought the man to the amphitheater and showed him, so he could see with his own eyes, just how a lion strangles a man. The lion then concluded, "A pretty picture is not proof: facts are the only evidence!"

When the evidence is fairly weighed, a colourfully painted lie is quickly refuted by the facts.[41]

Ademar's lion sounds like a member of the Vienna Circle – for instance, Rudolf Carnap saying to – or, rather, roaring at – metaphysicians, poets, Hegelians, and other liars: "Your assertion is no assertion at all; it does not speak about anything; it is nothing but a series of empty words; it is simply without sense."[42] The irony is that Ademar de Chabannes is mostly known as a very capable forger, who created ample documentary evidence to promote the cult of Saint Martial of Limoges.[43] No doubt that the relation between facts, representations, and truth was of special interest to him. In his version of the fable, he introduces an opposition between fact and image, whereas the older versions only oppose two images of reality, equally biased. Again the lion stands on the wise side of the dispute, but this time through taking the lack of representative or symbolic power of his species as a strength rather than as a sign of inferiority. By nature, lions stick to facts and are not deluded by words and images. The paradoxicality of the fable is also maintained, and even reinforced, since a Carnapean lion defending the prevalence of real facts (lions are mammals) over artistically arranged facts (lions that talk) would not escape Carnap's wrath: "Your assertion is no assertion at all, etc."

Marie, like Ademar, expands the plot and complicates the issues at stake. She stages no fewer than four lions (three real and one painted), two peasants (one real, one painted), one emperor (real), and one baron (real) in sixty-four lines. A lion and a peasant become friends. But when the lion boasts of his royal lineage, the peasant shows him a mural painting representing a peasant killing a lion. The lion asks who did the mural. Told it was a man, he acknowledges that lions do not know how to do such things. He asks the peasant to come with him and brings him to the emperor's castle, just in time to attend the public punishment of a disloyal baron who has been condemned to death, and is thrown to the emperor's lion – with immediate results. Neither the lion nor the peasant says anything about this, but on their way home they meet another lion on a deserted heath. The lion of the heath exhorts the philanthropic lion to kill the peasant, since he belongs to a race that is keen to trap and kill lions. The philanthropic lion refuses to do so. The peasant thanks him, and then the lion asks him if he still views things as he used to. The peasant agrees that his views have changed and the lion concludes by stating that what he has shown the peasant was more truthful than the mural painting the peasant showed him. The moral goes:

> Par essample nus veut aprendre
> Que nul ne deit nïent entendre
> A fable, ke est de mençuinge,
> Ne a peinture, que semble sunge.
> Ceo est a creire dunt hum veit l'ovre,
> Que la verité tut descovre.   (ll. 59–64, p. 124)

From this example we should be taught
That no one should learn anything
From a fable, for it is made of lies,
Nor from a painting, which is like a dream.
One must believe only what one sees in actions,
Of which one uncovers the whole truth.

Howard Bloch's commentary of this fable stresses its paradoxicality as a "fable that denounces even the falsity of fables." He also views the moral as reflecting a general "distrust of images and words [that] runs throughout the *Fables*, which depict a world in which meaning is often detached from intention, and in which neither the eyes nor the ears are to be trusted."[44] In this sense, this fable is the most openly meta-discursive fable of the collection, and, as such, the most philosophical for its questioning of the relation between words, images, and things or facts.

The older Greek versions implicitly question the veracity of fables and other similar modes of representation, but the medieval ones (by Ademar and Marie) make that issue explicit, both through the plot and through the moral. Thus, the fable "that denounces even the falsity of fables" demonstrates the power of narratives to call to mind ideas at the same time they "appellate" nonexistent individuals. We get more ideas from the fable as we get more characters, more events, more details such as the axe by which the painted peasant kills the painted lion (l. 11), the castle of the emperor (l. 23), the baron in chains (l. 30), the waste heath (ll. 36–7). Thus we are led to sketch a landscape that is more evocative than the bare stage of the Greek fable, which does not provide any sense of space or location except for the presence of a sculpture, perhaps of Herakles killing the Nemean lion. Ademar introduces two markers of space: a tombstone and an amphitheater, evoking an imaginary ancient landscape, which his contemporaries may have related to the Gallo-Roman ruins present in their midst. Marie medievalizes shamelessly, creating a hybrid landscape similar to the landscape of her lais, in that it includes both an Anglo-Norman topography (the mural painting, the castle, the heath), an Anglo-Norman society (the peasant and the baron), and exotic or fantastic elements (the speaking lions, the emperor).

Marie and her four lions

This expansion provides Marie with a larger stage on which more characters can be called to interact. The multiplication of individualized lions is in itself a lesson on denotation and connotation. The first line of the fable introduces the first lion: "*Ci recunte d'un liun*" [This story tells about a lion]. What comes to mind are a bunch of traits or attributes, varying from one reader to another, depending on one's personal experience with lions. For me, it brings pell-mell a mane, the enormous stone lion of the place Denfert-Rochereau in Paris, Titus (the lisping lion hero of a French television cartoon of a long time ago), Yvain's lion, Lionel (Lancelot's cousin), several Lionels I have met or heard about such as a former French prime minister, and Clarence (the cross-eyed, gentle lion in an American television show of the 1960s). My ideas of lions are all second-hand or fictional, as probably yours are and Marie's were, although she might have seen the real thing in a *menagerie*. The lion is an overfictionalized creature, which has a bearing on the way we abstract or adstract it or him. The second line of the poem puts a halt to the associative or connoting game: "*un liun / Que prist un vilein a cumpainun*" [a lion / Who took a peasant for a companion]. Since this is not a usual trait associated with lions, we quickly shift to a denoting mode, in which "a lion" becomes "this lion" to which now any traits, including atypical ones, can be attributed. In the rest of the fable, "*li lïuns*" [the lion] will function – as Saul Kripke says a proper name functions, that is – as a "rigid designator."[45] It points stubbornly toward an individual, independently of what is known or not known about the traits of this individual. The fable works because we accept this lion as an individual, rigidly designated. The other lions who appear in the story are not individualized to the same degree. Marie carefully reserves the noun phrase "*li lïuns*" [the lion] to the first one, in contradistinction with the ways the other lions are called. The painted lion appears only in one sentence:

> *Ileoc ad li leüns veü*
> *Defors la porte une peinture*
> *Cum un vilein par aventure*
> *Od sa hache oscist un leün.*   (ll. 8–11)

> There the lion saw
> A painting on the outside of the door
> Showing how a peasant, by chance,
> Had, with his axe, killed a lion.

The painted, silent lion remains "a lion," although one could argue that the trait of "being killed with an axe by a peasant" is as individualizing as "having a peasant as companion." This argument may work in logic but not in fiction. Lion 2 suffers from three disadvantages compared to Lion 1: (a) he is a fiction within a fiction; (b) he is "bestialized" rather than "humanized"; (c) he is dead from the outset of the story.

The next lion, or Lion 3, does not suffer from disadvantages a and c; on the contrary, he is presented as all too real and all too alive – particularly from the perspective of the wretched baron. Lion 3 appears in close relation to the emperor who "*sil fïst geter a sun liun*" [had him [the baron] thrown to his lion] (l. 28). Beside disadvantage b, Lion 3 suffers from the disadvantage of being introduced in the story as belonging to a human master and as being primarily an accessory to justice rather than an individual agent. Once Lion 3 has done his job, "*E il l'ocist ignelepas*" [And he (Lion 3) killed him [the baron] straightaway] (l. 31), he disappears from the story. The reader has no trouble identifying who is "the lion" who departs from the castle with the peasant: "*Li lïuns atant s'en depart / E li vileins que mut fu tart*" [The lion now departs / With the peasant since it was late] (ll. 33–4).

The last lion, or Lion 4, could create confusion, since he shares none of the disadvantages listed above for Lions 2 and 3. He is alive, not a fiction, acts on his own volition, and is capable of reasoning as Lion 1 is:

Par mi les landes trespasserent,
Un autre lïun encuntrerent.
A celui dit qu'il fet desrei
Qu'il meine le vilein od sei,
Ki seit la fosse apareiller –
U il purreient trebucher.
Autresi seivent tut si parent –
Ja l'ocireit, si le cunsent.
Li lïuns dist qu'il l(es) escharnist;
Ne suffera pas qu'il ocesist
Pur nule rien unc ne pensa!   (ll. 37–47)

As they went across the heath,
They encountered another lion.
To that one, he said he did wrong
To travel with a peasant
Who knows how to make a pit
Into which they could fall.
That is what all his kin know to do.
He'd kill him now, if he consents.
The lion says that he is kidding him/them;
He will not let him kill him.
He never thought of doing that.

Old French tolerates pronominal ambiguity more than modern French, and much more than modern English. I have maintained the pronouns as they appear in the text, translating the third person singular "*il*" constantly by "he" or "him" instead of "it" to avoid creating a distinction between masculine and neutral, since the Old French text does not make one. Lions 1 and 4 both share the same personal pronouns: explicit "il" refers to Lion 1 in lines 39 and 40 ("*il fet desrei*" "*il meine le vilein*"), Lion 4 in line 45 ("*il l[es] escharnist*"), and both Lions 1 and 4 in its plural sense ("*il purreient trebucher*"). Only Lion 1 is referred to as "*celui*" ("that one") in line 39 ("*A celui dit*"). And only Lion 1 is called "*li lïuns*" (l. 45).

In this passage, we can sort out who is who by attributing to Lion 4 a distinctive trait opposing him to Lion 1: he is not a philanthropist, as Lion 1 appears to be from the very beginning; he is a misanthrope. Although he is able to reason, he does so from the perspective and interests of his species. He does not base his deep distrust of all men on an image representing the rather improbable scene of a peasant killing a lion with an axe, but more realistically, on cunning trapping practices, by which man can compensate for his lack of physical strength. Lion 4 does to Lion 1 what Lion 1 does to the peasant with the help of Lion 3: he undermines the lesson imparted by

Lion 2, but from a lion's rather than from a human perspective. Lion 2 lies to both men and lions. To men, he conveys an overinflated idea of their physical strength and ability to fight one on one with a large beast at close range. To lions, he conveys the mistaken idea that this is how men usually attack lions. Lion 4 is a logical and reasonable lion, indeed, but that is not enough to make him win his argument against Lion 1.

Lion 1 concludes the discussion by flatly refusing to let Lion 4 kill his companion, without any logical or practical explanation. He seems to be motivated by a certainty of the heart similar to the movement that motivates Yvain to rescue the lion against the dragon.[46] This is the ultimate degree of humanization, and therefore of individualization, that Lion 1 reaches: the aptitude to act knowingly against reason, according to one's heart. This is why Lion 1 has the last word of the fable, before the fabulist adds the moral, and this is also why Lion 1 does not seem as ferocious a Carnapean as Ademar's lion:

> "Jo vu dis einz, fet li lïuns,
> Ainz que fussums cumpainuns,
> Me mustrastes une peinture
> Sur une pere par aventure.
> Mais jeo te ai plus verrur mustree,
> A descuvert l'as esgardee."   (ll. 53–8)

> "I tell you, the lion said,
> That in the past, before we were companions,
> You showed me a painting
> That happened to be on a stone.
> But I showed you a truer one;
> You saw it in the open."

The truer painting is at a first level the real scene that the lion brought the peasant to see, the scene involving Lion 3. But what is to be done with the encounter with Lion 4? The peasant saw "in the open" that a lion could threaten his life (a more pointed lesson than seeing a lion threatening the life of someone else), but also that another lion – the lion – could stand up on his behalf.

The lesson that Lion 4 taught both Lion 1 and the peasant seals their companionship, endangered not so much by their respective species as by their social difference. The whole exchange starts with Lion 1 boasting about his royal pedigree: "Li lïuns dist, 'Fiz sui a rei'" [The lion said: 'I am the son of a king'] (l. 5). The peasant, understandingly miffed by this lack of social sensitivity, turns to species discrimination: "OK you are a king, but you are only an animal, and I'll show you what we, humans, can do to you, animals." "What animals are you talking about? Lions painted on a tavern sign? I'll show you what a real lion can do to a real human." "Yeah, but that is the emperor's lion, and he does what his master tells him to do." The dispute could have continued for a long time, if the last lion had not showed up and forced them to perform their friendship "in the open." If facts are more truthful than words and images, they are still not all verifiable or quantifiable: such is the case for the extent and nature of a relationship between two individuals. This makes me think that it could be useful to add to denotation and connotation something like "internotation." "A lion" and "a peasant" become in this fable "the lion" and "the peasant" in a rigidly denotating fashion because of their companionship, which distinguishes them from any other lion or peasant, wild or tamed, reasonable or not. The lion is this peasant's lion as the peasant is this lion's peasant, in the same way that a certain lion becomes Yvain's lion, and a certain knight named Yvain becomes the Knight with the Lion.

Kripke describes the system of reference and naming that creates what he calls "rigid designators" as a historical and collective process: "In general our reference depends not just on what we think ourselves, but on other people in the community, the history of how the name reached one, and things like that."[47] Marie's fable "The Lion and the Peasant" shows that, besides its historical and collective aspects, naming involves an affective, intersubjective dimension. To be named means that one has been subject and object of affect, at least in one relationship. When we name beings that are unable to be affected, we pretend they are affected: we fictionalize them. Following the custom of the fables, Marie does not give proper names to any character, whether human or animal, but this does not prevent some of the characters, as we have seen, from being identified by common names as if they were called by a proper name. I used numeral designations for my lions by convenience and to parody the style of analytical philosophy but, at some point, Lion 1 became for me Lion the Humanheart, and that is the name he keeps in my mind.

Conclusion

In Chapter 1, I defined "adstraction" by contradistinction with "abstraction" and with regard to our various modes of thinking about things, imaginary or real and whether in general or in particular. In this chapter, instead of our grasp of things, I considered our ways of summoning individuals, through Anselm's reflection on naming and referencing individuals in common and logical language, and through Marie de France's use of fictional individuals to set up various viewpoints (the viewpoint of men, of a man, of this man; the viewpoint of lions, of a lion, of this lion). In the texts used in both chapters, humans and animals provide most examples of things and individuals, genus and species that logicians and storytellers use to develop their arguments or narratives. Rather than an anthropocentrism, I would call their fundamental position a zoocentrism, from which the human animal defines the world as the space of his domination above all other animals, as long as he forgets he is an animal – which he cannot for very long. The unstable distinction between animal and human is doubled by another unstable distinction between things and individuals. Marie de France's fable "The Lion and the Peasant" provides us a key for the main difference between grasping things and summoning individuals. When we grasp things (here is a table, there a lamp, over there a window, beyond the window there is a street, in the street people walk and cars pass. . .), we define ourselves as a non-thing privileged with a unique position of observer of things, which we do not expect to respond to us or to define us back as we define them. When we summon an individual, we define ourselves as an individual too, and we expect something back, whether friendship, hostility, or indifference (which is an affect, not a lack of affect). Adstracting is the first move toward creating imaginary realms full of nonexistent particulars, or things. The second move is a call for affect, which creates a space for intersubjectivity, or internotation, in which individuals name other individuals and are named by other individuals, call and are called – whether they are human or animals.

So far I have treated imaginary and real things or individuals without questioning their status as existent or nonexistent beings. This distinction needs to be addressed, for logic as well as fiction implies an awareness that thinking about a thing or an individual does not entail its existence, as Abelard had pointed out with the example of the rational crow. The relation between naming and existence will be the main focus of the next chapter.

CHAPTER 3

The fox and the unicorn: naming and existence

Introduction

Let us consider the following two sentences:

(1)   No unicorn is named Barbara.
(2)   Renard is the most famous fox.

Independently of their meaning or truth, these may remind readers of another sentence, which circulated among philosophers, logicians, and linguists during the twentieth century:

(3)   The King of France is bald.[1]

(3) is obviously absurd, for everyone knows that the King of France is never bald even when he is. Wig aside, it is also absurd because there is no King of France currently. But can we say that (1) and (2) are equally absurd because every one knows that unicorns and Renard, the talking fox, do not exist?

  This type of sentence has been used in the fields of logic, linguistics, and semantics to discuss reference and existence. It raises the question of non-existent objects, and the troubling fact that they can be referred to with the same linguistic and logical forms as real ones.[2] "The current King of France" mentioned on May 18, 2011 is likely to be understood as referring to an unreal person or to nothing, while the strikingly similar phrase "the current Queen of England" mentioned on the same date is likely to be understood as referring to a real person. "Hippolyte Hydulphe" is likely to be understood as ... what? It may be referring to a real or an unreal individual, or to nothing at all, but why is this not obvious? For that type of argument, philosophers and linguists usually pick names likely to be familiar to their intended audience, such as "Pavarotti" or "Sherlock Holmes."[3] Due to his lack of celebrity, Hippolyte Hydulphe's existence cannot be verified until I tell you whether he is a real person or a fictional character. In the meantime, the referential status of

(4)   Hippolyte Hydulphe is bald.

will remain a mystery for you.

The philosophical frame of my first two chapters is the quarrel of the universals, in its medieval version. In this chapter, I will use as philosophical frame the quarrel about the status of nonexistent objects that started around 1905. At the heart of this quarrel stands our relationship with the world and our ability to encounter and understand reality through reason and language. I will focus in particular on our habit of naming things, whether they exist or not.

This chapter is divided into four sections: in the first and the last, I study texts and ideas developed by modern logicians, mostly Bertrand Russell (1872–1970), Alexius Meinong (1853–1920), Rudolf Carnap (1891–1970), Saul Kripke (born in 1940), and Keith Donnellan (born in 1931). In the second and third sections, taking the lead that Kripke and Donnellan propose concerning the "historical trail" of nonexistent entities, I will compare the coming into historical existence of the unicorn and Renard the fox, using classical and medieval texts featuring them.

Reasoning on nonexistent objects

Russell versus Meinong

Bertrand Russell's essay "On Denoting," published in the journal *Mind* in 1905, is as fundamental as Aristotle's *Metaphysics* IV, Anselm of Canterbury's *Proslogion*, or Descartes's *Discours de la méthode* in the history of Western thought. This short text (fourteen pages), although addressed primarily to logicians and mathematicians, is mostly written in plain English. As its title indicates, the essay focuses on a concept, "denoting," that John Stuart Mill introduced in anglophone logic as meaning "to designate or be a name of; to be predicated of."[4] Russell starts with defining denoting phrases by a list of examples:

> By a "denoting phrase" I mean a phrase such as any one of the following: a man, some man, any man, every man, all men, the present King of England, the present King of France, the centre of mass of the Solar System at the first instant of the twentieth century, the revolution of the earth round the sun, the revolution of the sun round the earth. ("On Denoting," p. 479)

The only common point I see in all these "denoting phrases" is that they apparently point toward something, which is a vague and broad thing to do for a phrase. However, Russell soon qualifies his interest in this vague, broad notion. "The subject of denoting is of very great importance, not only in logic and mathematics, but also in theory of knowledge" (p. 479). Denoting is part of Russell's view of our relation to the world, which he presents as based on a fundamental dichotomy: "The distinction between *acquaintance* and *knowledge about* is the distinction between the things we have presentations of, and the things we only reach by means of denoting phrases" (p. 479). We are acquainted with things we perceive directly, whether they are external or internal, or, in other words, we are acquainted with what we feel (I use here "to feel" as a mode of cognition; Russell does not use this term in "On Denoting"). But we know what we think about through a logical and linguistic apparatus, which, for Russell, reaches out toward the world through the use of "denoting phrases." After establishing this dichotomy, Russell focuses on the knowing–thinking–denoting branch, leaving aside the acquaintance–feeling branch. Russell does not define what would be the equivalent of "denoting" on that side of our epistemological tree, although he states that "all thinking has to start from acquaintance; but it succeeds in thinking *about* many things with which we have no acquaintance" (p. 480). For Russell, the things with which we have no acquaintance but are able to think about are mostly real things that are out of our immediate perceptual reach, such as those that are too big, too small, or too far away, exist in the mind of other people, or do not exist anymore. We could add things that do not exist at all among the things that are known to us thanks to denoting phrases, such as some of the examples Russell introduces to present them: the present King of France and the revolution of the sun around the earth.

The main concern of Russell is to establish a logically and epistemologically sound relation between formal logic and empirical knowledge, which he attempts through finding a way to reduce any sentence containing a denoting phrase to a logical proposition devoid of denotation. Thus, for Russell, a denoting phrase such as "the father of Charles II" can be analyzed as asserting that it is true that there is a certain variable x, and only one, that has the characteristics of having fathered Charles II. This may sound uselessly contrived, but this logical reduction bases our indirect knowledge of the world on verification: everything we may think about through denoting phrases (that is, everything that does not come to our mind as an immediate perception or feeling) is verifiable, the current King of France, God, and unicorns included.

In his recent comment on "On Denoting," David Kaplan remarks, "there is something very odd about urging the epistemological importance of *denoting* at the beginning of a work whose purpose is to show that the propositions we entertain when we *know, judge, suppose,* etc. contain *no* denoting elements."[5] This oddity is what makes Russell's essay so interesting, for in the same movement that he establishes a fundamental aspect of our way of grasping things, he renounces it for a more austere one. Instead of throwing a wide net that may catch all sorts of things, including nonexistent ones, Russell imagines a fishing rod that catches only existent things.

Russell justifies his decision to reduce all propositions in such a way that they do not contain any denoting phrase by the necessity to avoid the "intolerable" contradiction that the theory of Alexius Meinong creates:[6]

> The evidence for the above theory is derived from the difficulties which seem unavoidable if we regard denoting phrases as standing for genuine constituents of the propositions in whose verbal expressions they occur. Of the possible theories which admit such constituents the simplest is that of Meinong. This theory regards any grammatically correct denoting phrase as standing for an *object*. Thus "the present King of France," "the round square," etc. are supposed to be genuine objects. It is admitted that such objects do not *subsist*, but nevertheless they are supposed to be objects. This is in itself a difficult view; but the chief objection is that such objects, admittedly, are apt to infringe the law of contradiction. It is contended, for example, that the existent present King of France exists, and also does not exist; that the present round square is round, and also not round; etc. But this is intolerable; and if any theory can be found to avoid this result, it is surely to be preferred. ("On Denoting," pp. 482–3; italics in the text)

Meinong plays the role of the curious character Aristotle created to establish the principle of non-contradiction (here named by Russell "the law of contradiction"), as we will see in Chapter 4 – a character who allegedly supports ways of thinking dangerous for the *logos*. For Russell, the danger is that by counting as objects nonexistent items included in some denoting phrases Meinong jeopardizes all that has been won by accepting the principle of non-contradiction as an absolute law.[7] Fiction invades reality and rationality collapses. The danger is so great that Russell finds an extreme measure to avoid it: discarding denoting phrases altogether, in order to filter our thoughts before we consider their objects. The goal is to make sure that there is no object of thought until it is submitted to verification and found robustly existent. Therefore there is no class of "unreal individuals" separate from the class of real ones:

> The whole realm of non-entities, such as the "round square," "the even prime other than 2," "Apollo," "Hamlet," etc. can now be satisfactorily dealt with. All these are denoting phrases which do not denote anything... With our theory of denoting, we are able to hold that there are no unreal individuals; so that the null-class is the class containing no members, not the class containing as members all unreal individuals. ("On Denoting," p. 491)

While Meinong would say "unicorns are unreal individuals," Russell would say "unicorns do not exist," which is not a simple difference in words but involves a different vision of the world, as Russell makes it clearer in another text, published in 1919, also directed against Meinong:

> In such theories, it seems to me, there is a failure of that feeling for reality which ought to be preserved even in the most abstract studies. Logic, I should maintain, should no more admit a unicorn than zoology can; for logic is concerned with the real world just as truly as zoology, though with its more abstract and general features. . . A robust sense of reality is very necessary in framing a correct analysis of propositions about unicorns, golden mountains, round squares and other such pseudo-objects.[8]

I agree with Russell about the advantage of retaining a "robust sense of reality," in general. But *my* robust sense of reality is disturbed by the fact that logicians such as Frege, Meinong, or Russell would bother "framing a correct analysis of propositions about unicorns, etc." at all. This, to me, indicates that these three contemporary thinkers had to fight ancient demons to affirm their rationalism. Rationality needs the nonexistent in order to exist, but rationalism has trouble admitting it.

Carnap's tale of the unicorn

Rudolf Carnap cannot be described as a man lacking a robust sense of reality. He was one of the major logicians of the twentieth century and a fierce champion of science against metaphysics, as we have seen in Chapter 2. In a supplement titled "Meaning and Synonymy in Natural Languages" added to *Meaning and Necessity*, Carnap resorts to a short fiction.[9] In order to demonstrate that "the analysis of intension for a natural language is a scientific procedure, methodologically just as sound as the analysis of extension" (p. 236), Carnap imagines linguists studying the German language, which they do not know at all, by questioning a native speaker of German named Karl:

> Suppose, for example, that one linguist, after an investigation of Karl's speaking behavior, writes in his dictionary the following:
>
> *Pferd*, horse,
>
> while another linguist writes:
>
> *Pferd*, horse or unicorn.
>
> Since there are no unicorns, the two intensions ascribed to the word "Pferd" by the two linguists, although different, have the same extension. (*Meaning and Necessity*, p. 238)

Carnap is not interested in the quarrel between Russell and Meinong, but in the logical consequences of discarding intensional definitions (defining words by what they mean) and keeping only extensional definitions (defining words by the inventory of what they refer to, or what they denote). However, by stating flatly that "there are no unicorns," Carnap seems to align himself with Russell: the extensional domain of the word "unicorn" is null – that is, not filled with nonexistent items. But Carnap admits that the intensional domain of "unicorn" is not null. Although unicorns do not exist, the word "unicorn" has a meaning, which native speakers of languages including a word with the same intension, such as *Einhorn* or *licorne*, can understand. Carnap shows this through comparing the definition of "unicorn" (*Einhorn*) with the definition of "horse" (*Pferd*), and then with the definition of "goblin" (*Kobold*) (pp. 238–9). In the second case, his point is to show that even if both "unicorn" and "goblin" have "the same extension, viz. the null class," they do not mean the same thing, and users of the languages in which such terms appear do not use them indiscriminately. Carnap does not develop his argument toward a discussion of the truth-value of sentences including nonexistent objects, but his examples imply that sentences such as "A unicorn is not a horse" or "Unicorns and goblins are the same thing" can be declared true or false.

It must be noted that Carnap uses bilingual examples whereas the point he makes about intension and extension does not need a comparison between languages. Examples in English suffice to prove that in a given natural language a null extension does not prevent a word from making sense and being distinguished from other words, including some with a null extension as well. The whole demonstration works as well without the German words. Their use is an effect of fiction. Carnap wants to establish the objectivity of the intensional method; therefore, his fictional linguists must appear as objective as possible. The linguists need to be ignorant of the language they study, so they are not biased by their own understanding of the language. This is not logically necessary, but makes the fiction more convincing for its intended audience.

Carnap could have simply imagined linguists who are non-native speakers of English interviewing native speakers of English through a translator, and then not bother to indicate the translating mechanism, since this mechanism is not logically relevant. One may say that Carnap consciously or unconsciously assimilated the scientific, objective position with the English language so much that he could not imagine his linguists as non-native speakers of English. But, since Carnap grew up in Germany and published his first books in German before emigrating to the USA, his choice of anglophone linguists so ignorant of German that they need a native to tell them what "*Pferd*" means may be a little jab at American attitudes toward foreign languages.

Another explanation is that Carnap, while writing *Meaning and Necessity* in English, thought his examples in German. When seeking an example of a word with a null extension class, he did not think "unicorn" but "*Einhorn*," not "goblin" but "*Kobold*." Carnap's argument demonstrates explicitly the importance of nonexistent items for understanding how natural language works intensionally and extensionally, and that the logical problems they introduce are not trivial. But the fictional setting he creates reveals something else about natural language as mother tongue and about fiction – not on a logical level but on a psychological level.

Carnap uses six German words in the six pages devoted to "The Determination of Extensions" and "The Determination of Intensions" (pp. 235–40): "*blau*" [blue], "*Hund*" [dog], "*Mensch*" [man], "*Pferd*" [horse], "*Einhorn*" [unicorn], and "*Kobold*" [goblin]. Perhaps with the exception of "*Mensch*," they all look like a segment of the vocabulary of a young child, or as if they were taken from a book for young children, perhaps a picture book or an ABC book (these words do not start with the same letter). "*Hund*," "*Pferd*," "*Einhorn*," and "*Kobold*" could come from fairy tales, legends, or a bestiary. Like medieval bestiaries, modern bestiaries for children blend real and unreal, familiar and exotic, wild and domestic animals. In any case, these German words seem to come from Carnap's early childhood, the time when he learned his mother tongue in oral, pictorial, and written forms, which is also the time when he learned how to divide the world into things, to classify them, and to tell stories about them. Since he was born in 1891, when he wrote *Meaning and Necessity* in the 1940s and 1950s,[10] these words were old acquaintances and witnesses of his first steps as a logician, for we all start as logicians.

Historical trails of nonexistent objects: Kripke and Donnellan

Saul Kripke gave the three lectures he titled "Naming and Necessity" at Princeton in 1970. They were published in 1972. Carnap is never mentioned, but a nod is given to the unicorn at the beginning of the first lecture.[11] Kripke warns his audience that the views he will disclose in the lectures are "quite different from what people are thinking today" and that some of them "may strike some as obviously wrong."[12] He then says:

It is a common claim in contemporary philosophy that there are certain predicates which, though, they are in fact empty – have null extension – have it as a matter of contingent fact and not as a matter of any sort of necessity. Well, *that* I don't dispute; but an example which is usually given is the example of the *unicorn*. So it is said that though we have all found out that there are no unicorns, of course there *might* have been unicorns. Under certain circumstances there *would* have been unicorns. And this is an example of something I think is not the case. Perhaps according to me the truth should not be put in terms of saying that it is necessary that there should be no unicorns, but just that we can't say under what circumstances there would have been unicorns. Further, I think that even if archeologists or geologists were to discover tomorrow some fossils conclusively showing the existence of animals in the past satisfying everything we know about unicorns from the myth of the unicorn, that would not show there were unicorns. (*Naming and Necessity*, pp. 23–4)

The unicorn does not appear as a childhood acquaintance in Kripke's prose as *Einhorn* does in Carnap's prose. Kripke's unicorn is a trite example philosophers use to make dubious claims about possible worlds. Kripke was thirty years old when he lectured on names at Princeton. This is not an age at which one is prone to reminisce about one's early childhood, particularly when one is about to challenge older people's theses and authority.

Kripke's point is to make a distinction between what could have been or may be one day more than a figment of our imagination, and what could not and will never be more than that. For him, the unicorn does not make the cut. Its nonexistence is a necessity, not a contingency. This may seem quite obvious to the non-logician: we all know that unicorns do not exist; therefore they do not exist; therefore they cannot exist. But for anyone acquainted with logic (even moderately), this is mere opinion. Kripke, whose intended audience is more than moderately acquainted with logic, presents the view that unicorns cannot exist as "surprising" (p. 24), which implies that most logicians of his time were inclined to grant unicorns a certificate of contingent nonexistence allowing them to strut in possible worlds as well as in fictional realms. On this matter, Kripke stands with the non-logician, which places on him the burden of finding a logically defensible explanation for his stance.

In an addendum, Kripke explains that the unicorn has two flaws that prevent it from being possible (pp. 156–7). Unicorns cannot fit into any natural species because the myth about them "provides insufficient information about their internal structure to determine a unique species." Kripke concludes: "then there is no actual or possible species of which we can say that it would have been the species of unicorns." The second flaw is that even if we discover a previously unknown species fitting the properties of the unicorn the mythical unicorn would still need to be historically related to this species, for it could have developed independently (p. 157). In other words, the unicorn fails to be a properly shaped species and to have a reputable historical trail as a properly shaped species. The first failure is what makes it impossible (it cannot exist), and the second is what makes it unreal (it does not exist and has never existed).

My robust sense of reality and my insufficient mastery of logic incline me to stand with Kripke and non-logicians on this matter. Moreover, I have never encountered a unicorn who told me, "If you'll believe in me, I'll believe in you. Is that a bargain?," as Alice did in *Through the Looking Glass*.[13] If that had been the case, with all due respect to Kripke, I do not think his argument would have prevailed against that bargain. Since it has not been the case and I am now much older than Alice when she encountered a unicorn, I admit that the possibility of my encountering a unicorn anywhere else than in a book, a film, a picture, a toy store, or a dream is so unlikely that it can safely be taken as an impossibility. As Kripke puts it, the unicorn is necessarily and not contingently inexistent.

However, as a literary scholar and a medievalist, I am not content to leave the unicorn alone without asking more questions about its historical trail as a famous fiction. First, because the discussion about unicorns (or any other fictions of similar notoriety) by logicians always comes short of explaining the success of certain nonexistent items, success marked by their fame and longevity, in contrast with others. To give an example, why did the unicorn take off and not the yale? The proof that the yale did not take off is that, most probably, you are wondering what this is and whether it has anything to do with a certain North American institution of higher education. The yale is, like the unicorn, a bestiary animal.[14] Second, because Kripke's explanation could be applied to other bestiary animals that we consider real. The bestiary description of the lion, for instance, does not fit with any species that we would recognize as a species. Which species is characterized by the fact that its offspring are stillborn until their father breathes on them? And, following Kripke, I could say that the fact that there are some animals, which we call "lions," sharing traits with the bestiary lion (for instance, the mane) is not enough to establish a historical connection between the mythical lion and the real one. One could claim that all the animals of medieval bestiaries are imaginary in a necessary fashion, despite the fact that some of them share the same name and some resemblances with animals we know for real. Or, to go the other way, one could say that, for its medieval users, all the animals of the bestiary were real.[15]

Around the same time Kripke worked on names and reference, Keith Donnellan developed a theory of reference based on "historical explanation":

> Suppose someone says, "Socrates was snub-nosed," and we ask to whom he is referring. The central idea is that this calls for a historical explanation; we search not for an individual who might best fit the speaker's description of the individual to whom he takes himself to be referring (though his descriptions are usually important data), but rather for an individual historically related to his use of the name "Socrates" on this occasion.[16]

This may seem fairly commonsensical to a literary critic or historian, but to introduce a certain sense of history within the philosophical debate on reference was a bold gesture. It opened a new perspective on the problem of nonexistent objects. Donnellan applies to Santa Claus the same method he uses for Socrates in order to show that the historical explanation can make an account of nonexistent objects by discovering a "block" in their history, such as the fact that parents tell a fiction about Santa Claus to their children (pp. 23–4), or that Santa Claus and *Père Noël* may be historically related as a tradition (p. 29). By "block" Donnellan means some fact blocking them, so to speak, from being real. Usually the type of fact that constitutes a "block" is the disclosure of a source for the object in question. If an individual or a group of individuals (a tradition) invented or authored it, then it belongs to the category of unreal objects, to speak like Meinong, or it does not exist, to speak like Russell.

Bringing together the unicorn, the golden mountain, the square circle, Santa Claus, Sherlock Holmes, and James Bond makes sense at a certain level of analysis based on their common trait of being unreal or not to exist, but it fails to improve our understanding of their role as mental tools that are shared by a large number of people and have a history. On the other hand, looking at their history without taking into account their logical and ontological aspect is also missing something important about these objects – something that may explain their appeal and resilience. To pursue my inquiry on fiction, I will now follow the "historical trail" of the unicorn, while trying to identify the "historical blocks" that demonstrate its necessary fictionality.

The historical trail of the unicorn

The unicorn is a well-documented creature. The question of its existence has been raised for a long time from various quarters, as a scientific, poetic, exegetic, iconographic, or logical matter. Moreover, it is today a fashionable, marketable item. I will take advantage of several of the numerous recent studies in unicornology to retrace the different phases of its coming into inexistence.[17]

The speculative phase

The unicorn is born out of Greek speculations about animal species living in the Far East. Ctesias of Cnidus, a Greek physician working for the Persian king Artaxerxes II in the fifth century BCE, wrote extensively on Persia, of which he had first-hand knowledge, and India, where he never went.[18] Without using the word *monokeros*, Ctesias describes a species of single-horned wild asses:

> There are wild asses in India the size of horses and even bigger. They have a white body, crimson head, and deep blue eyes. They have a horn in the middle of their brow one and a half cubits in length. The bottom part of the horn for as much as two palms toward the brow is bright white. The tip of the horn is sharp and deep vermillion in colour while the rest in the middle is black.[19]

The fact that such an interesting animal had never been brought to Persia, dead or alive, needed an explanation. The stories Ctesias heard about the wild asses are related to their wild nature, which make them impossible to domesticate and hard to hunt:

> This animal is extremely swift and strong and neither horse nor any other animal can overtake it in pursuit. It begins running slowly, but the longer it runs, the more speed it picks up as it exerts itself brilliantly. Usually this animal cannot be hunted but when they bring their young to pasture and are surrounded by many men on horseback, they choose not to flee and abandon their colts; rather they fight both with their horn and by kicking and biting. (*Ctesias: On India*, pp. 56–7)

It is impossible to find out what Ctesias modified or added to the information and stories he gathered. In any case, if the result is indeed a fiction, it is a fiction based on reflection and speculation on the natural world, and not a deliberately imagined species like Tolkien's hobbit.

Aristotle does not talk about unicorns either, but about unicorned species. They come after a presentation of the different types of feet to be found among large mammals: many-cloven feet (human, dog, lion, leopard); cloven in two (sheep, goat, deer, hippopotamus), uncloven feet (horse and mule), sometime cloven, sometime uncloven (pig).[20] Then Aristotle considers the distribution of horns in relation to the type of feet:

Table 1 Aristotle's classification of horned mammals

Horns⇒ Feet ⇓	hornless (akerōs) 0	single-horned (monokerōs) 1	double-horned (dikerōs) 2	[many-horned] > 2
[feetless] 0				
solid (askhidēs) 1	horse, mule, some pigs	wild ass of India		
cloven in two (diskhidēs) 2	hippopotamus, most pigs	oryx	ox, deer, goat	
many-cloven (poluskhidēs) > 2	human, dog, lion, leopard			

Furthermore, of animals some are horned, and some hornless. The great majority of the horned animals are cloven-footed by nature, as the ox, the stag, and the goat; and a solid-hooved animal with a pair of horns has never yet been met with. But a few animals are known to be single-horned and single-hooved, as the Indian ass; and the oryx is single-horned and cloven-hooved. (*History of Animals*, II, 499b, p. 794)

The word *monokerōs* is used twice in this passage, as an adjective meaning "single-horned" to be added to the series of cognates *keratophoros* (horn bearing), *akerōs* (hornless), and *dikerōs* (double-horned). *Monokerōs* is applied to two different species, one of asses and one of antelopes, but does not become a species of its own. In this passage, as in the rest of *History of Animals*, Aristotle fuses two ways of describing the world: the extensional way Ctesias uses to listing and describing specimens he knows directly or indirectly; the intensional way Aristotle designs by combining traits (see Table 1).

The many-horned and the feetless are not mentioned by Aristotle, because no report of any specimen can be associated with these hypothetical traits. Their niches remain empty until more news is obtained, or their impossibility as living creatures is demonstrated. The single-horned mammals appear in niches difficult to fill, but which, at first sight, cannot be easily demonstrated as impossible. Why would nature shy away from a single-horned mammal, since she does not shy away from single-hooved ones? Actually, the narwhal is a single-horned mammal, and its horn has been at time passed for a unicorn horn.[21] If modern zoology has not discovered a single-horned species of terrestrial mammals, proofs of the existence of single-horned individuals are available. The unusual adornment of certain deer, cows, or goats results from human manipulation, genetic anomaly, or accident.[22] This does not prove that unicorns exist, or are based on existing animals. It just proves that the idea of a single-horned animal emerged in the ancient Greek culture as a speculative fiction, made of two kinds of speculation: one sifting through various reports about what there is in the world, and one classifying what is known to exist as well as what is not yet known to exist but could exist. Speculations of this sort can produce accurate descriptions of real objects, but they can also produce inaccurate descriptions of real objects and descriptions of unreal objects (whether the description of an unreal object can be deemed "accurate" or "inaccurate" is a matter I leave to logicians). The unreal single-horned animal species of Ctesias or Aristotle result from a blend of accurate and inaccurate descriptions of a variety of real objects. That is in this sense that I call them "speculative fictions."

The philologic phase

The speculative fiction of single-horned animals was called into a new phase when the Septuagint translators encountered the noun *re'em* in a few isolated passages of the Hebrew bible.[23] All are included in a song: the blessing song of Balaam in Numbers, the blessing swan song of Moses in Deuteronomy, the thundering song of God in Job, the praising song of the psalmist, the prophetic song of Isaiah. The *re'em* of the Old Testament is clearly a wild animal, but it belongs to a poetic and not a narrative diction. It is not an adstraction like Balaam's ass or Yvain's lion, but a metaphor, emphasizing God's power and the power of those who worship God.[24]

Readers of ancient Hebrew do not encounter an interpretative problem about the sense of *re'em* in these passages, even if they do not know exactly to what animal it refers.[25] It indicates the power of wild, untamed nature in a positive or negative way. It is part of the wonders of the Creation and a representation of God's supreme power over nature and man. This word makes sense as long as one does not try to translate it into another language, as happened with the Septuagint, the first documented translation of the Bible.[26] In all the passages where *re'em* occurs, *re'em* is translated as *monokerōs*, except in one. In Isaiah 34:7, it is translated as *hadroi*, which means "the strong," "the powerful." *Re'em* is understood here as an animal metaphor for the human world.[27]

An analysis of these passages shows that because of their poetic or metaphoric style the problem that the translators met with the *re'em* was not a problem of reference or denotation (what is this animal?), as the readers of Ctesias and Aristotle encounter, but a problem of meaning (what does this word or phrase mean here?). The process that led the Septuagint to feature single-horned animals cannot be qualified as creative any more than the process that led Ctesias and Aristotle to write about single-horned asses or antelopes. The introduction of the noun *monokerōs* in the Bible yielded a philological fiction, which Jerome embedded in the Latin Bible.[28]

His first attempt to revise the Latin translations of the Old Testament was applied to the Psalms.[29] In Jerome's Latin rendition of the psalms "according to the Septuagint" he translates the three occurrences of the *re'em* / *monokerōs* in Psalms 21(22), 28(29), and 91(92) by the Latin calque *unicornis*, which was already in use in the old Latin translations.[30] In his translation of the Psalms "according to Hebrew," he does not reject the single-horned animal but uses three different words to name it: "*salva me ex ore leonis et de cornibus unicornium exaudi me*" (Ps. 22:22); "*et disperget eas quasi vitulus Libani et Sarion quasi filius rinocerotis*" (Ps. 28:6); "*et exaltabitur quasi monocerotis cornu meum*" (Ps. 91:11). Jerome knew that the Septuagint was consistent in its translation of *re'em* by *monokerōs*, and that this term was not representing different Hebrew words.[31] That in some cases he chose a transliteration of the Greek (*monoceros*) and in others the Latin calque (*unicornis*) may be a stylistic variation, a device that Jerome was prone to use in his translations.[32] The "*quasi filius rinocerotis*" of Psalm 28(29): 6 comes from Jerome's consultation of revisions of the Septuagint.[33] The search for an alternative to *monokerōs* betrays the translator's dismay in front of "a veritable *crux interpretum*" in the Septuagint.[34] The Greek text is incomprehensible. Jerome's *rhinoceros* does not help but does not make it worse. When he translated the rest of the Old Testament, Jerome applied the same ad hoc, cautious approach, using *rhinoceros* in Numbers 23:22 and 24:8, Deuteronomy 33:17, and Job 39: 9–10.

Jerome did not expunge single-horned beasts from the Bible, as modern translators and scholars do, probably because he viewed them both as existing creatures in the natural world and as useful symbols in the realm of representations. With regard to the natural world, he relied on the authority of classical Greco-Roman science.[35] With regard to the symbolic realm, he could rely on the authority of the Bible itself. A single-horned animal appears in one of Daniel's visions: "As I looked on, a he-goat came from the west, passing over the entire earth without touching the ground. The goat had a conspicuous horn on its forehead" (Daniel 8:5). This is the only passage of the Hebrew bible where *monokerōs* or *unicornis* would be appropriate as an adjective, but since the word *re'em* does not appear here ancient translators in Greek and Latin did not feel authorized to use *monokerōs* or *unicornis* in this passage. Moreover, this solitary he-goat appears in a vision and does not represent a species that could exist, but an idea of events to come.

At the time of Jerome, about 800 years after Ctesias, the presence or absence of single-horned animals in the world and the Book had become a minor issue, discussed in small circles of pagan, Jewish, and Christian *literati*. So far, there is no evidence that anyone deliberately fabricated the unicorn or that stories about unicorns circulated. We have seen that various operations of speculation, translation, and interpretation led to the apparition of the idea and lexicon of single-horned animals. There was room for suspicion and doubt about their existence and the possibility of their inexistence was part of the tradition from its inception.[36] They were not seen as a necessary fiction as Saul Kripke views them; they appeared as a species that may or may not exist in this world. In the realm of language and faith, they were also seen as an available sign. Yet speculation and translation did not suffice to lend the single-horned animal a distinctive identity, to make it easier to remember and pass on. To be detached from its scientific and biblical sources, it needed a narrative, a picture, a poem, or any other mental form of this kind. It received it from exegesis.

The exegetic phase

Exegesis can be defined as the answer to the question: "How could this mean that?" From a rationalist perspective, it is a hopelessly biased mode of thinking.[37] The relevant questions are "What is this?," "What is there?," "Why?," "What for?," or "What does this mean?" but not "How could this mean that?" And yet, this question has been productive for many centuries, and it still is in theology and literary criticism. We also use it unconsciously to process numerous utterances, rephrasing what we hear or read according to our expectations, rather than according to what was said or written. In most cases, this works well enough to spare us the effort of meticulous decoding, for what is said or written is not often unexpected.

From the perspective of believers, exegesis redirects our attention from the self toward God. Therefore the question "How this [anything that can be expressed in human language] could mean that [God, which cannot be

expressed in human language]?" is not only a relevant question, but the
most important question to ask, even if it is applied to a minor detail.
Nothing can be minor or insignificant in the Creation from the perspective
of its Creator.[38] It is also a dangerous question, for the divine "that" proposed
by one exegete can always be called a pseudo "that" or a mere "this" by
another exegete. Any exegesis is liable to be deemed self-directed instead of
God-directed, whether the self is an individual, a group, or an institution.
Jerome's wavering between rhinoceros, monoceros, and unicorn reveals the
anxieties that accompanied the controversial mission he undertook: to lay a
sound philological ground for future exegetes.[39]

Jewish exegesis had prepared the ground by working on the figurative
meanings (mostly power and strength) associated with the horns of various
animals.[40] Early Christian exegesis added its own interpretations in a "piling
up" of meanings to choose from in various contexts. The exegetic meanings
of the biblical unicorn can be classified under five major themes: (1) A sign
of the Cross; (2) A symbol of Christ as a single son united with the Father;
(3) An image of the Patriarchs, Prophets, and Christ as believers in a single
god; (4) A sign of the unity of the faith; (5) An image of the proud raising
their horn, the Jews attached to one testament, and evil.[41]

One of the earliest examples of the unicorn interpreted as a sign of the
Cross occurs in Tertullian (c.160–c.225).[42] Tertullian did not envision the
unicorn as a distinct species or even as a whole animal, but as a pointer
toward what was still in the first centuries of the Christian era an astonishing
event: the crucifixion of a god made man.[43] Tertullian contributed to the
eventual transformation of the unicorn into a symbol of Christ through a
poetic reworking of metaphors and a quest for indices in the old text
pointing toward the new one.

If the Church Fathers had had a monopoly on exegesis, it is unlikely that
the unicorn would have left the footnotes of their commentaries and
treatises against heresies to populate Alexius Meinong's jungle of nonexistent objects. All the scholars who have studied the unicorn agree that it owes
its popularity in the Western tradition mostly to the text known as the
Physiologus.[44]

The fabulous phase

It is in the *Physiologus* that the noun "unicorn" was associated with a single
species, attached to an emblematic narrative, and represented in pictures.
Thus, an object of thought became an imaginary acquaintance, that is, a
versatile, transportable item, usable in various forms of expression, for

various purposes, by people belonging to various social groups, with various degrees of education and literacy. Without the speculative, interpretative, and exegetic working on the *monokerōs/unicornis* I have traced so far, the *Physiologus* would not have invented the unicorn. But without the *Physiologus*'s treatment of the materials it inherited from Greco-Roman science and Christian interpretation, the unicorn would not have survived long enough to bother Bertrand Russell or haunt Rudolf Carnap, for it would not have become fabulous.

The *Physiologus* was composed probably in Alexandria, or at least in Egypt, between 200 and 400, by an anonymous author, nicknamed in the text itself "Physiologus," and identified during the Middle Ages as Solomon, Aristotle, Saint Basil, Saint Ambrose, Saint Jerome, Saint John Chrysostom, and a few others.[45] It was never accepted as a "canonical" authority by the Church,[46] but it may be its disputable authority that made it such a popular book. Alain Boureau explains the success of Peter the Lombard's *Sentences* as a handbook of theology by the fact that it "could be legitimately contested, without running the risk of being blasphemous or irreverent, without the contortions necessary to take some distance from Augustine."[47] In a similar fashion, the *Physiologus* was translated in many languages from its original Greek and modified according to the needs of its users.[48] It was also frequently illustrated.[49] Recycled in Isidore of Seville's *Etymologies* and Honorius of Autun's *De imagine mundi*, it became the main source of the medieval bestiaries, and thus continued to be a reference until the fourteenth century.[50]

One could think of the *Physiologus* as a medieval Wikipedia, in which users added, modified, or suppressed elements of knowledge, opinion, or fiction within a fixed format. But the *Physiologus* is not an encyclopedia of natural history. While it is organized as an inventory of natural things (mostly animals, a few stones, an occasional tree), the text under each entry is designed as a helper to "the non-literal interpretation of the Old Testament."[51] The *Physiologus* can be considered as a kind of exegetic manual, in which the sacred text is presented piecemeal and fitted into a structure that does not derive primarily from religious categories. As Jan Ziolkowski notes, medieval readers "would have associated the *Physiologus* and fable because of their general similarity in structure: fable consists of a narrative with a moral, *Physiologus* of nature observation with moralization."[52]

The chapter on Unicorn (in one of its short forms) reads thus:

> In Deuteronomy Moses said while blessing Joseph, "His beauty is that of the firstling bull, and his horns are the horns of the unicorn" [Deut. 33:17]. The

monoceras, that is, the unicorn, has this nature: he is a small animal like the kid, is exceedingly shrewd, and has one horn in the middle of his head. The hunter cannot approach him because he is extremely strong. How then do they hunt the beast? Hunters place a chaste virgin before him. He bounds forth into her lap and she warms and nourishes the animal and takes him into the palace of kings. The unicorn has one horn because the Savior said, "I and the Father are one" [John 10: 30]. "For he has raised up a horn of salvation for us in the house of his servant David" [Luke 1:69]. Coming down from heaven, he came into the womb of the Virgin Mary. "He was loved like the son of the unicorns" [cf. Ps. 22:21] as David said in the psalm.[53]

This text contains a potpourri of the speculative, philological, and exegetic processes we have followed in Greco-Roman and Judeo-Christian texts, plus something else. "How to hunt a unicorn" belongs at first sight to the category of descriptive/prescriptive texts, of which cookbooks provide, in our times, the most popular examples. This hunting recipe seems derived from Ctesias and other classical experts in exotic game, but with an odd twist in it. I am not talking of the practical difficulties of finding chaste virgins willing to hunt dangerous animals, but of the textual confusion that the hunting of unicorns with chaste virgins as bait creates in the mind of the reader, who cannot help thinking this sounds like a story, although it is not a story.[54]

Let's imagine that in its chapter "Wolf," *Physiologus* had inserted the following sentences:

> The wolf is extremely fierce. How do they hunt him? Hunters place a little girl wearing a red riding hood in his path, pretending she is going to visit her Grandma. The wolf jumps into Grandma's bed and devours her. Soothed by his digestion and the sweet words the little girl tells him, he becomes docile, easy to capture and kill.[55]

Conversely, one could easily make up a folktale with the ingredients given in the *Physiologus* entry for unicorn. One could also easily assume that the *Physiologus* adapted an existing story as a hunting recipe, to fit its exegetic goal and the format of its entries.

Taking their cue, experts in unicornology have looked everywhere to find the tale they assume to be folded into the chaste virgin recipe. Odell Shepard confesses that after reading so many tales, legends, and myths involving virgins and animals, he started to suspect that he was "looking for the origin of a belief which has never had any single beginning." However, he picks an Ethiopian hunting tale, which has the same structure as the *Physiologus* recipe for hunting unicorns, but concerns rhinoceros and uses female monkeys as bait.[56] In recent books on unicorns, the most frequent originary tale comes from the Mahabharata.[57]

Physiologus creates the fiction of a fiction. First, it solidifies disparate elements concerning various single-horned animals into a species, creating the illusion that the species had been known for a long time. Both Latin versions B and Y start with authoritative definitions:

> *Est animal quod graece dicitur monosceros, latine vero unicornis*
> [There is an animal that is called "monokeros" in Greek, and "unicornis" in Latin]. (*Physiologus Latinus*, versio B, LLTSA)
>
> *Monokeras, hoc est unicornus, hanc naturam habet*
> [The monokeros, that is, the unicorn, has this nature]. (*Physiologus Latinus*, versio Y, LLTSA)

In a similar fashion, it creates the illusion that unicorn stories were in circulation for a long time. Thus, under the guise of fact gathering, the *Physiologus* invents a lore that did not exist. It does so in a non-narrative way, leaving the task to retrieve or invent the implied story to its readers. Many have been happy to oblige until this day.

The *Physiologus* was not looking for tales to tell or fictions to develop as fictions. It was looking for signs to use for a didactic and religious purpose in a contrived semiotic system. The unicorn ought to be a biblical sign since its name appeared at some point in the biblical transmission – accidentally as we have seen – causing interpretive problems and opening exegetic opportunities. But it needed to appear as already loaded with the rich, variegated, and yet specific signification that things and beings acquire usually through a long accretion of myths, tales, natural histories, travel accounts, and recipes. This was the case for many of the other animals in the *Physiologus* (for instance, those belonging to the Aesopian tradition or to Egyptian or Greco-Roman mythology) but not for the unicorn. After reviewing examples of the numerous representations of the unicorn in medieval and early modern paintings, tapestries, heraldry, and poetry, Shepard remarks: "The unicorn has a less prominent role in the romances of the Middle Ages than one might expect, considering its potentialities." He is able to cite two French romances in which a unicorn appears as a character and not as a decorative figure painted on a shield or elsewhere, but they are late minor romances, in which the unicorn remains anonymous and does not play a major role, as the lion in Chrétien de Troyes's *Yvain* does.[58] Through time, the unicorn became a famous fiction but not a memorable adstraction such as Balaam's ass, Yvain's lion, or Tristan's dog.[59] Although the unicorn appears as a character in several contemporary novels, it remains more potent as a "detached fiction" providing symbolic or aesthetic value visually or poetically than as a narrative-bound character.[60]

No unicorn is named Barbara

On its trail toward fame and non-existence, the unicorn did not acquire a proper name. Unicorns remained anonymous individuals of a dubious species through a period that saw the creation of named animals, such as Ysengrin or Renard, and during which syllogisms were called by names, such as Barbara or Baralipton.[61] The lack of a proper name does not prevent adstraction to produce an imaginary singular individual, as we have seen in Chapter 2, with Marie de France's lions. Conversely, the use of coded short-hand names for syllogisms did not infuse them with life and individuality, except perhaps in students' pranks. There is no strict equivalence between proper name and individualized being whether real or not, but the proper name is one of the attributes that tend to strengthen individualization.

I cannot affirm the truth of my proposition (1) "No unicorn is named Barbara" because I don't know for sure. On proper names, Peter Strawson remarks: "At present, our choice of names is partly arbitrary, partly dependent on legal and social observances. It would be perfectly possible to have a thorough-going *system* of names, based *e.g.* on dates of birth, or on a minute classification of physiological and anatomical differences."[62] "Barbara" happens by coincidence to be a proper name in both ways Strawson describes: it is a semi-arbitrary, semi-conventional choice when applied to persons and a systematically constructed denomination when applied to syllogisms. It would be a perfect name for a unicorn, if a unicorn needed to be named. However, even if in some story a unicorn is named "Barbara," or if some child has named his or her toy unicorn "Barbara," or, for that matter, any other proper name, this would not suffice to remedy the lack of individuality the unicorn inherited from its half-speculative half-interpretive origins. The unicorn has been created mostly by people who like to speculate on what exists (translators, commentators, and poets), not by people who like to imagine what does not exist (children, logicians, and storytellers).

The historical trail and the various traits characterizing the unicorn confirm unsurprisingly Saul Kripke's stance on the necessary nonexistence of the unicorn as a species, no matter if people at different moments may have credited it with the benefit of the doubt. But, more interestingly, it seems that the lack of a well-founded connection with a real species and no more than one has something to do with the lack of development of the unicorn as an adstraction. This may be examined further through a comparison with another nonexistent object, named Renard.

The birth of Renard

Naming foxes and unicorns

My proposition

(2)   Renard is the most famous fox.

is not an interesting sentence from a logical perspective, since it duplicates sentences such as

(5)   Sherlock Holmes is the most famous detective.

without adding anything to the discussion on the referential or ontological status of such statements.[63] However, it becomes interesting when it is translated into French:

(6)   Renard est le renard le plus célèbre.

This apparent tautology results from a linguistic accident: *goupil* (the old French noun for "fox") was replaced by *renard* (the modern French noun for "fox"), under the influence of the fictional fox named "Renard," a masculine proper name with Germanic roots like Bernard or Richard. This linguistic accident demonstrates the truth of (2), that is the fame of Renard, although *en français seulement* as in (6).[64]

Both unicorns and French foxes owe their species names to an operation of renaming. In the case of the unicorns, it occurred through translation from Hebrew to Greek and involved the transformation of an adjective into a common name. In the case of foxes, it occurred within the same language, and involved the transformation of a proper into a common name. In modern languages, unicorns are named by a translation of the Greek adjective *monokerōs* or the Latin adjective/substantive *unicornis* into a noun (*licorne, unicornio, unicorno, unicorn, einhorn, eenhorn, enhjørning,* etc.). The description contained in the noun is thus retained through translations. This is another proof of the unicorn's bookish nature. Outside of France, the fictional Renard did not overcome the linguistic and cultural traditions associated with the animal that is named *zorro, volpe, raposa, fox, fuchs, vos, raev,* etc.[65] In both cases, fiction is involved in the process of nomination as much as naming is involved in the process of fictionalization, but the naming of the unicorn is an isolated linguistic act that is not supported or contested by the brushing with real things that acquaintance with foxes provides. I never met a unicorn, but, once, at dawn, in the woods, I met a live fox for a few seconds, and then it was gone. It was an object of direct acquaintance, as Russell would say. For me, it was a marvel. Unicorns are marvelous too, as elements of a marvelous semiotic system, for the beauty of the unicorn pertains to the beauty of the medieval bestiary.

There is no need to prove that foxes exist or that a talking fox is a necessary fiction, so understanding how Renard came into existence as a fiction that in turn came to rename reality requires a different method than the one I used with unicorns. The most interesting thing about unicorns is their history; the most interesting things about foxes are their stories. Their historical trail can be easily summed up. In the areas where humans coexist with foxes, numerous stories, descriptions, and recipes (from how to prevent the fox from killing your hens to the story of the beautiful woman who was in truth a female fox) circulate in forms mixing foreign with local lore, learned tradition with popular wisdom. The reports can be written, oral, or pictorial; their relation to truth and reality as well as their style and tone vary greatly. A similar assessment can be made for other animal species, which have in common the characteristics of being real, having been in contact with humans for a long time, and living in large habitats occupied by various human cultures. To give a short list relevant to Western Europe, I would count along with the fox, the wolf, the dog, the cat, the bear, the donkey, the goat, the cow, the horse, the crow, the owl, the pig, the rat, and the flea. These animals have been subjected to speculation and interpretation like the unicorn, and appear in the same ancient and medieval sources. All these species have not produced famous fictional characters, but have the potential to do so. The flea, for instance, is still waiting to be developed into a popular hero. I doubt it could reach the level of fame of the fox, but I may be wrong.[66]

The fox of the bestiary

In *Physiologus Latinus*, the fox does not benefit from any accident of translation or exegetic acrobatics, and keeps a simple, low profile. In the following excerpt the bracketed passages come from a variant version (version B):

> The fox is an entirely deceitful animal who plays tricks. If he is hungry and finds nothing to eat, he seeks out a rubbish pit [where there is red earth and rolls in it so that he appears bloodied all over; he then throw himself down and rolls over as though dead]. Then, throwing himself on his back, he stares upwards, draws in his breath, and thoroughly bloats himself up. Now the birds, thinking the fox dead, descend upon him to devour him. But he

stretches out and seizes them, and the birds themselves die a miserable death. [The fox is a figure of the devil. To those who live according to the flesh he pretends to be dead. Although he may hold sinners within his gullet, to spiritual men and those perfected in faith, however, he is dead and reduced to nothing.] The devil is, in fact, utterly dead as is the effect of his work. Whoever wishes to partake of his flesh will die, for his flesh is made of fornication, greed, desire, and hostile times [cf. Matt. 15:19]. For this reason Herod is likened to a fox [cf. Luke. 13:32]. And the scribe heard the Savior say, "The foxes have holes" [Matt. 8: 20]. And in the Song of Songs, "Catch us the little foxes that spoil the vineyards" [S. of S. 2:15]. And David in Psalm 62 said, "They shall be prey for foxes" [Ps. 63:10]. Physiologus, therefore, spoke wisely of the fox.[67]

The *Physiologus* does not waste time describing how the fox looks like for this is common knowledge. It focuses on one trait attributed to the fox: tricking preys through pretending to be dead.[68] This leads to two interpretations. In version Y, "*Et diabolus omnino mortuus est, et actus operi eius*" [the devil is, in fact, utterly dead as is the effect of his work].[69] The devil does not feign death: he is dead, and is death itself. In this interpretation, the ability of the fox to feign and lure is lost under the broader trait of pertaining to sin, death, and evil. In version B, "*Uulpis igitur figuram habet diaboli: omnibus enim secundum carnem uiuentibus fingit se esse mortuum*" [The fox is a figure of the devil. To those who live according to the flesh he pretends to be dead].[70] The devil pretends to be dead in order to lure humans to sin. The Latin verb form *fingit* comes from the verb *fingere*, which means to form, shape, compose, invent, make up, pretend. In this interpretation, both fox and devil are masters of fiction.

In the short narrative that constitutes the literal side of the comparison, the fox displays great acting skills. He picks the perfect stage: a rubbish pit presumably littered with carcasses. He uses make-up in the form of "*rubra terra*" [red earth], which makes him "*quasi cruenta appareat tota*" [look bloody all over]. Then "*et proicit se supina, sursum respiciens, et adducit flatos suos infra se: exspanditur omnino*" [throwing himself on his back, he stares upwards, draws in his breath, and thoroughly bloats himself up]. The bloating effect is probably the most difficult part to manage, but it is such a trait of verisimilitude that any actor willing to impersonate a decomposing corpse should strive to master it as well as the fox. In this short passage, our stern physiologist lets narrative pleasure take over. The devil has lured him into composing a vivid scene, which becomes independent from its moral and religious frame.[71] This is not the fiction of a fiction like the hunt of the unicorn, but the trace and seed of many past and future tales of the fox.

Renard and Genesis

The demonization of the fox in *Physiologus* was not an obstacle to its development as a fictional character in twelfth- and thirteenth-century Latin and vernacular literature. On the contrary, Jan Ziolkowski suggests that there is a correlation between negative exemplarity and individualization in *Ysengrimus*, a Latin beast poem dated from the mid-twelfth century, in which Reinardus the fox features as the accomplice and nemesis of Ysengrim the wolf: "One spectacular achievement of the *Ysengrimus'* poet was that he could make his characters exemplars of evil while managing at the same time to personalize the animals more fully than in any previous work of beast literature."[72] The use of proper names such as Reinardus and Ysengrimus marks a difference between *Ysengrimus* and other beast poems and prose works (including bestiaries and fables), but is not an invention of the *Ysengrimus* poet, who took it from a tradition that was most probably satirical and directed against clerics.[73] The Old French collection of tales known as the *Roman de Renart* (written between *c.*1170 and *c.*1250) shifted focus from the stupid wolf to the shrewd fox, which was a stroke of genius.[74] As he became a vernacular hero, Renard transformed durably the linguistic and cultural paradigm of the fox in French. He also provided the pretext for a reflection on naming and existence inserted in the prologue to one cycle of stories forming the *Roman*.

An anonymous thirteenth-century *remanieur* reorganized various existing Renard stories in order to create a narrative going from the childhood of the hero to his death.[75] The 200-line prologue of this cycle starts like a mock epic, and turns into a mock genesis accompanied by mock exegesis. In the epic introduction (ll. 1–23), the proper names "Renard" and "Ysengrin" appear after a recapitulation of tales that the audience is supposed to have already heard. These tales are designated either by their genre (tales, fables, epic songs, romances) or by the name of their heroes (Paris, Helen, Tristan) (ll. 1–10).[76] In the same way that these names call stories to minds, "Renard" and "Ysengrin" will call to mind other stories that are still to be told: "*Mais onques n'oïstes la guerre, / Qui mout fu dure de grant fin, / Entre Renart et Ysengrin*" [But you never heard about the war, / Which was so hard and so terrible, / Between Renard and Ysengrin] (ll. 11–13). The singer of tales promises to tell the origin of the war between the two "barons" (l. 14) but is unconcerned by the question of the origin of species, names, and fictions: "*Or orrez le commencement / Par qoi et par quel mesetance / Fu entre eux .II. la desfiance*" [You will hear from the beginning / how the misunderstanding happened / That led to their confrontation] (ll. 20–2). As soon as he has made this promise, he turns to something else: "*Je vous conteré par deduit / Conment il vindrent en avant, / Si con je l'ai trouvé lisant, / Qui fu Renart et Ysengrin*" [I will tell you for pleasure / How they came forward, / And who Renard and Ysengrin were, / As I found it while reading] (ll. 24–7). The singer of tales is now a reader and interpreter of books.

With this shift in style and scope comes a new proper name: "*Je trovai ja en .I. escrin / .I. livre: Aucupre avoit non*" [In a box I found / A book named Aucupre] (ll. 28–9). No one has identified "Aucupre" either as an author name or a book title. As a noun, "aucupre" may be related to a Latin word such as *aucupex* or *auceptor*, meaning "bird-catcher."[77] If such is the case, the source book itself (or its author) is like the fox of *Physiologus*, able to catch birds by playing dead:

> *La trovai je mainte reson*
> *Et de Renart et d'autre chose*
> *Dont l'en doit bien parler et ose.*
> *A une grant letre vermeille,*
> *La trovai je grant merveille.*
> *Se je ne la trovasse el livre,*
> *Je tenisse celui por yvre*
> *Qui dite eûst tele aventure,*
> *Mes l'en doit croire l'escripture.*
> *A desenor muert a bon droit*
> *Qui n'ainme livre ne ne croit.*   (ll. 30–40)

Here I found many stories
About Renard and other things
Of which one must dare to speak.
Next to a red capital,
I found a wonderful tale.
If I had not found it in this book,
I would have taken for a drunkard
Whoever would have told me that adventure,
But one must believe the Scripture / what is written.
He dies in disgrace – and rightly so –
He who does neither love nor believe books.

The reader is required to accept reading as a game of make-believe or a temporary suspension of disbelief. To read is to believe in what you read during the time you read it, but does not commit you to believe it outside of the book you read, because, obviously, that book is not the Book. The model of belief that this medieval theoretician has in mind is not children's games, as modern theoreticians of fiction do, but religious belief.[78] "*Mes l'en doit croire l'escripture*" (l. 38) plays on the double meaning of *escripture* and

could be translated in two ways, since medieval scribes did not use capitals
to make the distinction we make between "Scripture" and "scripture":

(7)   But one must believe Scripture.
(8)   But one must believe what is written.

In (7) "believe" should be better written "Believe," indicating that this kind
of belief implies a commitment to the truth of what you believe. One must
Believe that Scripture tells the Truth. In (8), the same commitment would
lead to absurd propositions, including some contradicting (7), such as:

(9)   Scripture is a fiction.

If one must Believe what is written, no matter what is written, then (9) is
true and (7) both true and not true. If one wants to maintain (7) as an
unquestionable Truth, then one needs to accept that "believe" in (8) means
something different than in (7), and that there are different ways to read
books and believe them.

   As a demonstration of how a belief that does not imply a commitment
to Truth works, Aucupre produces a narrative in which the main characters are Adam and Eve. If we are committed to Believe what is said about
Adam and Eve in the Bible, nothing of the same sort is required when we
read Aucupre's story about Adam and Eve. We are not even asked to
believe in Aucupre's existence. However, the story does not present itself
as a pure invention, but as belonging to the tradition of commentaries and
apocryphal texts growing around the Bible.[79] Since Genesis tells twice the
creation of animals (Gen. 1:24–8 and Gen. 2:18–20), Aucupre imitates this
repetition while avoiding attributing his text to God himself. He does
not rewrite the Bible but supplements it by proposing a story about what
Adam and Eve did between their banishment from Eden and the conception of Cain, that is, between Genesis 3 and 4.[80] Aucupre's Genesis 3½
starts thus:

> Aucupre dit en cele letre
> – Bien ait de Dieu qui l'i fist mettre! –
> Come Diex ot de paradis
> Et Adam et Evam fors mis
> Por ce qu'il orent trespassé
> Ce qu'il lor avoit conmandé.
> Pitiez l'en prist, si lor donna
> Une verge, si lor mostra
> Quant il de riens mestier avroient,
> De cele verge en mer ferroient.   (ll. 41–50)

After this letter, Aucupre says
– God bless him, who made him write here –
[alternative reading: – God bless him who wrote that here –]
How God out of Paradise
Expelled Adam and Eve
For they had disobeyed
His command.
He felt pity and gave them
A rod, and he showed them
How to strike the sea with the rod
When they needed something.

God helps Adam and Eve in the same way he helps Aucupre: through providing an initial boost and then leaving them to their own devices, for better or worse. When Adam strikes the sea, the ewe, the dog, and all the domesticable animals come out. When Eve strikes the sea, the wolf, the fox, and all the wild animals come out: "*Les Evain asauvagisoient, / Et les Adam aprivoisoient*" [Those from Eve became wild / And those from Adam became tamed] (ll. 97–8).

In Genesis, creating and naming are two separate acts, the former being the privilege of the Creator, the latter being granted by the Creator to one of his creatures, man. What complicates the matter is that, in Genesis 1, God creates by saying: "God said, 'Let the earth bring forth every kind of living creature: cattle, creeping things, and wild beasts of every kind'" (Gen. 1:24). But God's creative saying is not equivalent to naming. God does not need to name what he says and creates at once. Things are the words of God.[81] In Genesis 2, God creates living beings, including man, "from the dust of the earth" (Gen. 2:7), but then to man only he gives the power to name: "And the Lord God formed out of the earth all the wild beasts and all the birds of the sky, and brought them to the man to see what he would call them; and whatever the man called each living creature, that would be its name" (Gen. 2:19).

In Aucupre's story, Adam and Eve neither create new animals nor create the animals again, which would be taking the place of God and claiming that Aucupre's story is Scripture. With God's help, they call forth out of the sea species that were already potentially there. We could infer that God made a blueprint of living species in Eden, while on the rest of the earth life was potentially contained in the primary oceanic soup. This does not make of Aucupre a proto-Darwinian, since in his meditation on the origin of earthly species man plays an active role at the very beginning of evolution rather than being a late participant in it:

Adam tint la verge en sa main,
En mer feri devant Evain.
Si tost con en la mer feri,
Une brebiz fors en sailli.
Lors dist Adam: "Dame, prenez
Ceste brebiz, si la gardez:
Tant vos donra let et fronmage.
Ainsi i avrons compenage."   (ll. 51–8)

Adam held the rod in his hand,
And stroke the sea in front of Eve.
As soon as he had struck,
A ewe sprang out of the sea.
Adam said: "Lady, take
This ewe and keep her.
She will give you plenty of milk and cheese
To eat with our bread."

At a stroke of Adam's rod, a ewe comes out of the sea, whole with her vernacular name and dairy products. Adam has only to identify her, based on his Edenic knowledge of species. Apparently, he remembers the names he gave to animals when God asked him to name them.

With the fox, things are different. What comes out of the sea at one of Eve's strokes is not *a* fox but *the* fox: "*Entre les autres en issi / Le gorpil, si asauvagi*" [Among others, came out / The fox and he became wild] (ll. 99–100). This fox is not, like the ewe, the wolf, and the dog, the prototype of a species, but the whole species. In the next line, he is related to Renard: "*Rous ot le poil, conme Renart, / Mout par fu cointes et gaingnart: / Par son sens totes decevoit / Les bestes quanqu'il en trovoit*" [His hair was red, like Renard, / Very smart he was, and good at looting: / Using his wit, he deceived all / The animals he encountered] (ll. 101–4). Renard is born again. Genesis 3½ is now over and we can forget about Aucupre. The anonymous "I" that claimed to have found "Aucupre" in a box (ll. 28–9) is in charge of the text again: "*Sifaitement con je vos di*" [Exactly as I tell you] (l. 119).

God created animal species, Adam named them. This is the Truth to be Believed. But how humans divided animal species between wild and domestic, how they continue to manage this division, and how they use animals as signs, symbols, and fictions is a matter of inquiry that does not pertain directly to that Truth. Aucupre's apocryphal story works as a transition between Scripture and scripture, the Bible and romance, Belief and belief. It is still a tale of the origins, but when the fox enters the stage, the question of origins becomes moot. What matters is the significance of

Renard the fox for the readers, in the here and now of the reading experience:

> *Icil gorpil nos senefie*
> *Renart, qui tant sot de mestrie.*
> *Touz ceus qui sont d'engin et d'art*
> *Sont mes tuit apelé Renart,*
> *Por Renart et por le gorpil.*   (ll. 105–9)

> This fox signifies for us
> Renard, who was such a master.
> All those who are wily and crafty
> From now on are called Renard,
> For Renard and for the fox.

In a sense, Renard does not have any origin, for he is a creation of man rather than a creation of God like the fox. He is already here, on earth, when Eve conjures up the fox from the sea, since the fox has red hair "like Renard." He was surely already there, in Eden, when the first human couple tried to deceive God.[82] In another sense, Renard was already here when the author of this introduction and the compilation that follows started to work. As he admits, "from now on" ["*mes*"] (l. 108), "Renard" is the name of all individuals who know how to use guile, whether bipeds or quadrupeds. The author recognizes that he inherited the entanglement between the proper name and the common name, the foxy man and the manly fox. It seems that, at the time he writes, "Renard" is still in use as a proper name for men.[83] The author explains this conundrum as if it were an exegetic issue: "*Icil gorpil nos senefie / Renart, qui tant sot de mestrie*" [This fox signifies for us / Renard, who was such a master] (ll. 105–6). These two lines could be taken as a messianic announcement, "*mestrie*" meaning first "mastery," "authority," "power" before meaning a devious use of power and skills. The placement of "*Renart*" at the beginning of line 106, after the pause of the line break, can be heard as a mark of awe and respect. But, later on, Renard is explicitly connected to evil: "*Car cil Renart nos senefie / Ceus qui sont plain de male vie*" [For this Renard signifies for us / Those who live an evil life] (ll. 133–4). This brings the text back in line with the *Physiologus*' clear-cut interpretation (the fox represents evil), while it does not suppress the suspicion that the ambiguous lines 105–6 may raise against exegesis, and particularly its typological and moral aspects.[84] Renard the fox goes against the grain of *Physiologus*, bestiaries, and modern unicornology.

With *Ysengrimus* and *Le Roman de Renard*, the bestiary becomes pure fiction, and claims its status as fiction. The names "Ysengrin" and

"Renard" can be viewed as historical blocks in Donnellan's fashion. They claim the fictionality of the character they name. Aucupre's genesis is not apocryphal, but avowedly fictional. The birth of Renard is the birth of fiction as a realm independent from the major system of belief in place at the time.

Nonexistent objects and fictional realms

Rationalism and fictionalism

Following the historical trails of the unicorn and Renard led me to make a distinction between fictions resulting from speculation or interpretation, and fictions resulting from a conscious act of invention. But I do not think that people did not invent consciously before the twelfth century because they were not able to rationalize sufficiently their relation to the real world. Neither would I suggest that, in human history, after the time of myth came the time of fiction, or that fiction comes after myth in child development. Renard the fox does not replace the unicorn as a step on the road toward rationalism. I believe that both the unicorn and Renard pertain to our rationality as objects of thought, as well as all the other "nonentities," "nonexistent items," "nonsuches," "mere nothing," "fabulous entities," "figments," or "fictions," on which logicians of the twentieth and twenty-first centuries have pondered.[85]

The mock-speculation of Aucupre on the origin of species and the paradoxical lack of origin of Renard belong to the same type of investigation that Abelard led about the status of imaginary things. Like Marie de France's *Fables*, the whole *Roman de Renart* displays the same type of acumen about the way our language and reason name and summon things in the world that Anselm sharpens in *De grammatico*. The convergence of logic and fiction is not always present in the history of Western rationalism, which could be called as well "Western fictionalism." It occurred around 1100, and again around 1900, although logical and fictional thinking exist always and everywhere in human activities. What emerges in different forms, at different times and in different places, is a metadiscourse about these activities: reasoning about reasoning, reasoning about fiction, fiction-alizing reasoning, and fictionalizing fiction. To explain why this metadis-course emerges around 1100 and 1900 would be beyond my capacity and the scope of this book. I can only suggest that these moments seem to coincide with a major change in the form and medium of fictions. During the twelfth and thirteenth centuries, vernacular stories and songs started to be put in writing and gathered into books on a much larger scale than before in Western Europe. In the late nineteenth and early twentieth centuries, there appeared (again in Western Europe) a new form and medium, which is today the main vehicle of fictions for a large part of the world population: cinema. Did medieval and modern logicians anticipate these developments? Or did they, unwittingly, lay the ground for them with their investigations on the border between the real and the non-real, the true, the false, and the fictional? In any case, it seems that a reflection on nonexistent objects needs a certain development of fictional realms to occur, and that, conversely, fictional realms are developed when nonexistent objects are envisioned as objects of thought (even if it is to be denied as objects by philosophers like Russell).

The home and manners of nonexistent objects

An existent object exists in the world. I am in favor of saying "the world" following Russell's no-nonsense affirmation: "There is only one world, the 'real' world."[86] I affirm with Russellian poise that a nonexistent object does not exist in a nonexistent world for there are no fictional worlds. There are fictional realms, territories, domains, or whatever term delimiting a certain amount of complexity without aiming toward completeness and wholeness. The terms "fictional" and "world" brought together compose a clumsy metaphor creating more confusion than clarification.[87] Fiction is particularization and focalization; it does not tend to wholeness, no matter how many characters, places, and events it includes and no matter the time it spans. It does not require readers to construct a whole world around the details it gives (what a chore that would be, particularly for users who want to escape the world). It asks users to pay attention to and remember details. When authors of fiction talk about creating worlds, they brag. When users claim to live in a book, film, or game, they employ a tired metaphor.

If there is no fictional world, where do nonexistent objects exist? According to Terence Parsons, they do not exist (as their qualification "nonexistent" indicates), but they nonetheless are.[88] To investigate Kripke and Donnellan's historical trails and blocks one needs to look into archives not jungles, that is, repositories of human collective memory, such as the painted walls of a cave, a tomb, the memory of a storyteller, a mythology, a scroll, a book, a library, a computer, a language, a ritual, a song, and other devices we cannot yet imagine but may come into existence. Any inquiry related to nonexistent objects must be directed to archives, in the adequate corpus or through interviewing the adequate informants. The best place to study unicorns is not in central Asia, but in libraries.[89] Very little can be learned about Sherlock Holmes in Baker Street.

The fact that the nonexistent object finds its worldly home in archives has a consequence: its history is its nature. A nonexistent particular holds nothing innate, genetic, hereditary, or molecular. Its evolution is not without constraint, but the constraints are completely human-made. At any moment in the history of a nonexistent object, a human agent may introduce atypical features, reappropriate the object for different purposes and audiences, or transgress the rules of consistency, decency, and grammar that generally apply to fiction at a given time and place.

A nonexistent object rooted in an existent species does not behave like a nonexistent object that is not. Imaginary species are more difficult to manage than imaginary individuals of real species, for they are less fictionally flexible, and tend to become reduced to one specimen, which is neither quite an individual nor quite a species either. This said, there are spectacular successes beside the unicorn in this difficult niche (the phoenix, Melusine, the hobbit, and Godzilla come to mind).

The nonexistent object has a peculiar way of being. It is, to use a phrase favored by a notorious nonexistent man named Horace Rumpole, "a queer customer."[90] And this even if it represents normality and conformity. This queerness comes from the fact that it lacks the somethingness or somebodyness that supports the particularities of existent objects. The nonexistent object is an arrangement of particularities that presents itself in full light, even if all the particularities are not given at once, and even if it is not a complete set of particularities. Questions about nonexistent particulars such as, "What did Sherlock eat for dinner the day before that particular story starts?" are irrelevant if one expects to find out in the same fashion that you could find out what I had for dinner last night.[91] To answer such questions, one needs to create a fiction or to find out if someone has produced a fiction answering that question. When we encounter for the first time a new somebody or a new something, we have to do quickly a lot of guessing in order to choose how to behave and react (say hello, run away, do nothing, etc.). We pull at the few particularities we can observe, leaving the rest (the indistinct part of the something or somebody) open to guesswork. The nonexistent object appears with particularities and without indistinct parts. We don't have to do any guesswork if we don't feel like it. One can read and enjoy even a "whodunit" without trying to guess who did it. The stranger can remain strange and the mysterious events mysterious, without any danger for our body or soul.

The names of nonexistent objects

Nonexistent objects may or may not have a proper name. When they do, some philosophers like to call such names "empty names" in opposition to the "non-empty names" of real individuals.[92] Kenneth Taylor says that both empty names and non-empty names "serve as labels for and access points to conceptions of individuals."[93] It is true that proper names individualize (and, accessorily, anthropomorphize). But it may also be true that proper names fictionalize. It is actually in fiction that proper names function the most efficiently as "labels" calling up an individual. In real life, the individual may offer some resistance to labeling, unless we think that individualization is a matter of identification, in a legal and bureaucratic sense. I am wondering whether the first proper names were not all "empty names" attributed to individuals out of reach in everyday life such as ancestors, gods, and heroes, who could not be easily or properly designated by the handy deictics and nicknames (affectionate and otherwise) that people use for their relatives and neighbors, from "Hey you!" to "my little pumpkin."

Is "Hippolyte Hydulphe" an empty name? Can

(4)   Hippolyte Hydulphe is bald.

be deemed true or false? Does it say something about something, something about nothing, or nothing about nothing? On the issue of Hippolyte Hydulphe's baldness, I can only answer that I don't know. From this, you may guess that "Hippolyte Hydulphe" is not the empty name of a nonexistent object. For if I had made him up I could answer that question: I would just need to decide if I want him to be bald or not. I don't know because I never met this great-great-uncle of mine, who died a few years before I was born.

The fact that Hippolyte Hydulphe is known to me as a real (although departed) person may not be enough to make him real to you. You can still doubt my word or simply not bother. The troubling fact that nonexistent objects can be referred to with the same linguistic and logic forms (including proper names) as existent ones may be best explained by the degree of relevance any object has for us. What does matter for us is not primarily the distinction between existence and nonexistence, but the distinction between relevant and irrelevant, directly known, indirectly known, and unknown. There is no reason why my great-great-uncle should be relevant to you and your great-great-uncle should be relevant to me, unless we happen to share a common great-great-uncle. Would you not want to have a great-great-uncle named "Hippolyte Hydulphe"?

"On Denoting" revisited

For Russell, knowledge by direct acquaintance is a basic feature of the human relation to the world, of great interest to psychologists, anthropologists, or neurobiologists, but which does not need to be explored by the logician or the expert in natural sciences, since the question of existence or nonexistence, truth or falsity is to be judged through reasoning and knowing, that is through the use of denotation. The fact that nonexistent objects could be treated as objects of thought like existent ones was for him an aberration due to a lack of logical thinking on the subject. Russell was as aware as Abelard and Anselm that denotation involves imagination, guesswork, or worse. That is why he tried to reduce denotation to a system of logical propositions that could always be verifiable, and did not transgress the principle of non-contradiction. This was probably a necessary move in order to achieve progress in some aspects of knowledge, but it came at a cost: on the one hand, the inability to understand fiction and give it its proper place in human cultures; on the other, the cultivation of narcissistic illusions concerning our ability to use reason. Russell did not see that the principle of non-contradiction is a mental construction involving fiction and depending on an apparatus for the transmission of knowledge. Both the fictional construction and the epistemological apparatus were created by Aristotle, and will be the subject of the second and third parts of this book.

PART II

Figures of contradiction

CHAPTER 4

The opponent

Introduction

In Part I of this book, I considered logic and fiction in relation to things. Things are scattered – in our minds or in the world. Whether we address them through reasoning or imagining, we know that we cannot keep them in order for too long. Logic and fiction are different ways to impose a temporary truce on the disorder and scattering of things. There are other ways (all temporary): we may order and master language through poetry, space through obsessional cleaning, and the unknown through rituals. What logic and fiction have in common in this regard is their dependence on the principle of non-contradiction, as a founding rule for ordering things and transforming them into objects of statements. In Part II of this book, I want to study the principle of non-contradiction as a foundational fiction of Western thought, which involves going back to Aristotle's fourth book of *Metaphysics*.

If *Metaphysics* IV was a *Bildungsroman*, it could be summarized as an encounter between a young metaphysician and a shadowy character, called *ho amphisbētōn*, the opponent, who does not say anything but stands in denial of the most fundamental principle of all – the grail that our hero seeks. Without the opponent, the grail cannot be found and the principle cannot be defined, while in the presence of the opponent the grail loses its power and the principle loses its universality. Before studying this figure, I will first review briefly Aristotle's argument with the help of modern commentators.

The "most certain principle of all"

Metaphysics IV starts, as almost every book of *Metaphysics* does, with an attempt to define the object of the first science studied in the treaty. "There is a science which investigates being as being and the attributes which belong to this in virtue of its own nature" (*Metaphysics* IV, 1003a; p. 1584).[1] This object, or being *qua* being, makes the first science distinct from all other sciences aiming towards being only under particular respects. The first science examines the attributes of being, such as contraries (*Metaphysics* IV, 1004a; pp. 1585–6). It also establishes the basic axioms valid for all particular sciences, such as the principles of logical reasoning (*Metaphysics* IV, 1005a; p. 1587). At this point in the text, Aristotle shifts from a panoramic vision of the sciences to a close-up on the axiom referred to as the principle of non-contradiction and that he announces as "the most certain principle of all" (*Metaphysics* IV, 1005b; p. 1587). He defines it in the following terms: "It is, that the same attribute cannot at the same time belong and not belong to the same subject in the same respect" (*Metaphysics* IV, 1005b; p. 1588). Since, according to Aristotle, a principle cannot be demonstrated, the most fundamental principle of all can only be asserted through the refutation of arguments opposed to it. The rest of Book IV is devoted to this task.[2]

In a nutshell, his refutation consists in arguing that by refusing the principle of non-contradiction the opponent forfeits the possibility to make sense, and therefore to oppose the principle. Unable to speak sensibly, the opponent loses also the ability to act sensibly in the real world.[3] He who believes that it is possible to state that the same thing is this and not this at the same time and under the same respect, that a proposition can be both true and false, condemns himself to be like a "plant" – unable to speak, think, and act – or like a madman who jumps into a well because he cannot decide whether the well exists or not, whether it is better to avoid it or go straight into it (*Metaphysics* IV, 1008b, p. 1592).

Despite the limited scope of its argument, *Metaphysics* IV can be seen as one of the founding texts of Aristotelian ontology. For Jonathan Lear, the goal of this book is to demonstrate the adequacy between mind and reality:

> Aristotle's goal is neither to prove the principle of non-contradiction nor to convince an opponent of the principle to change his mind: in Aristotle's view, there is no such opponent. What Aristotle is trying to do is to show how the structure of reality constrains the structure of our thought. The very fact that the world is constituted of substances and properties forces us to think, speak, and act in certain ways. In a world made up of substances, any thinker must be someone who believes the principle of non-contradiction.[4]

In this perspective, the principle of non-contradiction, which emanates from the structure of reality, is the proof that such a structure exists outside of the mind. If we cannot think without abiding by the principle, Aristotle's vision of the world is true. Or could it be the other way around? The fact that the world, as Aristotle conceives it, is unthinkable without the principle of non-contradiction may not imply that the principle is an expression of the structure of reality, but, rather, that it is a condition necessary to Aristotle's thought. And the fact that he has to stage a nonexistent opponent in order to establish the principle points toward the structure of the mind rather than the structure of the world.

Enrico Berti accepts the broad implications about reality and cognition that Lear sees in the principle: for him, the principle allows Aristotle to affirm that the experience of the senses is intelligible.[5] He also underscores the link between the principle of non-contradiction and signification: "It appears as the very condition of thinking, saying and living, as the supreme criterion of significance in the global sense of the term."[6] In another essay, Berti discusses the theological implications of the principle, and concludes that it establishes "the transcendence of the absolute, that is the existence of God."[7] However, since Berti agrees with Pierre Aubenque that the theology of *Metaphysics* IV is a negative and problematic theology,[8] it seems that the principle plays a double role both as a stable foundation for Aristotle's thought and as a springboard for his most daring speculations.

Another modern reader of *Metaphysics* IV, Russell Dancy, chooses to emphasize the contradictions of Aristotle's position and comes to the conclusion that Aristotle has failed in his attempt to demonstrate the impossibility of denying the principle rationally.[9] As counter-examples, Dancy cites Kierkegaard and Engels, who both opposed the principle for different reasons and in different ways.[10] Although one may disagree with their arguments, no one can say that they stand out of the realm of rational discourse, like the speech of a plant or a madman. Dancy ends his book on this reflection: "One might deny the law of non-contradiction for all sorts of reasons. None that I have seen strike me as good reasons. But neither do I see any reason for saying that there never *could* be good reason for denying it."[11] Dancy underscores the strange nature of Aristotle's argument: even readers who tend to think intuitively that abiding by the principle of non-contradiction is a good thing to do may find the position of the opponent not so hopeless or unreasonable.

Aristotle introduces the opponent just after stating that the principle of non-contradiction cannot be demonstrated: "We can, however, demonstrate negatively even that this view [that the same thing is and is not] is impossible, if our opponent [*ho amphisbētōn*] will only say something" (*Metaphysics* IV, 1006a, p. 1588). This is the only time that he is called *ho amphisbētōn*, the opponent.[12] In the rest of the text, he is evoked only by pronouns or circumlocutions: "he," "him," "those who say that. . ."[13] Yet, despite his elusiveness, he is such a striking figure that Dancy feels the need to name him: "I hereby christen Aristotle's interlocutor, the man who wants to deny the law of non-contradiction in Gamma 4, 'Antiphasis'."[14] Dancy comments that the character is imaginary and does not represent any specific historical figure. Besides naming him, Dancy treats him mostly as a variable in the argumentation, to which Aristotle assigns different philosophical positions incompatible with the principle of non-contradiction.[15] Naming the opponent Antiphasis helps Dancy to reconstitute the arguments implicit in Aristotle's refutation, that is, the arguments that Antiphasis would say if he said anything, which he cannot since he does not abide by the principle of non-contradiction. In English, Antiphasis would be Contradiction, a fitting name – at first view – for the character opposing the principle of non-contradiction. However, since the opponent says nothing, it is misleading to call him Contradiction, which implies in Greek as in English to say something against something (*anti-phasis*, contra-diction). By defining him only as an opponent, Aristotle leaves room for a scenario in which the opponent remains silent. How does one refute a silence?

How to confound mistaken philosophers, obdurate sophists, or plants

Aristotle inherited the technique of refutation from the sophists, against whom he used it.[16] The Greek verb for "to refute" is "*elenkhein*," which in Homer means "to shame," "to treat with contempt," and in later authors such as Herodotus, Xenophon, and Plato, "to accuse," "to ridicule," "to confound." Even when *elenkhein* is used as a technical term in the field of dialectic, it retains a psychological connotation associated with the shame, defeat, and humiliation of the opponent. Such a connotation is not part of the semantic field of the Latin *refutare*, which means originally "to strike back."

Aristotle has the psychological connotation of *elenkhein* in mind in the sentence that follows the one introducing the opponent: "and if he says nothing, it is absurd to attempt to reason with one who will not reason about anything, in so far as he refuses to reason. For such a man, as such, is seen already to be no better than a mere plant" (*Metaphysics* IV, 1006a, p. 1588). Aristotle's concept of the "plant" is not related to our modern idea of the "vegetable," a human being maintained alive in a comatose state. When Aristotle ridicules and humiliates his opponent by assimilating him to a plant, he downgrades him to the level of the "nutritive soul" that is common to humans, animals, and plants.[17] But if the opponent attempted to speak and say something meaningful he would still lower himself to the status of plant simply because he opposes the principle of non-contradiction:

And if he makes no judgment but thinks and does not think, indiffer-
ently, what difference will there be between him and the plants? – Thus,
then, it is in the highest degree evident that neither any one of those who
maintain this view nor any one else is really in this position. For why
does a man walk to Megara and not stay at home thinking he ought to
walk? Why does he not walk early some morning into a well or over a
precipice, if one happens to be in his way? Why do we observe him
guarding against this, evidently not thinking that falling in is alike good
and not good? (*Metaphysics* IV, 1008b, p. 1592)

Aristotle's refutation is a trap, which the opponent of the principle cannot
avoid, whether he remains silent or speaks. If the opponent does not
argue, he is defeated without battle; if he argues – no matter what his
argument is – he demonstrates that he is a hypocrite or a superficial thinker,
because he cannot truly think what he claims to think (that the principle of
non-contradiction is false) without losing the ability to think and act
rationally. Are you a plant? Are you insane? Are you just playing with
words without realizing their full implication?

Metaphysics IV is not intended for an audience of plants. Those who oppose
the principle of non-contradiction are thinkers familiar with speculations on
contraries, being and non-being, truth and falsity. They are predecessors or
contemporaries of Aristotle.[18] The principle of non-contradiction may well
have been designed as a litmus test to separate the philosophers from the
dialecticians and sophists. At the beginning of *Metaphysics* IV, before starting
his refutation, Aristotle explains the distinction:

[D]ialecticians and sophists assume the same guise as the philosopher, for
sophistic is philosophy which exists only in semblance, and dialecticians
embrace all things in their dialectic, and being is common to all things; but
evidently their dialectic embraces these subjects because these are proper to
philosophy. – For sophistic and dialectic turn on the same class of things as
philosophy, but this differs from dialectic in the nature of the faculty required
and from sophistic in respect of the purpose of the philosophic life. Dialectic
is merely critical where philosophy claims to know, and sophistic is what
appears to be philosophy but is not. (*Metaphysics* IV, 1004b, p. 1586)

The distinction is crucial but difficult to establish since they all use the
same concepts and terms. The dialectician seems less dangerous than the
sophist, since Aristotle believes that dialectic is more limited in scope than
philosophy but prepares the philosopher to address the fundamental
questions that first science investigates, whereas the sophist is nothing
else than a pseudo-philosopher, his goal being not to reach truth but to
reap profit (*Metaphysics* IV, 1005b, p. 1587).

Amphisbeton may belong to one group or the other, which leads Aristotle to define two strategies:

> But the same method of discussion must not be used with all opponents; for some need persuasion, and others compulsion. Those who have been driven to this position [that all opinions and appearances are true] by difficulties in their thinking can easily be cured of their ignorance; for it is not their expressed argument but their thought that one has to meet. But those who argue for the sake of argument can be convinced only by emending (*elenkhein*) the argument as expressed in words. (*Metaphysics* IV, 1009a, p. 1593)

If Amphisbeton is a sincere but misled dialectician or philosopher, he can be convinced through persuasion (*peithō*) and a patient argumentation. If he is a sophist, then he must be vanquished and put to shame with his own arms, through refutation, seen as a forceful mode (*bia*). The pair *bia* and *peithō* evokes the Homeric opposition of Achilles, who fights with might and strength (*bia*), and Ulysses, who convinces with guile and ruse (*metis*).[19] Pierre Aubenque suggests that Aristotle adopts refutation as an anti-sophist weapon because he finds Plato's answer to the sophists lacking both in strength and persuasiveness. Myths or arguments *ad hominem* are useless against such opponents.[20]

The presence in the text of an opponent who is sometimes a philosopher, sometimes a sophist, makes Aristotle's voice and persona oscillate between the aggressive and the persuasive.[21] The rest of the passage is addressed to misled philosophers, whom Aristotle tries to help getting out of the metaphysical quagmire they have walked into, in good faith. He addresses at first both philosophers and sophists, attacking the belief that a fundamental principle could be demonstrated:

> There are, both among those who have these convictions and among those who merely profess these views, some who raise a difficulty by asking, who is the judge of the healthy man, and in general who is likely to judge rightly on each class of questions. But such inquiries are like puzzling over the question whether we are now asleep or awake. And all such questions have the same meaning. These people demand that a reason shall be given for everything; for they seek a starting-point, and they wish to get this by demonstration, while it is obvious from their actions that they have no conviction. But their mistake is what we have stated it to be; they seek a reason for that for which no reason can be given; for the starting-point of demonstration is not demonstration. (*Metaphysics* IV, 1011a, p. 1596)

Then the argument, which seems primarily to attack Protagoras's relativism, does not clearly follow one strategy or another. The passage in which Aristotle establishes the principle of the excluded third, starts like the refutation of an impossible position that can only be debunked by *bia*, strength: "But on the other hand there cannot be an intermediate between contradictories, but of one subject we must either affirm or deny any one predicate" (*Metaphysics* IV, 1011b, p. 1597). At the end of the passage, all the opponents (that is, all those who believe or claim that there is a third possibility beside "A" and "not A") are summoned to define clearly what they are talking about: "And the starting-point in dealing with all such people is definition. Now the definition rests on the necessity of their meaning something; for the formula, of which the word is a sign, becomes its definition."[22] Aristotle then mentions two philosophers, Heraclitus and Anaxagoras, as opponents who confuse the definition of truth and falsehood, and admit a third position between contraries (*Metaphysics* IV, 1012a, p. 1598). At this point, the reader forms the impression that strength has taken over persuasion, and that all opponents, in the end, are like sophists. The fellow philosopher, who starts opposing the principle of non-contradiction for honorable, philosophical reasons, turns into a sophist because he has deprived himself of the logical and moral foundation of philosophy. He cannot be treated as a colleague any more: he is an enemy who must be refuted and shamed by his own weapons. Moreover, if one agrees with Pierre Hadot that to practice philosophy in ancient Greece meant mostly to adopt a certain way of life,[23] the opponent is presented in terms that make him less and less able to embrace such a way of life. The warning is stern: if you are a philosopher, or wish to become one without admitting the principle of non-contradiction, you will successively become a mistaken philosopher bogged in a metaphysical quagmire, a sophist arguing only for the sake of arguing and the profit that can be made out of it, a madman jumping in a well instead of walking on the road, and, finally, a plant, vegetating silently.

Who is Amphisbeton?

This seems powerful enough, at least rhetorically or symbolically. The opponent stands utterly defeated from the very beginning. However, Aristotle is not satisfied when he has confounded him once; he needs to confound him repeatedly, which suggests that Amphisbeton somehow resists refutation. It is time now to look closely at the name Aristotle has chosen for his opponent. The noun *amphisbētōn*, "opponent," comes from the verb *amphisbētein*, to oppose, which is a compound of *bainein*, to walk, and the prefix *amphis*. Like many prefixes in Greek, *amphis* has various and at times opposite meanings. *Amphis* means "both" and "separately." It always involves two elements set in contradistinction or opposition, but it may either join or disjoin them. Aristotle could have chosen other terms to designate an opponent – terms prefixed with the less ambiguous prefix *anti*, like *antikeimenos*. By choosing a term in *amphis*, the joining-disjoining prefix, he indicates that this opponent is not an ordinary opponent, someone against (*anti*) whom one is set or disposed. Amphisbeton is both an opponent and an accomplice. Aristotle is plainly aware of this trait when he explains that this opponent does not say "yes" when one says "no" and "no" when one says "yes." Straightforward polemic does not breach the principle of non-contradiction; it reinforces it. Amphisbeton is more subtle and dangerous:

> And at the same time our discussion with him is evidently about nothing at all; for he says nothing. For he says neither "yes" nor "no"; and again he denies both of these and says "neither yes nor no"; for otherwise there would be something definite. (*Metaphysics* IV, 1008a. p. 1592)

If I say, "Beautiful weather, isn't it?," Amphisbeton does not say: "You find that beautiful? I find it awful." He says: "Beautiful and awful, beautifully awful and awfully beautiful." And then he adds: "Not at all beautiful and not at all awful, both and none." Such an interlocutor would be exasperating, but can he exist? Aristotle brings him to the verge of fictional existence but does not flesh him out, giving him only the textual status of a theoretical or rhetorical position. Then Aristotle invites a good number of philosophers (including Anaxagoras, Parmenides, Protagoras, and Cratylus) to occupy the inexistent seat on which Amphisbeton sits and does not sit, speaking without saying anything.

Aristotle himself is close to taking on the role of Amphisbeton when he tries to answer the argument of Democritus and Anaxagoras, according to whom "contradictories and contraries exist simultaneously in all beings."[24] Aristotle says: "To those, then, whose belief rests on these grounds, we shall say that in a sense they speak rightly and in a sense they err" (*Metaphysics* IV, 1009a, p. 1593). "You are right and you are wrong" sounds like a typical amphisbetian answer. What prevents Aristotle from becoming his own opponent is the careful addition of "in a sense . . . in a sense . . ." Aristotle explains this crucial nuance, which distinguishes ambivalence from ambiguity:

> For "that which is" has two meanings, so that in some sense a thing can come to be out of that which is not, while in some sense it cannot, and the same thing can at the same time be and not be – but not in the same respect (*ou kata tauto*). (*Metaphysics* IV, 1009a, p. 1593)

In his definition of the principle of non-contradiction, Aristotle insists that the principle is valid only if things are considered under the same perspective: "It is, that the same attribute cannot at the same time belong and not belong to the same subject in the same respect (*kata to auto*)" (*Metaphysics* IV, 1005b 20). Aristotle does not contradict the principle of non-contradiction when he says "you are both right and wrong" because he is aware of linguistic ambiguity. One single term or proposition may mean several things. The first sentence of *Categories* says: "When things have only a name in common and the definition of being which corresponds to the name is different, they are called *homonymous*" (*Categories*, 1a, p. 3).

Aristotle differs from the sophists because he does not consider language to be a tool perfectly adapted to reality or thought. Pierre Aubenque proposes that Aristotle's fight against the sophists led him to renounce believing in a divine power of human language. From divinely inspired, the *logos* becomes dialectic, but the price to pay for universalizing and abstracting is ambiguity.[25] Aristotle accepts ambiguity as a necessary condition of human language, but he refuses ambivalence as an unsustainable position for human thought. He refuses it so much that he does not give this position a name. The noun *amphis-bētōn*, used once and only once in *Metaphysics* IV, does not produce an abstract term equivalent to our modern *ambivalence*, which Eugen Bleuler, a Swiss psychiatrist, coined in German around 1909.[26]

In *Metaphysics* IV, ambivalence is prohibited as a theoretical position. However, it is not present in this text only as a theoretical position. The elusive figure of Amphisbeton suggests that someone could hold this impossible position, although Aristotle creates Amphisbeton only to deny his existence. As he builds and rebuilds his refutation, he indicates two locations where ambivalence could reside: poetry and madness.

Poets and madmen

Homer appears in one passage dealing with the idea that all perceptions and hence all thought is true, an idea shared, according to Aristotle, by Democritus, Empedocles, Parmenides, Anaxagoras, and Homer:

> A saying of Anaxagoras to some of his friends is also related – that things would be for them such as they supposed them to be. And they say that Homer also evidently had this opinion, because he made Hector, when he was unconscious from the blow, lie "thinking other thoughts" – which implies that even those who are bereft of thoughts have thoughts, though not the same. Evidently, then, if both are forms of thought, the real things also are at the same time so and not so. (*Metaphysics* IV, 1009b, p. 1594)

Modern translators indicate that the only passage in the *Iliad* that could correspond more or less to what Aristotle says is not about Hector but about Euryale.[27] Since for Aristotle and his contemporaries the Homeric tradition is still largely an oral one, the imprecision of the citation is nothing remarkable in itself.[28] However, the Homeric reminiscence is the kernel of Aristotle's thought in this passage and deserves attention. Aristotle remembers that Homer uses the expression "*keisthai allophroneonta*" meaning "to be lying with one's mind somewhere else." The verb *allophronein* appears in *Odyssey* X (l. 374), with the meaning "to think about other things," when Ulysses sits at Circe's table, his mind distracted by other thoughts from his immediate environment. In *Iliad* XXIII (l. 698), *allophronein* describes the mental state of a boxer (Euryale during the funeral games) who has just been knocked out. Aristotle associates the expression "*keisthai allophroneonta*" with Hector wounded, but whether it is Euryale knocked out or Hector wounded who has his mind elsewhere while lying down on the ground, this "elsewhere" is more comatose than thoughtful.

Aristotle works poetically and philosophically with Homer's wording in a way that is difficult to render in modern translations. *Allophronein* derives from *phrēn*, the diaphragm, which is also, in Greek, the heart, the soul, the mind, and the spirit. *Phronēsis*, thought, derives also from *phrēn*. In commenting on Homer's phrase, Aristotle uses four terms derived from *phrēn*:

> Homer [. . .] made Hector, when he was unconscious from the blow, lie "thinking other thoughts" (*allophroneonta*) – which implies that even those who are bereft of thoughts (*paraphronountas*) have thoughts (*phronountas*), though not the same. Evidently, then, if both are forms of thought (*phronēseis*), the real things also are at the same time so and not so. (*Metaphysics* IV, 1009b, p. 1594)

Can the thoughts produced by a mind dissociated from itself (as indicated by the prefixes *allos*, other, and *para*, beside) still be considered as *logoi*, bearing the discrimination between true and false? For Aristotle, it is necessary to answer these questions in the negative, for this type of thinking (other, elsewhere, or beside) is a threat for the principle of non-contradiction. If everything one thinks is true, and if what someone has in mind in a semi-comatose or delirious state can be considered as thought, then the bizarre ideas conceived in such states will be as true as any other ideas. As a consequence, the world will contain things that are simultaneously this and not this. The bottle I see as a single object when I am sober will also be in reality double, since I see it that way at other times. Moreover, in such a philosophy, the question of nonexistent things or beings is irrelevant, and, therefore, nothing can be viewed as a fiction. If everything one thinks is true and corresponds exactly to reality, there is no logic – and no fiction.

Aristotle may have a point but his critique of Homer's citation does not make his argument stronger or clearer. Obviously, when Homer uses the verb *allophronein* to describe the thoughts of a fighter who has just been hit on the head, he does not make any statement about the status of truth of these thoughts. To attack the position holding that "all thought is true," Aristotle blends two arguments: (1) All thought is not true; (2) All that happens in the mind is not a thought. In fact he needs only to demonstrate that all that happens in the mind is not true, whether it is called thought, perception, opinion, or anything else. If all that happens in my mind is true, then a bottle can be both one and two, which contradicts the principle of non-contradiction. If I admit that certain things happening in my mind are not true, then I can interpret my varying estimates of the number of bottles in such a way that I do not contradict the principle: the bottle is either one or two, but not both. In one case, my estimate is correct; in the other, I am mistaken because I am drunk or someone hit me on the head.

The citation of Homer brings the discussion from the general level that philosophers address to the particular level of individual lives that poets represent. When Aristotle introduces a philosopher's opinion, he uses a verb meaning "to say."[29] For Homer, he uses the verb *poiein* (to make) in the sense of making a poem: Homer "*epoiēse*" (made) Hector (*Metaphysics* IV, 1009b, p. 1594). By choosing this verb, Aristotle emphasizes Homer's poetic activity and suggests possible figures other than sophists and philosophers to sit on Amphisbeton's seat. Amphisbeton could be Hector or Euryale or anyone whose thoughts have been violently altered. He could also be the poet describing such a state of mind, himself experiencing a state of *allophronēsis* or *paraphronēsis* under poetic inspiration or through *mimēsis*. In all these cases, Amphisbeton cannot be so easily reduced to the category of plants. Humans may experience temporary alterations of their thoughts, without completely losing it. Poets are not deprived of the capacity of making sense. Altered thoughts and poetry can still mean something at the very moment they openly contradict the principle of non-contradiction, as the Anacreontic distich quoted by Dancy shows: "I love and I don't love / I am mad and I am not mad."[30] Dancy thinks that Aristotle eliminates contradictions in language and thought by ignoring or suppressing whole domains of his own culture. It could be argued that Aristotle indicates obliquely in the text of *Metaphysics* IV the domains where meaning and contradiction coexist, contradiction is meaningful, and contradiction does not threaten the principle of non-contradiction. Homer's *allophronēsis* and *paraphronēsis* allow Aristotle to indicate another argument in favor of the principle of non-contradiction. If I accept the principle, I will resolve my contradictory thoughts by admitting that one must be false in the language of philosophers, other or beside in the language of poets. The principle will not help me to determine which one is true, which one is false, but, in general, experience should be able to do this.[31] If, on the contrary, I do not accept the principle, I will have no motivation, no mental frame to distinguish between different sorts of thoughts or mental states. In a world where all is true and all is false, there is no reason to make distinctions between perceptions, thoughts, remembrances, dreams, illusions, and hallucinations. In such a world, again, the concept of fiction does not make sense.

Aristotle implies this line of argumentation but does not develop it in *Metaphysics* IV, perhaps because he does not want to descend from ontology to psychology – ontology being the first science he is at pains to isolate and address, and psychology being only a specific science among many. However, the principle of non-contradiction remains as fundamental for Aristotle's psychology as for his ontology.[32] It explains why Aristotle, so curious about everything, is not interested by the various manifestations of *mania*, madness, to which Plato pays much more attention, classifying it in four categories.[33] For Aristotle, if poets can still be assimilated to misled philosophers and considered as rational interlocutors, the madman ought to be excluded from the field of reason. Madness demonstrates the insanity of not complying with the principle of non-contradiction, as illustrated by the example of the man who wants to go to Megara and jumps into a well. The poet who imitates madness is in the city, and can be heard by all. The madman (a tragic Amphisbeton) is out in the wild, and his speech is inaudible. In her book on madness, history, and politics in nineteenth-century France, Laure Murat asks: "Would the madman be in essence the opponent? Or is it the opponent who is systematically considered as a madman?"[34] Her opponent is a political opponent, but the conflation she questions may have been embedded much earlier in the Western discourse on reason and madness.

Aristotle's unconscious

Poets and madmen experience states of the mind that baffle the principle of non-contradiction – which raises the issue of consciousness versus unconsciousness. There is no term in ancient Greek that corresponds to the Freudian unconscious. However, it is possible in *Metaphysics* IV to follow a line of thought addressing the discrepancy between what a subject says he or she thinks and what he or she truly thinks.[35] After Aristotle has presented the principle of non-contradiction as "the most certain of all" and as a principle about which "it is impossible to be mistaken," he explains,

> for such a principle must be both the best known (for all men may be mistaken about things about which they do not know), and non-hypothetical. For a principle which every one must have who knows anything about being, is not a hypothesis; and that which every one must know who knows anything, he must already have when he comes to a special study. (*Metaphysics* IV, 1005b, pp. 1587–8)

However, philosophers need to establish this principle, no matter how well known it is: "he whose subject is being *qua* being must be able to state the most certain principles of all things. This is the philosopher" (1005b, p. 1587). The beginning of *Metaphysics* IV makes clear that it is not for everybody to "know beings as beings." If all humans share a desire for knowledge, not all seek the principles of knowledge. The philosopher discovering the most fundamental and solid principles of all (*tas bebaiotatas archēs*) knows something that is not common knowledge. This is not contradictory since the fundamental nature of a principle does not imply that all know it consciously. On the contrary, if the principle is by definition "best known," "unmistakable," and "that which every one must know who knows anything," no one needs a philosopher or to be a philosopher to have access to such a principle. Still, the best-known principle needed Aristotle to give it to the world in an explicit and clear form. If Parmenides got close with his "being is, not being is not," Aristotle had to invent a formulation that did not exist before him.[36]

Let us admit that one may know a principle without being able to enunciate it, or without thinking about it as a formalized rule. What sort of knowledge is this? And what is the use of formalization if knowledge can exist without it? *Metaphysics* IV presents the principle of non-contradiction as a principle that a large number of people misunderstand, violate, or ignore. Among these people, only the madman or the man reduced to a vegetative state is sincerely opposed to the principle, which bans them from the realm of reason without hope of reintegration as long as they stay mad or vegetative. All other opponents are not sincere or do not know what they say when they claim anything that implies a rejection of the principle.

After having stated the principle of non-contradiction, Aristotle addresses the disjunction between thinking and saying:

This, then, is the most certain of all principles, since it answers to the definition given above. For it is impossible for any one to believe the same thing to be and not to be, as some think Heraclitus says; for what a man says he does not necessarily believe. If it is impossible that contrary attributes should belong at the same time to the same subject (the usual qualifications must be presupposed in this proposition too), and if an opinion which contradicts another is contrary to it, obviously it is impossible for the same man at the same time to believe the same thing to be and not to be; for if a man were mistaken in this point he would have contrary opinions at the same time. It is for this reason that all who are carrying out a demonstration refer it to this as an ultimate belief; for this is naturally the starting-point even for all the other axioms. (*Metaphysics* IV, 1005b, p. 1588)

According to Aristotle, reality and the constitution of the human mind constrain humans to think correctly about the principle of non-contradiction. Human thinking cannot, whether we like it or not, bear contradictory thoughts simultaneously. Human thinking can be mistaken but not contradictory. I can take John for Paul or vice versa, but I cannot sincerely believe that the man crossing the street is both John and Paul. Still, Aristotle needs to explain how some people do hold contradictory opinions despite the fact it is impossible to think in a contradictory fashion.

An opinion that some lend to Heraclitus helps Aristotle to open up a space of disjunction between thinking and saying: "for what a man says (*legei*) he does not necessarily believe (*hupolambanein*)." The verb *hupolambanein* means literally "to take from below," that is, "to under-stand." For Aristotle, thinking works in depth, whereas saying operates at the surface. David Ross comments on this passage in the following terms: "Aristotle is not accusing Heraclitus of insincerity, but suggesting that he did not express his meaning exactly, or did not understand the full meaning of the words he used."[37] But if Heraclitus is not insincere or lying when he says that the same thing is and is not, if he is not conscious that there is a discrepancy between what he thinks and what he says, then what sort of disjunction is at work here? The statement "What a man says he does not necessarily believe" suggests a distinction between a deeper level of *logos*, where contradiction is impossible to think, and a more external or superficial level where contradiction can be enunciated. However, this distinction does not imply the existence of an unknown continent in the human mind or soul. "It is not necessary that one may think everything one may say" does not lead automatically to "one does not know everything one thinks." The place that Aristotle assigns to logic and its fundamental principles is at the root of thinking, in the depth, that is, exactly where Freud denies it, when he claims that the unconscious does not know the laws of logic, and, in particular, the principle of non-contradiction.[38] The unconscious that appears in *Metaphysics* IV is deeply logical and is defined logically. Contradiction can be thought only at a more superficial level, the level of belief. Someone who believes that one can think contradictorily plays with ideas without thinking deeply. The terms Aristotle uses to describe this game are related to *doxa* (opinion) or *agnoia* (ignorance), or in general are located at the level of saying (*phēmi*) rather than thinking. For instance, "there are some who, as we have said, both themselves assert (*phēsin*) that it is possible for the same thing to be and not to be, and say that people can judge (*hupolambanein*) this to be the case" (*Metaphysics* IV, 1006a, p. 1588). Some people "say" that one can "think" contradictorily, but they are mistaken since they do not think that way themselves. The fact that they are able to say anything implies that at a deep level they abide by the principle of non-contradiction, which is the foundation of meaning.

They demonstrate the same thing in their daily actions and behavior:

> For he does not aim at and judge all things alike, when, thinking it desirable to drink water or to see a man, he proceeds to aim at these things; yet he ought, if the same thing were alike man and not-man. But, as was said, there is no one who does not obviously avoid some things and not others. Therefore, as it seems, all men make unqualified judgments, if not about all things, still about what is better and worse. (*Metaphysics* IV, 1008b, p. 1592)

Philosophers are like all other humans. They act according to principles agreeing with both reality and reason, but they do not necessarily know the principles that compel them to act in a certain way rather than in another. Their speeches and opinions are sometimes in agreement with the deep principles, and sometimes not. They suffer from contradiction as an intermittent disease that can be cured, either by strength or persuasion:

> Those who have been driven to this position [that all opinions and appearances are true] by difficulties in their thinking can easily be cured of their ignorance (*agnoia*); for it is not their expressed argument (*logon*) but their thought (*dianoian*) that one has to meet. But those who argue for the sake of argument (*logou kharin legousi*) can be convinced only by emending the argument (*logou*) as expressed in words. (*Metaphysics* IV, 1009a, p. 1593)

For Aristotle, a mental disease founded on error or ignorance is easier to cure than a disease caused by a passion for arguing. This difference may come from the fact that Aristotle's treatment consists in making conscious and known a knowledge that is already there, in language and thought, but is not necessarily perceived by those who think and speak. Again, Aristotle is opposed to Freud. Freud views contradiction as the repressed that needs to be patiently recuperated and brought back to consciousness. For Aristotle, the principle of non-contradiction is repressed by false beliefs and arguments. The philosophical cure makes the patients aware that the principle of non-contradiction is at work in them, and that thinking without abiding by it is a disease of the mind. Again, Aristotle presents contradiction as a degradation, this time not an ontological one (degrading a rational being down to the level of a vegetative one) but an epistemological one (from knowledge down to ignorance).

Conclusion

Metaphysics IV treats problems and themes that appear in other books of *Metaphysics*, but with a peculiar mood, rhythm, and tone. Truth is at stake as a logical and an ethical problem.[39] Refutation leads Aristotle to create an opponent, which is, at first, nothing other than a rhetorical device and an empty variable, but becomes an ominous presence revealing that contradiction cannot be so easily rejected from the realm of rational thinking and speaking. The opponent is both impossible and all too real. He sits like a guard dog at the threshold of the house, keeping mental disorder outside. His position at the threshold of rationality marks what we call ambivalence, which is unconceivable without the philosophical work Aristotle and his predecessors did on opposition. Aristotle developed his thoughts on this issue in such a way that ambivalence had to become unbearable and unspeakable for the rational subject as a sincere position.

Laurence Horn, in his *Natural History of Negation*, states that "it is with Aristotle that the locus of the study of negation leaves the realm of pure ontology and enters the domain of language and logic."[40] I would add that this relocation occurs through the representation of absolute negation in a fictional figure. The opponent negates the very possibility of negation and assertion. Aristotle, in creating this figure as a necessary nonexistent being (such as Kripke's unicorn), anchors the principle of non-contradiction in imagination and adstraction. This is why I have proposed at the end of Chapter 3 to consider Western rationalism as a "fictionalism." By fictionalizing ambivalence, contradiction, and other modes of being acquainted to the world that cannot be asserted or negated, Aristotle has divided the mind between a rational and an irrational side, using the irrational side to make the divide visible and understandable.

CHAPTER 5

The fool who says no to God

Introduction

In Chapter 2, we encountered Anselm as a dialectician and grammarian gifted with a sharp sense of words, images, and meaning not dissimilar to the sharpness in style and meaning evident in Marie de France's vernacular works, particularly in her fables. We will now return to the Anselm that is better known: the author of the so-called ontological argument.

Anselm of Canterbury occupies a peculiar position in philosophical lineages. He combines mystic and logic in an unprecedented fashion, culminating with the "proof of the existence of God," in which he uses the figure of Insipiens, the fool who denies the existence of God. Like Aristotle's opponent, the fool is a contradictor, a denier, and a trouble-maker, used to buttress a fundamental argument. Between the opponent and the fool, between the argument establishing the principle of non-contradiction and the argument establishing the logical impossibility of the inexistence of God, lies the same difference as between a sophist and a heretic, a philosophical error and a theological one. This chapter will examine the place of Insipiens in Anselm's *Proslogion*, a short "allocution" (which is the meaning of the Greek word "*proslogion*"), written in 1077 or 1078 as a sequel to the *Monologion*, a meditation in the form of a soliloquy on God's nature. Anselm claims at the beginning of both works that he wrote them at the request of brothers of the abbey of Le Bec, who wanted to have in writing what Anselm had presented to them orally.[1]

Some historians of ideas consider Anselm's speculation on the existence of God as an isolated, anomalous experiment, which did not have much influence on the evolution of Catholic theology and Western philosophy.[2] It is true that there is no Anselmian filiation as there are Platonist and Augustinian ones. The philosophers and theologians who discussed the ontological argument either to accept or reject it did so from a very different perspective than that of Anselm.[3] However, at that moment of "transition from a monastic to a scholastic view of rationality,"[4] Anselm's *Proslogion* appears as a key episode in the context of the late eleventh-century tension between reason and faith and the revival of logic.

Anselm's prayers

Anselm's relation to his predecessors is more complex than Aristotle's (which is not simple itself), because he is the heir of two lineages: the lineage of the fathers of dialectic and the lineage of the Church fathers; he is also the son of two sets of allegoric mothers: Philosophy/Reason and Church/Faith. The two lines and sets merge in the person of Boethius, translator of Greek logic into Latin, philosopher, poet, and Church father. In his major works, Anselm explicitly mentions only Aristotle and Augustine, while he implicitly refers numerous times to Boethius. In his letters, he makes explicit references primarily to Christian authors such as Gregory, Bede, Lanfranc, and Cassian. A few passing references demonstrate his acquaintance with classical authors such as Virgil, Horace, and Lucan.[5] Yet the text that most fills his mind and memory is the Bible – especially the Psalms.

In the prologue of the *Monologion*, Anselm claims that, obeying the prescription of his brothers, he included nothing in his meditation that "*quatenus auctoritate scripturae penitus nihil in ea persuaderetur*" [would be argued on the basis of the authority of Scripture] (p. 7; p. 5). However, he also claims in the same prologue that "*quam ego saepe retractans nihil potui invenire me in ea dixisse, quod non catholicorum patrum et maxime beati Augustini scriptis cohaerat*" [in the course of frequent rereadings of this treatise, I have been unable to find anything which is inconsistent with the writings of the Catholic fathers, and in particular with those of the Blessed Augustine] (p. 8; p. 6). Not referring to the authority of Scripture does not mean that Anselm has forgotten it, but rather that he has it very much in mind. If Anselm does not cite the Scripture or the Church fathers in the *Monologion*, he cannot help using them to build his argument. In his edition and translation of Anselm's *Œuvre*, Michel Corbin signals in notes numerous allusions to Augustine and Boethius's treatises on the Trinity, and a few allusions to the Scripture.[6] By explaining that he is arguing without the Scripture but in agreement with it, Anselm recognizes that his relation to theology, Church, and faith is of such a nature that he cannot set it into parentheses, even for a brief exercise. He is silent about his position with regard to the philosophical lineage that he activates. Perhaps the tools of dialectic were so foundational in his education that he did not consider himself to be indebted to the originators and transmitters of these tools and modes of thinking. Who would acknowledge an intellectual affiliation to Mr. Webster or M. Larousse? Anselm assimilates logic to the natural work of any rational mind, not to a historical development involving thinkers, masters, disciples, and schools. The alternative to not using the "authority of the Scripture" is to use *"plano stilo et vulgaribus argumentis simplicique disputatione"* [the plain style, with everyday arguments, and down-to-earth dialectic] (p. 7; p. 5). That the *Monologion* is anything but plain, unsophisticated, and straightforward is obvious as soon as the first chapter unfolds. The *topos* of modesty masks an intellectual affiliation that is embarrassing to admit. Claims of lack of sophistication often cover the fear of being associated with a sophistic master or school.

In the prologue of the *Proslogion*, Anselm presents his second attempt to demonstrate the existence of God as a more elegant and economic argument than his first one. Since the *Monologion* is *"considerans illud esse multorum concatenatione contextum argumentorum"* [made up of a connected chain of many arguments] (p. 93; p. 82), Anselm is now seeking a single argument:

> *coepi mecum quaerere, si forte posset inveniri unum argumentum, quod nullo alio ad se probandum quam se solo indigeret, et solum ad astruendum quia deus vere est, et quia est summum bonum nullo alio indigens, et quo omnia indigent ut sint et ut bene sint, et quaecumque de divina credimus substantia, sufficeret.* (p. 93)

> I began to wonder if perhaps it might be possible to find one single argument that for its proof required no other save itself, and that by itself would suffice to prove that God really exists, that he is the supreme good needing no other and is he whom all things have need of for their being and well-being, and also to prove whatever we believe about the Divine Being. (p. 82)

Anselm does not reiterate that he will not use the authority of the Scripture, but his explanation implies it, and reducing the series of arguments presented in the *Monologion* into a single one appears as a continuation of the exercise in an even more self-contained fashion. However, the very first chapter of the *Proslogion* contains about twenty biblical quotations, the majority from the Psalms.[7] This number approaches the thirty-two quotations of the first pages of Augustine's *Confessions*. Just as Augustine starts with an elaborate psalm praising God and asking his help ("Have mercy so I may find words . . . Speak to me so that I may hear . . . allow me to speak before your mercy," *Confessions* I: 5–7), Anselm starts with a psalm praising and beseeching: "Come then, Lord my God, teach my heart where and how to seek you, where and how to find you. . . My heart is made bitter by its desolation; I beseech you, Lord, sweeten it by your consolation . . . Teach me to seek you, and reveal yourself as I seek you" (*Proslogion*, pp. 84–7). In both cases, Scripture is not used as an authority but as what authorizes a man (i.e., a sinner) to seek God with human means (his memory or his ability to argue). For Anselm, Augustine is both a father in knowledge and a brother in sin and faith. By imitating Augustine's imitation of the psalms, Anselm places himself next to him as a praying figure turned toward God.[8] Where can Aristotle and Boethius stand in this picture or vision? At the heart of the argument contained in Anselm's psalm, argument that is the offering Anselm makes to his brothers and God, the principle of non-contradiction plays the role of the grain of sand in the oyster. It has to be here, unacknowledged, for the pearl to take shape.

Anselm's argument

The logical argument does not take much space in the whole structure of the *Proslogion*: chapters 2 and 3 contain it. Chapter 4 addresses human ability to think contradictory thoughts. The remaining twenty-two chapters examine the nature of the divine being, once it has been established that God is of such a nature that he cannot be thought not to exist. What makes the argument of *Proslogion* 2 and 3 work? According to Alexandre Koyré, the novelty of Anselm's argument lies in the combination of the "principle of perfection" and the "principle of non-contradiction."[9] The argument begins with the two following sentences: "*Et quidem credimus te esse aliquid quo nihil maius cogitari possit. An ergo non est aliqua talis natura, quia 'dixit insipiens in corde suo: non est deus'?*" (p. 101) [Now we believe that you are something than which nothing greater can be thought. Or can it be that a thing of such a nature does not exist, since "the Fool has said in his heart, there is no God"?] (p. 87). On one hand, we are asked to participate in the belief that God can be defined as a perfection expressed negatively (*aliquid quo nihil maius cogitari possit*); on the other hand, we see a contradictor intruding into the text to affirm that the God that has just been defined in such a way does not exist. The task at hand is not to disprove the contradictor but to disprove the possibility that such a contradictor might invalidate the definition of God proposed – a definition essential to the establishment of the necessity of his existence. Whereas Aristotle uses Amphisbeton in an aggressive fashion to destroy the position of his philosophical adversaries, Anselm introduces Insipiens defensively in order to protect his own position. The authority of the psalms serves as a shield against potential accusations of doctrinal error, or worse.[10] Anselm cannot be influenced directly by *Metaphysics*, since the only texts of

Aristotle that were available to him are *Categories* and *On Interpretation*.[11] However, his argument relies on the principle of non-contradiction, as well as on the evocation of an elusive character. Insipiens is a little bit less elusive than Amphisbeton since he has been given something to say: "*non est deus*," but this is said "*in corde suo*," and after that he keeps quiet for the rest of the *Proslogion*.

Insipiens or the opponent to God

Anselm did not invent the fool: he borrowed him from Psalms 9(10), 13(14), and 53(54).[12] In Psalm 9(10) appears the wicked figure of an oppressor of the poor:

> *Quare Domine stas a longe*
> *dispicis in temporibus angustiae*
> *in superbia impii ardet pauper*
> *capiantur in sceleribus quae cogitaverunt.*   (Ps. 9:22–3)

> Why stand far off, Lord?
> Why hide away in times of trouble?
> The wicked in their arrogance hunt down the afflicted;
> May their crafty schemes prove their undoing.   (Ps. 10:1–2)

The oppressors are qualified as *impii* in anticipation of the following verses, in which the psalmist establishes a correlation between wickedness and lack of faith:

> *Quia laudavit impius desiderium animae suae*
> *et avarus adplaudens sibi blasphemavit Dominum*
> *impius secundum altitudinem furoris sui non requiret*
> *neque est Deus in omnibus cogitationibus eius*
> *parturiunt viae eius in omni tempore*   (Ps. 9:24–6)

> The wicked boasts of the desires he harbours;
> in his greed he curses and reviles the Lord.
> The wicked in his pride does not seek God;
> there is no place for God in any of his schemes,
> His ways are always devious.   (Ps. 10:3–5)

This impious and sinful man is not yet a denier of God, but someone who challenges God's power, which implies that he believes in the existence of God. He abuses the poor and the humble because he thinks God will not notice: "*dixit in corde suo oblitus est Deus, abscondit faciem suam*" (Ps. 9:32) [He says in his heart: God has forgotten, he has hidden his face] (Ps. 10:11). This rebellious attitude is radicalized in the first lines of Psalm 13(14) – the lines Anselm quotes in *Proslogion* 2: "*Dixit insipiens in corde suo non est Deus*" (Ps. 13:1) [The fool says in his heart: There is no God] (Ps. 14:1). The rest of the psalm exposes the consequence of this denial: sin and wickedness that God has noticed, notices, and will notice.

> *Corrupti sunt et abominabiles facti sunt studiose:*
> *non est qui faciat bonum*
> *Dominus de caelo prospexit super filios hominum*
> *ut videret si esset intelligens requirens Deum.* (Ps.13:1–2)

> They are corrupt and their deeds are abominable:
> No one does good!
> The Lord has looked out from heaven upon the sons of men,
> to see if there be any that understand and seek God. (Ps.14:1–2)

Between Psalm 9(10) and Psalm 13(14), the argument goes into full circle: wickedness leads to rebellion, rebellion to denial, and denial to wickedness. The psalmist defines the inner life of the impious fool as lacking faith by lack of morality, and lacking morality by lack of faith. Moreover, Insipiens is also wanting in terms of intelligence and knowledge. Neither does he understand nor seek to understand God, and thus manifests a profound ignorance unaware of itself:

> *nonne cognoscent omnes qui operantur iniquitatem*
> *qui devorant populum meum ut cibum panis*
> *Dominum non invocaverunt.* (Ps.13:4)

> Have they no understanding, all those who commit iniquities,
> who devour my people as if eating bread?
> They have not called upon the Lord. (Ps.14:4)

By not calling or seeking God, the now large group of *insipientes* condemns itself not to know, in absolute terms: "*nonne cognoscent?*"

When Anselm gives his *Proslogion* the subtitle, "*Fides quaerens intellectum*" (p. 94) [Faith in Quest of Understanding] (p. 83), he may have in mind Psalm 13(14), v. 2: "*Dominus de caelo prospexit super filios hominum ut videret si esset intelligens requirens Deum*" [The Lord has looked out from heaven upon the sons of men, to see if there be any that understand and seek God]. Against the vicious circle linking denial and ignorance, or lack of faith and lack of intelligence, Anselm creates a virtuous circle in which faith and intelligence feed one another. For this virtuous circle to exist, and for the *pius sapiens* to replace the *impius insipiens*, the un-creed of the fool (*non est deus*) must be understood as a logical impossibility.

The man who does not understand what he thinks

Serendipitously, Anselm does not have to invent a character uttering such a blasphemy, but he needs to construct a logical apparatus to turn the blasphemy into a theological tool. Aristotle only needs to create a certain logical position without any specific enunciation: Amphisbeton is a character without lines to say. Insipiens has a line to say – if only to himself – but it carries its own contradiction in the same way that Amphisbeton's blank line does. More precisely, for Aristotle to say "X" (and no matter what X is as long as it makes sense) implies having the principle of non-contradiction in mind, *a priori*, even if one denies it *a posteriori*. For Anselm to say "God is not" implies having the necessary existence of God in mind *a priori*, even if one denies this existence or its necessary character *a posteriori*.

Aristotle and Anselm's arguments raise various logical and ontological problems. They also share a cognitive difficulty. Both of them need to maintain that it is possible for one "to say" or "to say in one's heart" things they demonstrate to be "unthinkable." As we have seen, Aristotle uses two hypotheses to separate what is said from what is thinkable. The first hypothesis is that the speaker lies, is not sincere when he says things that contradict the principle of non-contradiction, and that he says that for the sake of arguing. In the second hypothesis, the speaker is sincere but does not realize the full implications of what he says, thus creating a rift between what he thinks and what he thinks he thinks (*Metaphysics* IV, 5, 1009a). Anselm's solution is more complicated, and implies a modification of the biblical Insipiens.

Anselm never supposes that Insipiens is insincere when he affirms: *non est Deus*.[13] If he is a fool and an ignorant, he is sincerely so. In the psalms, Insipiens is clearly neither an atheist nor an agnostic but a rebel who says to God: "*Non es*," which is a contradictory statement. In Psalm 9(10), "*et avarus adplaudens sibi blasphemavit Dominum*" (Ps. 9:24) [the wicked curses and reviles the Lord] (Ps. 10:3). That provocative attitude is linked to the disappearance of God from his mind: "*neque est Deus in omnibus cogitationibus eius*" (Ps. 9:26) [there is no place for God in any of his schemes] (Ps. 10:4). Like children who believe they cannot be seen by people they cannot see, the rebellious sinner "*dixit enim in corde suo oblitus est Deus, abscondit faciam suam*" (Ps. 9:32) [says in his heart: God has forgotten, he has turned away his face] (Ps. 10:11). This Insipiens occupies an ambivalent position toward God, affirming his existence while denying his power (you exist but you cannot do anything against me) or affirming his power while denying his existence (you are powerful but you do not exist). The biblical Insipiens says something similar to what Amphisbeton would say if he was asked his opinion on the existence of God: "He is and he is not." At first sight, Anselm's Insipiens does not commit any sin against the principle of non-contradiction by saying "God is not." His proposition may be false but it does not seem contradictory. Anselm posits his contradictor within the sphere of rational thought, out of which Aristotle expelled his opponent, posting him just at the threshold of rationality. Insipiens is not an enemy of the principle of non-contradiction; he is an enemy of God who both warrants and transcends the principle. Insipiens, like Amphisbeton, is cornered in an impossible location, but inside, not outside, rationality.[14] It is important to note that Anselm never denies Insipiens a basic reasoning capacity, and never envisions him as a plant or an insane man jumping into a well instead of going to Megara.[15]

As soon as Insipiens appears in the *Proslogion*, he displays a capable intellect, which makes the distinction between what he says and what he thinks a subtle one:

> *Sed certe ipse idem insipiens, cum audit hoc ipso quod dico: "aliquid quo maius nihil cogitari potest", intelligit quod audit; et quod intelligit in intellectu eius est, etiam si non intelligat illud esse.* (p. 101)

> But surely, when this same Fool hears what I am speaking about, namely, "something-than-which-nothing-greater-can-be-thought," he understands what he hears, and what he understands is in his mind, even if he does not understand that it actually exists. (p. 87)

Insipiens is deprived neither of senses (he hears) nor of sense (he understands). But he does not understand all that is in his understanding or intellect. Anselm is aware that the distinction he tries to establish between what is in the intellect and what is understood by the intellect is so subtle that it may bring the faithless *insipiens* dangerously close to the faithful *sapiens* that Anselm hopes to present as a model to his brethren. In *Proslogion* 4, he comes back to this point:

> *Verum quomodo dixit in corde quod cogitare non potuit; aut quomodo cogitare non potuit quod dixit in corde, cum idem sit dicere in corde et cogitare? Quod si vere, immo quia vere et cogitavit quia dixit in corde, et non dixit in corde quia cogitare non potuit: non uno tantum modo dicitur aliquid in corde vel cogitatur. Aliter enim cogitatur res cum vox eam significans cogitatur, aliter cum id ipsum quod res est intelligitur. Illo itaque modo potest cogitari deus non esse, isto vero minime. Nullus quippe intelligens id quod deus est, potest cogitare quia deus non est, licet haec verba dicat in corde, aut sine ulla aut cum aliqua extranea significatione.* (pp. 103–4)

How indeed has he "said in his heart" what he could not think; or how could he not think what he "said in his heart," since to "say in one's heart" and to "think" are the same? But if he really (indeed, since he really) both thought because he "said in his heart" and did not "say in his heart" because he could not think, there is not only one sense in which something is "said in one's heart" or thought. For in one sense a thing is thought when the word signifying it is thought; in another sense when the very object, which the thing is is understood. In the first sense, then, God can be thought not to exist, but not at all in the second sense. No one, indeed, understanding what God is can think that God does not exist, even though he may say these words in his heart either without any signification or with some peculiar signification. (pp. 88–9)

This passage echoes three Aristotelian ideas: the principle of non-contradiction, the ambiguity (or "homonymy") of language, the adequacy between reality and thought. By first stating that "to say in one's heart" is a biblical synonym of "to think," Anselm acknowledges that the argument made in *Proslogion* 2 and 3 entails a contradiction: Insipiens thought X and Insipiens did not think X, since to think X is contradictory and therefore cannot be thought. However, it was necessary to state that "Insipiens thought X" in order to demonstrate that he could not do such a thing. Anselm uses the argument of homonymy[16] to solve this contradiction. "To think" means different things and language can help to make these different meanings clear. The distinction between "to think" [*cogitare*] and "to understand" [*intelligere*] solves the contradiction. Insipiens may have thought that "God is not" but he could not have understood it.

Anselm, like Aristotle, distinguishes two levels of thought, the level of words and their various associations, and the level of the relation between words and reality, or words and things.[17] At the level of words, "error is human" and one may think thoughts that do not match reality. But if one thinks and understands what one thinks, then the adequacy between reality and thought, or between reality and human reason, must prevent error and make "unthinkable" what does not match reality.[18] Error is human but human reason cannot err when it is well employed. Insipiens errs because he says something without analyzing the terms he uses, without pondering over their meaning and logical implications. When he says "God is not" he does not understand that this proposition contradicts the concept contained in the word "God." Insipiens thinks something like "God who cannot not be is not," but he does not understand that he is thinking such a thing, for otherwise, he would recognize that he is wrong.

Can Insipiens become a Catholic?

This passage of the *Proslogion* implies that there is hope for Insipiens. If only he could understand what he thinks, he would stop thinking such nonsense. And since Insipiens is able to understand, he only needs that someone explain to him his error. Can we imagine here that Anselm discovered a pedagogical tool able to convert to his faith *cum* understanding any reasonable human being? Can we view Insipiens as a *bon sauvage* ready to receive the message and waiting for it? Karl Barth, in his comment of the *Proslogion*, rejects such an anachronistic interpretation, which presents Anselm as an adept of a rational, natural, and universal theology.[19] However, Barth also thinks that Anselm may have in mind non-Christians of his time (Jews, Muslims, pagans, and heretics): "There is no question but that this other person who rejects the Christian revelation and therefore Anselm's presupposition is really before Anselm's mind as he writes and that he is speaking in opposition to him, addressing him, wishing to say something to him or at least wishing to reduce him to silence."[20] In this case, Insipiens represents someone who is outside the system in which faith founds the intellectual quest, the system in which Anselm locates himself. But then, further on, Barth states that none of Anselm's works can be viewed as "addressed directly to those outside, that is as 'apologetic' in the modern sense."[21] In this case, Anselm addresses his *Proslogion* to Christian theologians, or, even more specifically, to Benedictine theologians like himself. The argument is both *pro domo* and *in domo*. On this, Barth concludes that Anselm's argument is not "esoteric," which seems once more to open the field toward the outside, rather than to confine it to the converted.[22]

Barth's contradictory argument assigns to Insipiens at times the role of a contradictor external to faith, at times the role of a partner in faith, perhaps even of an alter ego of Anselm. This reflects the tension at work in Anselm's text and stresses the ambiguity of Insipiens's role in it. Anselm does not explain how Insipiens could transform his *cogitare* into an *intelligere* illuminated by faith, if he does not start by accepting faith itself, that is by saying "God is." Anselm adds to his distinction between thinking and understanding:

> *Deus enim est id quo maius cogitari non potest. Quod qui bene intelligit, utique intelligit id ipsum sic esse, ut nec cogitatione queat non esse. Qui ergo intelligit sic esse deum, nequit eum non esse cogitare.* (p. 104)

> For God is that-than-which-nothing-greater-can-be-thought. Whoever really understands this understands clearly that this same being so exists that not even in thought can it not exist. Thus whoever understands that God exists in such a way cannot think of him as not existing. (p. 89)

One needs to understand the word "God" in a peculiar way for the argument to work. But how can one come to understand that God "is that-than-which-nothing-greater-can-be-thought"? Chapter 4 ends on a prayer, which indicates that this understanding depends on the grace of God:

> *Gratias tibi, bone domine, gratias tibi, quia quod prius credidi te donante, iam sic intelligo te illuminante, ut si te esse nolim credere, non possim non intelligere.* (p. 104)

> I give thanks, good Lord, I give thanks to you, since what I believed before through your free gift I now so understand through your illumination, that if I did not want to believe that you existed, I should nevertheless be unable not to understand it. (p. 89)

The clause "if I did not want to believe that you existed" opens a new logical and psychological perspective on Insipiens. Instead of a poor, limited fellow, able to think (*cogitare*) but unable to understand (*intelligere*), a Thomas appears, who does not want to believe even when he sees. Moreover, this incredulous posture is attributed hypothetically to "I, Anselm," just at the moment in the mental journey retraced by *Proslogion* when "I, Anselm" has been granted with an illumination allowing him to become unable not to understand, even if he made the conscious choice of refusing to believe. Schufreider points out that the ending of chapter 4 is a "reversal of the famous saying that was the final note of *Proslogion* 1."[23] Responding to "I do not seek to understand so that I may believe; but I believe so that I may understand," the conclusion of chapter 4 claims that the understanding that has been reached through the two preceding chapters (which constitute the "argument") would prevail even if faith happened to be defective – at these dark hours when even an Anselm may be tempted to become an Insipiens.

Amphisbeton is an outsider, allowing insiders to find their place in the realm of reason. Insipiens is a halfway Amphisbeton, standing at the same time inside and outside the realm of divinely inspired reason. Insipiens does not oppose or ignore the principle of non-contradiction but he refuses to believe in what, for Anselm, is the foundation of the principle, that is, a being whose existence cannot be denied and who is the creator of all beings whose existence is contingent and *can* be denied. The principle of non-contradiction establishes that one cannot say at the same time "God is" and "God is not." According to Anselm, this is exactly what Insipiens does when he says in his heart "God is not." But this argument stands on the assumption that God is a concept that cannot be denied, and that cannot be submitted to the usual tools of verification. "It is possible that God exists" or "Either God exists or he does not" are unacceptable propositions according to Anselm's logic. Thus, the principle of non-contradiction itself takes a different value than it has for Aristotle: it holds only in so far as a major exception to it is accepted as rational. God is the font of rationality but he cannot be subject to its claims. In Anselm's works, reason and reasoning are at times allies given by God to help men to believe, at times enemies questioning what is unquestionable. This explains why some modern readers view Anselm as a pillar of scriptural authority and others as a pioneer of Christian rationalism.[24] This finally explains why Anselm accepted to integrate the counter-argument of a monk of Marmoutiers, named Gaunilo, in subsequent copies of his work, together with his answer.

Gaunilo's text is titled "*Quid ad haec respondeat quidam pro insipiente*" [What can be responded on behalf of the Fool].[25] Gaunilo assumes the position of Insipiens to argue that Anselm's argument does not convince him that he cannot truly think (*intelligere*) the proposition: "God does not exist." Anselm states at the beginning of his answer that Gaunilo is not a true Insipiens:

> *Quoniam non me reprehendit in his dictis ille 'insipiens', contra quem sum locutus in meo opusculo, sed quidam non insipiens et catholicus pro insipiente: sufficere mihi potest respondere catholico.* (p. 130)

> Since it is not the Fool, against whom I spoke in my tract, who takes me up, but one who, though speaking on the Fool's behalf, is an orthodox Christian and no fool, it will suffice if I reply to the Christian. (p. 111)

"*Catholicus pro insipiente*," a Catholic speaking for or as a fool who does not believe in God is exactly the position that Anselm assumes when he gives a voice and a role to play to the biblical Fool in the *Proslogion*. Anselm is making clear here that one can argue with Insipiens as long as Insipiens is a role and not a person. Gaunilo probably agrees with this premise. Both Gaunilo and Anselm use the same strategy but draw different conclusions – not about the existence of God but about the possibility of finding a logical argument to demonstrate it. This difference of view transforms the role Insipiens plays for them. For Gaunilo, Insipiens demonstrates that reason cannot turn someone who does not believe into a believer: one must believe to believe, and then understanding may follow – or not, depending on God's will. To start with "God is not" is not the best way to arrive at "God necessarily is." For Anselm, one needs to have faith in order to start reasoning about faith, but reasoning may at some point become an interlocutor of faith. Insipiens then is an internal voice of the Catholic, a voice that needs to be soon quieted but not until it has spoken out its disbelief.

Conclusion

If we were to read the *Proslogion* as a drama instead of a mystic treatise or a philosophical argument we would identify a chorus (the brethren) and three protagonists. In order of appearance: Anselm, God, and Insipiens. Each one of these protagonists represents a logical and ontological definition. Anselm is a being that can be thought not to exist. God is a being that cannot be thought not to exist. Which leaves us with Insipiens as a being that cannot be thought to exist. If the first and second protagonists can be related to two different modes of existence, that is, contingency and necessity, a third mode is needed to give Insipiens a status. Let us call it fiction. In such a configuration, fiction is not presented as the lower end of a succession of degraded mimetic images, but as a component in a logical and ontological structure expressing the relation between the mind and the world. Whether Anselm proves the necessity of God's existence both in the mind and the world or not, he opens for fiction a logical space symmetrically opposed to the space of God – a space necessary for humans to understand and explore their fundamental contingency.

CHAPTER 6

The man who says no to reason

Introduction

Aristotle's opponent and Anselm's fool are minimalist fictions, created by philosophers who had no intention to let these characters turn their arguments into tales. Once they have played their role in defining a logically impossible position, they vanish from the text. In this chapter I will examine a text in which opponents to reason and reasoning linger, having more to do than to say nothing at all or tell silently a blasphemy to their own heart. This text is usually considered a fiction, and, to the best of my knowledge, does not figure on syllabi for courses taught in philosophy departments. It is Guillaume de Lorris and Jean de Meung's *Roman de la Rose*, a vernacular *summa* of courtliness and scholasticism composed in the thirteenth century, in northern France.[1]

In the *Rose*, two characters stand up as self-conscious supporters of contradiction, irrationality, or plain foolishness: an allegorical figure named False Seeming (*Faux-Semblant*) and the hero and narrator of the whole romance, the Lover (*Amant*). I will first examine False Seeming's speech in relation, on one hand, to the liar paradox, and, on the other, to the positions occupied by Amphisbeton and Insipiens. I will then consider the Lover as an opponent to Reason, able to use his own reason to assert his choice to be a fool. I will conclude with a study of the Lover as a paradoxical "I," a plausible self, and a fictional subject.

False Seeming against God, logic, truth, and common sense

False Seeming as a liar

Since Susan Stakel's study of the semantic field of deceit in Jean de Meun's *Rose* and her rehabilitation of False Seeming as a key element of the text, several scholars have closely examined this figure.[2] Daniel Heller-Roazen connects False Seeming's assertion *"Parjurs sui"* (l. 11175) [I am a perjurer] (p. 196) to the paradox of the liar and the tradition of *insolubilia* in medieval logic.[3] Created in ancient Greece, the paradox has provoked logical investigations during Antiquity, the Middle Ages, and the twentieth century.[4] In modern logic, it has inspired in particular Bertrand Russell, Alfred Tarski, and Saul Kripke's works on truth theory and formal semantics.[5]

Treated as a logical problem, the liar paradox "arises when we try to assess the truth of a sentence or proposition that asserts its own falsity, e.g.: **(A)** Sentence (A) is not true."[6] In a more natural form, "This sentence is false" or "I lie" present the same properties. The paradox works best when it is as decontextualized as possible, but some logicians have considered it in relation to empirical contexts. For instance, instead of considering "I lie" or "I am a liar" as an absolute (this "I" can only and exclusively utter lies), other formulations of the paradox admit "contingent liars" who may occasionally tell the truth:

> Epimenides, himself from Crete, is said to have claimed that all Cretans are liars. This claim is paradoxical if interpreted to mean that Cretans always lie, or if interpreted to mean they sometimes lie and if no other claim made by Epimenides was a lie. On the former interpretation, this is a simple variation of the liar paradox; on the latter, it is a form of contingent liar.[7]

Naming the liar (in this case, Epimenides) and embedding the statement in an anecdote relative to Crete is an example of adstraction at the service of abstract modes of thinking.

Saul Kripke proposes another adstraction closer to our times in his 1975 article "Outline of a Theory of Truth," in which the Liar is named "Nixon." Kripke's scenario is more elaborate than having Nixon saying: "I am a liar." It involves a fictional character named "Jones" who would say: "Most (i.e. a majority) of Nixon's assertions about Watergate are false." As Kripke notes, "nothing is intrinsically wrong with [this statement], nor is it ill-formed." But, if Nixon was to retort, "Everything Jones says about Watergate is true," then the paradox of the liar would be triggered, and the two assertions would be "true if and only if they are false."[8] This could be boiled down to the following exchange between any two protagonists: "You are a liar." "Everything you say is true." Besides its interest for logicians, such an exchange seems to me aptly to represent the mutual positions of fiction makers and fiction users, with regard to truth. A fiction user is someone who never stops saying, "you are a liar," to which a fiction maker never fails to respond, "how right you are."

False Seeming expands the liar paradox into a liar speech of more than a thousand lines (ll. 10956–12013). The God of Love is assembling his troops to attack the castle in which Jealousy keeps the Rose locked away from the Lover. His barons advise him that he should enroll False Seeming in his army (ll. 10923–31). The God of Love agrees and asks False Seeming to come forward:

> *Sans faille, tu es maus traÿstres*
> *Et lerres trop desmesurez:*
> *.C. mile foiz t'es parjurez;*
> *Mais toutevois en audiance*
> *Pour nos gens oster de doutance,*
> *Commant je que tu leur ensaingnes,*
> *Au mains par generaus ensaingnes,*
> *En quel lieu mieus te troveroient*
> *Se du trover mestier en avoient*
> *Et comment l'en te connoistra,*
> *Car granz sens en toi connoistre a.*
> *Di nous en quel lieu tu converses.*   (ll. 10944–55)

Without fail, you are a wicked traitor and unrestrained thief. You have perjured yourself a hundred thousand times. But in any case, to relieve our people of their uncertainty, I command you in their hearing to teach them, at least with general indications, in what place they would best find you if they needed to, and how you will be recognized, for one needs good wits to recognize you.[9] Tell us what places you frequent. (p. 193)

The God of Love may be the king of fools, but he is no fool. He knows what False Seeming is up to and if he enrolls him it is not to reform him but to use his skills. The assertion "*tu es maus traÿstres*" [you are a wicked traitor] (l. 10944) is not paradoxical, but based on empirical facts: "*.C. mile fois t'es parjurez*" [You have perjured yourself a hundred thousand times] (l. 10946). Accusing someone else of being a liar does not produce a self-referential statement, but requesting that the alleged traitor teach and advise one's troops sounds paradoxical in a psychological and political sense: "You are a liar; now tell and teach us the truth about yourself." Moreover, the lines that caught Daniel Heller-Roazen's attention in False Seeming's speech are similar to the lines pronounced by the God of Love (see Table 2). By accepting literally the God of Love's definition, False Seeming retroactively turns the God of Love's statement into a paradox in the same way that Kripke's Nixon turns Jones's statement into a paradox when he says: "Everything Jones says about Watergate is true."

Table 2 *The liar paradox in the God of Love and False Seeming's speeches in* Roman de la Rose

God of Love	False Seeming
Sans faille, tu es maus traÿstres	*Sanz faille traÿstres sui gié,*
Et lerres trop desmesurez:	*Et pour larron m'a dieus jugié;*
.C. mile foiz t'es parjurez;	*Parjurs sui.*
(*Roman de la Rose*, ll. 10944–6)	(*Roman de la Rose*, ll. 11173–5)
Without fail, you are a wicked traitor and unrestrained thief. You have perjured yourself a hundred thousand times.	Without fail, I am a traitor, and God has judged me a thief. I am perjured.
(*The Romance of the Rose*, p. 193)	(*The Romance of the Rose*, p. 196)

False Seeming also casts ambiguity on the identity and power of the God of Love by saying: "*Et pour larron m'a dieus jugié*" [God has judged me a thief]. To which God is he referring? To the God of Love who has precisely accused him of being a thief? Or to another God (sometimes also called the God of Love), more powerful than the alleged "God of Love" who is willing to hire False Seeming in his troops?

The whole speech of False Seeming is a masterpiece of ambiguity and contradiction, for, as Susan Stakel says, "he seems unable to make an assertion without contradicting himself."[10] It should be noted though that self-contradictory assertions such as "*Sanz faille traÿstres sui gié*" [I am a perjurer] are rare in False Seeming's speech. Besides lines 11073–5, I find only line 11236, "*C'est voirs, mes je sui hypocrites*" [It is true but I am a hypocrite] (p. 197) that could be read as a version of the liar paradox. It is again a response to an assertion made by the God of Love: "*Tu sembles estre.i. sains hermites* (l. 11235) [You seem to be a holy hermit] (p. 197). Apart from these two lines, False Seeming contradicts himself by affirming things that he has denied earlier, or vice versa. For instance, when he claims "*Nus ne doit haïr pour l'abit / Le povre qui s'en est vestuz*" (ll. 11960–1) [No man should hate a poor man on account on the habit he is dressed in] (p. 208), he contradicts his earlier claim: "*J'ameroie mieus l'acointance /.C. mile tans dou roi de France / Que d'un povre, par nostre dame! / Tout eüst il ausi bonne ame*" (ll. 11245–8) [I would a hundred thousand times prefer the acquaintance of the King of France to that of a poor man, by our lady, even though he had as good a soul] (p. 197). False Seeming is above all a contradictor, that is, someone who does not abide by the principle of non-contradiction, since in his speech he juxtaposes contradictory statements without choosing between them.

False Seeming as a contradictor

I agree with Heller-Roazen that the character False Seeming is related to the liar paradox, but I view this paradox as a particular way of breaching the principle of non-contradiction, and, therefore, the liar as a species of the contradictor *genus*. The proposition

(1)   I am a liar.

entails that

(2)   Proposition 1 is true.

and

(3)   Proposition 1 is false.

are both true at the same time and under the same respect. This breach of the principle is particularly interesting in that it summons the issue of reflexivity in the arena. Reflexivity, as a logical concept, defines a relation "that, like identity, each thing bears to itself."[11] Although it is mostly applied to "things" that are abstract elements of sets and are designed by conventional signs such as letters (a, b, c, . . .), reflexivity involves the notion of "self." Mathematicians and logicians can relate a or b to itself without having to imagine a or b as selves. For philosophers reflecting on reason and rationality as human prerogatives, and trying to define thresholds of humanity through figures upholding impossible statements, the self cannot be avoided. Silent Amphisbeton led Aristotle to muse about the relation between what one thinks and what one says, what one believes one thinks and what one truly thinks. Anselm's Insipiens talks to his heart, that is, to himself. By giving False Seeming a fully developed first person speech, Jean de Meun indicates that the most interesting expression of the liar paradox may be: "I am a liar" with emphasis on "I." False Seeming lies mostly with regard to himself, and thus embodies what Jean de Meun views as a major sin and temptation of his times, hypocrisy.

This emphasis on the first person singular does not make False Seeming a more plausible figure than Amphisbeton or Insipiens. One can contradict oneself; one can deny God while invoking him; one can lie about oneself. But one cannot do these things constantly.[12] False Seeming's speech is so full of contradictions, deceits, and lies that the reader cannot figure out whether he is a consistent or an inconsistent liar or contradictor. Does he ever say anything unparadoxically true or sincere? This implausibility may be why Jean de Meun thought he could take the risk of making him question both Aristotle's logic and God's existence.

Describing the "*faus religieus*" (l. 11027) [false religious] (p. 194), False Seeming explains that they lead people to believe in the sophism "*Cist a robe religieuse / Donques est il religieus*" (ll. 11058–9) [this man has the robe of religion; therefore he is a religious] (p. 194). Although traditional wisdom has taken care of this sophism with the proverb "*Li abiz ne fait pas le moine*" (l. 11062) [the habit does not make the monk] (p. 194), according to False Seeming,

> *Nepourquans nus n'i set respondre,*
> *Tant sache haut sa teste tondre*
> *Voire rere au rasoir d'ellanches*
> *Qui barat trenche en.xiii. branches;*
> *Nus nel set si bien distinter*
> *Qu'il en ose.i. seul mot tinter.*
> *Mais en quelque lieu que je viengne,*
> *Ne comment que je m'i contiengne,*
> *Nient plus fors barat n'i chaz.*
> *Ausi com dant Tyberz li chaz*
> *N'entent qu'a soriz et a raz,*
> *N'entent je a riens fors a baraz.* (ll. 11063–74)

Nevertheless no one knows how to reply to the argument, no matter how high he tonsures his head, even if he shaves with the razor of the *Elenchis*, that cuts up fraud into thirteen branches. No man knows so well how to set up distinctions that he dare utter a single word about it. But whatever place I come to, no matter how I conduct myself, I pursue nothing except fraud. No more than Tibert the cat has his mind on anything but mice and rats do I think of anything except fraud. (pp. 194–5)

False Seeming is smart enough not to stand directly against the principle of non-contradiction. However, he flatly denies that the logical apparatus Aristotle created, in particular in his *Sophistical Refutations* (in Greek *Sophistikoi elenchoi*, in Latin *De sophisticis elenchis*), is a tool that could help us to separate falsehood from truth, and fallacy from genuine argument. Confronted by False Seeming and his followers, Aristotle himself would be like a rat caught by a cat. All his distinctions between categories of arguments would amount to nothing against the power of seduction and the determination of the masters of *barat* (fraud). Amphisbeton has returned, with a vengeance and an army of pious-looking sophists following him.

About God and Christianity, False Seeming, true to himself, remains doggedly ambivalent. He preaches "*la religion / selonc la droite entencion*" (ll. 11126–7) [religion based upon a right intention] (p. 195) against the simulacra of religion he described earlier. He accurately quotes the Bible (Proverbs: ll. 11281–6, p. 198; Gospels and Saint Paul: ll. 11379–410, p. 199; Matthew: ll. 11606–15, p. 203) and invokes the example of Christ and the apostles against begging (ll. 11297–303). But he also affirms that "*Car laborer ne me puet plaire: / De laborer n'ai je que faire; / Trop a grant paine en laborer; / J'aim mieus devant les genz orer / Et affubler ma renardie / Du mantel de papelardie* (ll. 11523–8) [working can give me no pleasure: I have nothing to do with it, for there is too great difficulty in working. I prefer to pray in front of people and cover my foxlike nature under the cloak of pope-holiness] (p. 202). Invoking "*renardie*" in the late thirteenth century is to invoke the famous trickster we have already encountered in Chapter 3. The devil is never far away when Renard appears.

The God of Love, who had been silent for a long time, interjects: "*– Qu'est-ce, dyable? Quel sont ti dit? / Qu'est-ce que tu as ici dit? / –Coi? Granz dyablie apertes! / – Dont ne croiz tu pas dieu? – Non certes!*" (ll. 11529–32) [– What's this? The devil! What are your words? What have you said here? – What? – Great and open disloyalty. Don't you fear God then? – Certainly not] (p. 202). As the disjunction between Dahlberg's translation and Strubel's edition points out, this passage is difficult to interpret. Some editors attribute the line "*Coi? Granz dyablie apertes!*" to the God of Love, some attribute it to False Seeming. Some manuscripts give "*crains*" [fear] where other give "*crois*" [believe].[13] Even the milder variant, in which False Seeming simply states that he does not fear God, is enough to evoke the fool of the Psalms and Anselm's *Proslogion*. In the bolder variant, False Seeming affirms that what he says is "*granz dyablies*" [greatly diabolical] and that he does not believe in God. Later on, he will claim "*Je sui des vallez antecrist*" (l. 11717) [I am one of Antichrist's boys] (p. 205) and "*Ainsi antecrist atendrons, / Tuit ensamble a lui nous tendrons*" (ll. 11849–50) [Thus we are awaiting Antichrist, and all together we will hold by him] (p. 207). False Seeming never says clearly "There is no God." He seems rather to hold that, "there may be a God but I don't care." Or, given his wide use of self-contradiction, False Seeming's position toward God could also be stated as: "There may be a God or not; therefore I do believe in him and I don't."

False Seeming merges the liar, Amphisbeton, and Insipiens in one as he defies both logic and God. Like them, he is less a character representing a plausible self than a figure representing a limit of language, an impossible speech that nonetheless must be spoken. The liar, Amphisbeton, and Insipiens are implausible because they say so little, and impossible because what they say would collapse the whole system of meaning they would use to say so. False Seeming is implausible because he is pure speech without limit: he could continue on and on as a sort of verbal machine. He is impossible because he makes daily communication impossible: he flouts all of Paul Grice's maxims of conversation at once.[14] But, as we have seen in preceding chapters, if Amphisbeton and Insipiens were conceived as weapons preempting counterarguments by demonstrating their fundamental impossibility, after having fulfilled their mission they continue to loom in the text as ambiguous presence, both denied and ascertained. Aristotle even points out human domains in which Amphisbeton would somehow make sense: madness, poetry, rhetorical games played by sophists. Anselm was unable to assign a fixed place to Insipiens inside or outside the Christian faith and made of him a dangerous, potential double of the questing Christian philosopher. With False Seeming, the opponent to rational discourse is allegorized in a way that makes of him both a pure figure of speech and a well-informed commentator of current events. He refers at length to the quarrel between the mendicant orders and the University of Paris, an event that was the Watergate of Jean's era.[15] To the logical and theological issues that were at stake for Aristotle and Anselm, Jean adds moral and political issues. How can people live in society if *barat* and *renardie* render most verbal communications ambiguous, ambivalent, deceptive, or self-contradictory? Like for Aristotle and Anselm, the opponent represents not only hostile others, but also a part of oneself that must be overcome: as Aristotle fought an inner sophist and Anselm an inner heretic or doubter, Jean, as he gives voice to False Seeming, seems to fight an inner hypocrite.

The *Roman de la Rose* is not an allegorized treatise of neo-Aristotelian philosophy, although some parts of it, in isolation, could be read as such. The speech of False Seeming is embedded in a first person narrative. It must be understood in relation to the fictional self whom False Seeming is summoned to help conquer a rose. By calling deceit, lies, and hypocrisy to support the Lover's amorous quest, the God of Love rewards his servant's devotion to Love and resistance to Reason. This time, the opponent to Reason is not only a plausible, fully developed character: he *is* the two authors of the text.

The Lover and Reason

Love as the antithesis of reason

When Reason appears for the first time in Guillaume de Lorris's *Rose*, the Lover is in great need of advice. After getting very close to his beloved rosebud, he had to back up in the face of Dangier, the fierce guardian of the rose's chastity. Reason starts her speech by explaining the origin of his suffering: "*Biaus amis, folie et enfance / T'ont mis en poine et en esmai. / Mar veïs le bel tens de mai / Qui fist ton cuer trop esgaier*" (ll. 2996–9) [Fair friend, folly and childishness have brought you this suffering and dismay. It was an evil hour when you saw the beauty of May that gladdened your heart so much] (p. 73). Then she adds idleness as another cause of his sorry state. She describes the obstacles he will encounter if he persists in his infatuation and, at last, she delivers her prescription, which can be summarized as: "Stop being in love if you want to keep your sanity."

In her seventy-four-line speech, Reason uses the noun "*folie*" six times, the noun "*folage*" once, the adverb "*folement*" once, and the verb "*foloier*" twice, demonstrating that she takes seriously her main function described by the Lover himself as the "*pooir et seignorie / De garder homme de folie*" (ll. 2991–2) [the power and the lordship to keep man from folly] (p. 73). The narrator claims that God has created Reason in his image to fulfill such a difficult task (ll. 2988–9). So Reason, according to her role, explains to the young man that to be a fool is to follow one's heart: "*Le cuer, que tu as trop volage, / Te fait entrer en cest folage*" (ll. 3058–9) [It is your too-fickle heart that makes you enter into such folly] (p. 74). Not to be a fool is to follow Reason's advice, that is, not to follow one's heart. In other words, Reason is saying to the Lover: "either you follow your heart and you are a fool, or you follow me and you are reasonable."

The message is simple but raises two problems. First, the state of reasonability is defined in a negative way, that is, as not to be a fool. So, in order not to be a fool, you have not to be a fool. Second, there is a strict disjunction between following Reason's advice and surrendering to Love: "*Onques mon consoil n'i atendis / Que tu au dieu d'amors te rendis*" (ll. 3055–6) [You did not heed any of my counsel when you gave yourself to the God of Love] (p. 74). If to surrender to Love is the opposite of following Reason's advice, then it seems that a lover cannot be reasonable, as Chrétien de Troyes states in the song "*Amors, tençon et bataille*": "*Molt m'a chier Amors vendue / S'onor et sa seignorie, / K'a l'entree ai despendue / Mesure et raison guerpie*" [Love sold me access to her land and realm for a high price, for at the gate I forfeited measure and abandoned reason].[16] Then, it would be unreasonable for Reason to talk to someone in love.

The Lover's reaction to her speech confirms this reading. He simply gets mad: "*Je respondi iriement*" (l. 3072) [I replied angrily]. The Lover rebels against his advisor, tells her to let him be in love and dismisses her. Reason meekly obeys his order: "*Atant Raisons s'est departie / Qui voit bien que par *sermoner / Ne m'en porroit de ce torner*" (ll. 3094–6) [Thereupon Reason left, since she saw that her preaching could not turn me from my purpose] (p. 75). The Lover returns to his sorry state: "*Je remains d'ire et de duel plains*" (l. 3097) [I remained, full of anger and sorrow] (p. 75). God's daughter, created by him in Paradise, in his own likeness, to guard humans against foolishness, appears singularly powerless when confronted by a banal, benign case of youthful love. However, if the Lover can be considered unreasonable, he certainly cannot be considered irrational.[17] He has understood the gist of Reason's speech and his response makes sense. Reason here seems to be an instance of self-control rather than the intellectual faculty that allows understanding, judgment, and thoughts, and her power seems to be limited by the free will of the self.

At the beginning of Jean de Meun's part of the *Rose*, the Lover is still obsessed, frustrated, and depressed, but he reflects on what Reason told him. After lamenting the fact that he cannot win access to the Rose, the Lover goes through a spell of self-criticism: "*Si n'ai de sens, ce croi, demie, / Ainz fi grant folie et grant rage / Quant au dieu d'amours fis homage*" (ll. 4129–31) [Nor, believe me, did I show a grain of sense, but rather folly and madness, when I gave homage to the God of Love] (p. 92). The Lover rephrases Reason's argument and applies it to himself: to be in love is foolish; I am in love, therefore I am a fool. He also credits Reason for the new turn of his thoughts: "*Bien le m'avoit raisons noté / Tenir me puis pour assoté / Quand des lors d'amer ne recrui / Et le conseill raison ne crui*" (ll. 4144–7) [Reason warned me well on this situation; I may count myself as an idiot when from that time I neither renounced love nor trusted Reason's advice] (p. 92). But when he starts to think about putting his reflection into practice, he realizes that in order to follow Reason he has to betray Love: "*Je m'en voill, ce croi, repentir. / Repentir! Las! Je que feroie? / Traytres, las, honniz seroie!*" (ll. 4151–3) [I think I want to repent. Repent? Alas! What would I be doing? As a traitor, alas, I should be dishonored!] (p. 92).

The first encounter of the Lover with Reason can be understood as the representation of an inner conflict, reminiscent of twelfth-century Ovidian romances such as *Eneas* or Chrétien de Troyes's *Cligès*, in which monologues often turn into inner dialogues between Reason and Love, or Mind and Heart.[18] But, as Sarah Kay pointed out, it is more difficult to imagine the personifications in Jean de Meun's *Rose* to be part of the mind of the Lover than in Guillaume de Lorris's *Rose*. As a result, "the model which is most widely applicable is that of teachers to (unwilling) pupil."[19] In Jean de Meun's *Rose*, Reason teaches the Lover in a series of speeches full of citations from and references to authorities such as Plato, Cicero, Aristotle, Ovid, Boethius, Andreas Capellanus, etc.[20]

The Lover does not dismiss her until line 7213: "*Et se je sui fols, ne vous chaille*" [It is none of your business if I am a fool] (p. 137). Although he lets Reason lecture most of the time, he intervenes repeatedly to ask or answer questions, or to dispute certain finer points of her lesson. For instance, when Reason asks if the Lover truly thinks she wants him to hate instead of to love (ll. 5367–70), the Lover answers by a fifty-line argument including a direct reference to Cicero's *De Amicitia* that he seems to have read on his own (ll. 5401–4).

Twelfth-century courtly lovers stage their divided state of mind in the inner room of the heart or the soul. Jean de Meun transforms this room into a classroom, in which the self not only feels, enjoys, and suffers, but also reasons, disputes, and learns. This may indicate that Reason can be understood as the Lover's reason (his own private capacity of reasoning) as well as a human trait, shared by all humans. Aristotle's opening statement, "All men by nature desire to know" (*Metaphysics* I, 980a, p. 1552), is put to the test of love. Does a man in love desire to know? The response in the *Rose* is: yes, indeed. The Lover wants to know what love is, and Reason easily convinces him that she can be his teacher on this matter. The Lover says, "*Mout i entendist volentiers / Mes cuers et plus en apreïst / S'il fust qui leçon l'en preïst*" (ll. 4270–2) [my heart would listen willingly and would learn more if there were someone who could teach it] (p. 94). And Reason agrees: "*Par mon chief, je la te vueill prendre / Puis que tes cuers i veult entendre*" (ll. 4273–4) [By my head, I want to teach you, since your heart wants to hear] (p. 94). Without being a philosopher or a sophist, a theologian or a heretic, the Lover is a man arguing with his reason, which implies that he is a man owning Reason (God's daughter) as a part of himself he needs to be whole and human, but that is not the whole of him. He is not an opponent to reason as a matter of principle or because of ineptitude: he opposes reason's dictatorial tendencies and questions her domination over himself. This is a sign that he is not such a fool and has got a sense of what learning from reason should be: based on debate and resistance to authority rather than on acquiescence and monologue. When Reason asks the Lover to renounce love because it is the antithesis of reason, she opens a trap for herself that the Lover shrewdly points out, by accusing her of wanting him to hate (ll. 4641–2). This forces both Reason and the Lover to distinguish various types of love, some of which are compatible with Reason.

Loving Reason

At the end of her speech, Reason offers her love to her student. "*Nepourquant, si ne vueill je mie / Que tu demeures sanz amie: / Met, s'il te plaist, en moi t'entente. / Sui je pas bele dame et gente / Digne de servir.i. preudomme / Et fust emperieres de Romme? / Si vueill t'amie devenir"* (ll. 5791–7) [Nevertheless I don't want you to live without a friend. If it pleases you, turn your attention to me. Am I not a lady beautiful, noble, fit to serve a worthy man, even the emperor of Rome? I want to become your friend] (pp. 116–17). This pedagogically unwise request signals a metaphorical shift. The relation between a young man and his reason has been so far represented as the relation between a master and a disciple. Reason proposes to transform it into a loving relation between *ami* and *amie*. This attempt to shift to another representation means that the relation between master and disciple is not sufficient to describe the relation between "me" and "my reason." From a superego figure towering over the ego and provoking much resistance from him, Reason turns into a seductive figure whose goal is to replace the Rose as love object. This passage is, for most readers, ludicrous, all the more since the Lover will not fall into Reason's snares. Reason's proposition sounds like the attempt of an old maid to master sex appeal, as long as we read it along the code that the Lover uses to talk and think about love. We laugh if we are like the Lover, convinced that the only love accessible to normal human beings is sexual, passionate, and courtly. But if we heed Reason's request to take *"l'entendement / D'amours un pou plus largement"* (ll. 5437–8) [to grasp a somewhat more comprehensive understanding of love] (p. 111), then after the first laugh, we may ponder upon the idea of loving Reason, and loving one's reason.

When Reason gives the Lover the example of Socrates as one of her *amis* (ll. 5843–64), she turns from comedy to tragedy. To a young man repeating that he will die of love if his desires are not promptly rewarded, she opposes the example of an old man who died for the love of *sophia*, a notion that encompasses reason, moderation, judgment, and self-denial. By proposing to be the Rose, Reason asks her audience to think of her in emotional terms. She too can provide joy, fear, anxiety, hope, and perhaps despair. Being reasonable means to tame one's passion out of experience and self-interest. Being in love with reason means to change the object of one's passion, while keeping passionate. Instead of passionately loving, drinking, eating, collecting, gambling, hunting, traveling, conquering, or any other activity usually linked with passion, one would become passionately engaged in thinking, meditating, analyzing, understanding, reading, writing, learning, teaching, abstracting, computing, or any other activity usually linked with reason. The *Rose* does not narrate the complete conversion of the passionate Lover into a passionate writer but it gives clues about the process. The Lover's resistance to Reason's preaching, teaching, and seducing forces her to change her strategy from an authoritarian, externalized approach to an

intimate, emotional exchange. In the narrative, she fails since the Lover
dismisses her once more to turn to other advisers. But her failure produces
the narrative and enables the Lover to become a narrator and two authors.[21]

Reasoning about one's love or Love and loving one's reason or Reason
intersect constantly in the exchange between the Lover and Reason, undermining the antithesis between love and reason that was established in their
first encounter as a psychological and ethical problem. The logical aspect of
the problem is addressed in their second encounter when Reason takes on
the task of teaching the Lover what love is. The lesson turns out to be a
master class in contrariness and contradiction.

Love is everything and its contrary

Reason, having obtained the Lover's attention by focusing on his obsession,
exposes her teaching plan:

> Or te demonstreré sanz [fable]
> Chose qui n'est pas de[monstrable],
> Et savras tantost sanz science
> Et connistras sanz connissance
> Ce qui ne puet estre seü
> Ne demonstré ne conneü.   (ll. 4275–80)

> I shall demonstrate you without fable what is not demonstrable. You shall
> know straightway without knowledge and learn without learning what
> cannot be known, demonstrated, or learned. (p. 94)

This is very advanced pedagogy, one that even the most enthusiastic
renovators of the art of teaching might hesitate to promote in today's
classrooms. As Catherine Brown has shown, several major medieval texts,
including the *Rose*, use contradiction as a "hermeneutic irritant" useful for
teaching.[22] The next stage looks like a shock therapy: Reason administers to
her student a heavy dose of oxymorons:

> Amours ce est pais hayneuse,
> Amours est hayne amoreuse,
> C'est loiautez la desloiaus,
> Ce est desloiautez loiaus,
> C'est paours toute asseüree,
> C'est esperance desesperee,
> C'est raison toute forsenable,
> C'est forsenerie raisnable (ll. 4290–7)
> . . .
> C'est fous sens, c'est sage folie (l. 4320)

Love is hateful peace and is loving hate. It is disloyal loyalty and loyal disloyalty, fear that is completely confident and despairing hope. It is reason gone mad and reasonable madness ... It is foolish sense, wise folly. (pp. 94–5)

The first two lines "love is hateful peace / love is loving hate" should suffice to make the point that love is an ambivalent instance composed of itself and its contrary. The rest of the list gives other pairs of contraries commonly associated with love (loyalty and disloyalty, sickness and health, heaven and hell, spring and winter, etc.), thus reinforcing the dizzying effect. Reason includes herself and her opposite in the list: "*C'est raison toute forsenable / C'est forsenerie raisnable*" [It is reason gone mad and reasonable madness] and a variation on the same theme "*C'est fous sens, c'est sage folie*" [It is foolish sense, wise folly]. The obvious message is that love creates in the mind a state of generalized instability, in which contraries clash instead of delimiting a scale from one pole to another. Love does not slide back and forth between the pole of reason and the pole of madness: it suppresses intermediate states and brings the polar opposites together. Love is madness and reason at the same time and in the same respect.

For Aristotle, contraries and contradictories are two different types of opposition. First, contraries are terms (black, white; ill, in good health) while contradictories are propositions (he is ill; he is not ill). Second, while both contraries and contradictories cannot be both true at the same time applied to the same subject (A cannot be both black and white, cannot sit and not sit at the same time in the same respect), some contraries can be false simultaneously: A may be neither black nor white, but pink or grey. Contradictories, according to Aristotle, cannot be false simultaneously. "A sits" and "A does not sit" cannot be false at the same time. One ought to be true while the other is false.[23] In Reason's list of oxymoronic sentences, this distinction is erased and contraries behave all like contradictories – otherwise, there would be no provocative fun in associating them. Reason presents love as a principle of generalized contradiction, following the lead of courtly poets claiming, for instance, "I shall write a poem of sheer nothing"[24] or "A stroke of joy hits me which kills me"[25] or "My joy turns into sorrow."[26] According to Reason, a Lover is an Amphisbeton able to sing – if not to speak.

The Lover's response proves that he does not view himself as an Amphisbeton, and does not understand what Reason is up to with this oxymoronic firework:

> *Dame, fis je, de ce ne me vant,*
> *Je ne sais pas plus que devant,*
> *A ce que m'en puisse retraire.*
> *En ma leçon a tant contraire,*
> *Que je n'en sai nul mot entendre.*
> *Si la sai je bien par cuer rendre,*
> *K'onc mes cuers rien n'en oublia,*
> *Voire entendre qanqu'il i a*
> *Pour lire en tout communement,*
> *Ne mais a moi tant seulement.*   (ll. 4357–66)

Lady, I flatter myself that I know no more than before of how I can extricate myself from love. There are so many contraries in this lesson that I cannot understand a word of it; and yet I can repeat it well by heart for my heart never forgot any of it. Indeed, I can understand enough of it to read it in public, but not to myself alone. (p. 95)

What the Lover would like to get from Reason is not a list of contraries, but a definition in which he may be able to recognize his own state of mind and which would allow him to understand it and remember the explanation: "*Prier vous vueill dou defenir / Si qu'il m'en puisse souvenir, / Car ne l'oy defenir onques*" (ll. 4369–71) [I beg you to define it in such a way that I may remember it, for I have never heard it defined] (p. 95). The allegedly foolish Lover is asking for a common sense approach to the topic in question – love – and does not accept one of the classic tropes of love in courtly literature: its contradictoriness. Is he starting to be cured, or just totally blind to his own condition?

Reason agrees to switch to another type of discourse about love, based on definition, examples, myths, borrowings from authorities, and arguments. Her speech about love expands into a speech about Fortune, language, justice, and other philosophical themes. In the end, the Lover refuses once more to renounce his way of loving, but this does not mean that he learned nothing from what Reason has said. His rebuke is more articulate than the first one:

> *Se je sui fols, c'est mes damages;*
> *Mais au moins fis je lors que sages,*
> *De ce cuit je bien estre fis,*
> *Quant hommage a mon maistre fis.*
> *Et se je sui fols, ne vous chaille!*
> *Je vueill amer comment qu'il aille,*
> *La rose ou je me sui vouez:*
> *Ja n'iert mes cuers d'autre douez.*
> *(Et se m'amor vous prometoie,*
> *Ja voir promesse n'en tendroie);*   (ll. 7209–18)

If I am a fool, it is my loss. At least – and I think that I am quite certain of it – I did what is wise when I paid homage to my master. If I am a fool, it is none of your business. However it goes, I want to love the rose to which I am pledged. No other will ever fill my heart. If I promised my love to you, I would never keep my promise. (p. 137)

As in his first dismissal speech, the Lover claims that he cannot serve two masters at the same time. Now he also claims that he has the right to be mad because "*c'est mes damages*" [it is my loss], and to choose the object of his love and the subject of his thoughts because it is "*m'amour*" and "*mi penser*" [my love and my thoughts]. The Lover declares his subjective sovereignty by using a rational discourse to support a choice not made on a rational basis.

Another later part of the text shows that the oxymoronic lesson of Reason has not been lost on him. Just before starting his final pilgrimage toward the rose, the Lover says: "*Ainsi va des contraires choses: / Les unes sont des autres gloses; / Et qui l'une en veult definer, / De l'autre li doit souvenir / Ou ja par nulle entencion / N'i metra diffinicion*" (ll. 21577–82) [So it goes with contrary things; one is the gloss of the other. If one wants to define one, he must remember the other, or he will never, by any intention, assign a definition to it] (p. 351). Now the Lover bases his idea of love on the power of contraries to explain or gloss each other, an idea he found incomprehensible when Reason exposed it to him. This indicates that reasoning, like loving, must be done in the first person. No one, not even Reason, can reason for me. In order to reason, I need to embrace Reason as my own, to love her as I love myself.

Loving and knowing in the first person singular

The major issue treated in the *Rose* may not be the question of the compatibility of celestial reason with physical passion within human beings, but the question of knowing, learning, and reasoning in the first person singular. Twelfth-century psycho-logicians (that is, vernacular lyric poets and fiction writers) created concepts and modes of representation that allowed them to study the first person singular mostly from the perspective of love, desire, and language. What does the ability to say, "I love," "I desire," "I sing," or "I say" imply for the subject? The troubadours and trouvères, Chrétien de Troyes, Marie de France, and others provided much to think and imagine on this matter. But upon the implications of statements such as "I learn," "I understand," "I know" vernacular poets did not provide clearly articulated opinions. For Zrinka Stahuljak, "the gap between experience and knowledge means that in the Chrétien romances knowledge in the wake of an experience appears only as a spectre of itself," and cannot lead to abstract thinking or pure *savoir*.[27]

In the twelfth and thirteenth centuries, the theorization of knowledge and learning knew important developments, among which an attempt to reconcile Augustine's imperative to look inside ourselves with Aristotle's imperative to look at the outside world.[28] By replacing Boethius's dialogue between Philosophy and an old unhappy philosopher condemned to death with a dialogue between Reason and a young unhappy lover condemned to write, Guillaume de Lorris and Jean de Meun rephrase the question of knowledge in new terms, using the first person method initiated by Augustine as well as the first person speech invented by the troubadours.[29] As Sarah Kay and Adrian Armstrong stress it, "the success and prestige of the *Rose* ensure an association between intellectual adventure and *poetic form*."[30] Thus the *Rose* renews vernacular courtly psycho-logic in framing it in an imposing network of philosophical and literary citations, paraphrases, borrowing, imitations, and references. It also unknowingly rewrites the scene in Aristotle's *Metaphysics* IV, in which a reasoning character encounters a figure resisting the most fundamental principle of reasoning.

A paradoxical "I"

The Lover is at once a plausible and impossible character, thus following Aristotle's advice in his *Poetics* that "for the purpose of poetry a convincing impossibility is preferable to an unconvincing possibility."[31] It may seem strange to us to consider the Lover (and the *Roman de la Rose*) as plausible, because we tend to assimilate the plausible to the esthetic of realism associated with the modern novel. If we step out of this cultural paradigm, we can identify elements of plausibility that allow readers to be seduced by the *Rose* and accept to conceive the Lover as a particular, plausible individual. Here, I extend David Hult's remark about Guillaume's section of the *Rose* to describe both parts of the romance: "Once one understands that Guillaume's poem works as a text of seduction, one that attempts to elicit an appropriate response from its reader, then one can see that seduction works on (at least) two levels. The most obvious is, of course, the seduction of the Lady, but the other, no less significant, is the seduction of the reader, the call to contemplate, to perpetuate, and possibly to continue the poetic journey."[32] In order to continue the "poetic journey" the reader must have identified in some ways with the narrative "I," despite its paradoxicality.

The *Roman de la Rose* is a long dream, retold in the first person by the dreamer. The prologue of Guillaume's *Rose* starts by quoting the common opinion, that "*qu'en songe / N'ait se fable non et mençonge*" (ll. 1–2) [there is nothing in dreams but fables and lies] (p. 31). But the first speech act of the narrative "I" is to hold the opposite opinion: "*Car endroit moi ai ge creance / Que songe sont senefiance / Des biens au genz et des anuiz*" (ll. 15–17) [but, for my part, I am convinced that a dream signifies the good and evil that come to men] (p. 31). As Daniel Poirion points out, "the theme of this prologue looks like a paradox: what the author will say is true precisely because it is about a dream."[33] The personal pronoun "I" reinforced by the contiguous "me" ("ge" and "moi") identifies itself in opposition to common opinion, that is, paradoxically, and in conjunction with a contradictory stance: establishing one's truthfulness upon a phenomenon usually associated with falsity. To justify his bold stance, the narrator gives the following reason: "*Que li plusor songent de nuiz / Maintes choses covertement / Que l'en voit puis apertement*" (ll. 18–20) [for most men at night dream many things in a hidden way which may afterward be seen openly] (p. 31). This introduces a temporal paradox in the story, which Emmanuèle Baumgartner summarizes thus: "[T]he dream fiction establishes a narrative voice, an 'I' who speaks in the present, rewrites his past, and projects himself into the future, always eluding our attempts to situate the story in space and time."[34]

Jean de Meun did not attempt to resolve the contradictions attached to the narrative "I" and the dream frame he received from Guillaume. He carried them on for thousands of lines, adding yet another paradox. Well into the narrative, the narrator and the readers learn from the God of Love that the narrator's name is Guillaume de Lorris, that he has not yet started to write the romance, that he will die without finishing it, and that another poet, named Jean Chopinel, not yet born, will pick up the interrupted dream and narrative, and inhabit the vacant "I" (Strubel, ll. 10497–682; Dahlberg, pp. 186–9).[35] The infractions committed by the Liar, Amphisbeton, Insipiens, and False Seeming seem relatively innocuous compared to the enormous paradox of attaching the same "I" to two different individuals, in a strange case of deictic reincarnation. However, after the God of Love's disturbing speech, the show continues, and the narrative "I" does not manifest any dismay or concern about his ontological status. He does not cry out: "But, then, *who* am I?" The reader who has accepted the dream frame, the allegorical conceit, the general tendency of the text to expand rather than to move on, and the reduction of the female protagonist to a plant, accepts this new development without ado and continues the journey with the Narrator, Dreamer, Lover, and two Authors as if they were a single referent.

The *Roman de la Rose* tests our obdurate assumption that personal pronouns are reliable shifters. Out of context they remain indeterminate, but, as soon as they are uttered in context, they refer to a specific referent because it is their job to do so. In speech, "I" refers to the speaker and "you" to the addressee, except in the case of reported speech.[36] But even in such cases we usually do not have trouble sorting out the referents of the "I" and "you" occurring in utterances such as: "But you told me: 'I'll see you tomorrow'." This may raise a dispute about what you said and meant and what I heard and understood, but it is unlikely to lead us to brood over the instability of our identities, and the possibility that I could be you and you could be me – or, worse, that "I" could be at once both you and me. In written forms, it is more complicated to establish the referent because the source of enunciation is lacking, but, in most cases, the readers interpret personal pronouns easily, thanks to textual, paratextual, and contextual clues.

There is a literary exception to this linguistic rule. The lyrical "I" that troubadours and trouvères fashioned has peculiar referential features. If it can be related to a specific poet (anonymous or named) as the *vidas* and *razos* demonstrate when they construct a biographical narrative out of poems,[37] it can also be taken as a shifter that continues shifting even after being enunciated. Any singer, performer, listener, or reader can take it on, without definitely fixing it.[38] However, this indefinite quality of the lyrical "I" does not constitute in itself a violation of our common understanding of reference and identity. This "I" refers to a generic "Lover" or "Poet" or "Poet in love," adding to the gnomic wisdom that poetry proffers the experiential authority of the only plausible witness of an inner state: the self. Only "I" can say something about what "I" feel, but it is understood that what one lover feels represents what all lovers feel. Perhaps, too, lovers need to be told what they are supposed to feel while in love. Whether courtly love poetry is descriptive or prescriptive, the first person lends it both depth and versatility, providing a seed capable of developing into a plausible fictional self when transplanted in a narrative context, such as a romance.

A plausible self

By playing with different known literary tropes and genres (the lyric poem, the dream vision, the allegorical didactic narrative, the courtly romance, and the love debate), Guillaume, and then Jean, have created a new standard of literary plausibility or fictional truthfulness.[39] The bafflement and helplessness of the main protagonist develops the trope of the idiotic hero (the *nice*) that Chrétien de Troyes uses in *The Tale of the Grail* – a work that is, like Guillaume's *Rose*, unfinished or suspended in an ambiguous closure.[40] A trait that readers could attribute to the atypical hero of an atypical Arthurian story becomes in the *Rose* the mark of the self that confronts the world and his desire. Baffled, disoriented, silent before the deluge of words pouring out of external and internal mouths, fascinated by images and easily lured by them, so stands "I" in his vulnerable majesty. "I" is sovereign over his dream for he needs only to wake up to reduce all the enemies and obstacles on his path toward the beloved to nothing. Unfortunately, by the same token, the beloved too would be reduced to nothing. Our power upon the *ficta* we create is absolute, but in order to make the *ficta* relative to the self plausible, that is, to make them look like *facta*, the self must be represented in a state of helplessness, bafflement, with little control on what happens to him. The apparent stupidity, passivity, and intellectual limitation of the narrator in the *Rose* is what makes readers identify with this "I" – except, perhaps, the readers who believe that their intellect and will are always in control, even when they dream.

This "far too easily awed and unnerved" character[41] finds his foils in the allegorical figures (Reason, Dangier, Nature, etc.) and stereotypical figures (Friend, the Old Woman) that populate his dream-world and become his protagonists. Although many of them use first person speech (as we have seen with False Seeming) and sound self-assertive and authoritative in comparison with the Lover, none of them confronts him with a full-fledged, individual, alternative "I." As Eric Hicks explains, personifications of qualities cannot logically receive attributes without edging toward tautology (Courtesy is courteous, Justice is just) or toward contradiction (if Poverty is shameful, what is Shame?).[42] Only the narrating "I" can be subjected to various attributions, whether complementary (the narrator may be courtly, young, and idle) or antagonistic (he may be ashamed, poor, and depressed at the same time he is courtly, young, and idle). The cast of the *Rose* emphasizes the plausibility of the main protagonist as it emphasizes the implausibility of the other protagonists, suggesting that, from the perspective of the self, "I" is the only true "I" around.

The only being in the dream and the garden who is presented as another individualized being (not a type or a class) is the rose – who never says "I." Individualized characters saying "I" can be found in embedded stories (such as the story of Pygmalion, ll. 20821–21214; pp. 340–6), but they are not part of the diegesis and do not interact with the narrator, who is the only one in the romance who possesses the following features: having multiple attributes, using the first person singular, and being part of the main plot.

These traits are not necessary in order to make a fiction of the self plausible: the rose could have been given a little first person speech, a rival lover could have entered the garden, the narrator may have encountered Pygmalion and talked with him, etc. But, given the circulation and influence of the *Rose*, they became a dominant template.

The paradoxical "I" set in the *Rose* yields a plausible self, able to reflect, remember, learn, or understand, as well as to feel, forget, ignore, or misunderstand. Is it enough to create a subject?

A fictional subject

The hero of the *Rose* is, according to Daniel Heller-Roazen, a "contingent subject" who "shows himself in his capacity to be someone other than himself, and, at the limit, not to be at all."[43] He is not "a character simply described in the course of the poem of Guillaume de Lorris and Jean de Meun"; he is rather "the fundamental figure for the language of the poem itself" (p. 60). And the poem "reveals itself in its capacity to be otherwise than it is" (p. 62). The argument links strongly the narrative "I," the poem, and contingency, but views the "I" as an "indeterminate *persona* through which the poem unfolds" (p. 62).

I find it difficult or counter-intuitive to associate contingency with something other than the particular, in a narrative context. Contingency can be considered in connection with concepts, classes, and types (e.g., the divine is necessary, the human is contingent, or vice versa), but thinking contingency in time and space usually leads to thinking that contingency particularizes the real and realizes particularity. The unfolding of events in the story – events that could happen or not, in one way or another – leaves a trace of this or that, not of indeterminacy. The strength of Heller-Roazen's argument is that the *Rose* has a particular, privileged relationship with contingency because of a number of specific features (formal and thematic). Its weakness is that, at times, it seems to imply that all poetic discourses are contingent, all personal pronouns are and remain indeterminate (even in context), and that contingency is a necessary trait of poetic, first person speech. To which it could be said that if a poem is in itself a contingent thing (it could have been not written, or written differently, or written and lost, etc.), once it comes to be heard or read, its contingency is fixed in the past and looks singularly like a necessity. Certainly, the text could have been different, but we need to accept it as it exists today, in about 320 known manuscripts.[44] The names "Guillaume de Lorris" and "Jean de Meun" could have remained unknown, or could have been different. But, to this day, no scholar has claimed these names are not part of the tradition, or proposed other ones. And names have the power to endure, once they have been attributed to something or someone. We cannot render the alleged authors of the *Rose* anonymous or rename them unless we deliberately produce a fiction, claiming, for instance, that the *Rose* was written by someone named Marcel Proust and continued by another person named Simone de Beauvoir.

To keep the argument about contingency tight, we need to keep it internal and related to the particular. This romance and this narrator are not contingent in general terms (if they are, it is in a trivial sense), but they fictionalize contingency in particularly ingenious ways, which Heller-Roazen brings convincingly to the fore. I defined fiction in Chapter 5 as the mode of being something that cannot be thought to exist. I have to explain now how it can be related to being something that can be thought not to exist and, therefore, to exist, that is, to being contingent.

Fiction, or "something that cannot be thought to exist," is not necessarily impossible or implausible. It cannot be thought to exist, even when it is possible and plausible, because, at some point in the chain of communication that brought it to us, it is obvious that someone invented it, or, it can be established that it results from a collective invention (I follow here Kripke and Donnellan's ideas about historical trails and blocks, which I discuss in Chapter 3). What I call fiction can be related to William of Ockham's *ficta*. Ockham developed a theory of mental objects that in some ways could replace the universals he rejected as real objects. These *ficta* also included inner objects provoking hallucinations, or presenting to the mind things not yet in existence (e.g., a castle that is still to be built) as well as non-existing things (e.g., a chimera). All of these objects he called "*ficta*." Later, he rejected this theory in order better to respect his own rule of parsimony.[45]

The authors of the *Rose* were certainly not constrained by any rule of parsimony, whether logical, ontological, or stylistic. They expand, multiply, duplicate, or replicate without compunction. However, the paradoxical "I" and plausible self of the *Rose* is not yet another abstraction, but an adstraction – that is, a particular although nonexistent figure. The fact that this "I" refers to different aspects of a person (as author, narrator, dreamer, or lover) and to two different proper names creates a "layered" and paradoxical referent, but tends to render this "I" more particular rather than more general.[46] At the same time, to follow Daniel Heller-Roazen, the main protagonist is presented as under the sway of Fortune, that is, as contingent in all respects. This prevents generalization, for, if what happens to "I" is contingent, or rather, is contingency itself, "I" can only be *this* "I" to which this (which could have been different but nonetheless befell this way) happened.

The confrontation between the allegorical figures and this particular contingent "I" creates a shift from a realist psycho-logic to a nominalist one. "I am reasonable," "I am courtly," "I am jealous," "I am poor" cannot mean anymore "I participate in or represent a quality which exists in the world as a universal." All the towering or prolix figures appearing in the dream affirm through their depictions and discourses that they exist only in a dream, that is one further degree away from reality than the dreaming "I," who can exist, albeit fictionally, outside of his dream. An allegoric poem and narrative such as the *Rose* can be deemed "nominalist" because the presence of allegory as a mode of representation and of allegories as figures does not lead to an allegorical representation of the world and the self. Wetherbee makes the following remark as he reviews medieval works influenced by the *Rose*: "In the *Canterbury Tales*, the elements of the great allegory become refracted and diffused into the fragmentary waking dream lives of ordinary human beings."[47] This could be applied to the *Rose* as well, with the plurality of "ordinary human beings" being reduced to a single human being, diffracting the great allegory in numerous fragments, often contradicting one another. Thus, the old dissenting figure of the opponent finds itself endowed with a new authority and stature: the consciousness of being oneself. The man who says no to Reason in the *Rose* is mortal, contingent, and particular, which entitles him to say "I" and carry on his loving, dreaming, and narrating as a single, adstract being.

Conclusion

In the *Roman de la Rose*, the opponent to the principle of non-contradiction and other reasonable assumptions is externalized as a social evil in the figure of False Seeming, and internalized as a prerogative of the Lover. His opposition to and negotiation with Reason appear as the mark of the free will of a contingent subject, whose very nature is constantly to change and differ from himself, but not to the extent that he becomes another self, or is even able to grant another being the status of "self." This may partly explain why the rose is deprived of selfhood and never says "I" in the romance that bears her name. The construction of an adstract self is a gendered undertaking.

It is also a social undertaking, depicting a city in which words and things are connected in an arbitrary fashion, and speech is never immune to ambiguity, ambivalence, paradoxicality, or deceit. In such a city and for such a subject, fiction appears to be the most appropriate mode of representation. It opens a space of thinking in which meaning can be found in that which cannot be thought to exist and exists only to be thought.

Fathers, sons, and friends

In the preceding chapters and parts of this book I have attempted to bring logic and fiction together as two closely related modes of thinking and knowing. Although I focused mostly on rather cerebral modes of thinking, and the modern theoreticians I referred to were mostly analytic philosophers, I often mentioned affect or emotions – in particular in Chapter 6 in which I studied the debate between a man in love, driven by his affect, and Reason or his reason. In Part III and the final three chapters I will address more directly the relation of affect with logic and fiction.

It may seem counter-intuitive to link logic and fiction, because at first sight logic has nothing to do with affect and fiction is mostly about affect. I believe this disjunction does not hold. I hope to have shown that fiction deals with fundamental logical issues such as the relation between the particular and the general, naming and referencing, the status of nonexistent objects, paradoxes, contradictions, and modalities. I also hope to have shown that logic not only uses fiction through creating examples, but is also wedded to fiction in a more fundamental way. The opponent to the principle of non-contradiction or rational thinking is a foundational fiction appearing first in ancient Greek clothing and reappearing in medieval garb. My final task consists in examining foundational phantasms appearing too at these two pivotal moments in the history of Western logic: the time of Aristotle and the time of Anselm of Canterbury and Abelard.

By "phantasm," I mean a mental image or series of images staging the self in relation to real events and people, like a memory, but with significant and consistent imaginative aspects.[1] I assume that phantasms are part of normal human mental life, offsetting our lack of direct acquaintance with the inner life of fellow human beings.[2] A phantasm can be minimal and close to reality. For instance, "I am sure she does not like my new haircut" may be true, but stages an imaginary scene in which an imaginary "she" expresses to an imaginary "I" her dislike of the new haircut. It can develop into more elaborate scenarios: "X hates my new haircut because she is jealous of anything I do that is out of the ordinary, but I don't care and one day I will come to work in high-heeled shoes, and she will say ... and I will respond ... etc." "Haircut" or "high-heeled shoes" can be replaced by "car" or "peer-reviewed article" or anything that may be a focus of affect. Some people are more likely to expand phantasms in daydreams or full-blown fictions than others, but no one is immune from phantasms – not even logicians.

In this section, I will study three interrelated phantasms. The first one is the phantasm of filiation as a mode of philosophic transmission from predecessor to successor. The second is the phantasm of hostility toward other philosophers perceived as rivals or traitors. The third is the phantasm of friendship as an ideal form of relationship, reachable only by male philosophers or men acquainted with philosophy.

My corpus of texts in these final chapters focuses primarily on works by Aristotle, Abelard, and Chrétien de Troyes. But I will also refer to Plato, Cicero, Anselm, Aelred of Rievaulx, and Jacques Derrida.

CHAPTER 7

Aristotle or the founding son

Introduction

Aristotle remarks at the end of his treatise *On Sophistical Refutations* that "On the subject of rhetoric there exists much that has been said long ago, whereas on the subject of deduction we had absolutely nothing else of an earlier date to mention, but were kept at work for a long time in experimental researches" (*Sophistical Refutations*, 184a–b; p. 314). Being first is nice but a little inconvenient. Aristotle concludes by asking his readers to forgive his mistakes and thank him for the discoveries he made in the absence of tradition and predecessors.

No modern philosopher or historian of ideas would refuse to grant Aristotle the title of "First Logician" in its chronological sense.[1] But what interests me more than his position as founding father of logic is his anxiety and pride about this role. In order to notice a lack of predecessors, one needs to operate within a narrative of succession. Aristotle views his logical discoveries and innovations within the larger frame of philosophy. He does not claim to be the first philosopher, indeed, but to belong to a succession of Greek philosophers. He presents his work as continuing (even if it is often by refuting) the work of his predecessors.[2] His reviews and remarks on his predecessors are scattered in various works (often in introductions), but, brought together, they cohere in a narrative that has proved to be remarkably enduring. It is still difficult today to think about early Greek philosophy without Aristotelizing in one way or another.

My main claim in this chapter is that Aristotle was the first Greek philosopher to locate himself explicitly in such a narrative. Philosophy did not start with him, but history of philosophy or philosophy as a historical process did. After examining how Greek philosophers before Aristotle viewed themselves in relation to those who came before them, I will focus on Aristotle as the founding son of Greek philosophy. In order to view philosophy as a succession of predecessors and successors, or fathers and sons, Aristotle had to first present himself as a son. This filiation was associated with the painful phantasm of an unavowed patricide. In this regard, Aristotle can be compared to Eneas, hero of the Old French translation of the Aeneid, whom Zrinka Stahuljak views as both a founding figure and a patricide. Following Stahuljak's insights about genealogy and filiation, I too consider that their link to nature "is not natural but rather is socially constructed; filiation is not synonymous with blood and procreation."[3]

Before Aristotle: the circle of eternal thinkers

What survives of pre-Socratic philosophy does not give any indication that the ancient philosophers were interested in their predecessors, or had historicized or genealogized their own practice. Heraclitus of Ephesus names the most other philosophers and poets – to dismiss them summarily: "Much learning does not teach insight. Otherwise it would have taught Hesiod and Pythagoras and moreover Xenophanes and Hecateus." Or: "Pythagoras the son of Mnesarchus practiced inquiries more than all other men, and making a selection of his own writings constructed his own wisdom, polymathy, evil trickery." Or: "Homer deserved to be expelled from the contests and flogged, and Archilochus likewise."[4] Rejection of common opinion, knowledge, and traditional Greek culture is one of the fundamental gestures characterizing the fragments or aphorisms regrouped under the name "Heraclitus of Ephesus."[5] Poets and philosophers are not to be sorted out and critically examined. They are to be summoned and rejected in order for the *logos* to emerge from an authentic inquiry within the self and outside of it, in the world. Such an inquiry is an act, not a discipline. It does not happen in history; it does not result from accumulation and transmission of knowledge; it is done anew with each inquirer. "Philosophy" and "philosopher" do not even figure in Heraclitus's lexicon. Presocratic thought is a pre-philosophical thought,[6] which has been preserved because eventually it came to be collected, classified, and taught, although it was not intended originally to be transmitted in this fashion.

During the fifth century BC, two sophists, Hippias and Gorgias, started to collect and disseminate various opinions on various things[7] by wise men, poets, and "philosophers" as a new terminology (*philosophia* and its cognates) now allowed them to make the distinction.[8] According to Jaap Mansfeld, these collections "had the purpose of providing easy access, perhaps mainly for rhetorical purposes, to what must have been an already bewildering variety of ideas." Mansfeld also surmises that these collections put to the fore agreements and disagreements among the wise.[9] If such is the case, Hippias and Gorgias's collections anticipate Abelard's *Sic et Non*, and probably cater to a similar need of ammunition for disputes, but with a difference: *auctoritas*. In the fifth century BC, ancient Greek poets and proto-philosophers did not have the *auctoritas* that the Church fathers had in the twelfth century AD, as Plato's treatment of other philosophers (predecessors or contemporaries of Socrates) demonstrates in his dialogues.[10]

In *Sophist*, Plato presents a compendium of previous theories on being through the voice of an unnamed visitor, coming from Elea.[11] Addressing the young Theaetetus in the presence of Socrates and the geometer Theodorus, the man from Elea exposes the "myths" used by philosophers, including those from Elea, to answer the questions: "How many beings are there?" and "What are they like?"

> They each appear to me to tell us a myth, as if we were children. One tells us that there are three beings, and that sometimes they're somehow at war with each other, while at other times they become friendly, marry, give birth, and bring up their offspring. Another one says that there are two beings, wet and dry or hot and cold. He marries them off and makes them set up house together. And our Eleatic tribe, starting from Xenophanes and even people before him, tells us their myth on the assumption that what they call "all things" are just one. Later on, some Ionian and Sicilian muses both had the idea that it was safer to weave the two together. They say that *that which is* is both many and one, and is bound by both hatred and friendship. According to the terser of these muses, in being taken apart they're brought together. The more relaxed muses, though, allow things to be free from that condition sometimes. They say that all that there is alternates, and sometimes it's one and friendly under Aphrodite's influence, but at other times it's many and at war with itself because of some kind of strife. (*Sophist*, 242c–243a; pp. 263–4)[12]

The visitor supposes that his audience will easily recognize the different philosophical schools through the "myths" he evokes playfully. Isocrates, less sure than Plato that his audience would know the philosophical "Who's Who," crafted a mnemonic to warn young men against being carried away by speculations on the nature of things:

> I would, therefore, advise young men to spend some time on these disciplines, but not to allow their minds to be dried up by these barren subtleties, nor to be stranded on the speculations of the ancient sophists, who maintain, some of them, that the sum of things is made up of infinite elements; Empedocles that it is made up of four, with strife and love operating among them; Ion, of not more than three; Alcmaeon, of only two; Parmenides and Melissus, of one; and Gorgias, of none at all.[13]

From infinity to naught, Isocrates declines the whole spectrum of "speculations of the ancient sophists" in a way that may remind modern readers of *Ten Little Indians*. "And then there were none" comes as the unavoidable conclusion of this entropic pattern. For Isocrates, the ultimate theory of "none at all" exposes the vanity of all theories of this sort. For Plato, if theorizing is not a vain activity, nonetheless the ancient way of theorizing leads to confusion:

VISITOR: [...] It's hard to say whether any one of these thinkers has told us the truth or not, and it wouldn't be appropriate for us to be critical of such renowned and venerable men. But it wouldn't be offensive to note the following thing, either.
THEAETETUS: What?
VISITOR: That they have been inconsistent and contemptuous toward us. They've simply been talking their way through their explanations, without paying any attention to whether we were following them or were left behind.

(*Sophist*, 243a–b; p. 264)

The visitor acknowledges that Xenophanes, Parmenides, Heraclitus, Empedocles, etc. own a status of fame and anteriority. However, and with all due respect, the task of present philosophers is to start the inquiry again and to question the ancients as if they were present:

VISITOR: [...] Let's ask – as if they were here – "Listen, you people who say that all things are just some two things, hot and cold or some such pair. What are you saying about them both when you say that they both *are* and each one *is*?"

(*Sophist*, 243d–e; p. 264)

The gesture recalls Heraclitus of Ephesus's dismissal, but is more graceful and humorous. The switch from aphorism to dialogue has the effect of turning the ancestors into fictionalized characters, protagonists of other fictionalized characters or subjects of their talk.

In her study of Plato's relation to ancient philosophers, Mary Margaret McCabe insists on the fictional turn of the dialogues: "the drama of the dialogues is fiction; all of these characters, including Socrates himself, are imaginary."[14] Pierre Hadot, too, points out that in the dialogues "Plato uses Socrates as a mask," thus "disappearing completely behind Socrates and avoiding systematically the use of 'I'."[15] Whether Plato uses a mask to avoid speaking in the first person or sets up imaginary scenes with fictional characters, he does not present himself as the successor of illustrious predecessors.

Socrates is an eternal contemporary in soul and spirit. The dialogues in which he appears bring him to life and celebrate his immortality. He comes with a mask that Hadot characterizes as "the mask of irony,"[16] a mask described by Alcibiades in *Symposium* as "a statue of Silenus," that is, a box shaped as a burlesque, coarse, and ugly figure and containing little statues of the gods (215a–b; p. 497). McCabe points out that the fictionalized ancestors are often introduced in the dialogues as absent, missing, or silent interlocutors.[17] This is true, and, as mentioned above, this recalls Heraclitus of Ephesus's gesture of rejection. But the invention of Socrates changes considerably the whole picture. As a fictionalized character, he is part of the group of ancestors and can address them as one of them. On the other hand, he is different and plays a different tune on his Silenian flute. In the passage of *Sophist* quoted above, Plato, through the voice of the man from Elea, presents the founding fathers of Greek philosophy as a band of venerable and likable Sileni, who somehow approached the truth while carousing – yet missed it. Socrates is not a Silenus, but someone who looks like one, intentionally. His carousing imitates the ancestors' dance, but turns out to be a dance of another kind, a reasoning dance, if such a thing can be imagined. The founding, mystifying, and carousing fathers do not need to be dismissed summarily any more. If a philosophy based on reasoning and not myth or storytelling is to become possible, they must be addressed as eternal interlocutors. In a similar fashion, the sophists contemporary with Socrates are both refuted and integrated in the dialogues. What would remain of Gorgias, Protagoras, and Hippias if they had not become some of Socrates's most memorable protagonists?

For Plato, the dancing with ancestors continues no matter how wrong they were; for Aristotle, the dance is over. We have seen Plato initiating a philosophical salvaging of a fabulous past, which probably took its initial shape in collections of opinions such as those attributed to Gorgias and Hippias. Aristotle pursued this undertaking in a more systematic and radical way. His invention of philosophy on a successional model results from a combination of gestures: abandoning the dialogical form, reviewing and sorting out predecessors, drafting a timeline, and declaring Socrates dead and philosophers mortal.

From Plato's dialogue to Aristotle's treatise

Aristotle wrote dialogues, of which only titles and fragments survive.[18] As a pupil of Plato for about twenty years, he started his philosophical career by writing within the Platonist mold – that is, the general form of the philosophical dialogue derived and adapted from Plato's dialogues and transmitted through his school, the Academy. However, what can be reconstructed of Aristotle's dialogues indicates that they did not have the dramatic vivacity of truly Socratic dialogues (such as *Charmides*, *Lysis*, *Laches*, *Protagoras*, *Gorgias*).[19] They probably tended toward the demonstrative exposé that appears in some of Plato's dialogues (such as *The Republic*, *Timaeus*, *Critias*, *Laws*), in which "the conversation takes on the character of a dogmatic exposition of doctrine by the main speaker to an audience."[20] However, since the chronology of Plato's works is far from being established with certainty, there is no clear evidence that Plato moved from one form to the other. *Philebus*, which scholarly agreement sees as a late work, is a Socratic dialogue.[21] And, in any case, even in his most "dogmatic" dialogues, Plato never uses a first person account in which the speaking "I" would refer to himself.

In Aristotle's work, exposition and demonstration replace dialogue and make this form obsolete.[22] In Cicero's brief description of the Aristotelian way of setting up a dialogue, the presence of an "I" referring to the writer is put to the fore: "*quae autem his temporibus scripsi Aristoteleion morem habent in quo ita sermo inducitur ceterorum ut penes ipsum sit principatus*" [But I have recently written texts following the Aristotelian custom, according to which the conversation of the others is so arranged that the main part is in the charge of the writer himself].[23] It seems then that in his early, Platonist works, Aristotle had already honed an "I, Aristotle," which would eventually become the voice preserved by posterity, that is, monologic and not fictionalized – which does not mean simplistic or fascistic.[24] This "I" is generally so discreet and unobtrusive that it rarely occurs as a first person singular, but manifests itself mostly through impersonal turns, which are common and handy in Greek, or as the first person plural, that is, the ancestor of our own academic "we."[25] Thus, the second person so characteristic of Plato's dialogues ("Tell me ..." "Do you think ..." "Would you agree ...") disappears entirely from Aristotle's treatises. We, the readers, are in charge of responding if we so wish or are able; on the other hand, we are free to do so without prompting.

By renouncing the masks and fictions that Plato used with such shrewdness and virtuosity, Aristotle was able to create the fiction of a stable authoritative voice speaking to contemporary and future peers and disciples. This was at the cost of poetry, myth, and irony. When Aristotle adopts this new didactic style, he does not renounce setting his own philosophy in dialogue with other philosophies, but he does it in a citational mode that isolates his own discourse while identifying its sources.

Sorting out predecessors

Aristotle was a collector of data, observations, opinions, traditions, and books. According to Strabo, he was the first book collector.[26] Pierre Hadot presents his school, the Lyceum, as a research organization, questing for materials of all kinds aimed to establish a classification of phenomena and to root reasoning in observation.[27] Even when delving into abstract intellectual activities such as metaphysics, Aristotle often starts by gathering and presenting the opinions and theses of those who are known to have said something about the specific issue he wants to address.[28] Suzanne Mansion views these typical exposés of others' opinions as a way for Aristotle to articulate his own inquiries, either through agreeing or disagreeing with philosophical traditions, but in any case by taking them seriously – without irony.[29]

At the beginning of *Physics*, in order to establish the principles of nature and a method to study natural things, Aristotle sketches a "tree" of the different positions occupied by previous thinkers:

> The principles in question must be either (a) one or (b) more than one.
> If (a) one, it must be either (i) motionless, as Parmenides and Melissus assert, or (ii) in motion, as the physicists hold, some declaring air to be the first principle, others water.
> If (b) more than one, then either (i) a finite or (ii) an infinite plurality. If (i) finite (but more than one), then either two or three or four or some other number. If (ii) infinite, then either as Democritus believed one in kind, but differing in shape or form; or different in kind and even contrary. (*Physics* I, 184b; p. 315)

The "a" "b" "i" and "ii" are added by the editor,[30] but they only make the syntactical and logical structure of the original text more explicit. Aristotle here uses in a condensed and non-dialogical form the mode of reasoning by divisions and subdivisions that Plato uses in dialogues such as *Statesman* and *Parmenides*. Ironically, it is old Parmenides himself who explains to Socrates (portrayed here as a young man) the method that Aristotle will eventually use to refute Parmenides in *Physics*:

> [Parmenides]: [. . .] But you must do the following in addition to that: if you want to be trained more thoroughly, you must not only hypothesize, if each thing is, and examine the consequences of that hypothesis; you must also hypothesize, if that same thing is not.
> "What do you mean?" [Socrates] asked.
> "If you like," said Parmenides, "take as an example this hypothesis that Zeno entertained: if many are, what must the consequences be both for the many themselves in relation to themselves and in relation to the one, and for the one in relation to itself and in relation to the many? And, in turn on the

> hypothesis, if many are not, you must again examine what the consequences
> will be both for the one and for the many in relation to themselves and in
> relation to each other. (*Parmenides* 136a; p. 370)

Moreover, Parmenides has just mentioned that he overheard a conversation
between Socrates and Aristotle (135d; p. 370), who, indeed, is not our
Aristotle; but, still, the presence of this homonym (who replaces Socrates
as the protagonist of Parmenides in the second part of the dialogue)
produces an eerie effect on any reader for whom "Aristotle" cannot not
help but evoke the First Logician.[31] In Plato's *Parmenides*, the transmission
of philosophy happens as a timeless event, collapsing the generational gaps
while depicting an idyllic passage of the torch from the very old philosopher
to the very young (and perhaps the unborn).

At the beginning of *Physics*, Aristotle, who has read *Parmenides*, disen-
tangles himself from the web of conversation between eternally contemporary philosophers. He was not there, even if by pure coincidence his name is
inscribed in the august company of Parmenides, Zeno, and Socrates.
Anyway, there is no "there" other than the space of the discourse with its
divisions and subdivisions, a discourse whose source is unified and which is
only contemporary to itself.

The classification of opinions is the primary frame in which Aristotle
pinpoints the ancestral giants, reduced to their arguments, neatly rearranged
in a succession of "either . . . or . . ." repartitions. Do not kill your fathers;
file them away. However, the neat classification announced at the beginning of the review is not followed systematically in the rest of the passage,
which mostly opposes those who deny motion to being to those who accept
motion as part of reality.[32] Aristotle is a compulsive "classifier" who does not
hold on to his classifications. Werner Jaeger has remarked that Aristotle is
not a systematic thinker but an analytical one, who likes to sort and
separate, but does not produce in the end a *sustēma*, or a closed set of
dogmas, a term invented by Hellenistic philosophers after Aristotle.[33] More
important than the resulting grouping of predecessors are the criteria and
lines of division that Aristotle uses to sort them out. I will now focus on the
division between poets and philosophers.

Although Aristotle is not sure whether Thales of Miletus took his view of
water as the primeval matter from ancient mythologies and cosmogonies, he
deliberately associates him with Anaximenes of Miletus and Diogenes of
Apollonia, and not with Homer and Hesiod (*Metaphysics* I, 983b–984a;
p. 1556).[34] Elsewhere he more clearly affirms the distinction. Discussing the
principles of perishable and imperishable things, he mentions Hesiod and

other cosmologists or mythologists' theory about ambrosia and nectar whose consumption makes all the difference between immortals and mortals (*Metaphysics* III, 1000a; p. 1579).[35] But after pointing out the logical problems that may be encountered by a metaphysics based on nectar and ambrosia as primal elements, Aristotle returns to serious people and *their* theories:

> But into the subtleties of the mythologists it is not worth our while to inquire seriously; those, however who use the language of proof we must cross-examine and ask why, after all, things which consist of the same elements are, some of them, eternal in nature, while others perish. (*Metaphysics* III, 1000a; p. 1580)[36]

At the beginning of *Poetics*, Aristotle uses a similar distinction but this time without dismissing poets. He simply states that there is nothing in common between Homer and Empedocles except meter, and suggests calling the former "poet" and the latter "physicist," that is, philosopher of nature (*Poetics*, 1447b; p. 2316).[37]

Drafting a timeline

Although Aristotle's first impulse is to classify philosophers according to thematic or formal criteria, and to put sixth-century Anaximander in the same basket as fifth-century Democritus, chronological concerns appear in the review at the beginning of *Physics*: "Even the more recent of the ancient thinkers (*hoi husteroi tōn arkhaiōn*) were in a pother lest the same thing should turn out in their hands both one and many" (*Physics* I, 185b; p. 317). Aristotle here presents a relative chronology within the group of the founding philosophers: they all belong to the *archē*, the beginning, a position of anteriority which, in Greek, is semantically attached to the notion of authority, principle, and rule. Those who came before predetermine what will come later, but they do not arrive all at once.

Those who come later can review and ponder the opinions of their predecessors, compare them, point out their flaws and strengths, and then proceed to exposing their own opinions, just as Aristotle does after spending several pages to explain why Parmenides and Melissus's positions on being are untenable, and reviewing the more acceptable, but still far from flawless theories of the physicists. Then, at last, he declares: "*Hōd'oun hēmeis legomen prōton peri pasēs geneseōs epelthontes*," which literally translated means "Now then we ourselves speak, starting first with becoming in all its meaning"

(*Physics* I, 189b, p. 324). A philosophy in becoming needs to address first what becoming is.

The treatise *On the Soul*, despite being much more limited in scope than *Physics* or *Metaphysics*, also begins with a reviewing of "the opinions of our predecessors" on the nature of the soul:

> For our study of soul it is necessary, while formulating the problems of which in our further advance we are to find the solutions, to call into council the views of those of our predecessors (*tas tōn proterōn doxas*) who have declared any opinion on this subject, in order that we may profit by whatever is sound in their suggestion and avoid their errors. (*On the Soul*, 403b; p. 643)

Once this is done, Aristotle may, as in *Physics*, authorize himself to add his opinion, or, rather, to propose his opinion as a better substitute for all of the above mentioned:

> Let the foregoing suffice as our account of the views concerning the soul which have been handed on by our predecessors; let us now make as it were a completely fresh start (*hōsper ex huparkhēs*), endeavouring to answer the question, What is the soul? i.e. to formulate the most general possible account of it. (*On the Soul*, 412a; p. 656)

Suzanne Mansion remarks that this review is more dismissive than those in *Physics* and *Metaphysics* since Aristotle comes to conclude that all his predecessors (including Anaxagoras, Democritus, Empedocles, Thales, the Pythagoreans, Xenocrates, Alcmeon, Critias, and Plato) started on the wrong foot.[38] To solve the riddle of the soul, a fresh start is in order: "*hōsper ex huparkhēs*" [as if going back to the beginning]. Aristotle cannot claim he is the first or among the first to attack the problem. He cannot ignore his predecessors. By acknowledging their anteriority, he construes his own theory on the soul as a "new beginning," that is, a fiction of beginning, an "as if it was the beginning again." No one can begin what has already begun; no one can be born again; but one can propose new solutions to old problems.

Aristotle is aware that temporal limitations apply to philosophers. By reviewing his predecessors and acknowledging their precedence, he signifies that his philosophy takes place in time, and not in eternity. He is so aware of the weight of tradition that he mentions that he has a predecessor in the tradition of collecting and reviewing the opinions of others:

> Gorgias declares that nothing exists; and if anything exists it is unknowable; and if it exists and is knowable, yet it cannot be indicated to others. To prove that nothing exists he collects the statements of others, who in speaking about what is seem to assert contrary opinions (some trying

to prove that what is is one and not many, others that it is many and not one; and some that existents are ungenerated, others that they have come to be), and he argues against both sides. (*On Melissus, Xenophanes, and Gorgias*, 979a, p. 1548)

For Aristotle, the disagreements and contradictions between philosophers do not demonstrate the impossibility of knowing, or, even less, the impossibility of stating that something *is*; on the contrary, disagreements and contradictions demonstrate that philosophy is, is in becoming, and has something to say about what is and what becomes. Aristotle uses Gorgias's method to debunk Gorgias's argument, and to demonstrate that a method invented to support what Aristotle views as a sophistical fallacy and a perversion of reasoning can be put to a more productive use.

It is at the beginning of *Metaphysics* that Aristotle exposes the most complete historical sketch of the tradition he both acknowledges and opposes. He starts, like in *Physics* and *On the Soul*, by calling up his predecessors: "We have studied these causes sufficiently in our work on nature, but yet let us call to our aid those who have attacked the investigation of beings and philosophized about reality before us" (*Metaphysics* I, 983b; p. 1555). This time, he frames the review in a sketch of the prehistory and history of philosophy, rooted in the anthropological approach to philosophy asserted in the very first sentence of *Metaphysics*: "All men by nature desire to know" (*Metaphysics* I, 980a; p. 1552). This claim establishes human nature as the non-historical substratum supporting the history of human knowledge. The desire to know is a potential that every human being owns by nature but will develop unequally depending on various factors, in particular the availability of leisure (*Metaphysics* I, 981b; p. 1553).[39] The opening pages of *Metaphysics* I suggest a pyramid of knowledge whose broad base is made of the knowledge that sensorial perception amply, daily, and indiscriminately provides to human beings, and whose apex consists in the *first philosophy* that Aristotle defines as the science "which investigates being as being"(*Metaphysics* IV, 1003a; p. 1584).[40]

This structure of knowledge mingles with the order of history when Aristotle imagines a relative chronology in which the more abstract arts and sciences are latecomers, and first philosophy becomes last invention:

> At first he who invented any art that went beyond the common perceptions of man was naturally admired by men, not only because there was something useful in the inventions, but because he was thought wise and superior to the rest. But as more arts were invented, and some were directed to the necessities of life, others to its recreation, the inventors of the latter were always regarded as wiser than the inventors of the former, because their branches of knowledge

did not aim at utility. Hence when all such inventions were already established, the sciences which do not aim at giving pleasure or at the necessities of life were discovered, and first in the places where men first began to have leisure. This is why the mathematical arts were founded in Egypt; for the priestly caste was allowed to be at leisure. (*Metaphysics* I, 981b; p. 1553)

"Egypt" signals the passage from prehistory to history and establishes a place of origin for Greek philosophy and sciences. Aristotle follows an epistemological tradition dating back at least to Herodotus, who attributed the invention of geometry to the Egyptians and of astronomy to the Babylonians.[41]

The history of ideas and knowledge becomes the "history of philosophy" when it becomes Greek; then, it also ceases to be anonymous. Aristotle, using pre-existing lore,[42] enthrones Thales of Miletus as the first of the earliest philosophers. Talking of "*prōtōn philosophēsantōn*" [the first who philosophized], Aristotle claims that most of them "thought the principles which were of the nature of matter were the only principles of all things" (*Metaphysics* I, 983b; pp. 1555–6). The following explanation is indeed "a strongly Aristotelian account of what a material cause is," as Richard McKirahan puts it.[43] Aristotle projects his own concerns and concepts on the ancestors, but that is exactly why he invented them.[44] Thales is a necessary "first of the firsts" in the distant past of Greek thought: "Thales, the founder of this kind of philosophy (*ho tēs toiautēs arkhēgos philosophias*), says the principle is water" (*Metaphysics* I, 983b; p. 1556). Whatever one thinks about the way Aristotle practices history, it is still customary to start a history or overview of early Greek philosophy with Thales: "As regards the beginning, this book follows the convention, authorized by Aristotle, of making Thales of Miletus the pioneer, and no *individual* claimant with a better title will ever be suggested."[45] Apparently, Aristotle chose his first philosophizing individual wisely since nobody to this day has found a better one. However, he did not call him a "pioneer" but a "founder" or "author" or "initiator." The term *arkhēgos* was also used to qualify a founding hero, a king, or a warrior chief.[46] Aristotle's first philosopher is not a conqueror, but a royal figure, founder of an intellectual dynasty and genealogy.

Genealogy and patricide

All successions are not genealogical. Before addressing the metaphorical and phantasmatic aspects of the intellectual genealogy founded by Thales of Miletus, according to Aristotle's script, I will first look at its historical and institutional aspects.

In the passage of the *Sophistical Refutations* where Aristotle affirms to be the first "on the subject of deduction," and which I cited at the beginning of this chapter, one finds a description of transmission of knowledge by succession valid for most arts.[47] After stating that the beginnings are always the most difficult stages, and that it is easier to add onto what has already been discovered, Aristotle says:

> This is in fact what has happened in regard to rhetorical speeches and to practically all the other arts; for those who discovered the beginnings of them (*hoi tas arkhas heurontes*) advanced them in all only a little way, whereas the celebrities of today are the heirs (so to speak) of a long succession (*ek diadokhēs*) of men who have advanced (*proagagontōn*) them bit by bit (*kata meros*), and so have developed them to their present form, Tisias coming next after the first founders (*meta tous prōtous*), then Thrasymachus after Tisias, and Theodorus next to him, while several people made their several contributions to it; and therefore it is not to be wondered at that the art has attained considerable dimensions. (*Sophistical Refutations* 183b; p. 314)

In this passage Aristotle delineates the process of intellectual transmission originating with those who discovered the first principles (*hoi tas arkhas heurontes*), also named the first founders (*hoi prōtoi*), developed by the succession (*ek diadokhēs*) of a numerous series of people who have advanced principles bit by bit (*para pollōn kata meros proagagontōn*). *Proagagontōn* also means "predecessors." Only the first founders can be viewed as absolute predecessors; the followers are inheritors who become predecessors in turn.

Jaap Mansfeld links this model, which is not yet institutionalized in Aristotle's description, with the institution of schools directed by a master, the first one being Plato's Academy:

> In these schools, the head of the association had a successor (*diadokhos*) who was appointed or chosen. Retrospectively, such lines of successions were also constructed for the Preplatonic period, and these successions of Preplatonics were in various ways linked with the later philosophical schools.[48]

Mansfeld dates the first work titled *Successions of the Philosophers* (*Diadokhai tōn philosophōn*) by a certain Sotion to the beginning of the third century BC, that is twenty to thirty years after Aristotle's death. It seems safe to assume that Sotion followed Aristotle's historicized view of Greek philosophy, which was preserved and transmitted in the school founded by Aristotle, the Lyceum.

The first successor (or *diadokhos*)[49] of Aristotle, Theophrastus, was chosen by the master himself, according to the model of intellectual transmission that Mansfeld describes, by which a school makes itself perennial through the passage of the baton from a master to a chosen disciple. But another model existed: transmission through secession. The first documented secession of this kind is Aristotle's foundation of the Lyceum around 335.[50] Instead of staying in Plato's Academy under the direction of Plato's successor, Speusippus, Aristotle created his own school.

The history of the relation between Aristotle and Plato, the Lyceum and the Academy is of great complexity and difficult to reconstitute. Socrates plays a crucial role in this history, both as a living philosopher and, after his death, as a legendary one. But Socrates is an ambivalent figure, surrounded with guilt and pain as well as with pride and laughter, an ambivalence that has durably marked the model of succession for post-Socratic philosophers. I will now examine how Aristotle presents Socrates in his reviews of predecessors.

Plato is much more visible in Aristotle's work than Socrates, since Aristotle, in his reviews of predecessors, presents Plato as the turning point in the history of philosophy. In *Metaphysics* I, after finishing his review of the earliest philosophers with the Pythagoreans, Aristotle draws a clear line between them and Plato:

> From the earlier philosophers, then, and from their successors we can learn this much.
>   After the systems we have named came the philosophy of Plato, which in most respects followed these thinkers, but had peculiarities that distinguished it from the philosophy of the Italians. (*Metaphysics* I, 987a; p. 1561)

This separation is embedded in the structure of *Metaphysics* I. After a section on principles in pre-Platonic theories comes a section on principles according to Plato (*Metaphysics* I, 985b–988a; pp. 1559–62). Then, on the question of causes, Aristotle first explains the opinions of pre-Platonic philosophers, criticizes them, and then moves on to explain and criticize Plato's theory about the Ideas as causes (*Metaphysics* I, 988a–993a; pp. 1562–9). As Long observes, "Aristotle has an implicit concept of *early* Greek philosophy, but it is more pre-Platonic than pre-Socratic."[51] The habit of calling early Greek philosophers "the Presocratics" is only a century old.[52] It simply models the divide indicated by Aristotle but sets Socrates instead of Plato as the borderline figure marking a major shift.

Aristotle neither assimilates him to the earlier philosophers nor views him as the turning point. He mentions him only three times in *Metaphysics*, assigning him the role of a marginal thinker who contributes to the first philosophy indirectly, while focusing on ethics:

> Socrates, however, was busying himself about ethical matters and neglecting the world of nature as a whole but seeking the universal (*to katholou*) in these

ethical matters, and fixed thought for the first time on definitions; Plato accepted his teaching, but held that the problem applied not to any sensible thing but to entities of another kind. (*Metaphysics* I, 987b; p. 1561)

In this passage Socrates is mentioned to explain how Plato came to conceive his theory of Ideas from an originally Heraclitean position. Socrates provides an external kernel – *to katholou* (the universal) – around which Plato's meditation reshapes (or perhaps re-founds) philosophy. In *Metaphysics* XIII, Aristotle discusses at length "whether there is or is not besides the sensible substances (*ousiai*) any which is immovable and eternal"(*Metaphysics* XIII, 1076a; p. 1701). Previous philosophies offer only two likely candidates: numbers and Ideas, which may or may not be the same thing, depending on which philosophy one turns to. In this book, Aristotle refines his presentation of Plato's Ideas and their origins, and refers to Socrates as a crucial influence on this doctrine:

> Socrates occupied himself with the excellences of character, and in connection with them became the first to raise the problem of universal (*katholou*) definitions ... For two things may fairly be ascribed to Socrates – inductive arguments and universal definition, both of which are concerned with the starting-point of science. But Socrates did not make the universals or the definitions exist apart; his successors, however, gave them separate existence, and this was the kind of thing they called Ideas. (*Metaphysics* XIII, 1078b; p. 1705)

According to Aristotle, Socrates must be credited with the systematic use of logical or dialectical reasoning in philosophy, even though he himself used it only on ethical questions. On the other hand, he must be exonerated from the separation between Ideas and sensible things, a fault committed by others.[53] Strikingly, Aristotle sets a clearly individualized Socrates against a nebulous *hoi* (they). The translation renders *hoi* by "his successors" to make the text more intelligible, but the Greek reads more literally: "But Socrates did not make the universals or the definitions exist apart; they, however, gave them separate existence, and this was the kind of thing they called Ideas." There is no definite antecedent to *hoi* in the preceding sentences, but "they" are defined at the end of the sentence as those who use the term *ideas* (Ideas) to name the things they have set apart, i.e., the universals (*ta katholou*) and the definitions (*tous horismous*) that Socrates did not set apart. It seems that "setting apart" is the gesture by which "they" set themselves apart from Socrates.

Aristotle does not explain the position of Plato with regard to Socrates. Is he the guilty one who separated the intelligible from the sensible, and himself from Socrates? Or should the guilt fall on anonymous disciples of Plato from whom Aristotle must now set himself apart? In any case, if Aristotle cannot be deemed responsible for the divide in the tradition, he may be credited with being the first to indicate its problematic nature. In other words (and in modern terms), Aristotle was not the one who killed the father, but the first one to acknowledge that a father has been killed and had to be killed. When we use the term "pre-Socratic" (and it would be the same if we used the term "pre-Platonic"), we actually whisper "pre-patricide." Socrates seems for historical reasons the most likely first expiatory victim of this new scheme of transmission, but, precisely for the same historical reasons, it was extremely difficult for his contemporary and immediate successors to admit they, too, had to kill him, symbolically. The story starts to read like *Murder on the Orient Express*: they all did it, so nobody was guilty.

For Aristotle, the separation between Socrates and "those" who created the theory of the Ideas is the source of a major metaphysical and logical conundrum, one that he himself is at pains to sort out. In another passage of *Metaphysics* XIII, Aristotle repeats what he has said about Socrates' role but provides more technical details on ideas, universals, particulars, and their relationship:

> Those who posit numbers only, and these mathematical, must be considered later; but as regards those who believe in the Ideas one might survey at the same time their way of thinking and the difficulties into which they fall. For they at the same time treat the Ideas as universal, and again as separable and individual. That this is not possible has been shown before. The reason why those who say substances are universal (*katholou*) combined these two views in one, is that they did not make them identical with sensible things. They thought that the sensible particulars were in a state of flux and none of them remained, but that the universal was apart from these and different. And Socrates gave impulse to this theory, as we said before, by means of his definitions, but he did not *separate* them from the particulars (*kath'hekaston*); and in this he thought rightly, in not separating them. This is plain from the results; for without the universal it is not possible to get knowledge, but the separation is the cause of the objections that arise with regards to the Ideas. (*Metaphysics* XIII, 1086b; pp. 1716–17)

On ethical issues (since, according to Aristotle, it is only on ethical issues that Socrates decided to focus his philosophizing), Socrates was able to think both *katholou* (according to the whole) and *kath'hekaston* (according to each) through the use of definitions. The term translated by "definitions" is *horismous*, which derives from *horos*, boundary stone, anything marking a limit, then the limit itself. The act of defining creates limits. Aristotle does not explain how Socratic definitions do not fall entirely on the side of the whole and maintain contact with particulars, and particularly those which are sensible things. The major problem in the theory of Ideas, as it is explained here, is that the Ideas need to be both universals and particulars without being related in any way to sensible things. The Ideas make the world intelligible by suppressing all that it contains. We understand, but we understand only that which does not exist and cannot be perceived. On the other hand, if we stick to that which exists and which we perceive, we may never understand anything. Aristotle exposes this problem at the end of *Metaphysics* III while trying to define what the "first principles" (*hoi arkhoi*) are:

> If they are universals, they will not be substances; for everything that is common indicates not a "this" but a "such," but substance is a "this." And if we can actually posit the common predicate as a single "this," Socrates will be several animals – himself and man and animal, if each of these indicates a "this" and a single thing. If, then, the principles are universals, this result follows; if they are not universals but of the nature of individuals, they will not be knowable; for the knowledge of anything is universal. Therefore if there is to be knowledge of the principles there must be other principles prior to them, which are universally predicated of them. (*Metaphysics* III, 1003a; p. 1584)

Socrates is present in this passage, not as the philosopher, but as example of an individual man. Plato did not use "Socrates" that way. It is possible that this was a common practice in the Academy, but our first written source of this custom is the Aristotelian corpus. "Socrates," "Plato," "Callias," and "Coriscus" stood for "every man" until they were replaced in this function by "John," "Harry," "Paul," and "Mary" or their equivalent in other modern languages, as I noted in Chapter 1. In ancient Greece, people had only one name, therefore "Socrates" can refer both to a specific individual such as the philosopher who drank a certain beverage in 399 (but not exclusively to him since there were other people named Socrates around),[54] and to an unspecified human individual used as an example for demonstrative purposes. In modern English, a "John" popping out in a philosophical text without any previous precision can only refer to an unspecified individual used for demonstrative purposes. "John" cannot refer to John Locke or "Paul" to Paul Grice, for instance. This change toward more anonymous exemplars underlines the fact that the "every man" of traditional philosophy was in fact an "every philosopher," often incarnated by a comic character derived from the historical Socrates, who had to endure all sorts of mistreatments and metamorphoses for the enjoyment and education of generation after generation of students in philosophy. This may seem to have nothing to do with Aristotle's problem of finding a substance that would not be universal but would still be intelligible, and that would not be particular but would still be "capable of independent existence."[55] But since this problem has to do with the way Aristotle envisions the philosophical legacy of Socrates and Plato, as he himself points out in the two passages of *Metaphysics* XIII cited above, it is worth investigating the shift from Socrates the martyred predecessor to Socrates the exemplary every man.

Jonathan Lear believes that Aristotle was able to solve his problem by changing his thoughts about what a substance (*ousia*) is. I will not evaluate the soundness of Lear's understanding of *Metaphysics* VII.[56] His argument, however, reflects Aristotle's search for a compromise that would both preserve the philosophical legacy he was setting in a historicized form and save the philosophical enterprise he was building from the Charybdis of unintelligibility (the world is unintelligible) and the Scylla of separation from reality (the World is intelligible but it is not the world). In *Categories*, primary substances are individuals, hence, Socrates is a primary substance that cannot be predicated of anything else (*Categories*, 2a; pp. 4–5).[57] In *Metaphysics* III, Aristotle comes to the conclusion that individuals, such as Socrates, are not knowable or intelligible. In *Metaphysics* VII, he attempts to find a solution: *ousia*, the primary substance, is not the individual any more, but the species-form that informs the individual and makes of it what it is in essence. "Socrates" as an individual is not knowable or definable; "Socrates" as "a man" – that is, "a rational animal" and other essential predicates – is knowable.[58] Whether this works or not, the conceptual move from the individual as substance to the species-form as substance is duplicated by the rhetorical move from Socrates the historical individual, the philosopher who tried not to separate philosophizing from the real (and maybe died for doing just that), to Socrates the "man," the conceptual intermediary that allows individuals to be thought about and understood while maintaining their opaque individuality.

Aristotle contributed to shaping philosophy as an institution according to a succession model, from predecessor to successor and master to disciple. But his account of Socrates' place in and contribution to the history of philosophy reveals the affective side of the succession model, deeply felt as a genealogical model. In Aristotle's narrative of the history of philosophy, Socrates' death appears like Charlemagne's sin in the stained glass window of Chartres: it is not told directly or explicitly, but is a fundamental element of the whole story. As Zrinka Stahuljak shows in her analysis of the window and its various restorations and interpretations, Charlemagne's sin (his incest with his sister) disrupts the grand narrative of filiation between uncle and nephew and makes it ambivalent.[59] There is no genealogical story without its sins and disruptions. Aristotle presents the most important disruption in the philosophical tradition as prepared by Socrates and enacted by Plato. The sin is a symbolic patricide that had to happen to allow philosophy to become historical, but which cannot be narrated or attributed to anyone. It occurred somehow between Plato and Aristotle. The deed is not yet done in Plato's dialogues. It is a *fait accompli* in Aristotle's treatises, in which the ghost of Socrates can be put to good (non-threatening) philosophical use when reworked into "a man."

Conclusion

Freud views our relation to our fathers, our masters, and our dead as fundamentally ambivalent.[60] By inventing the history of Western philosophy on a genealogical model, Aristotle inscribed ambivalence at the heart of the philosophical tradition, just as he inscribed contradiction at the heart of rationality when he established the principle of non-contradiction. Ambivalence and contradiction can be defined as the juxtaposition of two opposite propositions – psychological in the case of ambivalence (I love Socrates and I hate Socrates), logical in the case of contradiction (Socrates is dead and Socrates is not dead). These are Aristotelian definitions. A non-Aristotelian definition, based on affect, could be that ambivalence and contradiction result from the fear of choosing and, therefore, losing what has not been chosen. Or, it may result from the regret of having lost something that one has not chosen. Aristotle's ambivalence toward ambivalence may point toward a regret of this sort.

While I was studying Aristotle's texts concerning his predecessors, I was struck by the fact that Aristotle replaces Heraclitean brutality and Socratic irony with something much more insidious and radical. He treats his predecessors as dead people, who deserve respect and care, but do not have anything to say beside what the living philosophers have them say when they cite them. They are not within reach any more; they are within quotations marks. They are not immortal anymore either. Aristotle renounces any claim of immortality for the philosopher, the *theios anēr*, the divine man that some of his predecessors believed themselves to be.[61]

Jonathan Lear ends his book *The Desire to Understand* with the problem of the relation between humanity and divinity in Aristotle's philosophy: "What is so hard for a modern reader to take seriously is Aristotle's claim that man has a divine element in him."[62] Lear may mean "modern philosopher" rather than "modern reader" since many modern readers do not have any trouble envisioning the divine in man. More troublesome for many ancient and modern readers (including some philosophers) is the

juxtaposition of a belief in the presence of the divinity in man with a
disbelief in the possibility that the individual human soul survives death.
Lear adds:

> It is man's natural desire to understand that propels him forward through a
> life of inquiry and experience until he is able to realize what he truly is. It is
> this natural desire that propels him to transcend his nature. And yet there is a
> trace of humanity, which remains even in this divine life: it can only be lived
> for a short period. Death overtakes even the philosopher. But, while it lasts,
> the life of the mind is god-like. Aristotle, no doubt, thought that he had lived
> such a life.[63]

The price of living such a life is death and the knowledge that the rational
animal is a mortal god.

CHAPTER 8

Abelard or the fatherless son

Introduction

In Chapter 7, I have tried to reconstruct the phantasms that may have played a role in the vision Aristotle had of himself as a philosopher in relation with other philosophers. My guess is that Aristotle was the first consistently to view other philosophers as predecessors, contemporaries, and successors, instead of eternal interlocutors. I also surmise that in order to historicize and genealogize philosophy Aristotle had to involve a patricide in the story, which he did reluctantly and indirectly with the figure of Socrates, and bluntly with all philosophers past, present, and future, including himself, as he renounced the belief that philosophy could be a ticket for immortality.

Moving from the corpus of texts attributed to Aristotle to the corpus attributed to Abelard is like visiting someone's home after visiting a museum. Affects and phantasms no longer have to be surmised from shards and fragments: they are part of the furniture. This is why scholars who have studied Abelard's life and works often portray him in a vivid fashion. (Such depictions cannot be found in Aristotle's scholarship.) Among the traits most scholars attribute to Abelard are feistiness, contradictoriness, and arrogance.[1] This image of Abelard as someone who tended to disagree with others and himself finds its origin in Abelard's letters (in particular in the long autobiographical letter known as *Historia calamitatum* or *A History of my Calamities*), and in his adversaries' texts (especially thoses of Roscelin and Bernard de Clairvaux). However, in his study of Abelard's philosophy, John Marenbon insists on his capacity as a constructive thinker, his effort to reconcile opposed conceptions, his subtlety and flexibility in applying rationality to ethical and theological matters.[2] In her study of Abelard, Eileen Sweeney views his "tendency to turn all narratives into narratives of conflict [as] a manifestation of the desire for authenticity in his own work and an uncanny ability to sniff out the absence of it in others." She qualifies Abelard's *méthode* as "hermeneutics of suspicion" which does not lead to reconciliation but to "revealing the gaps that cannot be overcome."[3]

In this chapter, I will not attempt to reconcile the aggressive author of the letters with the flexible thinker of the philosophical works, the arrogant master with the melancholy critic of himself. I will try to assess how Abelard viewed himself as a philosopher in relation with his predecessors and contemporaries. I will focus first on the relationship of Abelard with his distant, pagan ancestors, Aristotle and Plato, and then on his relationship with his close, Christian, predecessors, Anselm of Canterbury and Roscelin. I will leave aside Guillaume de Champeaux, Anselme de Laon, and Heloise, not because I think they are negligible, but because, since they are more visible in the letters, their relations with Abelard have attracted more commentary and interpretations.[4] To understand the phantasms at stake in the construction and transmission of philosophy, I will focus on one of Abelard's logical works (*Dialectica*) and one of his theological works (*Theologia summi boni*). The difficulty of carrying on the legacy of Plato and Aristotle in a Christian culture will be central to this chapter. Abelard may have perversely loved to get himself into trouble, but he did not have to deploy much ingenuity to do so: claiming to be a Christian philosopher and daring to discuss the Trinity was enough for a lifetime of troubles.

Succeeding the "Prince of Peripatetics"

The great pagan ancestors are hardly mentioned in the *Historia calamitatum*, perhaps because Abelard does not view them as "calamities."[5] Or perhaps it is because Abelard prefers to mention or quote Christian sources in his confessional letter. In any case, Abelard's relationship to Aristotle and the Peripatetics must be studied in his dialectic writings, while his relationship to Plato and Neoplatonists must be studied in his theological writings.

In Abelard's *Dialectica*, Aristotle is mentioned so often that a modern editor renounced listing all these occurrences in his index.[6] This is not surprising since Abelard's logical oeuvre "is made mostly of glosses."[7] The oldest texts of Abelard that we know are his commentaries on Porphyry's *Isagoge*, Aristotle's *On Interpretation* and *Categories*, Boethius's *On Division* – texts dating from 1102 to 1104, when Abelard started to teach.[8] His two main treatises, *Dialectica* and *Logica*, dating from about 1117 to 1120,[9] keep much of the form and spirit of commentaries based on the logical canon available at the time, but they include critical discussion of various theses and, at times, Abelard's own theses on problems raised by the "old logic."[10] As Jolivet notes, Boethius is Abelard's main model, his logical work being mainly structured as a commentary, but Aristotle "who commented nobody" is also for him a model of independent thinking.[11]

His attitude toward Aristotle is cautiously critical and ironically reverent. For instance, about a disagreement between Aristotle and Plato, Abelard writes: "*Sed et si Aristotilem, Peripateticorum Principem, culpare presumamus, quem amplius in hac arte recipiemus?*" [But if we presume to accuse even Aristotle, the Prince of Peripatetics, whom else will we approve in this discipline [dialectic]?].[12] The title of "Prince" (or "First") of Peripatetics pays homage to the first logician while it reduces his principality to a small population of wanderers, the restless Peripatetics. John of Salisbury nicknames Abelard *Peripateticus Palatinus* (Peripatetic of Le Palet) with the same blend of irony and respect.[13] At the same time, Abelard presents Aristotle as the incarnation of the art (*hac arte*) that he practices and upholds in front of his adversaries.[14] To attack Aristotle would be to weaken one's own position as dialectician. But, when Aristotle disagrees with Plato, the "Prince of Peripatetics" stands up against the "*primum totius philosophie ducem*" [first leader of all philosophy] (*Dialectica*, p. 90). Aristotle's disagreement with his master Plato allows Abelard to disagree with Aristotle without disrupting the tradition or weakening the art. Disagreement between master and disciple is part of the tradition, and is loaded with passion:

> *Qui fortasse, si et scripta magistri eius Platonis in hac arte novissemus, utique et ea reciperemus nec forsitan calumnia discipuli de diffinitione magistri recta videretur. Novimus etiam ipsum Aristotilem et in aliis locis adversus eumdem magistrum suum et primum totius philosophie ducem, ex fomite fortassis invidie aut ex avaritia nominis <vel> ex manifestatione scientie, insurrexisse, quibusdam et sophisticis argumentationibus adversus eius sententias inhiantem dimicasse, ut in eo quod de motu anime Macrobius meminit. (Dialectica, p. 91)[15]*

> If we knew all the writings of his master Plato in this discipline, we would probably accept them and perhaps the disciple's calumny about the master's definition would not seem correct. In fact we know that in other places Aristotle stood up against his master, the first leader of all philosophy, perhaps kindled by the spark of envy, or out of jealousy for his good name, or to show off his knowledge. Eagerly, he attacked his theses by means of some sophisms, for instance about the motion of the soul, as Macrobius reports.

Abelard projects his own experience of the master–disciple relation onto Plato and Aristotle – a relation characterized by envy, jealousy, and rivalry. Thus, he also shows how difficult it is to draw a line between legitimate, rational criticism applied by one philosopher onto the opinions of another, and "calumnies" disguised as criticism but inspired by spite or envy. The anachronistic projection that leads Abelard to read "Plato" and "Aristotle" as if they were "Anselme de Laon" and "Abelard" leads him to give a lucid account of what is at stake in the model of mastery and transmission Greek philosophers founded. There is nothing better than one phantasm to tell the truth about another.

This relative lucidity is due to the fact that Abelard can distance himself from the psychological intensity that the direct transmission from a living master to a living disciple produces. His relationship to Aristotle, as far as it can be surmised from his logical texts, seems to be better described as a relation between nephew and uncle than one between son and father. "Uncle Aristotle" is a figure of authority, but not of unquestionable power. Abelard explains in the prologue of *Dialectica* that he wrote it for his nephews, the sons of his brother Dagobert.[16] Staging himself as "uncle Abelard" may have helped him to imagine a dispassionate relation with the ancient logicians he wanted to celebrate and criticize.

In the same prologue, Abelard affirms that he can improve upon what he has received. For instance, on the subject of hypothetical syllogisms, he claims:

> *post omnes tamen ad perfectionem doctrine locum studio nostro in utrisque reservatum non ignoro. Item que ab eis summatim designata sunt vel penitus omissa, labor noster in lucem proferat, interdum et quorundam male dicta corrigat, et schismaticas contemporaneorum nostro<rum> uniat, et dissensiones moderno-rum, si tantum audeam profiteri negotium, dissolvat.* (*Dialectica*, pp. 145–6)

> However, I do not fail to recognize that after all [these authors] there is place for our studies to perfect the doctrine by studying both [Theophrastus and Eudemos]. Our work will enlighten what they sketched summarily or completely omitted, while it will correct the errors of some, unify the divergent opinions of our contemporaries, and, if I am brave enough to undertake such a task, resolve the dissensions of the moderns.

Since logicians of the past made mistakes and did not finish the work, it behooves their present successors, the moderns, to correct them, in order to avoid falling into schisms and dissensions. Abelard endorses the successional model created by Aristotle, while displaying a staunch belief in his own personal capacity to be, in his time, *the* successor brave enough to finish the logical work. The passage from "we" (*labor noster*) to "I" (*audeam*) in the same sentence is telling.

A similar declaration introduces the fifth section of *Dialectica*: "*Non enim tanta fuit antiquorum scriptorum perfectio ut non et nostro doctrina indigeat studio nec tantum in nobis mortalibus scientia potest crescere ut non ultra possit augmentum recipere*" [For the perfection of ancient writings is not such as the doctrine would not need our work; knowledge does not grow in us, mortals, to the point that it could no longer receive any improvement] (p. 535). Here, instead of describing himself as the one able to solve, clarify, correct, unify, and enlighten, Abelard resorts to a true plural "we" (*in nobis mortalibus*) positing himself in the long chain of mortal beings who by necessity have to leave things unfinished after them. However, this real "we" does not lead to any defined community, since it embraces all of humanity. Logicians and philosophers are mortals, which allows them to correct and improve the work done by their predecessors, but exposes them to the knowledge that their successors will do the same to them.

The prologue of *Dialectica* ends with a list of the seven texts of the logical canon, followed by this statement:

> *Quorum omnium summam nostre* Dialectice *textus plenissime concludet et in lucem usumque legentium ponet, si nostre Creator vite tempora pauca concesserit et nostris livor operibus frena quandoque laxaverit.* (*Dialectica*, p. 146)

> The text of our *Dialectica* will contain a complete sum of these texts, which it will enlighten for the use of the readers, if the Creator of our life grants us a little bit of time, and if envy relaxes the bridle she sets on our works.

In comparison with Anselm's elaborate prayers in the *Monologion* and *Proslogion*, Abelard remains remarkably discreet about his relationship with God in *Dialectica*. His only request to God is to grant him not vision, illumination, or special intimacy, but just time. His most pressing request is directed toward his human fellows through an allegorical figure: "*et nostris livor operibus frena quandoque laxaverit*" [if envy relaxes the bridle she sets on our works]. *Livor*, describes first, the skin discoloration resulting from various ills, and second, a passion that may provoke such a discoloration. Envy is livid. Abelard allegorizes his relationship to his masters, peers, and disciples under the traits of a pale rider, whose goal is to keep the horse in the stable, while the horse is ready for the race. Imaginary or founded in reality, Abelard's metaphorical account of his position as master of dialectic in Paris around 1117 contrasts with his effort to find a synthesis among the *disjecta membra* of the logical body. "If God gives me the time, I will do the work I can do" sounds like a reasonable wish. "If only those envious people would leave me alone, I would prove them how great I am" does not.

Scholars agree that Abelard was a logician of considerable skill, although, for reasons independent of his competence (the availability of more of Aristotle's logical texts), his logic was soon to be superseded.[17] His claim to be a significant agent in the history of logic was supported by his teaching, and is still demonstrated in his writings. In the domain of dialectic, Abelard could truthfully play the role of the good disciple, respectful and critical of the masters, becoming in turn a good master, devoted to the defense and illustration of his art through conciliatory strategies and hard labor. The phantasm of being *the* successor of Aristotle worked happily in reality, but only as long as Abelard limited himself to being a dialectician. When he attempted to become a new, Christian Plato, a rift opened between dream and reality.

Becoming God's philosopher

In his article titled "The Platonisms of Peter Abelard," John Marenbon reviews all the mentions and references to Plato in Abelard's writings – that is, to the scant available Plato reduced to the *Timaeus* and to what was filtered through the Neoplatonist tradition and the first Church Fathers, such as Augustine.[18] Marenbon concludes: "Abelard's Platonism is, most of all, an attitude to the history of philosophy and the place of philosophy."[19] Since in the first decades of the twelfth century Aristotle was known only through some of his logical texts, his realm could be identified with the third art of the *trivium*. Plato, even reduced to one text, was associated with the nebulous realm of philosophy, whose relationship to another nebulous realm still in the making and named theology was a vexed issue.[20] Following Marenbon's suggestion on Abelard's Platonism, one could say that Plato provided Abelard with a model of inquiry that incited him to expand his domain out of the confines of dialectic.

At the end of *Dialectica*, in the section "On divisions and definitions," Abelard takes as example of division the soul divided in three powers (*Dialectica*, p. 555). This example leads him to a discussion of the soul that is more metaphysical than logical, and to Plato's "soul of the world" [*anima mundi*] in *Timaeus*:

> *Sunt autem nonnulli catholicorum qui allegorie nimis adherentes Sancte Trinitatis fidem in hac consideratione Platoni conantur ascribere, cum videlicet ex Summo Deo, quem T'Agathon appellant, Nou naturam intellexerunt quasi Filium ex Patre genitum; ex Nou vero Animam mundi esse, quasi ex Filio Spiritum Sanctum procedere.* (*Dialectica*, p. 558)

> Some Catholics, leaning excessively on allegory, strive to identify the faith in the Holy Trinity in this notion of Plato; they understand with certainty that the nature of the *Nous* comes from the supreme God, whom they call *To Agathon*, almost as the Son is brought forth by the Father, and that the Soul of the world comes from the *Nous*, almost as the Holy Spirit comes from the Son.

This "excessive" allegoric reading does not sustain a critical, rational analysis comparing the two notions:

> *Sed hec quidem fides platonica ex eo erronea esse convincitur quod illam quam mundi Animam vocat, non coeternam Deo, sed a Deo more creaturarum originem habere concedit. Spiritus enim Sanctus ita in perfectione Divine Trinitatis consistit, ut tam Patri quam Filio consubstantialis et coequalis et coeternus esse a nullo fidelium dubitetur. Unde nullo modo tenori catholice fidei ascribendum est quod de Anima mundi Platoni visum est constare, sed ab omni veritate figmentum huiusmodi alienissimum recte videtur, secundum quod duas in singulis hominibus animas esse contingit.* (*Dialectica*, pp. 558–9)

> But in fact, this Platonist faith shows itself to be mistaken, for Plato admits that what he calls Soul of the world is not co-eternal with God, but takes its origin from God in the same way as creatures. Whereas the Holy Spirit is included in the perfection of the Divine Trinity and, therefore, no one among the faithful can doubt that he is co-substantial, co-equal, and co-eternal with the Father as well as with the Son. This is why Plato's Soul of the world can in no way be identified with the tenor of the Catholic faith, but is correctly viewed as a fiction completely estranged from truth, and according to which two souls exist in each human.

Abelard demonstrates that what describes best the relation between Plato's account of the Creation and the Catholic account is not an analogy but an incompatibility. They are not almost the same (*quasi*); they are contradictory and cannot both be true. This could be argued without evaluating the truth content of both accounts, but, as a Christian logician, Abelard is compelled to move from the form of the argument to its substance – from logic to theology – and to clarify which one of the two accounts is true and which one is false. He ends by characterizing Plato's soul of the world as a fiction (*figmentum*), estranged from the truth (*ab omni veritate alienissimum*) leading to untenable consequences such as the presence of two souls in one body. Although this sounds like a definitive dismissal, Abelard, consciously or unconsciously, leaves the door open for a reassessment of Plato when he charges him with using a fiction, instead of accusing him of lying or erring. Fiction can be put at the service of the truth, in the same way that imagination can serve judgment.[21]

A few years after *Dialectica*, Abelard wrote his first treatise of theology, known as *Theologia summi boni*. Returning to Plato, Abelard now accepts to consider the Demiurge, *Nous*, and the Soul of the world as analogical to the Father, the Son, and the Holy Spirit. To justify this analogy, he explains that the passage on the soul of the world must be read as "*per pulcherrimam involucri figuram*" [the beautiful figure of a myth].[22] He then indicates that he changed his mind about the Soul of the world because he changed his way of reading Plato:

> *Quae enim quasi fabulosas antea videbantur et ab omni utilitate remota secundum litterae superficiem, gratiora sunt, cum magnis plena mysteriis postmodum reperta magnam in se doctrinae continent aedificationem.* (TSB, p. 32)

> In fact, what at first appeared, according to the surface of the text, close to a useless fabulation, becomes more attractive when it is found to be full of great mysteries and to contain a most instructive doctrine.

Like Augustine, who first found the sacred Christian texts uninteresting for their lack of sophistication, and had to learn to read them figuratively instead of literally in order to appreciate them,[23] Abelard found a mode of reading allowing him to inscribe Plato among the authorities useful for a Christian philosopher.[24] He also claims that it is necessary to read Plato figuratively to avoid contradicting the general opinion that Plato was a great philosopher:

> *Ex hac itaque Macrobii traditione clarum est ea quae a philosophis de anima mundi dicuntur, per involucrum accipienda esse. Alioquin summum philosophorum Platonem summum stultorum esse deprehenderemus. Quid enim magis ridiculosum, quam mundum totum arbitrari unum esse animal rationale, nisi hoc per integumentum sit prolatum?* (TSB, p. 36)

> From the tradition taught by Macrobius it is clear that what philosophers say about the soul of the world must be understood through a myth. Otherwise, we would discover that Plato, the greatest philosopher, is the greatest fool. For what is more ridiculous than to think the whole world is a rational animal – unless this is said in a veiled fashion?

Abelard then stresses a series of contradictions that appear when one reads *Timaeus* literally and analyzes it with the tools of dialectic.[25] Instead of concluding as he did in *Dialectica* that Plato's soul of the world is a fabulation divorced from truth, he agrees that dialectic cannot be applied to all texts. This argument is at the core of the exegetic tradition. As Abelard makes clear in *Dialectica* when he refers to Catholics reading Plato allegorically, the technique of figurative reading was not reserved to the Old Testament. It could be applied to other texts, with the same goal: reading pre-Christian texts in such a way that they would be compatible with or announce the New Testament. Reading Plato allegorically would reconcile philosophy and theology:

> *Quod si ad involucrum deflectamus ea quae de anima mundi magnus philosophorum astruit, facile est rationabiliter cuncta accipi nec a sacrae fidei tenore exorbitare.* (TSB, p. 38)

However, if we inflect toward the myth what the great philosopher claims about the soul of the world, it is easy to understand all of it in a rational way without straying away from the tenor of the sacred faith.

This may be all one needs to become God's philosopher. But can God's philosopher continue to be the successor of the first dialectician?

Reconciling Aristotle's *logos* with Plato's *sophia* and both with Christ

In *Dialectica*, no authority, even Aristotle's, is unquestionable. In *Theologia summi boni* Abelard keeps in check his dialectical tendency to assimilate truth with a lack of contradiction, in order to access truth through other means and ways, including the use of fables, myths, or fictions. Thus he builds up his Plato as a different figure of authority, more obscure, uncertain, and difficult to refer to than Aristotle, but able to anticipate the Christian truth and to build bridges between logic, philosophy and theology. Aristotle knew what he was saying but unfortunately he did not say much (we are talking of the early twelfth-century Aristotle). Plato did not know what he was saying, but he reached a higher truth. Abelard may have desired to incarnate a fusion of Aristotle and Plato in his own work and life, to be simultaneously a dialectician and a poet-philosopher.[26] This also meant to bring Aristotle in relation with the Christian truth.

In a letter defending dialectic against its detractors, Abelard writes:

> *Cum ergo uerbum patris, Dominus Iesus Christus, λόγος Graece dicatur, sicut et σοφία patris appellatur, plurimum ad eum pertinere uidetur ea scientia quae nomine quoque illi sit coniuncta et per deriuationem quandam a λόγος logica sit appellata et sicut a Christo christiani, ita a λόγος logica proprie dici uideatur. Cuius etiam amatores tanto uerius appellantur philosophi quanto ueriores sint illius sophiae superioris amatores. Quae profecto summi patris summa sophia cum nostram indueret naturam ut nos uerae sapientiae illustraret lumine et nos ab amore mundi in amorem conuerteret sui, profecto nos pariter christianos et ueros effecit philosophos.[27]*

Therefore, since the Word of the Father, Lord Jesus Christ, is called *logos* in Greek, just as it is named the *sophia* of the Father, this knowledge seems to relate very much to him which is connected with him also by name and which is by a certain derivation from *logos* called logic; and just as Christians seem properly to be so called from Christ, so is logic from *logos*.

In addition, lovers of logic are all the more truly called philosophers as they are truer lovers of that higher *sophia*. Indeed, when that highest wisdom of the highest Father assumed our nature so that it might illuminate us with the light of true understanding and turn us from love of the world toward love itself, it made us at once Christian and true philosophers.

Etymology and the Scriptures are called to the rescue of a dream that has already turned sour when Abelard writes this letter, in the early 1130s.[28] The fusion of *logos* and *sophia* in Christ may be a theological truth or an inspiring analogy; it neither resolves the problem of the relation between logic and philosophy, which Aristotle left unsolved, nor establishes a Christian philosophy. Even if one would accept that logic, philosophy, and Christian theology are compatible, one would not be bound to grant Abelard the title of "true Christian philosopher." No doubt that is what Abelard wanted to be and what he thought he was, but opinions about his achievement as a Christian philosopher have always been divided. Whatever the philosophical value of his work, he failed to turn a private phantasm of *grandeur* into a collective one recognizing him as the great man he hoped to be. On the other hand, he succeeded in becoming one of the most famous controversial men in Western history. This is due in good part to his vexed relationship with his close predecessors and contemporaries.

Smokescreens and mirrors

Abelard's intellectual formation involves four masters: one he probably did not meet – Anselm of Canterbury (1033–1109) – and three who were his schoolmasters: Roscelin (*c.*1050– *c.*1125), Guillaume de Champeaux (1070–1122), and Anselme de Laon (*c.*1055– *c.*1117). Abelard says much about his quarrels with the two latter clerics in the *Historia calamitatum*. But several studies show that Abelard appropriated their work and method in different aspects of his dialectics and theology.[29] He imitated those he rejected, or rejected those he imitated. He also repeated with Guillaume de Champeaux and Anselme de Laon a scene that had unfolded earlier, with other players. His narration, like a smokescreen, hides two other painful stories, the story of Anselm of Canterbury and Roscelin, and the story of Roscelin and Abelard.

Neither Roscelin nor Anselm of Canterbury is mentioned once in the *Historia calamitatum*. And yet, from 1120 until his death, Abelard wrote three books on the Trinity[30] – the question that initiated a controversy between Roscelin and Anselm in the years 1091–2 and that led Abelard to be condemned twice for heresy. The silence of Abelard about Roscelin could be explained by the desire to keep his distance from a man suspected of heresy. But his silence about Anselm, archbishop of Canterbury, is more difficult to explain. Anselm is mentioned only three times by name in other works than the *Historia*. Whether Abelard did not want to reveal the real influence Anselm had on him, or viewed him as representing the clerical power that censored him, we may never know for sure.[31] In any case, the story of Roscelin and Abelard eerily mirrors the story of Anselm and Roscelin. Both relationships evolve from close acquaintance based on a common interest in dialectics and theology to a bitter conflict culminating with a trial held in Soissons about opinions concerning the Trinity. The first trial was held against Roscelin in 1092, with Anselm among the accusers, the second against Abelard in 1121, with Roscelin among the accusers.

Roscelin de Compiègne remains a shadowy figure, known mostly by the allusions to him in other authors' writings.[32] Only one text is firmly attributed to him: a letter addressed to Abelard not long before 1121. He may be the author of anonymous texts dealing with logic, grammar, and theology.[33] He is considered as one of the first nominalists in the early stages of the quarrel of the universals.[34] I will not attempt to reconstruct an objective assessment of Roscelin's role in intellectual life around 1100, but will instead examine the subjective distortions appearing in Anselm and Abelard's texts mentioning him, as part of the game of mirrors in which they were involved.

As we have seen in Chapter 5, Anselm opened a path toward an exploration of the fundamentals of faith with the help of reason and reasoning. Like Aristotle, he used a fictional contradictor, Insipiens, to stage his argument. Insipiens, like Amphisbeton, represents an internal temptation (the temptation to contradict or deny) externalized as an impossible figure. As long as this figure remains a fiction, its closeness to the philosopher is not an issue. Gaunilo's argument integrated in the *Proslogion* shows that a real person could assume the contradictor's position without endangering Anselm's construction, as long as this impersonation was performed as role-playing for the sake of the argument. When a Roscelin or an Abelard takes on the role of the contradictor, fiction becomes phantasm. Then, judicious men become unable to recognize that their own position, which they view as orthodox, mirrors the position of their adversary, whose argument they view as heretical. The game of mirrors becomes warfare.

Anselm of Canterbury and his French friend

Between 1090 and 1093 – his last years at Le Bec – Anselm wrote several letters against Roscelin's ideas on the Trinity. These letters, intended to be circulated, present a public version of the story from the perspective of Anselm at a turning point of his life: he became archbishop of Canterbury in 1093. According to these texts, Anselm's intervention was triggered by one of his monks, named John, who wrote in 1091 or 1092 to ask Anselm his opinion on a question raised by Roscelin de Compiègne [*Roscelinus de Compendio*] concerning the Trinity and the consequences of thinking of the three persons as a single thing.[35] Jean adds that Roscelin claimed Lanfranc and Anselm had conceded him this opinion, but that it was in contradiction with Saint Augustine's authority.

We have Anselm's answer to this letter (Picavet, pp. 113–14). It is short: Anselm is too busy now, but he promises that he will write more on this question as soon as possible. In the meantime, he sketches an answer to the problem raised by "*de illo qui dicit . . .*" [the one who said . . .]. Without mentioning Roscelin by name, Anselm responds to his challenge. Roscelin, like Insipiens, is given the benefit of the doubt: he may claim something logically and theologically impossible because he does not understand the implications of his claim. If not, he is upholding polytheism:

> Quod si dicit tres personas esse tres res, secundum quod unaquaeque persona est Deus; aut tres deos vult constituere, aut non intelligere quod dicit. (Picavet, p. 114)

> And if he says that the three persons are three things according to the fact that each person is God, then either he wants to establish three gods, or he does not understand what he says.

Anselm gives Roscelin the choice between being a heretic or an idiot, a traitor to his faith or a fake who does not deserve his reputation as master of dialectic. Although Anselm stands against Roscelin, he still agrees to debate indirectly with him, using an argumentation that is not based solely on authority.

In a letter sent to Foulques, bishop of Beauvais, on the same issue, Anselm adopts a different tone.[36] He knows that a council presided over by the archbishop of Reims will examine Roscelin, and he wants it to be known that he does not share Roscelin's ideas on the Trinity. To this effect, he first reaffirms his faith in the Creed. Then he accuses Roscelin of blasphemy, and affirms that since he is a Christian there is no sense in trying to argue with him:

> Quod si baptizatus et inter Christianos est nutritus, nullo modo audiendus est; nec ulla ratio aut sui erroris est ab illo exigenda, aut nostrae veritatis illi est exhibenda; si mox, ut ejus perfidia absque dubietate innotuerit, aut anathematizet venenum quod proferendo evomuit, aut anathemizatur ab omnibus Catholicis, nisi resipuerit. (Picavet, p. 114)

> But if he was baptized and raised among Christians, he must not be heard at all; no explanation of his error should be asked of him, no explanation of our truth should be presented to him. On the contrary, as soon as his bad faith is known without a doubt, he must anathematize the venom that he has

vomited in uttering [this error], or be anathematized by all Catholics, if he does not recant.

Reason can be used only to convince a non-Christian of his error. Between Christians, there should be no discussion of this type: *"Fides enim nostra contra impios ratione defendenda est; non contra eos qui se Christiani nominis honore gaudere fatentur"* [For our faith must be defended rationally against miscreants, but not against those who say they enjoy the honor of being named Christians"] (Picavet, p. 114). Anselm puts behind him his past as an abbot not averse to discuss matters of faith rationally with his monks. Thus he appears to refuse any subsequent exchange of ideas with Roscelin.

In fact, he did continue to dispute with Roscelin on the Trinity through writing and rewriting a longer refutation, known as *Epistolae de incarnatione Verbi* [Letters on the Incarnation of the Word].[37] In its different versions, he never mentions Roscelin by name, but by periphrases such as *"Francigena quidam"* [a certain Frenchman] or *"a quodam clerico in Francia"* [a certain cleric in France].[38] In the earliest version, Anselm writes: *"hunc autem novi, quia amicus meus est"* [I knew this man because he is my friend] but this sentence disappears in all other versions.[39] In the later version, addressed to Pope Urban II after Roscelin's trial, Anselm insists on the difference between himself and his adversaries: *"illi utique nostri temporis dialectici, immo dialecticae haeretici"* [the dialecticians of our time, or rather, the heretics of dialectic].[40]

Nothing is known of the circumstances in which Anselm and Roscelin might have been friends, but given Anselm's interests in dialectics and Roscelin's stature as a dialectician, it would be surprising if they had not been in touch during the 1070s and 1080s, when Anselm was prior and abbot at Le Bec, in Normandy, and Roscelin canon at Compiègne, in Ile-de-France.[41] The *Monologion* and the *Proslogion* were written in 1076–8.

In this flurry of letters on the Trinity, Anselm distances himself from Roscelin in more and more violent terms, which indicates how close they were at some point.[42] Although Anselm might have sincerely believed that his dialectic had nothing to do with Roscelin's impious dialectic, he remains fascinated by the latter. The later version of *De incarnatione Verbi* starts with a long profession of faith, obedience, and humility, insisting on the preeminence of faith over understanding.[43] But after this cautious opening Anselm launches into a serious, detailed discussion of the logical and theological problems Roscelin posed. Despite what he had said in his letter to Foulques (that matters of faith should not be debated among Christians), this time he explains:

> *Huic homini non est respondendum auctoritate sacrae scripturae, quia aut ei non*
> *credit aut eam perverso sensu interpretatur. Quid enim apertius dicit scriptura*
> *sacra, quam quia deus unus et solus est? Ratione igitur qua se defendere nititur,*
> *eius error demonstrandus est. (Opera Omnia, vol. 2, p. 11).*

The authority of Sacred Scripture is not a sufficient response to such persons,
since they either do not believe in Scripture or interpret it in a perverse sense.
For what does Sacred Scripture say more openly than that there is one and
only one God? Therefore, their error is to be proved by the argument
whereby they strive to defend themselves. (*Major Works*, p. 238)

Dialectic misapplied to matters of belief needs to be opposed by dialectic
illuminated by faith. In the rest of the letter, Anselm becomes so engrossed in
the discussion that he stages an imaginary dialogue between himself and
Roscelin, punctuated by "he says" or "he will say" or "he would say." He even
ventures to try to think like Roscelin: "*Puto quia sic ratiocinatur secum*" (*Opera
Omnia*, vol. 2, p. 14) [When he says this, I think that he reasons with himself
as follows] (*Major Works*, p. 241). The discussion evolves like the *Proslogion*
from a logical argumentation (here about whole and parts, unity and multiplicity, the meaning of terms such as "persons" or "things") toward a religious
meditation. In the *Proslogion*, the meditation is about the nature and power of
God; in *De incarnatione Verbi*, it is about the Trinity and Incarnation.
Roscelin plays the role of intellectual trigger that Anselm's students at Le
Bec played when he wrote *Monologion* and *Proslogion*. Roscelin, though, is not
the faithful son and student of a father abbot. He is a rival, a dangerous peer,
an inimical brother, whose musing on the Trinity undermines the potent
symbolism of the father and son relation. At the beginning of the discussion,
Anselm shifts the argument from the three persons of the Trinity to the Father
and the Son:

> *Ut autem facilius et brevius hoc faciam, loquar tantum de patre et filio, quoniam*
> *hae duae personae suis propriis vocibus aliae ab invicem aperte designantur.*
> *Nam nomen spiritus sancti non est alienum a patre et filio, quia uterque est et*
> *spiritus et sanctus. Quod autem in patre et filio de unitate substantiae vel*
> *pluralitate personarum inveniemus, hoc in tribus absque dubio cognoscemus.*
> *(Opera Omnia*, vol. 2, p. 11)

And in order that I do this more easily and more briefly, I shall speak only of
the Father and the Son, since these two persons by their own names are
openly denoted as distinct from one another. (For the name "Holy Spirit" is
not foreign to the Father or the Son, since each of them is both spirit and
holy.) And we shall undoubtedly know in the case of all three what we shall
discover in the case of the Father and the Son regarding unity of substance
and plurality of persons. (*Major Works*, p. 238)

It makes sense logically to reduce the argument to two elements instead of three, but Anselm could have picked the Father and the Holy Spirit, or the Son and the Holy Spirit. He admits that the Holy Spirit does not hold the same symbolic power and is not related in the same fashion to the Father and the Son as they are related to one another. Logical convenience supports Anselm's intellectual and affective interest in the Father and the Son. This interest was so strong that Anselm wrote eventually another work titled "*Cur Deus homo*" [Why God Became Man], presented as a dialogue between Anselm and one of his fellow monks, Boso.[44] I view Boso as a tamed version of Roscelin, allowing Anselm to pursue the endless conversation started with Roscelin, when they were "friends."

Abelard and his insane master

At the Council of Soissons, Roscelin recanted all the opinions attributed to him, summarized in the formula: "*tres deos vere posse dici si usus admitteret*" [one could say there are three gods if it was admitted by usage] (Picavet, p. 49). He avoided condemnation, and after some time of exile in England he came back to pursue his career as master of dialectic at Loches and Tours. It is still unclear when Roscelin taught Abelard: it could have been shortly before his trial and exile, or after his return, or both.[45]

Abelard did not become champion of his master Roscelin's honor. Neither did he play a role similar to Anselm's role in the Church of his time. Rather than the heir of Roscelin or Anselm, he became the heir of the quarrel itself, perpetuating its tone and dynamic in the next generation of disputing clerics. He defended dialecticians against those attacking them in the name of the faith, and attacked "pseudo-dialecticians" for using their art to question faith.[46] He internalized the ambivalence toward language and logic that Aristotle had projected on Amphisbeton and the ambivalence toward God and faith that Anselm had projected on Insipiens. The desire to reconcile two opposed positions or to find a third way appears in Abelard's relation with Roscelin and Anselm, as it appears in his relation with Aristotle and Plato. The stakes were higher, however, involving fundamental aspects of the Christian faith and basic philosophical concepts. It may have been an opportunity for Abelard to replay the game of "hyperbolic parricide," which Claire Nouvet defines as the main feature of his relation to his biological father and intellectual fathers.[47] It was also a moment when, for Abelard, a discussion on the unity and trinity of God became entangled with the questions of his own identity, as a philosopher, a Christian, a master, and a man.

There is no direct documentation of Roscelin and Abelard's relation as master and student. An allusion to Roscelin's teaching appears in *Dialectica*, concerning the whole and the parts:

> *Fuit autem, memini, magistri nostri Roscellini tam insana sententia ut nullam rem partibus constare vellet, sed sicut solis vocibus species, ita et partes adscribebat.*[48]

> I recall that our master Roscelin was of the insane opinion that no thing is composed of parts, but as he viewed species only as words, he viewed parts only as words too.

Abelard recalls then the example of a house and its walls that Roscelin used to support his "insane opinion" about whole and parts. In other parts of his logical texts, Abelard appropriates the vocalism that Roscelin taught him.[49] Here, he ridicules it. Without trying to assess the philosophical validity of Roscelin's theses,[50] we can try to understand the position Abelard assumes in this passage with regard to his former master. He still names him *"magister noster"* [our master] and vividly remembers something he heard from him probably more than twenty years before. Abelard (like Anselm) acknowledges the fascination that Roscelin's ideas on language exercised on him by expressing revulsion against him. The master of reasoning is insane. In the name of the reason he was supposed to teach, it is the duty of his disciple to expose his lack of reason. At the same time, in attacking Roscelin's dialectic, Abelard risks undermining his own dialectic, which has incorporated many elements from Roscelin's teaching. This is perhaps why there is no real debate about the universals between Roscelin and Abelard appearing in the texts. Instead, the confrontation took place on the theological question already disputed between Anselm and Roscelin: the Trinity, which has also to do with wholes and parts.

The conflict between Roscelin and Abelard erupts around the time when Abelard's first work of theology, *Theologia summi boni*, circulated. No one is sure which one started to attack the other.[51] What can be established are the following facts. *Theologia summi boni* contains attacks clearly directed against Roscelin although he is not named in it. Roscelin may have read *Theologia summi boni* or heard about Abelard's teaching on the Trinity that precedes and prepares the treatise. Abelard wrote a letter to the canons of Saint Martin accusing Roscelin of various things (this letter is lost). Roscelin wrote Abelard a letter to defend himself against the accusations made in the letter to the canons (this letter is preserved). Abelard wrote a letter to Gilbert bishop of Paris to defend himself against things Roscelin might have said to him or will say to him about Abelard (this letter is preserved). The chronological order is not certain, except that all this happened before 1121, when the Council of Soissons condemned *Theologia summi boni*.

This book supports the opinion that the Catholic dogma of the Trinity is not in contradiction with logic and reason, although it is also beyond logic and reason.[52] It includes three passages titled "Invectives," one against Jews (book I, ch. V), one against "pseudo-dialecticians" (book II, prologue), and one against dialecticians (book II, ch. III). "Jews" are a traditional target of invectives for defenders of the Christian faith. In this passage they appear as an abstraction representing a certain understanding of God, eternity, and Creation, rather than as a real group of real human beings. The "pseudo-dialecticians" (a term that Abelard apparently invented)[53] take shape and life, if not individuality, in the vivid description of their relentless, destructive, and self-satisfied verbiage. They recall Anselm's "heretics of dialectic" in the letter *De incarnatione Verbi*. The third passage addresses one adversary in the second person singular: "*Responde tu mihi, astute dialectice seu versipellis sophista*" [Answer me, crafty dialectician or sophist able to take all skins] (TSB, p. 118). It is impossible to refrain from identifying "you, shrewd dialectician" with a real person. "There is little doubt that this 'sophist' is Roscelin," Marenbon writes.[54] No doubt either that if Roscelin read the *Theologia* he would recognize himself.

In the second invective, Abelard seems first to agree with what Anselm wrote in his letter about Roscelin to Foulques de Beauvais: Reason must be used only to convince non-Christians (e.g., Jews) of their error, and not to discuss matters of faith with other Christians. But since Abelard eagerly wants to dismiss Roscelin's position on the Trinity with rational arguments, he assimilates the pseudodialecticians with non-Christians:

> *Invectio in pseudodialecticos*
> *Supra universos autem inimicos Christi tam haereticos quam Iudaeos sive gentiles subtilius fidem sanctae trinitatis perquirunt et acutius arguendo contendunt professores dialecticae seu importunitas "sophistarum," quos "verborum agmine atque sermonum inundatione" beatos esse Plato irridendo iudicat.* (TSB, p. 66)

> Invective against Pseudodialecticians
> They investigate faith in the Holy Trinity with more subtlety than all the enemies of Christ – heretics as well as Jews and pagans – and attack it with sharper arguments, those experts in dialectic or those relentless sophists, which Plato mockingly considers happy with "their army of words and their flood of speech."

As he dismisses Roscelin's position (though not yet his person) by associating it to a contingent of the legion of "Christ's enemies" including non-Christians, such as pagans and Jews, and pseudo-Christians such as heretics, Abelard pursues the intellectual project of theological dialectic that Roscelin may haved tried to launch through his remarks on the three persons. As he contradicts Anselm's cautious warning about disputes between Christians, he also continues Anselm's own inquiry into the issues Roscelin had raised. Therefore it can be said that in *Theologia summi boni* Abelard takes over the positions of both Anselm the inquirer and Anselm the censor. He also identifies himself as a new Plato fighting modern sophists.

The third invective not only individualizes the enemy, but also presents him as dangerously similar to the author of the invective. The passage is titled "Invective against Dialecticians," which, under the pen of someone who viewed himself as the leading dialectician of his time, could be read as "Invective against Myself."

> *Invectio in dialecticos*
> *Responde tu mihi, astute seu versipellis sophista, qui auctoritate Peripateticorum*
> *me arguere niteris, de differentia personarum, quae in deo sunt, quomodo ipsos*
> *doctores tuos absolvis secundum traditiones quorum, ut iam ostendimus, nec deum*
> *substantiam esse nec aliquid aliud confiteri?* (TSB, pp. 118–20)

> Invective against Dialecticians
> Answer me, shrewd dialectician or sophist able to take all skins, who strives to refute me with the authority of the Peripatetics on the difference between the persons that are in God, how do you acquit your teachers when their lessons force you, as we have shown, to admit that God is neither a substance nor anything else?

The best way to win over an enemy who is using the authority of the Peripatetics is to prove that he is using it the wrong way, against the teachings of Aristotle and his followers, and against the tenets of Christian faith. No one else but a true dialectician, and moreover a Christian dialectician able to reconcile Aristotle and Plato, can fight back an enemy armed with the tool of dialectic. At the end of the third invective, Abelard writes:

> *Quas tamen possumus aggrediemur, maxime ut pseudodialecticorum importuni-*
> *tatem refellamus, quorum disciplinas et nos paululum attigimus atque in studiis*
> *ipsorum adeo profecimus, ut domino adiuvante ipsis in hac re per humanas*
> *rationes, quas solas desiderant, satisfacere nos posse confidamus. Habet enim*
> *humanas etiam rationes conditor ipse rationis, quibus animalium hominum ora*
> *obstruere possit, qui nos per sapientem illum admonet dicens: "Responde stulto*
> *iuxta stultitiam suam, ne sibi sapiens esse videatur".* (TSB, p. 122)

Let us use [the analogies] we can, mostly to rebut these relentless pseudo-dialecticians. We too have brushed a little with their discipline and we went as far in this study as to be confident that we could, with the help of the Lord, answer their challenge on this subject with human reasons, which are the only ones they want. For the creator of reason too holds human reasons, by which he can close the mouth of human animals, he who exhorts us through the voice of the wise: "Answer the fool according to his foolishness, so he may not believe himself to be wise."

Could the boy who studied with Roscelin have anticipated that he needed to learn what Roscelin had to teach in order eventually to stand against him? Abelard here reorders his past to give it a providential justification, as he will do in the *Historia calamitatum*. His association with Roscelin cannot be held against him once it is presented as part of a plan the creator of reason designed. Reason comes from God, but, since humans have free will, they can use it in agreement or in disagreement with the divine will. Therefore, the best, or only, Christian response to the misuse of reason in matters of faith is not to renounce using it but on the contrary to use it to fight its misuses. Again, we find Abelard following Anselm.

At the time of his first trial, around 1120, Abelard tries, consciously or unconsciously, to present himself as a successor of Anselm. However, his attempt only underlines the difficulty of the task and his inability to fit in the role of God's philosopher he imagined for himself. The more Abelard tried to look like an Anselm, the more he was viewed as a Roscelin – including by Roscelin himself.

Abelard's letter to Gilbert, bishop of Paris confirms this interpretation:

> *Relatum est nobis a quibusdam discipulorum nostrorum supervientibus, quod electus (erectus) ille et semper inflatus catholicae fidei hostis antiquus, cujus haeresis detestabilis tres deos confiteri, imo et praedicare Suessionensi concilio a Patribus convicta est, atque insuper exsilio punita, multas in me contumelias et minas evomuerit viso opusculo quodam nostro de fide sanctae Trinitatis, maxime adversus haeresim praefatam, qua ipse infamis est, conscripto.* (Picavet, p. 128)

> It has been reported to us by certain students of ours as they arrived that the proud and ever conceited old foe of the Catholic faith, whose detestable heresy to confess and even to preach three gods has been condemned at the Council of Soissons by Catholic fathers and in addition has been punished in exile, spewed forth many slanders and threats against me after he saw a certain work of mine *On Faith in the Holy Trinity*, which I had written especially against the aforementioned heresy by which he had earned infamy.[55]

Roscelin is demonized as the "*hostis antiquus*" [old enemy] of orthodoxy, which allows Abelard to present himself as a champion of Catholic faith and a victim of Roscelin's foul mouth. In the same breath, Abelard reveals that he has intended his own writings about the Trinity to attack Roscelin – therefore, that he has knowingly started the present conflict. He also shows that he is well aware of the dangers related to expressing opinions about the

Trinity: he knows that Roscelin had to face a trial in Soissons. By presenting his treatise as a reaction against Roscelin's heretic statements on the Trinity, he hopes to appear as a second Anselm, whose letter *De incarnatione Verbi* was a response to Roscelin's alleged tritheism. He actually names Anselm in the same letter as one of the victims of Roscelin's slandering, Robert of Arbrissel being another. Abelard praises Anselm as that *"magnificum Ecclesiae doctorem"* [magnificent doctor of the Church] and Robert as *"illum praeconem Christi"* [that outstanding herald of Christ].[56] At the same time, his defensive attack against Roscelin repeats Roscelin's attacks against married priests and clerics supporting them or lenient to them, and against those who may encourage wives to escape from their husband's power, as Robert of Arbrissel was said to have done.[57] Roscelin might have been sincerely convinced of the immorality of such behaviors. Still, after his trial, it was certainly good for his reputation to show himself as a stern enforcer of Church morality. Abelard's strategy is similar, except that it precedes and anticipates a trial, instead of following it. By presenting himself as standing against Roscelin, in the camp of the enemies of the Enemy, Abelard stands as a new Roscelin, attempting to rebuild a damaged reputation.

How to contradict the Trinity and survive

Roscelin's long letter to Abelard begins and ends with invectives and insults, but its bulk is a discussion of the unity and trinity of God.[58] As in Anselm's letter *De incarnatione Verbi*, it seems that the aggressive posturing and feelings surrounding the issue act as a warm-up for the deployment of intellectual power.

Amidst insults and invectives, Roscelin indicates strategies that Abelard should be well advised to follow, if he really wants to take the path Roscelin took thirty years ago:

> *Si enim aliquando vel in verbo lapsus fui vel a veritate deviavi, nec casum verbi nec assertionem falsi pertinaciter deffendi, sed semper paratior discere quam docere animum ad correptionem praeparavi, neque enim haereticus est qui, licet erret, errorem tamen non defendit.* (Picavet, p. 131)

> For, if I fell into error in words or if I deviated from truth, I did not defend obstinately this word use or false assertion, but I was always more disposed to learn my lesson than to teach corruption to a soul. He is not a heretic who, although he errs, does not defend his error.

If we turn this passage into an advice, it would be: "Since a heretic is not someone who errs but someone who persists in his error, do not persist when you are accused of error. Abjure as I did at Soissons." The second advice Roscelin gives is to quote as many Christian authorities as possible:

> *Si igitur apud istos quos impudenter me persequi declamasti aliquid sacrae Scripturae contrarium reperimus, cur miraris in dictis tuis aliquid reprehendi potuisse, cum te in sacrae Scripturae eruditione manifestum sit nullatenus laborasse? Huic enim singularitati, quam divinae substantiae tribuisti, sanctorum Patrum Ambrosii, Augustini, Isidori, scripta nequaquam consentiunt. Quae collecta ideo subjicere curavi, ut non ex mea sed ex auctoritate divina quod mihi tenendum est roboretur.* (Picavet, p. 133)

> If we find things opposed to the Holy Scriptures in those you impudently accuse me of persecuting [Anselm and Robert of Arbrissel], you should not be surprised that we find something reprehensible in your sayings, as your erudition in Holy Scriptures makes clear that you have not worked at all [in this field]. The writings of the Holy Fathers Ambrosius, Augustine, and Isidore do not accept the singularity you attribute to the divine substance. Therefore, I have gathered and presented [citations] in order to reinforce by a divine authority and not by mine what is to be held true.

Roscelin then gives a three-page-long list of citations from the Old and New Testaments, Ambrose, Augustine, Isidore, and others (Picavet, pp. 133–5). In the first book of *Theologia summi boni*, Abelard had reviewed biblical citations about the Trinity from the Old and the New Testaments, and philosophical testimonies, using Cicero, Hermes Trismegist, and, above all, Plato (TSB, pp. 4–63). A few Church Fathers (Augustine, Boethius, Isidore, and Lactantius) are mentioned occasionally. Roscelin is right to claim that Abelard had not done a thorough review of patristic authorities on the subject. It seems that Abelard started to compile citations soon after the Council of Soissons, which eventually led to the composition of *Sic et Non*. Roscelin's advice on this matter was not lost on him.[59]

Finally, Roscelin recommends that Abelard apply all the resources of logic to theological issues, but accept their limits and stop using them when they lose their efficiency and purpose: "*Dicat melius qui potest. Ego melius non valeo. Sed neque quod dico importune defendo*" [May he say better who can. I am unable to do better. And I do not defend obstinately what I say] (Picavet, p. 137). This can be heard as a lesson of humility, but also as a lesson in hypocrisy or freedom of mind: say what they want you to say and think what you want – a lesson that Renard and False Seeming were eventually to spread in *roman*.

Roscelin's argument about the Trinity is probably best understood as part of a larger debate about language and signification involving Anselm of Canterbury, Abelard, and other thinkers of their times. Alain de Libera

understands the disagreement between Roscelin and Abelard on this question as being the confrontation of "two semantics," one based on signification (Abelard) and the other on reference (Roscelin).[60] Constant Mews
observes that, for Roscelin, "all utterances used of God had to obey the rules
of language. One of these rules was that every noun, even those used of God,
signified a substance."[61] The case of God cannot constitute an exception, or
otherwise the language would collapse. Roscelin applies the principle of
non-contradiction in a strict Aristotelian fashion: God cannot be said to be
one and not one at the same time. But since Roscelin does not reach
the conclusion that the dogma of the Trinity is unbelievable, he has to
admit that human language cannot give an appropriate account of what the
Trinity is:

> Soli enim Trinitati ideo Dei singularis numerus relictus est, ut in ea et intra
> eam omnimodam aequalitatem significet. Hominibus vero ideo pluraliter
> datur, ut non idem meritum nec ejusdem dignitatis monstretur, ut "ego dixi:
> dei estis" (Ps. 82:6) et "Audi, Israel, Dominus Deus tuus Deus unus est" (Deut.
> 6:4). (Picavet, p. 137)

> The singular number of God is granted only to the Trinity in order that, in
> and within the Trinity, this number signifies any kind of equality. But to
> humans it is given only as plurality, to demonstrate that it is not of the
> same merit or the same dignity: "I have said: You are gods" (Ps. 82:6) and
> "Hear, O Israel! the Lord our God is one Lord" (Deut. 6:4).

As humans, we can name and understand the plurality; we can only name
the unity and singularity of God without understanding it. For Mews, this
is where Anselm and Roscelin are most opposed: "Where Anselm tended to
emphasize the continuity between human and divine language, Roscelin
focused on the gulf between human language and divine simplicity."[62] I
would add that Roscelin assigned to the logician the perilous role of gatekeeper of human language – a difficult, perhaps impossible task if the
divinity who transcends all rules forbids the gatekeeper from contradicting
himself and from contradicting the divinity's contradictory essence, at the
same time and under the same respect.

Roscelin ends his argument about the Trinity with surprisingly conciliatory words:

> Itaque cum de divinae substantiae unitate discrepare videamur, tu quidem de
> ingenioli tui tenui conatu praesumendo solitudinem ei singularitatis adscribens, ego
> autem divinarum Scripturarum sententiis armatus similitudinis et aequalitatis
> unitatem defendens. In hoc tamen convenire nos convenit ut Deum qui unus et
> trinus est, quoquo modo illud intelligendum sit, unanimiter deprecemur quatenus

in nobis ignorantiae tenebras illuminet, seu infidelitatis maculam lavet mentibus-que nostris cognitionem veritatis suae infundat, et nos sopito contentionis desiderio idipsum invicem sentire concedat Jesus Christus Dominus noster. Amen. (Picavet, p. 137)

We seem to be in disagreement on the unity of the divine substance – you, presuming on the moderate strength of your genius, endow it with the loneliness of singularity; I, armed with sayings from the Divine Scriptures, defend unity of similarity and equality. However, we happen to be in agreement when we pray unanimously to a God who is one and trine, no matter how we understand it, to enlighten the darkness of ignorance in us, to wash the stain of faithlessness, to infuse in our minds the knowledge of truth, and that, once our contentious mood is overcome, we receive all these from Jesus Christ our Lord. Amen.

Although Roscelin contrasts Abelard's presumption with his own reliance on scriptural authority, he proposes a terrain of conciliation. Whatever they may argue about the Trinity, and no matter how opposed their explanations of the Trinity are, they both pray to the same God, one and three.

Insult your enemy like yourself

It would be nice if the letter ended here. The next sentence is: "*in merdae nostrae detractionis immunditio suino more saturatus es*" [you have filled yourself like a pig in the shit and garbage of your defamation of me] (Picavet, p. 138). The letter ends as it started – with attacks against Abelard's person and life.

Roscelin's violence certainly mirrors Abelard's own violence toward his contemporary masters.[63] Roscelin provides support for this argument in his letter when he claims to rejoice to see himself depicted truly, as in a mirror, in Abelard's accusations:

> *Initium litterarum tuarum de mea immunditia et de ecclesiae Beati Martini contumelia est. De ecclesia doleo, de me autem laetus sum quia in veritate talem me esse recognosco qualem me scribendo depingis. Dixisti enim me omni vitae spurcitia notabilem. Quod cum ita est, hanc tuam veritatis assertionem quasi quibusdam brachiis charitatis amplector, et in verbis tuis quasi in speculo me totum aspicio.* (Picavet, p. 130)

The beginning of your letter reveals my dirt and insults the church of Blessed Martin. I am sorry for the church, but I am happy with what concerns me, since in truth I recognize myself as you depict me in your letter. You said that I was notorious for the filth of my life. Since it is so, I open the arms of love to embrace this truthful assertion of yours, and I see myself entirely in your words almost as in a mirror.

Given the general tone of the letter, this cannot be read as a sincere statement. Roscelin, sarcastically, claims to see himself *"quasi in speculo"* [almost
as in a mirror] in Abelard's words, whereas he means that what Abelard
describes is not Roscelin but himself. *"Mea immunditia"* and *"omni vitae
spurcitia notabilem"* apply perfectly, according to the last part of Roscelin's
letter, to Abelard. Insults and slanders mirror insults and slanders.

   Another way to interpret the relation between dialectical argumentation
and attacks *ad hominem* in Roscelin's letter is to locate it in a broader context
than an interpersonal one. Constant Mews depicts the first half of the
twelfth century as a time of "profound transformation" of the intellectual
life, but not centered around Abelard: "Most philosophical and theological
texts and glosses from the period remain anonymous, and largely unread.
Any attemps at a synthesis must remain provisional. Nonetheless, it is clear
that Abelard, far from being the first original thinker, issued from over half a
century of vigorous intellectual debate."[64] As I claimed earlier, Abelard did
not inherit his temper and ideas from one master or another in a father-to-
son pattern, but from the interactions between the preceding masters: he
inherited quarrels and ways of quarrelling.

   Roscelin and Abelard knew philosophy was not a solitary activity, and
located their talks and thoughts within concrete communities. Roscelin
starts his letter by insisting on the fact that they are both Christian and
churchmen: he as a canon of the churches of Loches, Tours, and Besançon,
and Abelard as a monk at Saint-Denis.

> *Quia vero spiritu immundo quasi cum quodam vomitu locutionis me infamem
> atque in concilio damnatum eructas, utrumque esse falsissimum praefatarum
> Ecclesiarum testimonio apud quas et sub quibus natus et educatus et edoctus sum
> comprobabo, cum apud Sanctum Dionysium cujus monachus esse videris, licet
> diffugias, modo tecum acturus venero. Neque vero timeas, quasi te noster lateat
> adventus, qui in veritate per tuum abbatem eum tibi nuntiabo, et quantum
> volueris ibi te expectabo.* (Picavet, p. 131)

> But, since in a foul breath you disgorged like verbal vomit that I had been
> declared infamous and condemned in a council, I will prove these two accusa-
> tions are absolutely false by using the testimony of the two churches I have
> mentioned – churches in and under which I was born, educated, and instructed.
> This I shall do when I will come to the church of Saint Denis, of which you
> seem to be a monk, even if you have run from it, in order to plead against you.
> Do not fear that our arrival would be hidden from you, for I will have your
> abbot announce it to you, and when you want, I shall wait for you there.

Roscelin points out the dubious status of Abelard as monk *"esse videris"* [as
you seem to be], as a counter-attack to the suspicion Abelard throws on

him, describing him as a Church outcast (which Roscelin was not). He also parallels the proposition made by Abelard in his letter to the bishop of Paris to have an open confrontation with Roscelin "*coram catholicis et discretis viris*" [before catholic men of discernment] (Picavet, p. 128; *Beyond the Personal*, p. 195) by a proposition focused on their respective status in the Church and not on theological discussion. If Abelard is a true monk, he should accept a confrontation in an arena suitable for a monk: in the cloister and in the presence of his abbot. The tone is violent, but Roscelin is actually giving an opportunity to Abelard to prove he is an obedient member of the Church and his community.

Whether in a monastory, a cathedral school, or what would eventually become the university, masters thought, taught, spoke, debated, and wrote in company. The conditions may have changed in important ways from the cloister to the urban school; still, a collective setting remained the background of philosophical and religious activities. The main challenge for medieval philosophers was the integration of the topics of debate they received from the tradition within their present communities, whether the largest one (Christianity) or the smallest ones (the canons of Besançon or the monks of Saint-Denis). The Aristotelian model of philosophical succession was adapted and modified by the notion of orthodoxy, to be understood as the norm distinguishing between a community of faithful and a community of heretics. In his letter to Abelard, Roscelin does not reproach Abelard for having ideas opposed to his own, or for having misrepresented or misunderstood his ideas, but for having presented him to others as an outcast and a heretic. If their discussion of the Trinity involves important differences in their understanding of language, Roscelin explicitly locates their respective positions with regard to known heresies: Abelard is erring on the side of the Sabellians, Roscelin on the side of the Arians (Picavet, p. 135). Ideas do not reflect a personal, individual choice; they represent the adherence of an individual to a group.[65] In this regard, Roscelin and Abelard were perfectly of their times and perfectly understood one another.

And yet, the endless dispute on the three persons that are one, the unity that is a plurality, and the plurality that is indivisible also allows private phantasms to emerge in the light of philosophical reasoning, or perhaps as a side effect of philosophical reasoning. My ideas on universals, particulars, the three persons, and the one God may not belong to me but to my community; my "calamities" happen only to me. Claire Nouvet is right to emphasize Abelard's identification with Christ and the phantasmatic dimension of his claim of mastery, his feeling of persecution, and his parricidal and fratricidal violence.[66] What is left unexplained is the articulation between logic, fiction, and phantasm. I defined a phantasm as a mental image or series of images staging the self in relation to real events and people, like a memory, but with significant and consistent fictional aspects. If the quest for truth, traditionally claimed by philosophers, has to be in cahoots with a claim for orthodoxy (in the sense of belonging to the correct group), the gain made in focus and consistency is counterbalanced by the necessity to imagine oneself as living among close enemies and in constant danger of being confused by others with those enemies. Everyone can be turned into an Amphisbeton or an Insipiens at any moment. The practice of philosophy becomes strongly associated with hostility rather than with friendship – both being equally phantasmatic.

This affective instability, or ambivalence, of the self with regard to other individuals coincides with considerable changes in the intellectual field. At the same time that logic was recognized as an art of language (including grammar, rhetoric, and dialectic) and that theology emerged as a field germane but not identical with philosophy, the notion of "person" became a key element linking thoughts dealing with fundamental categories such as the particular, the singular, the plural, the diverse, the same, the divine, the human, and the grammatical persons. Looking for an analogy showing that plurality of persons can be compatible with unity of essence, Abelard uses the three grammatical persons, which can refer to a single being through three "persons": the person who speaks ("I"), the person to whom I speak ("you"), and the person about whom one speaks ("he/she") (TSB, p. 178). This may or may not help to understand the divine Trinity, but it certainly opens a path to musings about the sort of being I am, as a linguistic entity in three persons, which can be imaginatively related to the Father (when I speak I am like the Father), the Son (when I am spoken to, I am like the Son), and the Holy Spirit (when I am spoken about, I am like the Spirit). I am immortal as the Father, I am mortal and immortal as the Son, and I am neither mortal nor immortal as the Spirit. Abelard and his contemporaries' reflections and disputes on the persons of the Trinity open the way toward the fictional first person singular discourse blooming in the *Roman de la Rose*. A Latin absolute subject (*Pater, filius et spiritus sanctus*) as ideal of the self will eventually lead to a vernacular contingent subject (*Au vuintieme an de mon aage ...*) as fiction of the self.

Conclusion

While reading the texts I analyze in this chapter, I felt both admiration for the boldness and creativity thinkers of this period deployed in logic, philosophy, and theology and pity for their endless and bitter struggles. It seems that their modernity (they called themselves *moderni*) was won at the price of making the self very vulnerable, and, therefore, defensive and aggressive. Their major fear seems to have been losing one's identity to become a negative mirror image of oneself. The attacks they wrote against each other can always be returned to the sender. Moreover, they were unable to view their own masters as father figures. Fathers needed to be dead or divine to become bearable.

There is nothing preventing a founding son from becoming a father. Although the foundation of philosophy involved ambivalence and parricide, Aristotle succeeded in creating a form and field of knowledge that could be reused in various places and times. The philosophic lineage being an imaginary one (that is, to use Zrinka Stahuljak's terms, a bloodless genealogy), it is not a continuous line. When it resurfaces in history, it needs to be founded again, according to local conditions and circumstances.

Two major sites of difference between Aristotle and Abelard's times are Latin and Christianity. Both involve inner rifts. Greek was Aristotle's mother tongue, whereas Latin was not Abelard's. For him, the language of the Father was *not* the language of the father, and the father through the flesh was incommensurably different from the Father through the Spirit, as Anselm of Canterbury stresses in his discussion of the Incarnation:

> *Et omnes sciunt in deo patrem non esse filium et filium non esse patrem, quamvis in uno homine pater sit filius et filius sit pater, si idem homo est pater et filius. Quod ideo fit, quia in deo dicuntur opposite, in uno vero homine non ad invicem, sed ad alium filium pater et ad alium patrem filius dicitur.* (*Opera Omnia*, vol. 2, p. 12)

> And everyone knows that, in the case of God, the Father is not the Son, and the Son is not the Father, although, in the case of human beings, if the same man is a father and a son, the father is a son, and the son a father. And this is so because we in the case of God predicate father and son in opposition to one another, while we in the case of human beings predicate father in relation to one man as son, and son in relation to another man as father, not father and son in relation to one another. (*Major Works*, p. 239)

The Father is not a/the Son, and the Son is not a/the Father. But at the same time They are related in a fashion that no human being can experience or even, perhaps, understand (although Anselm goes to great length to understand).

So, no one can claim to be the Father or the Son. All human males can claim to be father or son in the natural, sinful fashion (Abelard did), which does not grant the type of spiritual or symbolic authority that could refound philosophy as a genealogy. Within the Church, men can become Fathers, as figures of authority and power, including intellectual power. But since neither Plato not Aristotle could be turned into a Church Father, the grafting of the philosophical lineage onto the theological one failed to produce a single tree. Instead, a culture of debate flourished in competing schools, and fatherless sons turned into master speakers and writers.[67] In these new times, the old ideal of philosophical friendship was renewed and tested, as we will see in the next chapter.

CHAPTER 9

The dialectics of friendship

For Plato and his successors, philosophy is etymologically and conceptually associated to *philia* or friendship.[1] Derrida reaffirms this association when he says: "*La question 'Qu'est-ce que l'amitié?', mais aussi 'qui est l'ami(e)?' n'est autre que la question 'Qu'est-ce que la philosophie?'*" [The question 'What is friendship?', but also 'Who is the friend (both or either sex)?' is nothing but the question 'What is philosophy?'].[2]

In this chapter, I will examine friendship as both an affect and a phantasm, using ancient and medieval philosophical works, and one medieval romance. Aristotle's ideal friend is as much a fiction as his opponent, and both are part of his vision of philosophy. Mortal philosophers may find some comfort in the idea that true friends will mourn them appropriately and make sure that something of their work will be passed onto posterity. I will look at various aspects of friendship in texts by Plato, Aristotle, and Cicero, such as the distinction between perfect and imperfect friendship, the rejection of unstable or ambivalent friendship as incongruent with perfect friendship, and the exclusion of women from perfect friendship, that is, from philosophy. Then I will examine the way Aelred of Rievaulx, a twelfth-century English Cistercian abbot, adapted classical friendship to the intellectual and affective needs of monks, thus opening a more pragmatic understanding of friendship. I will finish by returning to Chrétien de Troyes's romance, *Yvain or the Knight with the Lion*, in which a mock dialectical debate demonstrates that love and hate can coexist within the same mind or heart toward the same friend/enemy, and that logic and fiction can at times work together to loosen up old phantasms.

Lovers and friends

There is no doubt that friendship exists, or, to say it in a nominalist fashion, that friends exist. People usually do not have trouble identifying their friends and explaining what friendship means in their lives. But, when it

193

comes to definitions and analyses, friendship becomes elusive. It is often dwarfed by love or self-interest, allegedly the two great Western passions. Friendship is not viewed as a passion, but rather as a reasonable, moderate affect, or a sort of social benefit. Ancient Greek and Roman philosophy thought it a virtue, that is, a disposition of the mind under the control of reason, tending toward the best, and belonging to men [*vires*]. As such, it was accorded a good deal of philosophical attention. Plato returned several times to this topic.[3] Aristotle devoted "about a fifth of a course in practical philosophy" to it, whereas, according to A. W. Price, "a modern work on ethics and moral psychology which gave that much space to friendship would seem quaint." For Price, one of the reasons of this fading away of friendship from philosophical discourse is "because modern moral philosophy has become obsessed with one's obligation towards people one doesn't know."[4] It may also be because, since friendship has been traditionally thought as involving people of the same gender (and preferably of the male one), the public and private discourse about homosexuality and queerness has considerably changed the affective landscape in which friendship is located and defined.[5] I cannot here take into account all the elements in ancient, medieval, and contemporary cultures that have a bearing on the notion, representation, and practice of friendship, but I will try to point out a few important shifts appearing in writings on friendship that are relevant to logic and fiction, focusing first on Plato's *Lysis*, a dialogue "*peri philias*" [on friendship].

Lysis starts with a first person verbal phrase, "I was on my way," and the "I" who speaks is Socrates (*Lysis*, 203a, p. 688). Socrates relates a conversation he had with two young men, Hippothales and Ctesippus, and two boys, Lysis and Menexenus, at a wrestling school. The very first exchange between Socrates, Hippothales, and Ctesippus is unequivocally about erotic and romantic love between older boys or men and boys. The wrestling school is a place where boys learn to wrestle, to address sacrifices to the gods, to dispute and converse as educated free citizens of Athens, and to pick up boyfriends or to be picked up as boyfriends. Physical beauty may not be the only criterion of choice, but it is a very important one. When Hippothales invites old, ugly Socrates to join him and his friends, he first lets him know that there are many boys there – and good-looking ones [*polloi kai kaloi*] (*Lysis*, 204a, p. 688). And when Socrates considers joining them, he asks Hippothales who is the best-looking one [*tis ho kalos*] (*Lysis*, 204b, p. 688). Blushing Hippothales cannot hide for long the name of his current infatuation – "Lysis" – from Socrates, who gently teases and advises him on his love affair. This part of the dialogue belongs to Eros: Socrates congratulates Hippothales for choosing such a well-bred and handsome "*erōs*" [object of love] (*Lysis*, 204e, p. 689), while Ctesippus describes Hippothales as an "*erastēs*" [lover], and Lysis as a "*pais*" [boy], that is, the normal object of love of an older boy or a man (*Lysis*, 205b, p. 689).

But the dialogue shifts when Socrates starts to speak with the two younger boys, Lysis and Menexenus, and asks questions about their "*philia*" [friendship]. They are not qualified as "lovers" but as "*philoi*" [friends] (*Lysis*, 207c, p. 691). The shift from "eros" to "philia" coincides with the moment when Socrates, after chatting in a light, comedic fashion with Hippothales and Ctesippus, switches to dialectics with Lysis and Menexenus. When Lysis asks him to "*ithi dialogou*" [go discuss] with Menexenus instead of him, Socrates answers: "*dialekteon*" [discuss, I shall] (*Lysis*, 211c, p. 695). It is not that erotic relations cannot be discussed, i.e., submitted to a dialectic treatment: they are discussed in *Symposium* and *Phaedrus*. In *Lysis*, Socrates chooses to talk about friendship with the younger boys because, on one hand, they are too young to talk about their experience of erotic love, whether they had one or not, and, on the other hand, they are better interlocutors for such a discussion than the older boys, obsessed with the pursuit of erotic love and pleasures. Here, Socrates proves to be much wiser than Reason in the *Roman de la Rose*. Lysis and Menexenus can still distance themselves from desire and view their friendship as a relation, therefore susceptible to being considered from the logical perspective of a relationship between opposites, contraries, or contradictories. Although Socrates can very well understand Hippothales's desire for Lysis, he avoids playing the role of an older lover (an *erastēs*), and treats Lysis like a young friend.[6]

To find out what friendship is, Socrates first uses common knowledge to show its shortcomings. He quotes Solon's lines: "Happy the man who has as friends his children and solid-hoofed horses, / his hunting hounds and a host abroad" (*Lysis*, 212e; p. 696). The first circle of friendship is located in the household, the second, in nature, and the third, in the outer world – away from one's home and land. Wherever you are, some beings can make your life happier if they are your friends, or can make it miserable if they are not your friends. Think about a rebellious child, a vicious horse, an unruly dog, and an inhospitable host. The fragment does not say whether the friendliness of children, horses, hounds, and hosts results from sheer luck or hard labor, but only that they may be hoped for. However, what interests Socrates is not friendliness but friendship. Solon's saying is wise at the level of a wisdom based on "life-as-it-is," but it becomes an obstacle to a wisdom that considers life never being "as-it-is." Through logical (and a tad sophistical) reasoning, Socrates pushes Solon's aphorism to a dead end. If friendship is based on necessity and prudence (turn into friends those who would risk turning into harmful enemies if not befriended), then the distinction between a "friend" and a "nonfriend," an "enemy" and a "non-enemy" cannot be stabilized. The choice of a friend is dictated by external circumstances and by my perception of who would be most useful or most detrimental to me. Therefore a friend cannot be defined in itself, according to specific qualities or traits, but in function of his or her relative position of helpfulness and harmfulness. In this sense, there are truly no friends, but rather networks of friendship, in which I myself figure as potentially helpful or harmful to other beings.

Demosthenes describes such a state of things in his speech *Against Aristocrates*: "For there is no natural category of friends or of enemies; but their actions makes them such, and the law gives us freedom to punish as enemies those who accomplish enemy acts."[7] What Socrates treats as the remnant of an ancient wisdom is presented by Demosthenes as the basis of the current law, a law that does not know friends and enemies *per se* but rather friendly and hostile acts, just and unjust acts. In the same speech, Demosthenes recommends "*hugiainontōn anthrōpōn*" [healthy human beings] to be ready for the transformation of friends into foes and vice versa: "One ought to love and to hate, I believe, just so far as not to overshoot the occasion of either."[8]

Demosthenes and Solon speak as men living in a world that men rule, but not a world without women. Solon's lines, cited by Socrates, can be translated in the feminine: "Happy the woman who has as friends her children and milk-giving goats, / her hens and the housewife next door." Socrates evokes Lysis's mother at her loom in a charming vignette of maternal business and authority,[9] but it is in his presentation of the traditional view that friendship is based on usefulness, a view that Socrates does not completely deny but deems insufficient.[10] The philosophical exploration of friendship he pursues in *Lysis*, *Phaedrus*, and *Symposium* takes place among men, and as it becomes more abstract it becomes more masculine.[11]

Moving toward a better definition of friendship, Socrates examines ideas about likeness and opposition in the universe proposed by poets (Homer, Hesiod) and poet-philosophers (Empedocles, Heraclitus). Whether the universe is ruled by the attraction of the likes or of contraries leads to unsolvable contradictions when applied to human affairs – a treat for the sophist, a defeat for the philosopher:

> "Then should we say that the opposite is its opposite's best friend?"
> "Absolutely."
> "But Menexenus," I said, "this is absurd. In no time at all those virtuosos [*hoi passophoi andres*], the contradiction mongers [*hoi antilogikoi*], are going

to jump on us gleefully and ask us whether enmity is not the thing most opposite to friendship. How are we going to answer them? Won't we have to admit that what they say is true?"

"Yes, we will."

"So then, they will continue, is the enemy a friend to the friend, or the friend a friend to the enemy?" (*Lysis*, 216a–b; p. 700)

Those who claim to be knowledgeable in everything [*hoi passophoi andres*] and at the same time are openly *antilogikoi*, that is, do not accept to submit their argument to logical rules, will only arrive at contradictory or trivial definitions of friendship. While ancient poets and philosophers may be admired for their contribution toward a more abstract conception of friendship than the pragmatic, utilitarian one of rulers and lawyers such as Solon or Demosthenes, they, too, arrive at an entanglement in which the friend and the enemy, friendship and enmity shift too easily into one another. Socrates deliberately chooses to open another way of thinking about friendship, a way that will not be *antilogical* and will not end in contradictions.

Friendship as virtue

In his ethics, Aristotle, more decisively than Plato, defines friendship as a human trait that needs to be separated from natural philosophy, or physics.[12] After briefly recalling pre-Socratic theories about the affinity of the likes and the attraction of contraries, he concludes: "The scientific problems we may leave alone (for they do not belong to the present inquiry); let us examine those which are human and involve character and feeling, e.g., whether friendship can arise between any two people or people cannot be friends if they are wicked, and whether there is one species of friendship or more than one" (*Nicomachean Ethics* VIII, 1155b, p. 1826). In *Eudemian Ethics*, Aristotle tries to integrate the idea of friendship as related to similarity or opposition into his own conceptual frame of the three kinds of friendship (based on pleasure, based on usefulness, for its own sake). The reasoning is not limpid, but it establishes some of the major traits of the "first friendship" (*prōtē philia*) in *Eudemian Ethics*, or the "perfect friendship" (*teleia philia*) in *Nicomachean Ethics*. From the notion of likeness, Aristotle moves to the notion of stability:

> The like is brought both under the pleasant and under the good, for the good is simple, but the bad various in form; and the good man is ever like himself and does not change in character; but the bad and the foolish are quite different in the evening from what they were in the morning. Therefore

> unless the bad come to some agreement, they are not friends to one another
> but are parted; but unstable friendship is not friendship. (*Eudemian Ethics*
> VII: 1239b; p. 1964)

Here friendship must be understood as its most achieved form, not its most
common. About the attraction of the opposites, Aristotle views it as coming
from usefulness, either for the sake of complementarity or for the search of
the mean:

> But opposites are friendly through usefulness; for the like is useless to itself;
> therefore master needs slave, and slave master; man and woman need one
> another, and the opposite is pleasant and desired *qua* useful, not as included
> in the end but as contributing towards it... Yet in a sense the love of the
> contrary is love of the good; for the opposites desire one another because of
> the mean; they desire one another like tallies because thus out of the two
> arises a single mean. Further, the love is accidentally of the opposite, but *per
> se* of the mean, for opposites desire not one another but the mean. (*Eudemian
> Ethics* VII: 1239b; p. 1964)

This aspect of friendship is accidental and not essential, and characterizes
unequal forms of friendship (slave and master, man and woman) rather than
the perfect friendship, which has to be equal (*Nicomachean Ethics* VIII,
1157b and 1158b; pp. 1829–31). In order to present friendship as both a
common human practice and a philosophical ideal, Aristotle eliminates
enmity and foe from his reflection on friendship and friend. Aristotle is
certainly as aware as Demosthenes that friends can turn into enemies and
vice versa. For him, this unstableness is a contingency that does not define
friendship but only signals its limits.

   When Aristotle describes and defines friendship according to the traits to
be found in its most rare manifestation,[13] it is as if he was describing and
defining siblinghood according to Siamese twins. The monstrous and the
perfect have rarity in common. Women, children, and slaves only have
commonalty in common. They even share this trait with many men, particularly men with little means and power, and of low birth – men who are
subjugated to other men. If children, slaves, and subjects are excluded from
egalitarian, perfect friendship as well as women (*Nicomachean Ethics* VIII: 7,
1158b; p. 1831), their exclusion is commutable: children grow, slaves can be
freed, and subjects can take power. Women never cease to be women. They
do not grow out of it, cannot be freed from it, and thus, they will not be
allowed to take power, or even to think or speak about it. As Barbara Cassin
says about Aristotle's view of human nature applied to slaves, children, and
women, "no amount of education will ever free women from the world of
silence."[14] If Aristotle states about the slave that "*qua* slave then, one cannot be

friends with him; but *qua* man one can" (*Nicomachean Ethics* VIII: 11, 1161b; p. 1835), he does not apply the same reasoning toward women, although he grants that, in the best cases, the friendship of husband and wife "may be based also on virtue, if the parties are good; for each has its own virtue and they will delight in the fact" (*Nicomachean Ethics* VIII, 1162a; p. 1836). This is the maximum of inclusivity that Aristotle can offer to women, which is not negligible.[15] Women have some place in the common forms of friendship, even in the virtuous ones – although Aristotle never discusses friendship between women, which theoretically could be both virtuous and equal – but they cannot contribute to its essential definition, except as the hidden opposite of a friend. The true opposite of a friend is not a foe but a woman; reciprocally, a friend can be defined as the opposite of a woman. Thus, when a woman practices friendship, she has either to be enemy of herself, or forfeit any claim toward perfect friendship. The latter may not be such a bad deal after all.

By setting the bar of friendship so high, Aristotle puts his own experience of friendship under restraint. At the beginning of *Nicomachean Ethics*, he evokes his friendship with Plato and some of Plato's disciples:

> We had perhaps better consider the universal good and discuss thoroughly what is meant by it, although such an inquiry is made an uphill one by the fact that the Forms have been introduced by friends of our own (*philous andras*). Yet, it would perhaps be thought to be better, indeed to be our duty, for the sake of maintaining the truth even to destroy what touches us closely, especially as we are philosophers; for, while both are dear, piety requires us to honour truth above our friends. (*Nicomachean Ethics* I, 1096a; p. 1732)

For Aristotle, *philosophia* and *philia* may be theoretically bound to each other; in practice, they are not so easy to reconcile. A philosopher may have to consider a philosopher friend as an opponent. In this sense, friendship between philosophers is no more immune to variation and reversal than other friendships. It may even be particularly conducive to it, given the issue at stake: what can be more divisive than truth between truth seekers? Hence, friendship between philosophers should not be a privileged candidate for perfect friendship. But this, Aristotle does not say. By devoting such an important part of his ethical treatises to friendship, he solidifies the notion that philosophers are expert in friendship, are particularly gifted for it, can tell the truth about it, even if they ought to prefer truth to their own friends. On the other hand, besides this passing remark alluding to his own experience of friendship, Aristotle restricts his speech on friendship to generalities and does not use examples of particular friendships (legendary or historical), leaving to readers the task of fiction-alizing friendship (perfect or otherwise) as they wish.

In his dialogue *De amicitia* [*On Friendship*] (also known as *Laelius*), Cicero uses a fictional frame in the model of the Platonic dialogues. In 129 BC, a few days after the death of Scipio Africanus, Scipio's best friend Gaius Laelius talked about friendship to his two sons-in-law, Gaius Fannius and Quintus Mucius Scaevola. Almost forty years later, in 90 BC, Scaevola repeated this conversation to a small group of friends, including young Cicero. In 44 BC, one year before his death, Cicero wrote down Laelius's words, transmitted by Scaevola, for his friend Atticus. Cicero claims at the beginning, "*sic hoc libro ad amicum amicissimus scripsi de amicitia*" [in this book, I have written as a most affectionate friend to a friend on the subject of friendship] (*De amicitia* i. 5; p. 113).[16] If friendship is what friends should be interested in conversing about, it should not be their own friendship, or at least not as they are still both alive. Cicero gives Atticus a model of speech that could be adapted to their friendship by one of them once the other has died. The frame is openly presented as a fictional re-creation of a scene that deserves to be immortalized and commemorated:

> *Eius disputationis sententias memoriae mandavi, quas hoc libro exposui arbitratu meo; quasi enim ipsos induxi loquentis, ne "inquam" et "inquit" saepius interponeretur atque ut tamquam a praesentibus coram haberi sermo videretur.* (*De amicitia* i. 3; p. 111)

> I committed the main points of that discussion to memory, and have set them out in the present book in my own way; for I have, so to speak, brought the actors themselves on the stage in order to avoid the too frequent repetition of "said I" and "said he," and to create the impression that they are present and speaking in person.

The frame itself defines etiquette of friendship, or, rather, of discourses about friendship. True friendship occurs between equals, but must be taught by an older man to younger men.[17] The fact that Fannius and Scaevola were Laelius's sons-in-law, and Cicero was sent to Scaevola by his own father to learn politics, law, and ethics, emphasizes the strictly masculine lineage of friendship. From the start, Scaevola's reminiscence of Laelius's speech points out how difficult and rare true friendship is, for it is triggered by a friendship that turned into hate. After discussing the separation "*capitali odio*" [in deadly hatred] of two great friends, Publius Sulpicius and Quintus Pompeius, Scaevola "*exposuit nobis sermonum Laeli de amicitia habitum ab illo secum*" [proceeded to repeat to us a discussion on friendship, which Laelius had had with him] (*De amicitia* i. 3; p. 111). A clear separation between friends and foes is not always possible in life as it is (and particularly *as it was* for men in power at the time of Cicero and Caesar),[18] but Laelius affirms that true friendship must be absolutely and lastingly positive: "*ut ne quando amare inciperemus eum quem aliquando odisse possemus*" [we should never begin to love anyone whom we might sometime hate] (*De amicitia* xvi. 60; p. 171). Friendship must be stable in order to be true and passed on to posterity. That love and hate could be present at the same time in the same heart for the same object is no more thinkable in this frame and according to this etiquette than the idea that women could be *vera amica*.[19]

From Plato's youthful *philia*, hardly separated from *eros*, to Aristotle's first and perfect friendship, to Cicero's Roman virtue, friendship looks more and more like a cult of virile perfection, allowing men to speak about their emotions without sounding effeminate or dominated by the sway of passion. It also looks more and more like a mourning ritual. Of true friends, one can only talk when they are dead or as if they were dead.[20] We may not know the extent of our attachment to someone until this person is dead, but this does not oblige us to think, talk, or write about this person and attachment in a melancholy tone. The rigidity of the discourse on friendship does not come from the real work of mourning, but from the mythologizing of friendship, which makes of it a variation of the cult of great men.[21]

Friends in sin, friends in Christ

In the prologue to his book on *Spiritual Friendship*, Aelred of Rievaulx (1110–67), obviously imitating the tone and intent of Augustine's *Confessions*, explains that his book was born from his wondering whether Cicero's ideas on friendship "*si forte possent Scripturarum auctoritate fulciri*" [could not be supported by the authority of the Scriptures].[22] Christianizing Cicero and paraphrasing Augustine were nothing new. However, Aelred's friendship is his own, and expresses new ideas and a new sensibility.[23] For Damien Boquet, Aelred's discourse on friendship completes his anthropology – an anthropology based on the rehabilitation of affect as a potential tool for salvation.[24] But since affect cannot be completely disconnected from the flesh and the Fall, Aelred's discourse on a friendship rooted in affect cannot avoid ambiguity and tensions:

> Thus, the dialectic of friendship explains some tensions in Aelred's writings about interpersonal relationships within the cloister. In this sense, *amicitia carnalis*, for instance, possesses a fundamentally ambiguous status in so far as it is marked by the polarization of *affectus carnalis*, damnable when it turns man into a slave of his carnal passions, and tolerable when it is used as a basis

for ascending toward virtue. This tension is what makes Aelred's discourse consistent.[25]

This tension allows Aelred to reintroduce enmity within the Ciceronian model of perfect friendship. When Cicero evokes friendships that turned sour or short for various reasons, he concludes:

> *Sed nescio quo pacto ab amicitiis perfectorum hominum, id est sapientium – de hac dico sapientia, quae videtur in hominem cadere posse – ad levis amicitias defluxit oratio. (De amicitia* xxvi. 100; p. 206)

> But in some unaccountable way I have drifted away from the friendship of faultless men – that is, men of wisdom, such wisdom I mean as is observed to fall to the lot of man – and I have rambled on to a discussion of friendship of the frivolous kind.

Wise men fall into friendship only with other wise men; therefore perfect friendship is like a perfect, eternal summer: no frost ever affects it. When Aelred treats the question of choosing one's friends, he starts from a Ciceronian position. Since a friend is *"consors tui animi"* [the sharer of your soul], he must be chosen and tried with great care: *"Stabilis enim debet esse amicitia, et quamdam aeternitatis speciem praeferre, semper perseverans in affectu"* (*De spiritali amicitia*, p. 98) [Friendship ought to be stable and to offer a certain prospect of eternity, always persevering in affection] (*Spiritual Friendship*, pp. 58–9). Instead of being rooted in virtue, as was Cicero's friendship, Aelred's friendship is rooted in the love of God, but besides that, at this point in the text, it still unambiguously fits the etiquette and frame of philosophical tradition. *"Cum vera amicitia nisi inter bonos esse non possit, qui nichil contra fidem vel bonos mores velle possint aut facere"* (*De spiritali amicitia*, p. 100) [Since true friendship cannot exist except among good people – I mean those who can neither desire nor actually do anything contrary to faith or good morals] (*Spiritual Friendship*, pp. 58–9), then the consequence is that Aelred will not examine all forms of friendship but only the "true" one.[26]

Aelred gets derailed from this model when, as a good abbot, he supplies concrete details to help the younger monks he addresses to choose their friends. They are four kinds of people one should not elect as friends: *"iracundi, instabiles, suspiciosi, verbosi"* (*De spiritali amicitia*, p. 102) [people who may be prone to anger, or flightiness, or those who may be distrustful or talkative] (*Spiritual Friendship*, p. 60). Cicero says that, stability being central to friendship, one should avoid unfaithful friends: *"nihil est enim stabile, quod infidum est"* [nothing is stable that is unfaithful] (*De amicitia* xvii. 63; p. 174). He also rails at length against flatterers (*De amicitia*, xxiv–xxvi;

pp. 196–206). If flatterers in search of patronage and other advantages were a common pest of the late Roman Republic, the irascible, the suspicious, and the garrulous are creatures of the cloister that Aelred had to deal with on a daily basis. As he explains why one should avoid having irascible friends, one of his two interlocutors, Walter, interrupts him:

> *Et nos te vidimus, si non fallimur, cum iracundissimo homine summa religione colere amicitiam; quem usque ad vitae eius finem numquam a te laesum, quamquam ipse te saepe laesisset, audivimus.* (*De spiritali amicitia*, p. 104)

> But, unless we are mistaken, we have seen you have cultivated a friendship of the highest devotion with a man who was very prone to anger, a man to whom you never did any harm even to the end of his life, although – we have heard – he often harmed you. (*Spiritual Friendship*, p. 60)

Such a mischievous quip is unthinkable in the mouth of any of the reverent sons-in-law featured in Cicero's dialogue. Whether a real Walter said it to a real Aelred or not does not matter: Aelred chooses to include vivid, personal exchanges between abbot and monks in his dialogue, because, if friendship is founded in affect (as Plato's *philia* was founded in *eros*), and if spiritual friendship implies dealing with emotions, moods, and tempers in order to progress toward salvation, stormy episodes should not be brushed under the rug of ideal friendship. Aelred answers with a pragmatic, yet optimistic advice:

> *Sunt quidam ex naturali conspersione iracundi, qui tamen ita hanc comprimere et temperare soliti sunt passionem, ut in quinque quibus, teste Scriptura, amicitia dissolvitur, atque corrumpitur, numquam prosiliant; quamvis nonnumquam amicum inconsiderato sermone, vel actu, vel zelo minus discreto offendant. Tales si forte in amicitiam receperimus, patienter tolerandi sunt, et cum nobis constet de affectu certitudo, si quis fuerit vel sermonis, vel actionis excessus, amico id indulgendum est; vel certe sine aliquo dolore iocunde insuper, in quo excesserit, commonendum.* (*De spiritali amicitia*, p. 104)

> There are some who, through their natural constitution, are prone to anger, but who are so accustomed to control, and moderate their passion, that they never fall into those five sins which, as Scripture bears witness, can cause a friendship to dissolve. However, they may sometimes offend a friend by an inconsiderate word, or by an action, or by a zeal that is less than discrete. If by chance we have taken such people into our friendship, we must put up with them patiently; and since we have some certainty about their affection for us, if there is any excessive speech or action on their part, we must indulge it because they are our friends, or certainly we ought to admonish them, but do it without causing grief, or even do it pleasantly. (*Spiritual Friendship*, p. 60)

About another of his friends, who, according to Walter and Gratien, acted unpleasantly in public toward him, Aelred recognizes that his friendship leads him to bear with his ill-tempered manner as long as honesty and good faith are not in jeopardy, because: *"Homo ille certe michi carissimus est; et semel a me receptus in amicitiam, a me numquam poterit non amari"* (*De spiritali amicitia*, p. 106) [Indeed that man is most dear to me, and at the same time, since I have received him in friendship, it will never be possible for me not to love him] (*Spiritual Friendship*, p. 61). Aelred explains the favoritism that other monks see in his indulgence as dictated by his evaluation of the exact balance that must be struck between fairness and the amount of rebuke his friend could bear with. He also implies, without giving details, that his friend might have had a point although he acted rashly to make it. From a psychology of explicit elitism (only true gentlemen can be true friends, and therefore they cannot behave in an unseemly, vulgar way toward one another), we have moved into a psychology of checks and balances between imperfect beings striving toward improvement – together. This certainly opens the door to admitting that a certain amount of hostility is possible, or even unavoidable, between the best friends and within the highest form of friendship.

Aelred's spiritual friendship is indeed declined in the masculine: his friends and the famous friends he evokes from classical and biblical traditions are men. However, in the whole treatise, there is not a single remark that deems women unable to partake in friendship at a similar level of perfection (or imperfection tending toward perfection) as men. Moreover, to justify his conviction that friendship is natural and good for humans, Aelred calls upon *Genesis* and the creation of man and woman:

> *Postremo cum hominem condidisset, ut bonum societatis altius commendaret: Non est bonum, inquit, esse hominem solum; faciamus ei adiutorium simile sibi. Nec certe de simili, vel saltem de eadem materia hoc adiutorium divina virtus formavit; sed ad expressius caritatis et amicitiae incentivum, de ipsius substantia masculi feminam procreavit. Pulchre autem de latere primi hominis secundus assumitur; ut natura doceret omnes aequales, et quasi collaterales; nec esset in rebus humanis superior vel inferior, quod est amicitiae proprium. Ita natura mentibus humanis, ab ipso exordio amicitiae et caritatis impressit affectum; quem interior mox sensus amandi quodam gustu suavitatis adauxit.* (*De spiritali amicitia*, pp. 36–8)

And when God created mankind afterward, in order to commend more highly the good conferred by human society, he said, "It is not good for man to be alone; let us make for him a helper fit for him." Certainly divine virtue did not simply form this helper from similar or even from the same material, but woman was created expressly as an incentive for happiness and friendship, from the very substance of the man himself. And so it is beautiful that the second created being was taken from the side of the first, so that nature might teach that all are equals, as it were "collateral." In human affairs there is to be neither superior nor inferior; this is the appropriate mark of friendship. So from the very beginning nature impressed upon human minds the emotional desire for friendship and affection, a desire which mankind's inner sense of love increased with a certain taste of sweetness. (*Spiritual Friendship*, p. 39)

Even in the passage that evokes the degradation of universal friendship into particular friendships after the Fall, Aelred does not distinguish in this regard between men and women (*Spiritual Friendship*, pp. 39–40, *De spiritali amicitia*, p. 38). Does this indicate a real opening toward women and a different understanding of gender with regard to friendship?[27] Or does this result from the common confusion of masculine with the universal associated with Aelred's personal disinterest in the feminine (or the feminine in women)?[28] Or, despite the passage on humans being all "collateral," and the absence of explicit rebuke, should we read *On Spiritual Friendship* as the counterpart of *On the Rule for Recluses*, which implies that if men can achieve spiritual fulfillment through friendship, women should seek it only in solitude?[29]

The fact that Aelred's texts can be interpreted so differently with regard to gender indicates that he is not simply reproducing the Ciceronian model of friendship in a Christian society. Aelred is not a philosopher or a master of dialectics, but he is a contemporary of Roscelin, Abelard, and Bernard de Clairvaux.[30] The emotional instability that he admits in his understanding of friendship echoes the phantasms we have seen at work in the relationship between Anselm of Canterbury and Roscelin, and Roscelin and Abelard. Aelred is not overly concerned about orthodoxy and heresy, though, but about the contiguity between friendship and erotic attraction, and therefore the feelings of jealousy and competition that often accompany passionate friendships. Instead of seeing the friend turned into a negative mirror image of the self, Aelred sees the friend as engaged in a similar work on the self, struggling with contradictory impulses, while aiming toward a perfection that cannot be reached on earth.

Don't they love each other? yes and no

Toward the end of *Yvain* or *The Knight of the Lion*, a remarkable digression interrupts the narrative for about one hundred lines, just before the judicial fight between Yvain and Gauvain. Instead of vicariously jousting, the reader is invited to debate whether or not, in one person, love and hate toward another person can coexist. Can we simultaneously love and hate the same object? The answer is immediately provided: indeed, yes. But how and why? That is the question the digression claims to answer. Jean Frappier might have been the first to associate this passage to Abelard's *Sic et Non*, on the basis of the line "*Oïl, vous respont, et nenil*" (l. 5998) [Yes, I answer you, and no], which echoes and translates the title of Abelard's compilation of contradictory citations answering 158 theological questions.[31] As Frappier points out, it also playfully evokes the disputes *pro et contra*, real or simulated, practiced as pedagogical exercises in twelfth-century schools, and in particular by Abelard as a master.[32] There is no doubt that this passage, packed with antitheses, paradoxes, and contradictions, has a distinct, dialectical flavor, but there is no consensus among scholars on its *raison d'être* or signification.[33]

For me, the interest of this passage lies in the disruption of the narrative by logical reasoning morphing into metaphor and allegory. The contraries, love and hate, become Love and Hate fighting like the fictional knights, Yvain and Gauvain, whom the digression left ready to fight each other in a trial by combat. As champions of two enemy sisters, the knights must perform incognito, which does not diminish the crowd's excitement: "*Et toz li pueples aprés court / Si com a tel afaire seulent / Courre les gens qui veoir veulent / Cops de bataille et d'escremie*" (ll. 5990–3) [And the crowd runs like crowds usually do when people want to see the blows exchanged in fight or joust]. Like the crowd, we the readers are ready for blood and gore, with the added excitement that we know the identity of the two knights. But, there is a "but" to defer our enjoyment:

> *Mais ne s'entreconoissent mie*
> *Cil qui combatre se voloient,*
> *Que molt entr'amer se soloient.*
> *Et or donc ne s'entr'aiment il?*
> *"Oïl", vous respont, et "nenil",*
> *Et l'un et l'autre prouverai*
> *Si que raison i trouverai.*   (ll. 5994–6000)

> But, they don't recognize each other,
> Those two who want to fight each other
> Although they used to love each other.
> Why, don't they love each other now?
> "Yes," I answer you, and "no,"
> And I shall argue for both answers
> In such a way that I shall find reasons to support both.

The first three lines are still part of the story, the fourth breaks away by asking a question that could not be asked by any character to another character. At first, it seems that the question "Don't they love each other now?" is asked by the narrator to the reader, a common feature of Chrétien's romances.[34] In fact, the following line "'Yes,' I answer you . . ." implies that this question is asked by the reader to the narrator, or, rather, that the reader should have asked this question, but did not, because the reader, like the crowd, is more interested in spectacular blows than in logical snags. The ideal reader would spontaneously detect contradictions and enjoy teasing them out. For that exceptional reader, the digression would be a treat, while the common reader may view it as a punishment.[35] The real question may be, "What sort of reader are you?" or "What are you reading for?" To which the reader can answer back, "What sort of writer are you?" and "What are you writing for?" In any case, no matter what sort of reader or writer I am, the question *"Et or donc ne s'entr'aiment il?"* [Don't they love each other now?] implies the "each-otherness" of two fictitious knights and the "each-otherness" of writer and reader – that is the relation of reciprocity indicated by the prefix *"entre"* and the reflexive pronoun in the verb *"s'entraimer."* Do you still love me and do I still love you as I put my story on hold? Do you still love me and do I still love you as I skip the logic to run to the fight? Are we still friends even when we pretend to debate? You are as much fictitious to me as you are real to yourself, and I am as real to myself as I am fictitious to you. Do we even qualify for friendship, given this peculiar dissymmetry? But why would we spend time in each other's company, trying to read each other's mind, if we were not in a relation of friendship? Friendship, in Old French, is commonly called *amor*,[36] and that is what the digression is about: the nature or essence of friendship viewed as a passion rather than as a virtue, and its logical and psychological relation with its opposite, *haine*, whether it concerns knights, author and reader, or other sorts of friends.

Yvain and Gauvain love each other: *"Pour voir, mesire Gavains aime / Yvain et compeignon le claime, / Et Yvains lui, ou quë il soit"* (ll. 6001–3) [In truth, sir Gauvain loves / Yvain and calls him his companion, / And Yvain does the same for him, wherever he is]. "Wherever he is" indicates that friendship does not depend on proximity or presence, but on reciprocity and acknowledgment. Wherever they are, and no matter how far or long apart, as long as each claims the other as his friend, they are friends. The problem is that at the very moment they are physically present to one another they are cognitively absent: *"Nes ici, së il le savoit, / Feroit il ja de luy grant feste / Et si mestroit pour lui sa teste"* (ll. 6004–6) [Even here, if this

one knew [who that one is], / He would greet him now joyfully / And
would give his life for him]. The sentence applies to Gauvain as well as to
Yvain, as the two next lines indicate: "*Et cil la siue ausi pour lui / Anchois
qu'en li feïst anuy*" (ll. 6007–8) [And that one would do the same for this
one, / To spare him trouble]. All hangs on the "if" clause: "If he knew."
They would behave like friends if they knew they were physically present
to one another.

   Friendship is a mental thing that can exist even when friends are physically apart. Moreover, friendship is actual even if one of its essential
premises remains potential. Friends can be defined as individuals who
would sacrifice their life for one another if they had to; if they never have
to, their friendship remains as actual as if the potential willingness to
sacrifice was actualized. Theoretically, if we agree that friendship can exist
in absentia and be actual when one of its premises remains potential, we
have to agree with the verse that follows: "*N'est cë amors entiere et fine?/ Oïl
certes*" (ll. 6009–10) [Isn't that whole and perfect friendship? / Yes, indeed].
The friendship between Gauvain and Yvain remains whole, perfect, and
actual even when they are away from one another and do not do anything to
prove their friendship. But can that be pushed to the point where one could
assert "Yvain and Gauvain remain perfect, actual friends at the very moment
they are going to fight each other to death"? The brutal juxtaposition of
friendship and hostility staged in the romance calls into question the
construction of perfect friendship as something independent of, or at least
resistant to, contingencies:

> *N'est cë amors entiere et fine?*
> *Oïl certes. Et la haïne,*
> *Dont ne rest ele toute aperte?*
> *Oïl, car ço est cose certe*
> *Que li uns a l'autre sans doute*
> *Voldroit avoir la gorge route,*
> *Ou tant avoir fait li voldroit*
> *De honte que pis en vaudroit.*   (ll. 6009–16)

> Isn't that whole and perfect friendship?
> Yes, indeed. But isn't hate
> Evidently present?
> Yes, for it is certain
> That each one – no doubt –
> Would like to break the neck of the other,
> Or to shame him so much
> That his worth would be lessened.

The desire to break another knight's neck does not sound especially chivalric.[37] Chivalric combat is presented here not as a display of sportsmanship, which is still compatible with the idea of perfect friendship, or of courtly love [*amors entiere et fine*], but as the enactment of the desire to destroy or demean the other, which is not.[38] The text simultaneously calls into question the nature of chivalry and the link between friendship and virtue.

The initial question the ideal reader should have asked the narrator was about a contradictory statement: "Don't they love each other at the same time that they don't love each other?" Socrates, in *Lysis*, tries to avoid this logical hurdle by understanding *philia* in relation to desire and lack, rather than in relation to its opposite or contradictory. Chrétien does not avoid the hurdle but makes it more manageable by slipping from contradiction (A and non-A) to contrariness (A and its contrary B), and from verbs to substantives. From the conjunction of "to love" and "not to love" the argument moves to the juxtaposition of love and hate or the cohabitation of Love and Hate:

> *Par foy, c'est merveille prouvee*
> *Qu'en a en un vaissel trouvee*
> *Amor et Haïne mortel.*
> *Dex! Meïsmes en un ostel*
> *Comment puet estre li repaires*
> *A choses qui si sont contraires?* (ll. 6017–22)

> By faith, it is truly prodigious
> To find in one vessel
> Love and deadly Hate.
> God! How can such contrary things
> Dwell in the same house?

It must be noted that, in Old French, allegories are not signaled by capitals or the absence of an article as in modern French: *Amour* et *Haine* versus *l'amour* et *la haine*. In modern English or French, we have to choose between concept and allegory, whereas, in Old French, they can be expressed altogether. The metaphor of the "vessel" is so vague and commonplace that it can still be understood on a conceptual level: love and hate, as feelings or affects, coexist in a single vessel, i.e., the heart or mind of one person. But, when in the next line, the vessel becomes a house [*ostel*], that is a place where people dwell [*li repaires*], love and hate turn into lodgers or dwellers, e.g., Lady Love and Sir Hate, or Dr. Love and Mr. Hate, or any other characters the reader may imagine. At this point, logic, abstraction, and rhetoric shift toward psychology, adstraction, and poetry.

The metaphor of the house appears in numerous ancient and medieval philosophical or rhetorical treatises as a *topos* or *topicum*, often used as a mnemonic device.[39] Boethius uses it to illustrate the topic of the whole and the parts.[40] But if Boethius's house supports reasoning such as "what is proper to the whole is proper to the part" or "what is in the part must be in the whole," Chrétien's house stands as a whole made of disconnected parts, which explains the coexistence of love and hate, and the cohabitation of Love and Hate:

> *En un ostel, si com moi samble,*
> *Ne püent eles estre emsamble,*
> *Que ne porroit pas remanoir*
> *L'une aveuc l'autre en un manoir*
> *Que noise et tenchon n'i eüst*
> *Se l'une l'autrë i seüst.*
> *Mais en un cors a plusors menbres,*
> *Quë il i a loges et chambres.*   (ll. 6023–30)

It seems to me that in the same house,
They cannot stay together
For they could not live
One with the other in the same place
Without disputes and wrangles,
If they were aware of each other's presence.
But, as in a body there are several members,
Here there are several rooms and alcoves.

Chrétien freely uses a traditional *topos* to describe a subject who knows that he does not know himself. According to his house metaphor, self-consciousness is the awareness of the dissociation of the self. Moreover, self-consciousness occurs only within an intersubjective setting, in which the self defines itself as it awakens to the presence of another self: friend or foe, friend and foe. The house of mischief in which Love and Hate take their quarters is not specifically Yvain's self or Gauvain's self; it is their selves (or themselves) involved with each other.

Earlier in the romance, Yvain had been trapped in the castle of the Lady of the Fountain, who is aware of his presence but unable to locate and see him, since he can make himself invisible thanks to a ring a maid named Lunete gave him (ll. 1020–37).[41] The debate on love and hate suggests that the castle could be read metaphorically as the invaded self of both Yvain and the Lady of the Fountain. First, Yvain plays the role of Love, as an intruder in the Lady's estate. But, further on, Love "squats" within Yvain himself:

Chele playe a mesire Yvains
Dont il ne sera jamais sains,
C'Amours s'est toute a lui rendue.
Les lieus ou ele est espandue
Va recherchant et si s'en hoste;
Ne veut avoir hostel ne hoste
Se chestui non, et que prous fait
Quant de mauvais lieu se retrait,
Por ce q'a lui tote se doint. (ll. 1379–87)

Sir Yvain has received a wound
Of which he will never be cured,
For Love gave herself entirely to him.
She searches all the places
Where she has spread herself, and leaves them.
She does not want any other hostelry nor host
But that one, and she is right
To remove herself from bad places
For giving herself entirely to him.

Love, like an errant knight, is a character moving from dwelling to dwelling. Despite the solidity attached to the idea of a house, here the metaphor expresses the mutability of the self, presented as inhabitant and inhabited, settled and unsettled, owner and tenant, aware and ignorant, known and unknown. Such a subject can very well love and hate the same object at the same time, and such a text can bear with ambivalence. Then, subject and text do not fit any more in the traditional philosophical discourse on friendship, mostly known by twelfth-century readers through Cicero's *Laelius*, but pertain to the modern landscape of dialectics and affect, promoted by Abelard, Aelred, and a few others (including Abelard's arch-enemy, Bernard de Clairvaux).

Once the fight starts, at line 6104, the two champions display an equal mastery in the noble art of hacking people up. Although they still do not identify each other, they cannot help being puzzled:

S'esmerveillent et esbahissent;
Que par ingal s'envaïssent
Qu'a grant merveille a chascun vient
Qui est cil qui se contretient
Encontre lui si fierement. (ll. 6197–201)

They marvel and wonder,
For they assault one another with such equal strength
That each is deeply amazed and wonders
Who this man is who resists
Him so fiercely.

Friendship, like the phoenix, is reborn out of its own destruction. By
fighting blindly, they rediscover the source of their friendship in their
equal strength and resilience, which implies that matching opponents are
only one step away from perfect friends. As critics have noted, the whole
episode of the fight between Yvain and Gauvain cannot be taken without a
grain of salt.[42] Once they finally figure out that this excellent knight is no
one other than his own alter ego, the physical fight to kill turns into a verbal
fight to lose: "I am the loser!," "No, I am the loser!" (this is the gist of lines
6280–98). So, does the reader have to plod through a debate on hate and
love only to be rewarded with an indecisive fight that demonstrates that our
two knights are doomed to friendship because neither one can physically
dominate the other? Does our friend, the author, intend only to frustrate
and tease us? Or are we frustrated because we expect more from fiction than
to be amused? Which Aristotelian form of friendship do we entertain with
the author: friendship for fun, interest, or its own sake?

   The attitude of King Arthur in front of the reversal of affects between the
two champions turned into friends may be a template for the ideal, friendly
reader:

> Mais li roys la tenchon depieche
> Quant oï les ot une piece;
> Car li oïrs molt li plaisoit
> Et cë aveuc quë il veoit
> Qu'il s'estoit entra'colé
> S'avoit li uns l'autre afolé
> Et enpirié en pluseurs lex.
> "Seigneur, fait il, entre vous dex
> A grant amor, bien le moustrez,
> Que chascuns dit qu'il est outrés.
> Mais or vous en metés sor moy.
> Et je l'amenderai, je croi,
> Si bien quë honnors vous sera
> Et touz siecles m'en loera."   (ll. 6355–68)

The king ends their quarrel,
But only after he has listened for a while,
For he enjoyed listening to them
And also seeing them
Now hugging each other
Although they had hurt and wounded
Each other in several places.
"Lords, he says, between you two
There is great love, as you demonstrate

When each one of you says that he has lost.
But now, leave it to me:
I will resolve the issue in such a way, I believe,
That the honor will be for you
And people will praise me for this."

The King is amused and detached while also involved. He remembers that the whole episode is not gratuitous, but rather has a function in the narrative: to resolve a quarrel between two enemy sisters. The resolution of this serious matter should be left to the friendly, kingly, reader.

Friendships that work

Renée Allen remarks that "in their eagerness to see Yvain's adventures as a series of women being rescued from male aggression, many critics gloss over the fact that the climactic battle between Yvain and Gauvain is a direct result of the quarrel of the Noire Espine sisters."[43] The question of juxtaposition of love and hate toward the same object is introduced by a story that begins like a Greek myth or fable.

> *Mais dedens chou fu avenu*
> *Quë a la Mort ot plait tenu*
> *Li sires de la Noire Espine;*
> *Si prinst a li tele aatine*
> *La Mors, que morir le couvint.*
> *Aprés la mort, ainsi avint*
> *De deux filles quë il avoit.*   (ll. 4697–703)

> But in the meantime it happened
> That the lord of the Black Thorn
> Had a dispute with Death.
> Death got so worked up against him
> That he had to die.
> After his death, this is what happened
> To his two daughters.

The lord of the Black Thorn[44] wedded Death as Proserpina wedded Pluto. They had two daughters, born out of *plaid* [dispute] and *aatine* [quarrel]. Death does not give birth from an act of love. True to their lineage, the two sisters quarrel about their inheritance: "*L'ainsnee dit quele aroit / Trestoute la tere a delivre / Tous les jourz qu'ele aroit a vivre, / Que ja sa seur n'i partiroit*" (ll. 4704–7) [The elder says that she will have / All the land at her discretion / All the days of her life / And that her sister will never share any of it]. The youngest is willing to share even her part of the inheritance but does not push sisterly love to the point where she would accept to be entirely spoliated: "*Et sache ma seur toute voie / C'avoir porroit avoir du mien / Par amour, s'ele en voloit rien; / Que ja par forche, que je puisse / Et que conseil n'ayeüe truise, / Ne li lairai mon hiretage*" (ll. 4774–9) [My sister should know, however, / That she could have some of my own, / For love, if she wants some; / But, never by force, as much as it is in my power / And that I can find support and help, / Will I leave my inheritance to her]. The digression about love and hate suggests that each champion fights for both sisters at the same time, even if Gauvain is nominally the champion of the eldest, or Hate, and Yvain, the champion of the youngest, or Love. No wonder no one can win or lose. The opposition of the two sisters is not only an opposition of good and bad (although it is clear that one is right and the other wrong), which in Aristotelian terms would be an opposition of contraries. It is also an opposition of contradictories: all against something (and not: all against nothing).[45] The elder wants all for herself and nothing for her sister, the younger wants something for both. Both are willing to use strength to defend their position, but the younger demonstrates that she is able to change her position and to act as a friend if possible, as an enemy if necessary.[46] The elder stays entrenched in her position of hostility, and, when her sister proposes to share some of her own and affirms that she does not want anything that does not belong to her, she answers: "– *Ne je ne veul, fait el, du tien / Que tu n'as riens ne ja n'aras. / Ja tant preechier ne saras / Que riens em pors pour preechier: / Tout em porras de duel sechier* (ll. 5956–60) [I don't want, she says, anything of your own either, / For you have nothing and will never have anything. / No matter how long you preach, / your preaching will get you nothing. / You will dry out in your grief]. Elsewhere, she wishes that her sister "*vivra dolente et caitive*" (l. 5904) [will live in sorrow and misery]. She does not wish her sister's death, but a miserable life for her, which would be the condition of her own happiness: "*S'est or mais drois que je me raille / En mon eritaigë em pais*" (ll. 5900–1) [It is right that I return now / In peace to what I inherited].

Yvain and Gauvain do not only fight for the sharing of land; they fight for the sharing of life and death, which is what Death and the Lord of the Black Thorn left to their daughters. The elder wants all the life for herself and all the death for her sister, but without her dying, because then she would inherit death from her. The younger can accept to receive death as her share, but only if her sister renounces her claim to immortality. The elder would like them to be immortal enemies; the younger would like them to be mortal friends. An indecisive judicial fight between two friends turned mortal enemies leaves the conflict of the two sisters unsolved. A third party is needed to cut the knot of love and hate, death and life, enmity and friendship. The king – no matter how senile, inefficient, or imaginary he is – can impose mortality as the rule, decree sharing as the means, and establish a space in which the two sisters can live together. In *Yvain*, this space is described in feudal and familial terms. After the elder sister reluctantly agrees to give her sister her share of inheritance, with the king as warrant, he says: "*Revesté l'ent tout orendroit, / Fait li roys, et ele en deviegne / Vostre fame et de vous le tiegne! / Si l'amés comme vostre fame / Et ele vous comme sa dame / Et comme sa serour germaine*" (ll. 6428–33) [Invest her on the spot, / The king says, so she can become / Your vassal and hold it from you. / Then love her as your vassal, / And she should love you as her lady / And as her blood sister]. The king can enforce feudal and familial love, which means keeping at peace with one another, not acting hostilely to one another, and, in case of necessity, supporting one another. He cannot enforce the affective love of friendship, as Aelred understood it. So Arthur, wisely, does not ask the two sisters to love each other like two friends or two brothers.

The story of the two sisters seems to narrate the contrary of ideal friendship: first, it happens between two women, and, second, they hate each other. But the story of the friendship between Yvain and Gauvain seems, too, a strange illustration of the "Great Friends" theme. Gauvain incites Yvain to abandon his new wife and new lordship to live again like a bachelor with the other bachelors, going from tournament to tournament (ll. 2484–538). As a consequence, Yvain is repudiated by his wife, becomes insane, and has to fight numerous monsters and evil knights to recover his wife and social status. Moreover, as we have seen, the two best friends almost kill each other for lack of recognition. In truth, they had not met for a long time and did not seem particularly worried about it.

Is there any friendship that works in this story? Yes: the friendship of a man and an animal, and the friendship of a man and a woman. While Gauvain is never here when one needs him,[47] Yvain finds, in the lion and the servant Lunete, two friends of a rare kind: reliable. And Yvain becomes as reliable as his friends: he helps them when they badly need help, which also in the end helps him to recover from the sorry state caused by his great friend Gauvain's advice. In the philosophical tradition, friendships between subjects who are (allegedly) unequal by nature are doomed to imperfection. In the fictional universe of this romance, there is no perfect human relationship (since love and hate can be housemates and since life and death are our inheritance, how could that be?); but, on a scale of relative value, a non-human friend and a non-male friend score the highest marks for Yvain. A lion and a girl are a knight's best friends.

Conclusion

I opened this chapter with a citation from Derrida's *Politics of Friendship*, a text that continues the tradition of philosophical treatises on friendship while recognizing its major flaw, the exclusion of women. This recognition appears in footnotes and parentheses. For instance, in a long footnote about brotherhood, Derrida balances with exquisite delicacy his own friendships for Nietzsche, Bataille, Blanchot, and Nancy with a truth he cannot repress: "*Il y a peut-être encore quelque fraternité, chez Bataille, Blanchot et Nancy, dont je me demande, du fond de mon admirative amitié, si elle ne mérite pas quelque déprise*" (*Politiques de l'amitié*, p. 57) [There is still perhaps some brotherhood in Bataille, Blanchot, and Nancy, and I wonder, in the innermost recess of my admiring friendship, if it does not deserve a little loosening up] (*Politics of Friendship*, p. 48). In chapter 3, a long parenthesis explains the nature of the trouble with a friendship conceived as a brotherhood:

> (*Vous n'aurez peut-être pas manqué d'en prendre acte: nous écrivons et décrivons les amis au masculin, au neutre-masculin. N'y voyez pas une distraction ou un lapsus. Ce serait plutôt une manière laborieuse de creuser le sillon d'une question. Par elle, vers elle nous sommes peut-être portés depuis le premier pas: qu'est-ce qu'une amie? Et l'amie d'une amie?*) (*Politiques de l'amitié*, p. 74)

> (You will not, perhaps, have failed to register the fact that we are writing and describing friends as masculine – neuter-masculine. Do not consider this a distraction or a slip. It is, rather, a laborious way of letting a question furrow deeper. We are perhaps borne from the very first step by and towards this question: what is a friend in the feminine, and who, in the feminine, is her friend?) (*Politics of Friendship*, p. 56)

In this chapter I neither asked nor answered the question of the "friend in the feminine." With the help of dialectic, a few fictions, and my own life experience, I take friendship in the feminine for granted. Otherwise, *O mes amies* . . . why and for whom would I write if there were no *amies*?[48]

Conclusion

When Sherlock Holmes reappears in front of John Watson, three years after his death at the falls of Reichenbach, "for the first and last time in [his] life," Watson faints. For once it is Holmes who is surprised by his friend: "'My dear Watson,' said the well-remembered voice, 'I owe you a thousand apologies. I had no idea that you would be so affected.'"[1] There is no discussion of friendship in the Sherlock Holmes stories. Friendship is just part of the setting, like 221B Baker Street. Holmes and Watson share most of the traits that perfect friends are supposed to possess: they are male, of equal status, educated and mostly virtuous (addictions aside). They do not belong to the highest classes, but they do not belong to the lower classes either. If Conan Doyle had stopped writing his Holmes stories after "The Final Problem," the whole corpus could have been viewed as belonging to the genre of the melancholy encomium that perfect friends compose for their departed friend, fusing friendship with the cult of great dead men. Watson ends his report of Holmes's last fight against Moriarty with: "If I have now been compelled to make a clear statement of his career, it is due to those injudicious champions who have endeavoured to clear his memory by attacks upon him whom I shall ever regard as the best and wisest man whom I have ever known."[2] But, in 1903, Conan Doyle resurrected Holmes in "The Adventure of the Empty House" at the cost of making Watson faint for the first and only time in his life. Holmes and Watson's friendship becomes eternal and the reasons for Watson's reporting less clear. Melancholy may be tainted with hysteria. I suggest in my last chapter that the relation between writer and reader could be called friendship, if one accepts friendship as being imperfect, ambivalent, and as happening between all kinds of people. Conan Doyle killed Holmes for various reasons including, I surmise, exasperation with his readers. He resuscitated him out of friendship for them (and perhaps for him), after all.

My friend, the reader, may still ask me what friendship has to do with particulars, adstraction, naming, reference, animals, nonexistent objects, rationalism, fictionalism, the principle of non-contradiction, the logical argument of the existence of God, the liar paradox, love, fictional representations of the self, the philosopher as mortal, Socrates as a ghostly father or a fatherly ghost, scholarly disputes full of phantasms, and the Trinity. I could answer that this list would not be less eclectic if friendship were added to it. But that would be treating lightly my reader's effort to understand and undermining my own attempt explicitly to connect all these elements. I may have failed in this regard, but I have tried. So I will try to explain why I could not avoid speaking about friendship as an enduring philosophical phantasm, which fiction may, at times, loosen up.

The Friend (or the perfect friend in Western philosophy) is the counterweight of the Opponent (or the contradictor, enemy of rationality and rationalism). Friendship offers a stable, controlled space of affect between peers. It is a rational or rationalized emotion, sidestepping ambivalence and contradiction, transcending its homoerotic roots (still visible in Plato's *Lysis*) to become an ideal of human perfection. The Friend and the Opponent are imaginary creatures or nonexistent objects like the unicorn and Renard. Both were created at the time when Greek philosophy was becoming a field of knowledge, a way of life, and a tradition to be transmitted from generation to generation. Like the unicorn, but unlike Renard, they were not deliberately created as fictions. The Opponent was an argumentative tool serving to establish a first principle for all philosophical thinking, and especially for logic. The Friend appears when philosophy attempts to rationalize the interpersonal relationship that is necessary for the practice of dialectics (Greek philosophy was much more dialogical than meditative). Philosophy also had to integrate affect as the part of human nature dominant in interpersonal relations. While recognizing themselves as simply human, and, as such, sharing human affectivity, philosophers hoped to attain a state of reasonable sensibility. Their idea of Friendship reflects this hope, which, without irony, I find beautiful. Unfortunately, it is an idea from which women were excluded from the very beginning. "Ho amphisbeton" is gendered in the masculine in Aristotle's *Metaphysics* IV because Aristotle was thinking of sophists and philosophers as his main interlocutors. In his mind, they were men betraying a male ideal and prerogative: feeling and thinking rationally. For sure, women too were rational animals, but they could not reach the top of the pyramid of knowledge and understanding in order to become philosophers. This inability was not due to dogged contradictoriness, but to women's involvement with everyday life, down-to-earth, routine tasks. Women were too reasonable (and too busy) to be rationalists.

I have talked so far mostly of Greek philosophy and phantasm. Still, how does Friendship relate to logic and fiction, and what about medieval philosophy and medieval literature? The first section of this book attempted to demonstrate that logic and fiction are rooted in similar processes of the mind. They are both games, tending toward abstraction or adstraction and operating in imaginary spaces of freedom detached from the contingencies of daily life, but reflecting them in a playful fashion. In the literary and philosophical cultures of the twelfth and thirteenth centuries, I find a remarkable understanding and enjoyment of this playfulness in both Latin texts on logic and ontology and Old French romances. Logic and fiction were not invented, then, but reinvented, as ancient Greek and Roman philosophy and literature became more accessible to a larger (although still limited) audience, in Latin or in Old French. The Opponent reappeared in new clothes as heretic, hypocrite, friar, or lover, while the Friend entered the cloister. Friendship had to become more humble and Friends more like friends, imperfect and variable, and, at times, carnally attracted to one another. Friendship, while still striving toward a form of perfection, began to look more like love, with its highs and lows, good fortunes and misfortunes. Thus, friendship could be fictionalized like love, and tested through multiple stories and characters, including female ones. That is not to say that women were invited with open arms into the schools where lovers of Reason and friends of Wisdom argued and debated. But something like a seed had been planted in the imaginary gardens of logic and fiction. It would not grow into a rose. I see it growing into a tree – many trees, a forest. Perhaps I am just dreaming.

Notes

INTRODUCTION

1. See Dominique Meyer-Bolzinger, *La Méthode de Sherlock Holmes: De la clinique à la critique* (Paris: Campagne Première, 2012).
2. John Woods, "Fictionality and the Logic of Relations," *Southern Journal of Philosophy* 7.1 (1969): 51–63 (p. 51).
3. Bertrand Russell, "On Denoting," *Mind*, new series 14.4 (1905): 479–93. Accessible online: http://revueltaredaccion.files.wordpress.com/2012/08/russell_on_denoting.pdf. On this controversy, see the two overviews of the problem of nonexistent objects published in 2009: Peter Lamarque, *The Philosophy of Literature* (Oxford: Blackwell, 2009), pp. 174–219 and Gabriele Contessa, "Who is Afraid of Imaginary Objects?," in Nicholas Griffin and Dale Jacquette (eds.), *Russell vs. Meinong: The Legacy of "On Denoting"* (London: Routledge, 2009), pp. 248–65. In "On Denoting" (p. 54) and *Introduction to Mathematical Philosophy* (London: George Allen & Unwin, 1919), p. 169 Russell uses Hamlet as an example of a fictional character. Nelson Goodman uses Pickwick in "About," *Mind* 70 (January 1961): 1–24 (pp. 18–22).
4. For instance, in *The Philosophy of Literature*, philosopher Peter Lamarque is willing to use an "analytical method" to approach literature without seeking "confrontation with other methodologies" (p. vii), and although he expresses numerous grudges against literary theory he acknowledges that "many of the concerns of Theorists are also concerns of the philosopher of literature." Moreover, since Theory is dead, and "there is evidence of a tamer post-theory theory emerging among literary critics," at last philosophers and literary critics may be able to talk to or read each other (p. 10).
5. On the development of medieval dialectic, see Alain de Libera, *La Philosophie médiévale*, 2nd edn. (Paris: Presses universitaires de France, 1995 [1993]), pp. 310–13.
6. On the development of Old French literature, and the changes and innovations that medieval authors and readers in this language experienced in the twelfth and thirteenth centuries, see Sarah Kay's presentation in Sarah Kay, Terence Cave, and Malcolm Bowie, *A Short History of French Literature* (Oxford: Oxford University Press, 2003), pp. 15–19.

7. On the idea of a medieval Renaissance, see Charles Homer Haskins, *The Renaissance of the Twelfth Century* (Cambridge, Mass.: Harvard University Press, 1927) and Robert L. Benson, Giles Constable, and Carol D. Lanham (eds.), *Renaissance and Renewal in the Twelfth Century* (Cambridge, Mass.: Harvard University Press, 1991).

8. For instance: Tony Hunt, "The Dialectic of Yvain," *Modern Language Review* 72 (1977): 285–99 (p. 298) and "Aristotle, Dialectic, and Courtly Literature," *Viator* 10 (1979): 95–129; Eugene Vance, *From Topic to Tale: Logic and Narrativity in the Middle Ages* (Minneapolis: University of Minnesota Press, 1987); Catherine Brown, *Contrary Things: Exegesis, Dialectic, and the Poetics of Didacticism* (Stanford, Calif.: Stanford University Press, 1998); Matilda Tomaryn Bruckner, "Mathematical Bodies and Fuzzy Logic in the Couplings of Troubadour Lyric," *Tenso* 14:1 (1999): 1–22; Sarah Kay, *Courtly Contradictions: The Emergence of the Literary Object in the Twelfth Century* (Stanford, Calif.: Stanford University Press, 2001); Daniel Heller-Roazen, *Fortune's Faces: The* Roman de la Rose *and the Poetics of Contingency* (Baltimore, Md.: The Johns Hopkins University Press, 2003); Eileen Sweeney, *Logic, Theology, and Poetry in Boethius, Abelard, and Alan of Lille: Words in the Absence of Things* (New York: Palgrave Macmillan, 2006).

9. This is a fairly basic idea, which must have been formulated in numerous sources. My source is Russell, "On Denoting," p. 479. This article will be examined in Chapter 3.

10. To destabilize our mental habits and reexamine induction, Nelson Goodman has created curious predicates such as "grue," which applies to "all things examined before *t* just in case they are green but to other things just in case they are blue." *Fact, Fiction, and Forecast*, 4th edn. (Cambridge, Mass.: Harvard University Press, 1983 [1954]), p. 74.

11. The texts I consider are Abelard's glosses on Porphyry's *Isagoge* and his treatise *On Intellections*.

12. Eugen Bleuler (1857–1939) used *Ambivalenz* in print for the first time in his article "Vortrag über Ambivalenz," *Zentralblatt fur Psychoanalyse* 1 (1910), p. 266 and then in his book *Dementia praecox oder Gruppe der Schizophrenien* (1911) (Tübingen: Edition Diskord, 1988), pp. 43–4. Bleuler is also credited for coining "Schizophrenie" and "Autismus."

13. This is the position developed by Avicenna and Thomas Aquinas. See Stephen Menn, "Metaphysics: God and Being," in A. S. McGrade (ed.), *The Cambridge Companion to Medieval Philosophy* (Cambridge: Cambridge University Press, 2003), pp. 147–70 (pp. 157–8).

14. I use and discuss D. Heller-Roazen's notion of "poetics of contingency" developed in his book on the *Roman de la Rose* (*Fortune's Faces*).

15. John Marenbon emphasizes Abelard's conciliatory tendency (*The Philosophy of Peter Abelard* (Cambridge: Cambridge University Press, 1997), pp. 332–9) while Eileen Sweeney emphasizes the "hermeneutics of suspicion" driving him to question relentlessly the relation between appearance and reality, surface and depth (*Logic, Theology, and Poetry*, pp. 63–6).

1 ABELARD'S DONKEY: THE NONEXISTENT PARTICULAR

1. I am playing here with Aristotle's classification of negation and opposition, in particular with his distinction between contraries (bad v. good) and contradictories (he sits v. he does not sit). For a summary of Aristotle's theory of negation, see Laurence R. Horn, *A Natural History of Negation* (Stanford, Calif.: Center for the Study of Language and Information, Stanford University, 2001 [1989]), pp. 6–21.

2. *Le Roman de Renart*, ed. Naoyuki Fukumoto, Noboru Harano, and Satoru Suzuki (Paris: Livre de Poche, 2005), p. 386 (ll. 1553–8). My translation. Harano and Suzuki have established the Old French text of this edition, from which come my Old French citations, except when indicated otherwise.

3. John Marenbon, "Life, Milieu, and Intellectual Context," in Jeffrey E. Brower and Kevin Guilfoy (eds.), *The Cambridge Companion to Abelard* (Cambridge: Cambridge University Press, 2004), pp. 13–44 (pp. 18–19).

4. Diane J. Reilly, "Bernard of Clairvaux and Christian Art," in Brian Patrick McGuire (ed.), *A Companion to Bernard of Clairvaux* (Boston, Mass.: Brill, 2011), pp. 279–304 (p. 291).

5. *Yvain* may have been composed between 1177 and 1181. See David Hult's introduction to Chrétien de Troyes, *Le Chevalier au lion* (Paris: Livre de Poche, 1994), p. 8.

6. See Naoyuki Fukumoto, Noboru Harano, and Satoru Suzuki, "Les Manuscrits du *Roman de Renart*," in *Le Roman de Renart*, pp. 48–59.

7. Alain de Libera, *La Querelle des universaux: De Platon à la fin du moyen âge* (Paris: Seuil, 1996), p. 452.

8. I was not thinking of Husserl when I wrote this description of things in my immediate surroundings. When Husserl talks about the sheet of paper on which he writes, the books, pencils, and inkstand that are in the vicinity of the sheet, he is trying to give an example of a "cogitatio, a mental process of consciousness." E. Husserl, *Collected Works*, vol. 2, *General Introduction to a Pure Phenomenology*, trans. F. Kersten (The Hague: Martinus Nijhoff, 1982), pp. 69–70. This is a step in the spiritual exercise that he calls "phenomenological *epoché*" or "parenthesizing" or "phenomenological reduction" (p. 66). I don't think that what I did with the plant and the lamp (and I genuinely *did* something with them) would qualify as part of a Husserlian exercise because I neither focused my attention onto my mental process (or my "cogito" at this moment) nor abandoned my "natural attitude" toward the world (pp. 60–2). I tried to find different words from those usually used to describe such things as a plant or a lamp.

9. This is, indeed, a simplified presentation of Aristotle's formulations. On Aristotle and Plato's thoughts on universals, see Libera, *La Querelle*, pp. 29–64.

10. Porphyry, *Introduction*, trans. Jonathan Barnes (Oxford: Clarendon Press, 2003), p. 3. The original Greek text and its Latin translation by Boethius can be consulted in [Porphyre], *Isagoge*, ed. and trans. Alain de Libera and Alain-Philippe Segonds (Paris: Vrin, 1998), p. 1.

11. Marenbon, "Life," p. 32.

12. Comparing Abelard's position on the universals with Boethius's position, Eileen Sweeney finds that their main difference is that "Boethius's goal in his logical commentaries is to distinguish in order to unite, Abelard's goal seems simply to distinguish." *Logic, Theology, and Poetry*, p. 66.

13. Marenbon, "Life," p. 34.

14. Libera, *La Querelle*, pp. 156–7.

15. I base my sketch of Abelard's ontology on Peter King's essay "Metaphysics," in Brower and Guilfoy, *The Cambridge Companion to Abelard*, pp. 65–125. On possibilities and powers, see pp. 83–4.

16. King, "Metaphysics," pp. 102–3.

17. Augustine, *Confessions*, Book 11, para. 15 (18). Latin text: Augustine, *Confessions: Introduction and Text*, ed. James J. O'Donnell, 3 vols. (Oxford: Clarendon Press, 1992), vol. 1, p. 154. English: *Confessions*, trans. Henry Chadwick (Oxford: Oxford University Press, 1991), p. 231.

18. King, "Metaphysics," p. 106. On the ontological difficulties that this conception of the *dictum* raises, see John Marenbon, "*Dicta*, Non-things and the Limits of Abelard's Ontology," *The Philosophy of Peter Abelard*, pp. 202–9. On the idea of non-things and its logical and linguistic aspects, see Martin Tweedale, "Abailard and Non-Things," *Journal of the History of Philosophy* 5.4 (October 1967): 329–42.

19. King, "Metaphysics," p. 108.

20. Michael Clanchy, *Abelard: A Medieval Life* (Oxford: Blackwell, 1997), pp. 169–72.

21. See L. Engels, "Abélard écrivain," in E. M. Buytaert (ed.), *Peter Abelard: Proceedings of the International Conference, Louvain, May 10–12, 1971* (Leuven and The Hague: Leuven University Press/Martinus Nijhoff, 1974), pp. 12–37; Winthrop Wetherbee, "Literary Works," in Brower and Guilfoy, *The Cambridge Companion to Abelard*, pp. 45–64. E. Sweeney studies Abelard's laments as innovative liturgical poetry in which Abelard pursues the same goals as in his logical, theological, and ethical works. *Logic, Theology, and Poetry*, pp. 95–7.

22. He might have written a *Grammatica* and at least planned to write a *Rhetorica*, of which nothing more than allusions remain. Constant Mews, "On Dating the Works of Peter Abelard," *Archives d'histoire doctrinale et littéraire du moyen âge* 52 (1985): 73–134 (pp. 92–3).

23. See Engels, "Abélard écrivain," pp. 27–8.

24. On philosophical exempla of abstract individual or universal singular, see V. Greene, "Nothingness and Otherness in *L'Être et le Néant* or 'Pierre, Paul, Anny et les autres,'" *Journal of Romance Studies* 6.1–2 (2006): 143–53.

25. Latin text in *Peter Abaelards philosophische Schriften: I. Die Logica "Ingredientibus": 1. Die Glossen zu Porphyrius*, ed. Bernhard Geyer, *Beiträge zur Geschichte der Philosophie des Mittelalters*, 21 (Münster: Aschendorffschen Verlagsbuchhandlung, 1919) (hereafter: Geyer).

26. English translation of the *Glossae super Porphyrium*, in *Five Texts on the Mediaeval Problem of Universals: Porphyry, Boethius, Abelard, Duns Scotus,*

Ockham, ed. and trans. Paul Vincent Spade (Indianapolis, Ind.: Hackett, 1994) (hereafter: Spade).

27. Sweeney, *Logic, Theology, and Poetry*, p. 68.

28. Spade notes: "*Burnellus* or *Brunellus* ('Browny') is the name of an ass, the paradigm of an irrational animal. The example is a favorite one in Abelard." Spade, p. 31, n. 7. On Abelard's use of examples in logic, see Clanchy, *Abelard*, pp. 111–14 (but he does not mention Browny).

29. See Nigel de Longchamp [or Nigellus Wireker], *A Mirror for Fools: The Book of Burnel the Ass*, trans. J. H. Mozley (Notre Dame, Ind.: University of Notre Dame Press, 1963).

30. Umberto Eco, *The Name of the Rose*, trans. William Weaver (New York: Harcourt Brace Jovanovich, 1983), p. 24.

31. W. V. O. Quine, "On What There Is," *Review of Metaphysics* 2.1 (1948), reprinted in *The Problem of Universals*, ed. Andrew B. Schoedinger (London: Humanity Press, 1992), pp. 156–70 (p. 158).

32. *Le Roman de Renart*, pp. 784–6 and 880–96.

33. Quoted and translated by Peter King in "Metaphysics," pp. 83–4. The original text is in Petrus Abaelardus, *Dialectica*, ed. L. M. de Rijk (Assen: van Gorcum, 1970), pp. 193–4.

34. "*Statum autem hominis ipsum esse hominem, quod non est res, vocamus*" (Geyer, p. 20) [Now someone's being a man, which is not a thing, we call the *status* of man] (Spade, p. 42).

35. "*Ostensa autem significatione universalium de scilicet rebus per nominationem et communi causa impositionis eorum monstrata, quid sint eorum intellectus, quos constituunt, ostendamus*" (Geyer, p. 20) [Now that the signification of universals has been shown (they signify things by naming them) and the common cause of their imposition has been pointed out, let us show what the understandings are that they constitute] (Spade, p. 42).

36. Marenbon, *The Philosophy of Peter Abelard*, p. 164. Abelard's theory of perception and knowledge is complex and varies in significant ways in the different texts in which he elaborates on this matter: the glosses on Porphyry's *Isagoge*, the glosses on Aristotle's *De interpretatione* (both are parts of *Logica Ingredientibus*), and the treatise *De intellectibus*. See Lucia Urbani Ulivi, *La Psicologia di Abelardo e il "Tractatus de Intellectibus"* (Rome: Edizioni di Storia e Letteratura, 1976); Marenbon, *The Philosophy of Peter Abelard*, pp. 162–73; Kevin Guilfoy, "Mind and Cognition," in Brower and Guilfoy, *The Cambridge Companion to Abelard*, pp. 200–22.

37. On Abelard's pessimism about human possibility of knowing, see Guilfoy, "Mind and Cognition," pp. 216–17 and Urbani Ulivi, *Psicologia*, p. 28.

38. Marenbon, *The Philosophy of Peter Abelard*, p. 164.

39. "l'immaginazione è insomma uno strumento in più offerto all'intelletto, che non sarà legato al solo momento della sensazione, ed appare, più del senso, una presenza costante dell'anima" (Urbani Ulivi, *Psicologia*, p. 29). My translation.

40. Guilfoy, "Mind and Cognition," p. 214.

41. Sweeney, *Logic, Theology, and Poetry*, p. 72.

42. Henry I of England for instance had one and brought a lion and other animals to Caen in 1105. Willene B. Clark, *A Medieval Book of Beasts: The Second-Family Bestiary: Commentary, Art, Text and Translation* (Woodbridge: Boydell, 2006), p. 18.

43. On imagination and its relation with experience and knowledge in medieval intellectual culture, see Giorgio Agamben, *Infancy and History: On the Destruction of Experience*, trans. Liz Heron (London: Verso, 2007), pp. 15–17. In my essay "Imagination" I tried to apply Agamben's general assessment to medieval literature. See V. Greene, "Imagination," in Zrinka Stahuljak, et al., *Thinking Through Chrétien de Troyes* (Cambridge: D. S. Brewer, 2011), pp. 41–74.

44. Chimera, centaur, sirens, and goat-stag (*hircocervus*) are mentioned in the *Glosses on Porphyry* (Geyer, p. 28; Spade, p. 51) and in *Des Intellections*, ed. and trans. Patrick Morin (Paris: Vrin, 1994), pp. 90 and 94–6.

45. This story appears in branch II, which is not included in the 2005 Poche edition by Fukumoto, et al. See *Le Roman de Renart*, ed. Armand Strubel, et al. (Paris: Gallimard, 1998), pp. 291–2 (ll. 36–42).

46. Jean Jolivet, "Trois variations médiévales sur l'universel et l'individu: Roscelin, Abélard, Gilbert de la Porrée," *Revue de métaphysique et de morale* 97.1 (January–March 1992): 111–55 (p. 119).

47. Jean Jolivet, *Arts du langage et théologie chez Abélard* (Paris: Vrin, 1982), pp. 72–4. See also Sweeney, *Logic, Theology, and Poetry*, p. 67.

48. Matilda Bruckner, *Shaping Romance: Interpretation, Truth, and Closure in Twelfth-Century French Fictions* (Philadelphia: University of Pennsylvania Press, 1993), p. 4.

49. The Latin prefix "ad" followed by a word starting with a "t" normally gives "att" rather than "ads." But "attraction" already exists, with a range of meanings that does not work for what I want "adstraction" to mean. I thank the anonymous reader for pointing out this etymological issue. As badly formed as "adstraction" may be, I cannot remove it from my argumentation without losing a pivotal moment.

50. "There is reason to doubt that we can form an image that is at once iconically representative but which could not be representative of any particular item." Guilfoy, "Mind and Cognition," p. 209. A similar comment on the same passage has been made by Sofia Vanni Rovighi: "nous pourrions objecter que l'on ne peut pas peindre un lion qui n'ait aucun caractère propre à ce lion-ci ou à ce lion-là, comme le voudrait Abélard." "Intentionnel et universel chez Abélard," *Cahiers de la revue de théologie et de philosophie* 6 (1981) (issue titled: *Abélard: Le "dialogue": La philosophie de la logique*): 21–30 (p. 24).

51. Michel Pastoureau, *Les Armoiries: Typologie des sources du moyen âge occidental* 20 (Turnhout: Brepols, 1976), p. 25. Pastoureau also points out that animal figures were very common in twelfth-century armorials, the most popular ones being the lion and the eagle (p. 29).

52. Marenbon dates the comments on Porphyry from the period between 1117 and 1120, and the *De Intellectibus* from c.1123 to 1126. Marenbon, "Life," pp. 18–19.

53. Bernard de Clairvaux, *Éloge de la nouvelle chevalerie*, in *Œuvres complètes*, ed. Pierre-Yves Emery, 31 vols. to date (Paris: Le Cerf, 1990–), vol. 31, p. 56. My translation.

54. Mary Carruthers points out that Bernard is not against images and ornaments as long as they are interiorized: "What Bernard counsels is lavish decoration of one's own making within the 'temple' of one's soul, fiction-making which is 'supported' by the plain surfaces and clear articulation of the unadorned church and cloister." *The Craft of Thought: Meditation, Rhetoric, and the Making of Images, 400–1200* (Cambridge: Cambridge University Press, 1998), pp. 86–7.

55. Chrétien de Troyes, *Yvain ou Le chevalier au lion*, p. 821 (ll. 3347–55). My translation.

56. The usual example of this type is: All men are mortal; Socrates is a man; Socrates is mortal. On medieval syllogisms, see Robert Blanché and Jacques Dubucs, *La Logique et son histoire* (Paris: Armand Colin, 2002), pp. 138–9 and 148–55.

57. Blanché and Dubucs, *La Logique et son histoire*, p. 139.

58. According to bestiaries, dragons are species of snakes and represent the Devil, whereas the lion is a figure of Christ. See the Aberdeen bestiary (*c*.1200) online: www.abdn.ac.uk/bestiary. The lion can be found on fols. 7^r–8^r and the dragon on fols. 65^v–66^r.

59. "*Leo fortissimus bestiarum.*" Aberdeen bestiary, fol. 7^r.

60. Z. Stahuljak remarks that "despite the urgency and speed at which their protagonists move, romances create a temporality in which a process of thinking about events, both presently occurring and past adventures, is at work." "Adventures in Wonderland," *Thinking Through Chrétien*, pp. 75–109 (p. 78).

61. Marcia Colish, *Medieval Foundations of the Western Intellectual Tradition 400–1400* (New Haven, Conn.: Yale University Press, 1997), p. 165.

62. Stephen Jaeger, *The Envy of Angels: Cathedral Schools and Social Ideals in Medieval Europe, 950–1200* (Philadelphia: University of Pennsylvania Press, 1994), p. 128.

63. Pierre Abélard, *Des Intellections*, p. 24. The word "memory" is listed in neither the index of Marenbon's *The Philosophy of Abelard* nor the index of Brower and Guilfoy, *The Cambridge Companion to Abelard*.

64. Carruthers, *The Craft of Thought*, p. 7.

65. Ibid., p. 2.

66. Libera, *La Querelle*, p. 73. On "Psychologic", see Greene, "Imagination," pp. 41–74.

67. Quine, "On What There Is," p. 167.

2 THE LITERATE ANIMAL: NAMING AND REFERENCE

1. Colish, *Medieval Foundations*, p. 165.

2. "No historian has been able to escape the opacity of the historical record with regard not just to Roscelin but to intellectual life in the late eleventh century in general." Constant Mews, "St Anselm and Roscelin: Some New Texts and their

Implications," *Archives d'histoire doctrinale et littéraire du moyen âge* 58 (1991): 55–98 (p. 56).

3. Proposed dates vary from before 1040 to c.1100. See Eleonore Stump, *Dialectic and its Place in the Development of Medieval Logic* (Ithaca, NY: Cornell University Press, 1989), p. 67; Martin Tweedale, "Logic (i): From the Late Eleventh Century to the Time of Abelard," in Peter Dronke (ed.), *A History of Twelfth-Century Western Philosophy* (Cambridge: Cambridge University Press, 1988), pp. 196–226 (p. 198); Yukio Iwakuma, "*Vocales*, or Early Nominalists," *Traditio* 47 (1992): 37–111 (p. 53). For the place and name, see the introduction to Garlandus Compotista, *Dialectica*, ed. L. M. de Rijk (Assen: van Gorcum, 1959), pp. ix–xxii and xlv.

4. Iwakuma, "*Vocales*," p. 54. The term *nominales* appeared later in the twelfth century; the precursors of this movement called themselves and were called *vocales* (p. 37).

5. Tweedale, "Logic," p. 199. In a more nuanced way, L. M. de Rijk arrives at a similar conclusion on Garlandus's formalism (Garlandus Compotista, *Dialectica*, pp. xlix–lii). About the mysterious John (*Jean*), master of Roscelin and probably one of the first vocalists, Iwakuma says: "John purified logic, in a sense, reducing it to a study of *voces*, while cutting off the ontological aspects" ("*Vocales*," p. 46).

6. Berengar of Tours and Lanfranc debated the Eucharist, Anselm of Canterbury and the school of Laon debated the Incarnation, Anselm and Roscelin debated the Trinity. Colish, *Medieval Foundations*, pp. 165–70; Michael Haren, *Medieval Thought: The Western Intellectual Tradition from Antiquity to the Thirteenth Century*, 2nd edn. (Toronto: University of Toronto Press, 1992), pp. 94–6 and 102–3. On the controversy on the Eucharist, see Irène Rosier-Catach, *La Parole efficace: signe, rituel, sacré* (Paris: Seuil, 2004), pp. 36–40.

7. To show that God does not have to obey the principle of non-contradiction, Peter Damian holds that God can change the past (Haren, *Medieval Thought*, p. 94; Colish, *Medieval Foundations*, pp. 161–2). But his position toward logic can also be seen as a "truce" and a way to circumscribe logic to human affairs rather than to dismiss it entirely. See Giulio d'Onofrio, "La Dialectique anselmienne," in Coloman Viola and Frederick Van Fleteren (eds.), *Saint Anselm: A Thinker for Yesterday and Today*, Proceedings of the International Anselm Conference, Paris, 2–4 July 1990 (Lewiston, Maine: Edwin Mellen Press, 2002), pp. 29–49 (p. 38).

8. "utiliser la dialectique pour combattre ceux qui l'utilisent, et ainsi la retourner contre elle-même." Alain de Libera, *La Philosophie médiévale* (Paris: Presses universitaires de France, 1995), p. 289.

9. E. Sweeney holds a similar opinion about Anselm, Berengar of Tours, and Roscelin, as having in common the use of dialectical arguments, even if in the end they did not stand on the same side of orthodoxy. *Anselm of Canterbury and the Desire for the Word* (Washington, DC: Catholic University of America Press, 2012), pp. 262–3.

10. The recent bibliography on Anselm is extensive. For an idea of the aspects of Anselm's life and works on which philosophers and theologians work today,

     see Brian Davies and Brian Leftow (eds.), *The Cambridge Companion to Anselm of Canterbury* (Cambridge: Cambridge University Press, 2004); Eileen Sweeney, *Anselm.*

11. Anselm of Canterbury, *Opera Omnia*, ed. F. S. Schmitt, 6 vols. (Edinburgh: Thomas Nelson & Sons, Ltd., 1940–61). Online version (Charlottesville, Va.: InteLex, 1998), vol. 1, p. 173.

12. Anselm of Canterbury, *The Major Works of Anselm of Canterbury*, ed. Brian Davies and G. R. Evans (Oxford: Oxford University Press, 1998). Online version, in Intelex Past Masters series (Charlottesville, Va.: InteLex, 2006), p. 151.

13. "Son *De grammatico* peut même être regardé comme le point de départ médiéval des théories de la signification et de la référence." Libera, *La Philosophie médiévale*, p. 293. Colish also insists on the originality and importance of this work in semantics (*Medieval Foundations*, pp. 167–8). For an overview of scholarly assessment of the *De grammatico*, see Sweeney, *Anselm*, pp. 74–6.

14. In the *De magistro*, the student is Augustine's son, Adeodatus. See Emmanuel Bermon, *La Signification et l'enseignement: texte latin, traduction française et commentaire du* De magistro *de Saint Augustin* (Paris: Vrin, 2007).

15. The English edition of Aristotle's works used throughout is *The Complete Works of Aristotle: The Revised Oxford Translation*, ed. Jonathan Barnes, Bollingen Series 71.2, 2 vols. (Princeton, NJ: Princeton University Press, 1984). The numbers and letters given before the page number give the reference to Immanuel Bekker's 1831 edition of the Greek text. So "*Categories*, 1a, p. 3" means that the passage of *Categories* can be found in Greek on page 1, column a, in Bekker, and in English on p. 3 of the *Complete Works* (the pagination of the 2 volumes is continuous).

16. For a summary of the logic and semantic issues raised in the *De grammatico*, see Libera, *La Philosophie médiévale*, pp. 293–7; Peter King, "Anselm's Philosophy of Language," in Davies and Leftow, *The Cambridge Companion to Anselm of Canterbury*, pp. 84–110; Sweeney, *Anselm*, pp. 82–93.

17. Brian Davies and Rosemary Evans translate the title *Dialogue on Literacy and the Literate* to expose the ambiguity of "*grammatico*," which can be used as an adjective or a noun. In the text itself they translate it as "literate" since it can also be used as a noun. It is difficult to know what "grammaticus" as a noun meant for Anselm. It could be only the masters and students in the arts of grammar, rhetoric, and dialectic in the schools and cloisters of his time, and the ancient authors they studied and commented on. It could also be a slightly larger slice of the (human) population, including well-educated lords and ladies.

18. John the Scot points out this contradiction by opposing the physical and irrational aspects of man, which makes of man an animal, to his spiritual and rational aspects, which sets man apart from all animals. Johannes Scotus Erigena (*De divisione naturae* 4.5) *Periphyseon: On the Division of Nature*, trans. Myra L. Uhlfelder (Indianapolis, Ind.: Bobbs-Merrill, 1976),

p. 220. Cited in Debra Hassig, *Medieval Bestiaries: Text, Image, Ideology* (Cambridge: Cambridge University Press, 1995), p. 168.

19. Sarah Kay has shown that in fact the relation between literacy and animality is made more complex in the Middle Ages by the fact that medieval readers had to look at and touch animal skins (parchment) in order to exercise their literacy. Sarah Kay, "Legible Skins: Animals and the Ethics of Medieval Reading," *Postmedieval* 2.1(2011): 13–32.

20. For Bernard the archpriest, see *Roman de Renart*, pp. 784–5 and 880–90; for the camel, see pp. 230–3.

21. Karl Steel shows how, in medieval texts, the repeated denial of animal–human likeness only betrays how much this strict division is fragile and can never be secured: "the human requires a continual reenactment of subjugation to attempt a stabilization it can never attain." *How to Make a Human: Animals and Violence in the Middle Ages* (Columbus: The Ohio State University Press, 2011), p. 44.

22. One modern definition of the proper name is a "set of sets" or the intersection of a sufficient number of sets (i.e., "humans" "Greeks" "males" "philosophers" "who died by poisoning") to obtain a set of one. See Gennaro Chierchia and Sally McConnell-Ginet, *Meaning and Grammar: An Introduction to Semantics*, 2nd edn. (Cambridge, Mass.: MIT Press, 2000), pp. 512–13. Anselm views the proper name as referring to a "collection of distinctive properties" that does not belong to any other individual. King, "Anselm's Philosophy of Language," pp. 90–1.

23. Jonathan Barnes, *Truth, etc. Six Lectures on Ancient Logic* (Oxford: Clarendon Press, 2007), p. 155.

24. See Radu J. Bogdan, *Predicative Minds: The Social Ontogeny of Propositional Thinking* (Cambridge: MIT Press, 2009), p. 87.

25. King, "Anselm's Philosophy of Language," p. 93.

26. John Woods, *The Logic of Fiction*, Studies in Logic 23 (London: College Publications, 1974), pp. 63–4.

27. E. Sweeney has argued that "the logical and theological texts in Anselm are related in a way that does not make logic the mere servant of apologetics nor reduce theology to an area for making linguistic distinctions. The kind of logical and linguistic analysis in these texts is present throughout his corpus and is at the core of a profoundly metaphysical and theological project." *Anselm*, p. 107.

28. On the imbrication between language, reason, senses, and the categories "animal" and "human" in Greek philosophy, see Daniel Heller-Roazen, *The Inner Touch: Archaeology of a Sensation* (New York: Zone Books, 2007), pp. 91–7. Heller-Roazen points out that Aristotle defined humans as the "living beings possessing language," which turned out to be translated in Latin as the "rational animal" based on the polysemy of *logos*, meaning both language and reason (p. 91).

29. If there is a consistent medieval system for naming living beings and places, there is not such a system for artworks. Literary and visual works are more

often designated by modern titles than by medieval ones. There are indeed exceptions, such as Marie de France's anxious insistence on naming her *lais*. See Bruckner, *Shaping Romance*, pp. 177–87; Howard Bloch, *The Anonymous Marie de France* (Chicago: University of Chicago Press, 2003), pp. 116–17.

30. See the index of *Le Roman de Renart* for the names of all the animals mentioned in the various branches. Animals' names appear also in the Old French fabliaux: e.g., Browny (*Brunain*) the Cow, or Browny (*Morel*) the horse. Thanks to Stefanie Goyette for signaling these examples.

31. See Bloch, *The Anonymous Marie de France*, pp. 1–9; Sharon Kinoshita and Peggy McCracken, *Marie de France: A Critical Companion* (Cambridge: D. S. Brewer, 2012), pp. 1–3.

32. Marie de France, *Fables*, ed. and trans. Harriet Spiegel (Toronto: University of Toronto Press, 1994), p. 9. On the general spirit of innovation that characterizes medieval fabulists, see Arnold Clayton Henderson, "Medieval Beasts and Modern Cages: The Making of Meaning in Fables and Bestiaries," *PMLA* 97.1 (January 1982): 40–9.

33. The Old French text comes from Harriet Spiegel's edition; I modified her translation.

34. Marie de France, "Prologue," in *Lais*, ed. Laurence Harf-Lancner (Paris: Livre de Poche, 1990). My translation.

35. My translation reflects one possible way to understand the passage (I follow the French translation of Laurence Harf-Lancner). But other plausible renderings have been proposed, such as: "Men of learning were aware of this and their experience had taught them that the more time they spent studying texts the more subtle would be their understanding of them and they would be better able to avoid future mistakes." Marie de France, *The Lais of Marie de France*, ed. and trans. Glyn Burgess and Keith Busby (Harmondsworth: Penguin, 1999), p. 41. Among the comments, see Leo Spitzer, "The Prologue to the *Lais* of Marie de France and Medieval Poetics," *Modern Philology* 41 (1943): 96–102; Tony Hunt, "Glossing Marie de France," *Romanische Forschungen* 86 (1974): 396–418; Alfred Foulet and Karl D. Uitti, "The Prologue to the *Lais* of Marie de France: A Reconsideration," *Romance Philology* 35 (1981): 242–9; Bruckner, *Shaping Romance*, pp. 193–4; Bloch, *The Anonymous Marie de France*, pp. 32–6.

36. Comparing Marie's prologue with a similar passage in a Latin text, Sharon Kinoshita and Peggy McCracken note that, when the Latin text considers readers as easily distracted and forgetful, Marie "vaunts the faculty of human reason, and specifically that of her modern contemporaries." *Marie de France*, pp. 21–2.

37. Leslie Kurke, *Aesopic Conversations: Popular Tradition, Cultural Dialogues, and the Invention of Greek Prose* (Princeton, NJ: Princeton University Press, 2011), p. 47.

38. I thank Matilda Bruckner for bringing this fable to my attention.

39. *Aesop's Fables*, ed. and trans. Laura Gibbs (Oxford: Oxford University Press, 2002), p. 95. Aphtonius compiled forty fables in the fourth century CE.

40. Latin text online: http://mythfolklore.net/aesopica/ademar/52.htm (accessed October 20, 2013). Text taken from the edition of Léopold Hervieux, *Les*

Fabulistes latins depuis le siècle d'Auguste jusqu'à la fin du moyen âge, 5 vols., 2nd edn. (Paris: Firmin-Didot, 1893), vol. 2, pp. 150–1.

41. *Aesop's Fables*, p. 96.
42. Rudolf Carnap, *Philosophy and Logical Syntax* (London: Kegan Paul, 1934), p. 14. Arthur Danto calls the position that Carnap epitomized "verification-ism" and considers it as a form of pathology. He nonetheless finds a "certain stammering grandeur in the manner with which in scarcely three sentences Carnap casts into the limbo of incoherence the sonnets of Shakespeare and *The World as Will and Idea*." Arthur Danto, *The Philosophical Disenfranchisement of Art* (New York: Columbia University Press, 2005), pp. 163–5.
43. See Richard Allen Landes, *Relics, Apocalypse, and the Deceits of History: Ademar of Chabannes, 989–1034* (Cambridge, Mass.: Harvard University Press, 1995).
44. Bloch, *The Anonymous Marie de France*, p. 133.
45. Saul Kripke, *Naming and Necessity*, 2nd edn. (Malden, Mass.: Blackwell, 1981), pp. 48–9.
46. I borrow the phrase "certainty of the heart" from Patricia Terry, "Certainties of the Heart: The Poisoned Fruit Episode as a Unifying Example in *La Mort le Roi Artu*," *Romance Languages Annual* 1 (1990): 329–31.
47. Kripke, *Naming and Necessity*, p. 95.

3 THE FOX AND THE UNICORN: NAMING AND EXISTENCE

1. Bertrand Russell invented this sentence in "On Denoting." Philosophers of language quoted it so often that John Woods counts it as one of the "minor classics" of philosophical *exempla*, in Woods, *The Logic of Fiction*, p. 82. Variants were also used: "The King of France is wise," in P. F. Strawson, "On Referring," *Mind* 59.235 (July 1950): 320–44 (p. 321) and Oswald Ducrot, "'Le Roi de France est sage': Implication logique et présupposition linguistique," in Ducrot, *La Preuve et le dire* (Paris: Mame, 1974), pp. 211–23.
2. Beside the works cited in n. 1, see Gottlob Frege, "On *Sinn* and *Bedeutung*," in *The Frege Reader*, ed. Michael Beaney (Oxford: Blackwell, 1997), pp. 151–71; Rudolf Carnap, *Meaning and Necessity: A Study in Semantics and Modal Logic*, 2nd edn. (Chicago: University of Chicago Press, 1956); John R. Searle, *Speech Acts: An Essay in the Philosophy of Language* (Cambridge: Cambridge University Press, 1969); Saul Kripke, *Naming and Necessity*; Terence Parsons, *Nonexistent Objects* (New Haven, Conn.: Yale University Press, 1980).
3. Gennaro Chierchia uses "Pavarotti" as an example of a real individual in *Meaning and Grammar*, pp. 55–113.
4. The *Oxford English Dictionary* indicates that John Stuart Mill was the first to use the verb "to denote," in contradistinction with "to connote," in his *System of Logic* published in 1843 (London: John W. Parker).
5. David Kaplan, "Reading 'On Denoting' on its Centenary," *Mind* 114.456 (2005): 934–1003 (p. 977).

6. On Alexius Meinong, see Richard Routley, *Exploring Meinong's Jungle and Beyond: An Investigation of Noneism and the Theory of Items* (Canberra: Australian National University, 1980) and Dale Jacquette, *Meinongian Logic: The Semantics of Existence and Nonexistence* (New York: Walter de Gruyter, 1996).

7. It must be noted that before 1905 Russell expressed interest in and agreement with Meinong's ideas. See Parsons, *Nonexistent Objects*, pp. 1–2.

8. Bertrand Russell, *Introduction to Mathematical Philosophy* (London: George Allen & Unwin, 1919), pp. 169–70. Quoted by Stephen Neale in "A Century Later," *Mind* 114.456 (October 2005): 809–71 (p. 815, n. 24).

9. Carnap, *Meaning and Necessity*, pp. 233–47.

10. Carnap's first edition of *Meaning and Necessity* appeared in 1947, the second edition in 1956.

11. See Avrom Faderman, "On Myth," in Anthony Everett and Thomas Hofweber (eds.), *Empty Names, Fictions, and the Puzzles of Non-Existence* (Stanford, Calif.: SCLI Publications, 2000), pp. 61–6. According to this article, Faderman worked in the late 1990s on a book project titled *Kripke and the Unicorns*. This book does not seem to have been published.

12. Kripke, *Naming and Necessity*, p. 23.

13. Lewis Carroll, *Through the Looking Glass*, in *The Complete Works of Lewis Carroll* (New York: The Modern Library, 1936), p. 229.

14. See the yale in the Aberdeen bestiary available online: www.abdn.ac.uk/bestiary.

15. Pamela Gravestock notes that "in the bestiaries, the imaginary animals are given the same treatment – both pictorially and textually – as those animals that were known to exist." "Did Imaginary Animals Exist?," in Debra Hassig (ed.), *The Mark of the Beast: The Medieval Bestiary in Art, Life, and Literature* (New York: Garland, 1999), pp. 119–35 (p. 120).

16. Keith Donnellan, "Speaking of Nothing," *The Philosophical Review* 83.1 (1974): 2–31 (p. 16). Saul Kripke acknowledges that his views are similar to those of Donnellan on the matter of "historical trail" in *Naming and Necessity*, pp. 163–4.

17. On medieval unicorns, the most complete study, with the richest iconographic dossier, remains Jürgen W. Einhorn [*sic*], *Spiritalis Unicornis: Das Einhorn als Bedeutungsträger in Literatur und Kunst des Mittelalters* (Munich: Fink, 1976). The author acknowledges briefly that he has a personal interest in unicorns (p. 14), but, appropriately since he is a Franciscan, he does not develop the personal angle.

18. On Ctesias's life and works, see Andrew Nichols's introduction to his English translation: Ctesias, *Ctesias: On India and Fragments of his Minor Works* (London: Bristol Classical Press, 2011), pp. 27–34; on their influence, pp. 13–18.

19. *Ctesias: On India*, p. 56. For the Greek text, see Ctesias of Cnidus [Ctésias de Cnide], *La Perse, l'Inde, autres fragments*, ed. and trans. Dominique Lenfant (Paris: Les Belles Lettres, 2004), pp. 182–3.

20. In modern terminology, horses, mules, and donkeys are odd-toed ungulates or perissodactyles, and animals with cloven hooves are even-toed ungulates or artiodactyles.

21. Thanks to Stefanie Goyette for reminding me that the narwhal is not a fish!
22. See, for instance, Dr. Franklin Dove's single-horned cow born in 1933 (Nancy Hathaway, *The Unicorn*, New York: Tess Press, 2005, pp. 146–8) and the single-horned deer found in a nature preserve at Prato, near Florence, in 2008 (www.dailymail.co.uk/news/article-1025793/The-horned-deer-solve-mystery-unicorn.html).
23. Numbers 23:22 and 24:8, Deuteronomy 33:17, Job 39:9–10, Psalm 21(22):22, Psalm 28(29):6, Psalm 91(92):11, Isaiah 34:7. J. L. W. Schaper lists and analyzes these passages in "The Unicorn in the Messianic Imagery of the Greek Bible," *Journal of Theological Studies* 45.1 (1994): 117–36. Chris Lavers gives a simplified summary in *The Natural History of Unicorns* (New York: HarperCollins, 2009), pp. 44–51.
24. The people of Israel have the strength of a re'em, since their God "is for them like the horns of the [re'em]" (Num. 23:22 and 24:8). Joseph, blessed by Moses, is endowed figuratively with the horns of the [re'em], which allows him to fight victoriously against neighbouring peoples (Deut. 33:17). "He [the Lord] makes Lebanon skip like a calf, Sirion like a young [re'em]" (Ps. 28(29): 6). For God, Mount Lebanon and Mount Sirion are as calves and young [re'ems] are for man. In Psalm 91(92), the psalmist compares himself to a [re'em], in order to thank God for his support: "You raise my horn like that of a [re'em]," which can be understood as a simile for righteous aggressivity against one's foes, or for high standing in earthly life, or for fertile virility. English translations are from *Tanakh: A New Translation of the Holy Scriptures According to the Traditional Hebrew Text* (Philadelphia, Pa.: The Jewish Publication Society, 1985). In this translation, "re'em" is translated consistently as "wild ox."
25. Rashi comments on the re'em of Psalm 22 as "a metaphor for the Amorite," and the son of re'em of Psalm 29 as a calf, but in neither case does he feel that he has to explain what type of animal a re'em is. Rashi, *Rashi's Commentary on Psalms 1–89 (Books I–III)*, trans. Mayer I. Gruber (Atlanta, GA.: Scholars Press, 1998), pp. 127 and 151.
26. Alexis Léonas, *L'aube des traducteurs: De l'hébreu au grec: traducteurs et lecteurs de la Bible des Septante (IIIe s. av. J.-C. – IVe s. apr. J.-C.)* (Paris: Éditions du Cerf, 2007), p. 9.
27. Lancelot Brenton translates it as "the mighty ones" in *The Septuagint with Apocrypha: Greek and English* (1851) (repr. 1986), p. 868. Moises Silva translates it as "the eminent ones" in *The New English Translation of the Septuagint*, ed. Albert Pietersma and Benjamin Wright (Oxford: Oxford University Press, 2009), p. 850. This edition is usually referred to as NETS, and is available online: http://ccat.sas.upenn.edu/nets/.
28. The twelfth-century Old French psalter translates all the re'em/monokerōs/ unicornis/ as "*unicornes.*" For instance, it translates Psalm 21:22 as: "Salve mei de la buche del liun, e des cornes des unicornes oi mei." *Le Livre des psaumes: Ancienne traduction française*, ed. Francisque Michel (Paris: Imprimerie Nationale, 1876), pp. 34, 44, 144, 171. The Tyndale Bible translates "the strength of an unicorn" for Numbers 23:22 and 24:8 and "the horns of an

unicorn" for Deuteronomy 33:17. See William Tyndale, *Tyndale's Old Testament*, ed. David Daniell (New Haven, Conn.: Yale University Press, 1992), pp. 235, 236, 303. The King James Bible translates all the occurrences of monokerōs/unicornis as "unicorn" except in one case. See *The New Cambridge Paragraph Bible with the Apocrypha, King James Version*, ed. David Norton (Cambridge: Cambridge University Press, 2005), pp. 200, 201, 267, 672. The exception is on p. 750 (see below, n. 31).

29. Jerome wrote two revisions of the Latin psalter in the years 384–92, the first using the Septuagint, the second using also other later Greek translations. This second revision of the Septuagint, known as the "Gallican Psalter," is included in the Vulgate edition under the name *psalmi iuxta LXX* in parallel with the translation called *psalmi iuxta hebraicum*. See Colette Estin, *Les Psautiers de Jérôme à la lumière des traductions juives antérieures*, Collectanea Biblica Latina 15 (Rome: San Girolamo, 1984), pp. 25–30; Dennis Brown, *Vir Trilinguis: A Study in the Biblical Exegesis of Saint Jerome* (Kampen: Kok Pharos, 1992), pp. 101–2. I use here the Latin text of both psalters edited in *Biblia sacra juxta vulgatam versionem*, ed. B. Fischer (Stuttgart: Deutsche Bibelgesellschaft, 1983).

30. Tertullian (*c.*160–*c.*225) cites a Latin translation of Deuteronomy 33:17 in which "unicornis" is used as a noun ("cornua unicornis cornua eius"). Tertullian [Tertullien], *Contre Marcion*, Book III, ed. and trans. René Braun, Sources Chrétiennes 399 (Paris: Éditions du Cerf, 1994), p. 160. In his *Historia naturalis*, Pliny the Elder (23–79) uses "unicornis" only as an adjective, applied to oxen ("unicornes boves") in Book VIII: 72 and 76, and to asses ("unicornis asinus") in Book XI: 255. He once uses "monokeros" as a noun (Book VIII: 76). Pliny the Elder [Pline l'Ancien], *Histoire naturelle*, ed. and trans. A. Ernout (Paris: Les Belles Lettres, 1947 (Book XI); 1952 (Book VIII)).

31. For the sake of brevity, I leave aside the case of Psalm 77(78):69, in which the Septuagint translator read "re'mim" for "ramim" (high places) and translated: "And he built his holy precinct like that of unicorns." This verse sounded suspicious to the translators of the King James Bible, who corrected it: "And he built his sanctuary like high palaces" (p. 750) despite the fact that Jerome keeps "monoceros" here even in his "Psalms according to Hebrew."

32. Brown gives several examples of passages in which Jerome uses different Latin synonyms to translate a single Hebrew or Greek word. *Vir Trilinguis*, pp. 112–13.

33. Einhorn, *Spiritalis Unicornis*, p. 48. On the revisions of the Septuagint, see Gilles Dorival, Marguerite Harl, and Olivier Munnich, *La Bible grecque des Septante du judaïsme hellénistique au christianisme ancien* (Paris: Cerf/ Centre national de la recherche scientifique, 1988), pp. 142–7.

34. Schaper, "The Unicorn in the Messianic Imagery of the Greek Bible," p. 117.

35. Jerome may have consulted Pliny the Elder, who describes various species of single-horned animals in his *Natural Histories*, including the rhinoceros, Indian oxen, and the frightening monokeros – part horse, part deer, part elephant, and part boar. [Pline l'Ancien], *Histoire naturelle*, Book VIII: 71–6 (pp. 48–50 in A. Ernout's edition (1952)). Odell Shepard remarks that unicorned species grew

from two in Ctesias and Aristotle to seven in Aelian and Pliny. *The Lore of the Unicorn* (New York: Barnes & Noble, 1967), p. 34.

36. Matti Megged, *The Animal that Never Was (In Search of the Unicorn)* (New York: Lumen Books, 1992), p. 3.

37. For instance, Shepard does not hide his strong feelings about medieval and early modern Christian exegesis, which, for him, has perverted an otherwise beautiful imaginary creature (*The Lore of the Unicorn*, pp. 45–52). This is an anachronistic bias, but the issues raised about the exegetic uses of the unicorn, in particular against the Jews, deserve to be addressed.

38. Lactanctius says that small things are the *figurae* of the great (*Divinae institutiones* VII, 14). Cited in Erich Auerbach, *Figura*, trans. Diane Meur (Paris: Macula, 2003), p. 41.

39. Jerome viewed the polemical, contradictory, and arduous aspects of his task as an *askesis* that allowed him "to fuse the identities of scholar and monk." Megan Hale Williams, *The Monk and the Book: Jerome and the Making of Christian Scholarship* (Chicago: University of Chicago Press, 2006), p. 5.

40. "It was already a symbol or emblem of strength when called the Horn of David, but it also included the ingredients of a universal myth about redemption and the symbolism of the Messiah." Megged, *The Animal that Never Was*, p. 57.

41. Hugo Brandenburg, "Einhorn," in *Reallexikon für Antike und Christentum* 4 (1959), cols. 840–62. Cited and summarized in Einhorn, *Spiritalis Unicornis*, p. 48.

42. Tertullian, *Contre Marcion*, Book III, p. 158. Tertullian is not the first to use the relation between the horns and the Cross: he relies on the earlier exegete Justin. See the footnotes, ibid., pp. 160–1.

43. Other early Church fathers' commentaries show that there was no unanimity about the way the unicorn should be interpreted. For instance, Theodoret of Cyrus, a later Greek Church Father (*c.*393–*c.*457), interprets the unicorns of the Psalms to signify monotheism, and, in one case, to represent evil. Theodoret of Cyrus, *Commentary on the Psalms*, trans. Robert C. Hill, The Fathers of the Church, vols. 101–2 (Washington, DC: The Catholic University of America Press, 2000–1), vol. 101, p. 39, 151,184; vol. 102, p. 39, 109–10. In the commentary on Psalm 91(92), one finds a couple of sentences mentioning "the horn of the cross," but the translator takes it as a later interpolation (vol. 102, pp. 109–10; p. 109, n. 2, and also introduction to vol. 101, pp. 4–7).

44. Shepard, *The Lore of the Unicorn*, pp. 45–9; Einhorn, *Spiritalis Unicornis*, pp. 50–3; Megged, *The Animal*, pp. 51–3; Lise Gotfredsen, *The Unicorn*, trans. Anne Born (London: Harvill Press, 1999), pp. 40–4; Lavers, *The Natural History*, pp. 63–70.

45. *Physiologus: A Medieval Book of Nature Lore*, trans. Michael J. Curley (Chicago: University of Chicago Press, 2009), pp. xvi–xx. One of the Greek versions of *Physiologus* is edited and translated in *Physiologus: The Greek and the Armenian Versions with a Study of Translation Technique*, ed. and trans. Gohar Muradyan

(Leuven and Paris: Peeters, 2005). The monoceros appears on pp. 38–40, 128–9, and 157–8.

46. Curley, *Physiologus*, p. xxii.

47. "qui pouvait légitimement se contester, sans risques de blasphème ou d'irrévérence, sans les contorsions nécessaires pour prendre distance par rapport à Augustin." Alain Boureau, *L'Empire du livre: Pour une histoire du savoir scholastique (1200–1380)* (Paris: Les Belles Lettres, 2007), p. 31. My translation.

48. "In the very synthetic spirit of the work itself, the material was constantly manipulated to suit particular audiences." Curley, *Physiologus*, p. xxxii.

49. Einhorn, *Spiritalis Unicornis*, pp. 60–2, 68–72, illus. 11–14 and 51–2.

50. On the translations and adaptations of *Physiologus* in the Middle Ages, see Curley, *Physiologus*, pp. xxvi–xxxiii. For a discussion of the date when bestiaries and, through them, the *Physiologus* became obsolete, see Ron Baxter, *Bestiaries and their Users in the Middle Ages* (London: Sutton, 1998), pp. 22–5.

51. Baxter, *Bestiaries and their Users*, p. 33. Michael Curley understands the term "physiologus" as meaning not "the naturalist" but "one who interpreted metaphysically, morally and finally, mystically the transcendent significance of the natural world." Curley, *Physiologus*, p. xv.

52. Jan Ziolkowski, *Talking Animals: Medieval Latin Beast Poetry 750–1150* (Philadelphia: University of Pennsylvania Press, 1993), p. 34.

53. Curley, *Physiologus*, p. 51. Two versions of the Latin text can be consulted online in Library of Latin Texts, Series A (Turnhout: Brepols, 2002–) (hereafter: LLTSA). Curley translates from version Y, although there are differences between his translation and the text given in LLTSA. Einhorn gives the texts of four Latin versions of the *Physiologus* (p. 275).

54. Most scholars call it a story or a fable (Shepard, p. 47, Hathaway, p. 14, Gotfredsen, p. 40, Lavers, p. 69). Jan Ziolkowski makes a distinction I view as crucial: "Rather than picturing the imaginary exploits of supposedly real individual animals ... each entry in the *Physiologus* purports to record the behavior and traits typical of an entire species" (*Talking Animals*, p. 34).

55. I recognize that it would be difficult to use that tale for exegetic purposes, for the "little red riding hood" is hard to find literally or figuratively even in the Septuagint version of the Bible.

56. Shepard thinks that the story is very ancient, although it is recorded in a sixteenth-century document. Shepard, *The Lore of the Unicorn*, pp. 65–8.

57. See Einhorn, pp. 35–7, Megged, pp. 22–5, Lavers, pp. 225–8, Hathaway, pp. 65–72, Gotfredsen, pp. 10–12. Other tales proposed include the story of Enkidu, the wild man in the Gilgamesh epic poem (Lavers, pp. 229–33) and a story/recipe related to the karkadann, a Persian unicorned beast (Hathaway, p. 62).

58. The two romances are the fourteenth-century *Le Romans de la dame a la lycorne et du biau chevalier au lyon* and the fifteenth-century *Chevalier du Papegau* (Shepard, *The Lore of the Unicorn*, pp. 84–5).

59. The unicorn is not used in the Aesopian tradition until the fourteenth century, when John of Sheppey, bishop of Rochester, composed a fable in Latin titled

The Lion and the Unicorn. English translation in *Æsop's Fables*, trans. Laura Gibbs (Oxford: Oxford University Press, 2002), p. 57.

60. On recent unicorns, see Hathaway, *The Unicorn*, pp. 163–9.

61. See Blanché, *La Logique et son histoire*, pp. 148–55; Louis Vax, "Barbara, Celarent, Darii, Ferio, Baralipton," *Le Portique: Revue de philosophie et de sciences humaines* 7 (2001): 81–103.

62. Strawson, "On Referring," pp. 340–1.

63. For a recent summary of this discussion, see Jody Azzouni, *Talking about Nothing: Numbers, Hallucinations, and Fictions* (Oxford: Oxford University Press, 2010), pp. 3–19 and for Azzouni's own solution to this problem, pp. 110–49.

64. In fact, "Renard" has influenced the lexicon of English, but on a much smaller scale. According to the *OED*, "Reynard" is a "proper name applied traditionally (chiefly in literature) to: a fox; also occasionally as a common noun."

65. Despite the popularity of medieval translations of the *Roman de Renart* in German and Dutch, "der Fuchs" did not become "der Reinhart" and "de vos" did not become "de reynaerde." On the first German translation, see Jean-Marc Pastré, "Morals, Justice and Geopolitics in the *Reinhart Fuchs* of the Alsatian Heinrich der Glichezaere," in Kenneth Varty (ed)., *Reynard the Fox: Social Engagement and Cultural Metamorphoses in the Beast Epic from the Middle Ages to the Present* (New York: Berghahn Books, 2000), pp. 37–53; on the Dutch renardian tradition, see in the same volume, Paul Wackers, "Medieval French and Dutch Renardian Epics: Between Literature and Society," pp. 55–72.

66. I have been told that the tick has become a famous character, named the Tick, in comics and a television series.

67. Curley, *The Physiologus*, pp. 27–8. The parts in brackets come from the longer version (version B).

68. The source of this is Aelian's *Historia animalia* 6.24. See Curley, *The Physiologus*, p. 78.

69. *Physiologus Latinus*, versio Y, in LLTSA, cap. 18, p. 116.

70. *Physiologus Latinus*, versio B, in LLTSA, cap. 15, para. 20, p. 30.

71. Later illustrators often represented this scene in bestiaries. See, for instance, Wilma George and Brunsdon Yapp, *The Naming of the Beasts: Natural History in the Medieval Bestiary* (London: Duckworth, 1991), pp. 13 and 19. See also the Aberdeen Bestiary, fol. 16ʳ. www.abdn.ac.uk/bestiary/translat/16r.hti.

72. Ziolkowski, *Talking Animals*, p. 234.

73. See ibid., pp. 209–10; Jill Mann, "The Satiric Fiction of the *Ysengrimus*," in Varty, *Reynard the Fox: Social Engagement*, pp. 1–15 (p. 3).

74. See Fukumoto, Harano, and Suzuki, "Les Manuscrits du *Roman de Renart*."

75. This introduction usually begins the branch 25, titled by modern critics "Les enfances de Renard." *Roman de Renart*, p. 54.

76. I leave aside the enigmatic line 8: "*Romanz de lui et de sa geste*" in the Livre de Poche edition, "*Romanz dou lin et de la beste*," in *Le Roman de Renart*, ed. Armand Strubel, et al. (Paris: Gallimard, 1998), and other variants that show

that copyists did not recognize the reference. See Jean Scheidegger, *Le Roman de Renart ou le texte de la dérision* (Geneva: Droz, 1989), pp. 81–8.

77. See *Roman de Renart* (Gallimard), p. 1375; and Scheidegger, *Dérision*, p. 177.
78. "Tous ceux qui ont étudié le développement affectif et cognitif du petit enfant s'accordent pour reconnaître que la naissance de la compétence fictionnelle, du 'faire-comme-si', du 'pour de faux', coïncide avec celle des comportements ludiques." Jean-Marie Schaeffer, *Pourquoi la fiction?* (Paris: Seuil, 1999), p. 175. See also Kendall Walton, *Mimesis as Make-Believe: On the Foundations of the Representational Arts* (Cambridge, Mass.: Harvard University Press, 1990), pp. 2 and 11–12.
79. Scheidegger suggests in particular the model of the Talmud, as well as Christian apocryphal stories such as those found in *La Queste del Saint Graal*. Scheidegger, *Dérision*, pp. 180–4. On Jewish sources and influence on the *Roman de Renard*, see also Jean Batany, *Scène et coulisses du* Roman de Renart (Paris: Société d'édition d'enseignement supérieur, 1989), pp. 96–101.
80. A similar strategy has been used with Arthurian tales when a copyist inserted Chrétien de Troyes's five romances in Wace's *Brut*, just after Wace mentions twelve years of peace in the reign of Arthur. See Ad Putter, "Finding Time for Romance: Mediaeval Arthurian Literary History," *Medium Ævum* 63 (1994): 1–16.
81. This idea was elaborated by many theologians, from Origen to Alain de Lille. It links things and signs, nature and writing. James R. Simpson describes the conceptual context of the *Roman de Renart* as a "system of thought where 'writing' constituted everything from the sum total of Scripture and all subsequent interpretation thereof, to the 'books' of the world itself: 'omnis creatura Deum loquitur' – every created thing speaks [of] God." *Animal Body, Literary Corpus: The Old French* Roman de Renart (Amsterdam: Rodopi, 1996), pp. 2–3. See also Francesco Zambon, "*Figura bestialis:* Les fondements théoriques du bestiaire médiéval," in Gabriel Bianciotto and Michel Salvat (eds.), *Epopée animale, Fable, Fabliau: Actes du IVe Colloque de la Société Internationale Renardienne Evreux, 7–11 septembre 1981* (Paris: Presses universitaires de France, 1984), pp. 709–17.
82. Scheidegger mentions a passage in the branch II of manuscript B, in which Renard explains to Noble that his "renardie" existed before the Creation, and that when Nature created his body preexisting renardie came into it. *Dérision*, pp. 350–1.
83. Jean Batany suggests that "Renard" came to be associated with guile and rebellion because of several earls of Sens named Renard (in Latin "Raginardus" or "Rainardus"), living in the tenth and eleventh centuries. Batany, *Scène et coulisses*, pp. 73–91. In another branch (18) of the *Roman de Renart*, Renard uses as a proof of his death the tombstone of a peasant named "Renard" (p. 950, l. 1627). I do not know when "Renard" ceased to be given as a first name. It is still a last name (including author Jules Renard).
84. See Jean Batany's suggestion that the *Roman de Renart* might have been influenced by Jewish milieux and traditions. "Et si Renard, sous son

déguisement de grand baron (mais parfois teint en jaune), n'était, à l'origine, qu'un 'sale petit juif,' offrant leur revanche imaginaire aux victimes des pogroms?" Batany, *Scène et coulisses*, p. 101. Certain forms of Christian exegesis could have been felt as a spiritual pogrom, and the ambiguous game on the Scriptures and exegesis in this passage may pertain to this "imaginary revenge." It may also pertain to the general character of "*dérision*" that marks the Renardian text (Scheidegger, *Dérision*, pp. 361–422).

85. I borrow these terms from the theories about fiction that Richard Routley surveys (*Exploring Meinong's Jungle*, pp. 537–55).
86. Russell, *Introduction to Mathematical Philosophy*, p. 169.
87. In particular a confusion between "possible world" and "fictional world." See Schaeffer's useful clarification on this point (*Pourquoi la fiction?*, pp. 206–7). John Woods's discussion of possible world theory in relation to a logic of fiction is too technical for me, but, if I am not mistaken, his conclusion is rather pessimistic: "The question is, do we need to countenance possible worlds in order to produce an adequate theory of fictionality? In the light of Buridan's problem, we might better look elsewhere." Woods, *The Logic of Fiction*, p. 108.
88. Parsons explains that the philosophical vulgate of his time and place (the 1980s in the USA) imposes the conviction that "everything exists" as a central tenet that he calls "the Russellian rut." Therefore to talk about nonexistent things like Pegasus or Holmes is to talk about nothing. In a *renardian* move, Parsons claims not to have trouble with that view but to have a strong desire "to look over the edges of that rut." Parsons, *Nonexistent Objects*, pp. 1–9.
89. I view Odell Shepard and Chris Lavers' stories about Indian rhinos, Tibetan antelopes, and donkeys as part of the fictionality of the unicorn rather than an explanation of it. See Shepard, *The Lore of the Unicorn*, pp. 28–33 and Lavers, *The Natural History of Unicorns*, pp. 7–21.
90. I would like to pay homage here to John Mortimer, the "creator" of the Rumpole novels and television series. "Queer Customer" is a Rumpolian interpretation of QC – "Queen's Counsel" – the title that Rumpole never obtains.
91. I rephrase here what Terence Parsons says about the "incompleteness" of fictional objects: "There is no clue in the novels about whether or not Holmes has a mole on his back, and no reason to extrapolate to either side of the story." Parsons, *Nonexistent Objects*, p. 182.
92. See the introduction to Everett and Hofweber, *Empty Names*, p. xii.
93. Kenneth Taylor, "Emptiness without Compromise: A Referentialist Semantic for Empty Names," ibid., pp. 17–36 (p. 30).

4 THE OPPONENT

1. For similar sentences at the beginning of other books of *Metaphysics*, see *Metaphysics* I, 982a, pp. 1553–4; *Metaphysics* III, 995a, p. 1572; *Metaphysics* VI, 1025b, p. 1619; *Metaphysics* VIII, 1042a, p. 1645.
2. On the use of refutation in *Metaphysics* IV, see Enrico Berti, "Il principio di non contraddizione come criterio supremo di significanza nella metafisica aristotelica,"

Studi Aristotelici (L'Aquila: L. U. Japadre, 1975), pp. 76–7; R. M. Dancy, *Sense and Contradiction: A Study in Aristotle* (Boston, Mass.: D. Reidel, 1975), pp. 14–21; Jonathan Lear, *Aristotle: The Desire to Understand* (Cambridge: Cambridge University Press, 1988), pp. 261–2.

3. See Berti's two studies: "Il principio di non contraddizione" and "Il valore 'teologico' del principio di non contraddizione nella metafisica aristotelica," *Studi Aristotelici*, pp. 89–108.

4. Lear, *The Desire to Understand*, p. 264.

5. Berti, *Studi Aristotelici*, p. 87.

6. "Esso ci appare in tal modo come la condizione stessa del pensare, del dire e del vivere, come il criterio supremo di significanza nel senso globale del termine." Ibid., p. 88. My translation.

7. "Nel corso di tale confutazione si manifesta infatti quello che si può chiamare il valore 'teologico' del principio di non contraddizione, ossia la possibilità di dimostrare per mezzo di esso, o meglio per mezzo della distruzione di ogni sua negazione, la trascendenza stessa dell'assoluto, vale a dire l'esistenza di Dio." Ibid., p. 90.

8. Ibid., p. 100.

9. Dancy, *Sense and Contradiction*.

10. Ibid., pp. 36 and 142 for Engels, and p. 54 for Kierkegaard.

11. Ibid., p. 142.

12. In Book IV, Aristotle uses two cognates of *amphisbētōn*: the adjective *amphisbētēsimos* (disputable) qualifies the position of Heraclitus and Cratylus according to which all changes constantly and therefore nothing can be said to be true (*Metaphysics* IV, 1010a, p. 1595); the verb *amphisbētein* (to disagree) is used negatively to assert that our senses do not give us contradictory information (*Metaphysics* IV, 1010b, p. 1595).

13. For instance: "And in general those who use this argument (*hoi touto legontes*) do away with substance and essence" (*Metaphysics* IV, 1007a, p. 1590).

14. Dancy, *Sense and Contradiction*, p. 14.

15. "Let us have one thing clear now: Antiphasis, for all I know, never existed... I shall try to construct a position for him using various historical elements. But he is, for my purpose, *only* a construction out of those elements and what Aristotle says to him." Dancy, *Sense and Contradiction*, p. 14. Italics in the text.

16. Most explicitly in *Sophistic Refutations*. On Aristotle and the sophists, see Pierre Aubenque, *Le Problème de l'être chez Aristote* (Paris: Presses universitaires de France, 1972), p. 97.

17. The nutritive soul is able to grow, absorb nutriment, and reproduce. Aristotle, *On the Soul*, 413a–416b, pp. 659–63.

18. The following philosophers and sophists are named in *Metaphysics* IV: Protagoras (1007b, p. 1591; 1009a, p. 1593), Anaxagoras (1007b, p. 1591; 1009a, p. 1593; 1009b, p. 1594; 1012a, p. 1598), Democritus (1009a, p. 1593; 1009b, p. 1594), Empedocles (1009b, p. 1594), Parmenides (1009b, p. 1594), Epicharmus (1010a, p. 1594), Xenophanes (1010a, p. 1594), Heraclitus (1010a, pp. 1594–5; 1012a, p. 1598); Cratylus (1010a, p. 1594). Aristotle alludes to others

without naming them (Dancy, *Sense and Contradiction*, pp. 63–73 and Aubenque, *Le Problème de l'être*, pp. 94–106).

19. See Gregory Nagy, *The Best of the Achaeans* (Baltimore, Md.: The Johns Hopkins University Press, 1979), pp. 42–58 and 317–47. On the idea of *metis*, see Marcel Detienne and Jean-Pierre Vernant, *Les Ruses de l'intelligence: la mêtis des Grecs* (Paris: Flammarion, 1974).

20. "Au discours on ne peut répondre que par le discours, et à sa contrainte que par une contrainte de même nature. Il faut donc accepter le terrain que nous imposent les sophistes, mais en retournant contre eux leurs propres armes." Aubenque, *Le Problème de l'être*, p. 97.

21. Each of Enrico Berti's two articles on *Metaphysics* IV ("Il principio di non contraddizione" and "Il valore 'teologico'," both published in *Studi Aristotelici*) focus on one group of opponents and one strategy, as Berti explains at the beginning of the second article, "Il valore 'teologico'" (pp. 89–90).

22. Editors and translators understand this passage differently. See, for instance, W. D. Ross in his edition of *Aristotle's Metaphysics*, 2 vols. (Oxford: Clarendon Press, 1953), vol. 1, pp. 284 and 287.

23. Pierre Hadot, *Éloge de la philosophie antique* (Paris: Allia, 2003). See also Hadot's *Philosophy as a Way of Life: Spiritual Exercises from Socrates to Foucault*, ed. Arnold Davidson, trans. Michael Chase (Oxford: Blackwell, 1995).

24. On Democritus, Plato, and Aristotle's ideas about being and non-being, see Harold J. Johnson, "Three Ancient Meanings of Matter: Democritus, Plato, and Aristotle," *Journal of the History of Ideas* 28 (1967): 3–16. Johnson states: "for Aristotle matter is the substratum of all natural contraries; for both Democritus and Plato it *is* one of the contraries" (p. 11).

25. Aubenque, *Le Problème de l'être*, pp. 115–17. Berti remarks that, for Aristotle, being is not contradictory but "multivocal" (*Studi Aristotelici*, p. 92).

26. See Introduction, above, n. 12.

27. Both the Tricot (*Métaphysique* vol. 1, p. 142, n. 1) and Tredennick (*Metaphysics*, Loeb Classic Library 271, p. 187, n. d.) translations say that this is to be found in *Iliad* XXIII, l. 698.

28. See Nagy, *The Best of the Achaeans*, p. 42.

29. "And this is why Democritus, at any rate, says (*phēsin*) ..."; "For Empedocles says (*phēsi*) ..."; "and elsewhere he [Empedocles] says (*legei*) ..."; "Parmenides also expresses himself (*apophainetai*) ..." (*Metaphysics* IV, 1009b, p. 1594). *Apophanetai* means "to make apparent."

30. "*Ereō te dēute kouk ereō / kai mainomai kou mainomai.*" Anacreon in *Lyra graeca*, ed. J. M. Edmonds, 3 vols. (Cambridge, Mass.: Harvard University Press, 1922–8), vol. 2, p. 102. Cited by Dancy, *Sense and Contradiction*, p. 37.

31. Cristina Rossitto, "Opposizione e non contraddizione nella 'Metafisica' di Aristotele," in E. Berti et al. (eds.), *La Contraddizione* (Rome: Città Nuova, 1977), pp. 43–69 (p. 62).

32. Aristotle's "psychological" works are *On the Soul*, and the short treatises *Sense and Sensibilia, On Memory, On Sleep, On Dreams, On Divination in Sleep*. On

the psychological aspects of the argument on the principle of non-contradiction, see Maria Cristina Bartolomei, "Problemi concernenti l'opposizione e la contraddizione in Aristotele," *Verifiche* 10 (1981): 163–93 (pp. 192–3).

33. Plato, *Phaedrus*, 244a–245a and 265b in *Plato's Complete Works*, ed. John M. Cooper (Indianapolis, Ind.: Hackett, 1997). E. R. Dodds, *The Greeks and the Irrational* (Berkeley: University of California Press, 1951), pp. 64–7.

34. "Le fou, serait-il, par essence, l'opposant? Ou est-ce l'opposant qui est systématiquement considéré comme un fou?" Laure Murat, *L'Homme qui se prenait pour Napoléon: pour une histoire politique de la folie* (Paris: Gallimard, 2011), p. 18.

35. On a conception of the unconscious turning back to Aristotle and working on the distinction between enunciation and enunciated, see Vincent Descombes, *L'inconscient malgré lui* (Paris: Gallimard, 1977, 2004), pp. 116–18.

36. Berti discusses what Aristotle adds to Parmenides (*Studi Aristotelici*, pp. 72–3).

37. Ross, *Aristotle's Metaphysics*, vol. 1, p. 264.

38. "The logical laws of thought do not apply in the id, and this is true above all of the laws of contradiction." Sigmund Freud, *New Introductory Lectures on Psychoanalysis* (1933 [1932]), *The Standard Edition of the Complete Psychological Works of Sigmund Freud*, ed. James Strachey, 24 vols. (London: Hogarth Press, 1957–74), vol. 22, p. 73. "The governing rules of logic carry no weight in the unconscious; it might be called the Realm of the Illogical." Freud, *An Outline of Psychoanalysis* (1940 [1938]), ibid., vol. 23, pp. 168–9. Berti discusses the logical and epistemological difficulties that Freud's thesis entails in "A partire dalla logica aristotelica della non-contraddizione: Confronto con i paradigmi delle scienze clinico-psicologiche," in Maria Giordano (ed.), *Episteme e inconscio* (Lecce: Milella, 1990), pp. 3–23 (pp. 15–23).

39. Marian Wesoly, "In margine al principio aristotelico di non contraddizione ed al problema della verità," *Eos: Commentarii Societatis Philologiae Polonorum* 70 (1982): 41–8 (pp. 47–8).

40. Laurence R. Horn, *A Natural History of Negation*, p. 1

5 THE FOOL WHO SAYS NO TO GOD

1. Anselm's introduction to the *Monologion* is at pp. 3–4 in *The Major Works*, and pp. 7–8 in *Opera Omnia*; his introduction to the *Proslogion* is at pp. 82–3 and pp. 93–4.

2. Among those who saw Anselm as an "isolated" thinker: Alexandre Koyré, *L'idée de Dieu dans la philosophie de St. Anselme* (Paris: Ernest Leroux, 1923), pp. 11–12; Étienne Gilson, *La Philosophie au moyen âge*, 2 vols. (Paris: Payot, 1976), vol. 1, p. 250; Frederick Charles Copleston, *A History of Philosophy*, vol. 2. *Medieval Philosophy, Augustine to Scotus* (New York: Doubleday, 1950), p. 161. More recently, scholars have argued that Anselm had more influence on his contemporaries and medieval successors than it was thought: Clanchy, *Abelard*, pp. 75–80; Gregory Schufreider, *Confessions of a Rational Mystic* (West Lafayette, Ind.: Purdue University Press, 1994), p. 15; G. R. Evans, "Anselm's

Life, Works, and Immediate Influence," in Davies and Leftow, *The Cambridge Companion to Anselm of Canterbury*, pp. 5–31 (pp. 24–8).

3. Among those who reject the argument: Thomas Aquinas, Hume, and Kant. Among those who use the argument: Descartes, Spinoza, Leibniz, and Hegel. Robert Brecher, *Anselm's Argument: The Logic of Divine Existence* (Aldershot: Gower, 1985), pp. 3–4. See also Bernard Pautrat's preface and the texts annexed to his translation of *Proslogion. Suivi de sa réfutation par Gaunilon et de la réponse d'Anselme* (Paris: Flammarion, 1993), pp. 15–30 and 111–44.

4. Schufreider, *Confessions*, p. 6.

5. Ian Logan, *Reading Anselm's* Proslogion: *The History of Anselm's Argument and its Significance Today* (Farnham: Ashgate, 2009), pp. 8–10.

6. *L'Œuvre d'Anselme de Cantorbéry*, ed. Michel Corbin, 7 vols. (Paris: Éditions du Cerf, 1986), vol. 1, pp. 40–3.

7. In their order of appearance in the text: Matt. 6:6; Ps. 26:8; 1 Tim. 6:16; Ps. 31:22; Ps. 77:25; Ps. 126:2; Ps. 121:9; Jer. 14:19; Ps. 114:3; Ps. 37:9; Ps. 6:4; Ps. 12:1; Ps. 12:4; Ps. 79:4; Ps. 78:9; Job 3:4; Ps. 37:5; Ps. 68:16; Isa. 7:9. These references appear parenthetically in Davies and Evans's translation, pp. 85–7 and in the footnotes of Corbin's edition, pp. 236–43.

8. Schufreider views the beginning of the *Proslogion* as a prayer focusing on the "quest for the vision of God" (*Confessions*, p. 104). Sweeney describes both the *Monologion* and the *Proslogion* as belonging to the Benedictine tradition of meditation and as "acts of imaginative reflection" (*Anselm*, p. 118).

9. Koyré, *L'idée de Dieu*, p. 196. Philosophers are not all understanding the argument in the same way. For surveys or discussion of the different philosophical reconstructions of the argument, see Graham Oppy, *Ontological Arguments and Beliefs in God* (Cambridge: Cambridge University Press, 1995); Brian Davies, "Anselm and the Ontological Argument," in Davies and Leftow, *The Cambridge Companion to Anselm of Canterbury*, pp. 157–78; Logan, *Reading Anselm's* Proslogion, pp. 151–202; Sweeney, *Anselm*, pp. 147–65. The general tendency in recent works on Anselm is to view his argument as much more complex and sophisticated than earlier modern readers have often assumed.

10. Sweeney argues that the fool "is virtually identical to the figure of someone ignorant or disbelieving created in the *Monologion*." Thus Anselm links both texts to scripture at the same time that he sets as his opponent a "rational unbeliever." *Anselm*, p. 113.

11. John Marenbon argues that *Categories* and *On Interpretation* are not purely logical, and introduce some of the philosophical issues that will be treated more in depth in *Metaphysics*. "Anselm and the Early Medieval Aristotle," in *Aristotelian Logic, Platonism, and the Context of Early Medieval Philosophy in the West* (Aldershot: Ashgate, 2000), article viii: pp. 1–19 (pp. 1–2).

12. I use Jerome's Latin version from the Hebrew – in which Psalms 9 and 10 are combined in a single psalm (9) – from *Biblia sacra juxta vulgatam versionem* (Stuttgart: Deutsche Bibelgesellschaft, 1983). The English translation is taken from *The Revised English Bible* (Cambridge: Cambridge University Press, 1989), with emendations to follow the Latin text more closely. I have also

consulted the *Holy Bible Douay-Rheims Version*, whose English is archaic but closer to the Latin text (Rockford, Ill.: TAN Books, 1989).

13. For Karl Barth, Anselm does not present any "malevolent inconsistency on the part of the *insipiens*." *Anselm: Fides Quaerens Intellectum: Anselm's Proof of the Existence of God in the Context of his Theological Scheme*, trans. I. W. Robertson (London: SCM Press, 1960), p. 165.

14. I had not read Sweeney's book on Anselm when I came to a similar understanding of the fool "not as sectarian but as generic and rational." *Anselm*, p. 148.

15. Giulio d'Onofrio shows that Insipiens is neither a madman nor a mentally challenged man, but that he represents a form of rationality that Anselm rejects because it does not accept the authority of Revelation. "Chi è l' 'Insipiens'? L'argomento di Anselmo e la dialettica dell'Alto Medioevo," *Archivio di Filosofia* 58 (1990): 95–109.

16. Aristotle explains what is homonymy at the beginning of *Categories* (1a, p. 3), and uses this argument against the sophists in *Sophistical Refutations* (165a, p. 278, 165b–166b, pp. 280–1 and *passim*).

17. On these different levels, see Joseph Moreau, *Pour ou contre l'insensé? Essai sur la preuve anselmienne* (Paris: Librairie philosophique J. Vrin, 1967), pp. 17–18 and Schufreider, *Confessions*, pp. 177–82.

18. For Sweeney, Anselm holds a paradoxical view of reason and language, "reasoning as if reason can understand God, the most supremely intelligible object, and praying as if reason is completely unequal to the task of grasping anything about God even in the most incomplete sense." *Anselm*, p. 170.

19. "The dialogue form and the desire for proof in no sense indicate that Anselm has accepted a position where faith and unbelief, the voice of the Church and every other voice, have equal rights ... Obviously this is no free school of free convictions." Barth, *Anselm*, p. 60.

20. Ibid., p. 62.

21. Ibid., pp. 62–3.

22. "The readers whom he visualizes and for whom he caters are the Christian theologians, or more exactly, the Benedictine theologians of his day. Anselm's theology is therefore no esoteric wisdom." Ibid., p. 63.

23. Schufreider, *Confessions*, p. 200.

24. See Marilyn McCord Adams, "Anselm on Faith and Reason," in Davies and Leftow, *The Cambridge Companion to Anselm of Canterbury*, pp. 32–60; Ermanno Bencivenga, *Logic and Other Nonsense: The Case of Anselm and his God* (Princeton, NJ: Princeton University Press, 1993), pp. 60–1 and 74; Sweeney, *Anselm*, p. 119.

25. Anselm, *Omnia Opera*, p. 125; the Oxford translation reads: "*Pro Insipiente:* On Behalf of the Fool by Gaunilo of Marmoutiers," *Major Works*, p. 105.

6 THE MAN WHO SAYS NO TO REASON

1. Very little is known about Guillaume de Lorris (*c*.1200?–*c*.1240?), while Jean de Meun has left a historical trail (*c*.1240–*c*.1305). "Lorris" and "Meun" are place names located in the *Orléanais*. Jean de Meun spent most of his active life in

Paris. On these two authors, see Sarah Kay, *The Romance of the Rose* (London: Grant and Cutler, 1995), pp. 9–11 and Daniel Poirion, *Le Roman de la Rose* (Paris: Hatier, 1973), pp. 3–5. On the question of authorship in the *Rose*, see Stephen G. Nichols, "The Medieval 'Author': An Idea Whose Time Hadn't Come?," in V. Greene (ed.), *The Medieval Author in Medieval French Literature* (New York: Palgrave Macmillan, 2006), pp. 77–101.

2. Susan Stakel summarizes the different positions on *Faux Semblant* before 1991 in *False Roses: Structures of Duality and Deceit in Jean de Meun's* Roman de la Rose, Stanford French and Italian Studies 49 (Saratoga, Calif.: Anma Libri, 1991), pp. 46–8. Daniel Heller-Roazen summarizes more recent works, up to 2003 (*Fortune's Faces*, p. 135).

3. Heller-Roazen, *Fortune's Faces*, pp. 133–4. Except when otherwise indicated, all citations of the *Roman de la Rose* are from Guillaume de Lorris and Jean de Meun, *Le Roman de la Rose*, ed. and trans. Armand Strubel (Paris: Livre de Poche, 1992). The translation (occasionally slightly modified) comes from *The Romance of the Rose*, ed. and trans. Charles Dahlberg (Princeton, NJ: Princeton University Press, 1971).

4. Diogenes Laertius attributes the paradox of the liar to Eubulides of Miletus. See Diogenes Laertius, *Lives of Eminent Philosophers*, trans. R. D. Hicks, Loeb Classical Library 184 (Cambridge, Mass.: Harvard University Press, 1925), p. 237. On the history of this (and other) paradoxes and fallacies, see C. L. Hamblin, *Fallacies* (London: Methuen, 1970); Paul Spade, *The Mediaeval Liar: A Catalogue of the* Insolubilia-*Literature* (Toronto: Pontifical Institute of Mediaeval Studies, 1975). (This is not a study on this question, but a catalogue that gives a good sense of its pervasiveness in medieval logic.)

5. "Semantic Paradoxes," in *Cambridge Dictionary of Philosophy*, ed. Robert Audi, 2nd edn. (Cambridge: Cambridge University Press, 1999), pp. 831–2.

6. Ibid., p. 830.

7. Ibid., p. 831.

8. Saul Kripke, "Outline of a Theory of Truth," *Journal of Philosophy* 72.19 (November 6, 1975): 690–716 (pp. 691–2).

9. Strubel and Dahlberg understand l. 10954 differently: "*Car granz sens en toi connoistre a.*" Dahlberg understands "*granz sens*" as brain power (one needs to be very smart to recognize False Seeming under his masks and disguises); Strubel translates "*car il est fort sage de te connaître*" understanding "*granz sens*" as wisdom (it is wise to be able to identify False Seeming despite his masks and disguises).

10. Stakel, *False Roses*, p. 51.

11. "Relation," in *Cambridge Dictionary of Philosophy*, p. 788.

12. As Gennaro Chierchia remarks, "it is hard to see how our species could have survived without being endowed with this disposition to utter truths." Chierchia and McConnell-Ginet, *Meaning and Grammar*, p. 101.

13. For instance, in Ernest Langlois's edition, the passages read: "*– Qu'est ce? diable! quel sont ti dit? / Qu'est ce que tu as ici dit? – Quei? – Granz desleiautez apertes. / Don ne crains tu pas Deu? – Non, certes.*" Guillaume de Lorris and Jean de

Meun, *Le Roman de la Rose*, ed. Ernest Langlois, Société des anciens textes français, 5 vols. (Paris: Champion, 1921), vol. 3, p. 204.

14. Paul Grice, *Studies in the Way of Words* (Cambridge, Mass.: Harvard University Press, 1989), pp. 28–9.

15. False Seeming claims to be both the champion and the enemy of Guillaume de Saint-Amour (*Rose*, pp. 201–2 and ll. 11492–528), a master of theology at the University of Paris, who, in the 1250s, defended the secular masters' monopoly on higher education against mendicant masters. See Michel-Marie Dufeil, *Guillaume de Saint-Amour et la polémique universitaire parisienne 1250–1259* (Paris: Picard, 1972); Penn R. Szittya, *The Antifraternal Tradition in Medieval Literature* (Princeton, NJ: Princeton University Press, 1986), pp. 11–61 and 186–90; G. Geltner's introduction to his edition: Guillaume de Saint-Amour (or William of Saint-Amour), *De periculis novissimorum temporum*, Dallas Medieval Texts and Translations 8 (Leuven: Peeters, 2008), pp. 1–27.

16. Text of the song edited by Marie-Claire Gérard-Zai, in Chrétien de Troyes, *Cligès*, ed. and trans. Charles Méla and Olivier Collet (Paris: Livre de Poche, 1994), p. 458. My translation.

17. John Fleming has stressed "the obdurate willfulness and ineducability of Reason's interlocutor," in order to present Reason as a figure of authority, expressing the moral and philosophical stance of the author. The relation of the Lover and Reason seems to me more complex, if only because the ineducable Lover is allegedly the author(s) of the Rose. John V. Fleming, *Reason and the Lover* (Princeton, NJ: Princeton University Press, 1984), p. 187.

18. *Le Roman d'Eneas*, ed. and trans. Aimé Petit (Paris: Livre de Poche, 1997), p. 500 (ll. 8196–212); Chrétien de Troyes, *Cligès*, pp. 82–4 (ll. 686–704).

19. Kay, *The Romance of the Rose*, p. 28.

20. See Ernest Langlois, *Origines et sources du* Roman de la Rose (Paris: E. Thorin, 1891). More recently: John V. Fleming, "Jean de Meun and the Ancient Poets," in Kevin Brownlee and Sylvia Huot (eds.), *Rethinking the* Romance of the Rose: *Text, Image, Reception* (Philadelphia: University of Pennsylvania Press, 1992), pp. 81–97; Alastair Minnis, *Magister Amoris: The* Roman de la Rose *and Vernacular Hermeneutics* (Oxford: Oxford University Press, 2001).

21. On the failure of Reason to educate the Lover, or her failure to grasp love, see Stakel, *False Roses*, pp. 76–7.

22. Brown, *Contrary Things*, p. 3.

23. For a summary of Aristotle's theory of opposites, see Horn, *A Natural History of Negation*, pp. 6–9.

24. Guilhem de Peitieu, "Farai un vers de dreyt nien," in *Troubadour Lyrics: A Bilingual Anthology*, ed. and trans. Frede Jensen (New York: Peter Lang, 1998), p. 66.

25. "Colp de joy me fier que m'auci": Jaufré Rudel, "Non sap chanter qui so non di," in *The Songs of Jaufré Rudel*, ed. and trans. Rupert Pickens (Toronto: Pontifical Institute of Mediaeval Studies, 1978), p. 100.

26. "La moie joie est tornee a pesance." Thibaut de Champagne, "Chançon ferai car talent m'en est pris," in S. N. Rosenberg, H. Tischler, and M.-G. Grossel (eds.), *Chansons des trouvères* (Paris: Librairie générale française, 1995), p. 594. My translation.

27. Stahuljak, "Adventures in Wonderland," p. 109.

28. Robert Pasnau qualifies Augustine's imperative "Return to yourself" (*Of True Religion*, 39.72) a "first person method." "Human Nature," in A. S. McGrade (ed.), *Cambridge Companion to Medieval Philosophy* (Cambridge: Cambridge University Press, 2003), pp. 208–30 (pp. 208–9). On Augustinian and Aristotelian trends in the thirteenth century, see R. Pasnau, *Theories of Cognition in the Later Middle Ages* (Cambridge: Cambridge University Press, 1997), pp. 9–11.

29. On the first person narrative and subjectivity in the *Rose*, see Charles Dahlberg, "First Person and Personification in the *Roman de la Rose*: Amant and Danger," *Mediaevalia* 3 (1977): 37–58 (pp. 37–9); Evelyn Birge Vitz, "Inside/Outside: First Person Narrative in Guillaume de Lorris's *Roman de la Rose*," *Yale French Studies* 58 (1979): 148–64; Michel Zink, *La Subjectivité littéraire autour du siècle de Saint Louis* (Paris: Presses universitaires de France, 1985), pp. 127–40, translated into English by David Sices as: *The Invention of Literary Subjectivity* (Baltimore, Md.: The Johns Hopkins University Press, 1999), pp. 112–24. On the relation of the *Rose* and Boethius's *Consolation of Philosophy*, see Adrian Armstrong and Sarah Kay, *Knowing Poetry: Verse in Medieval France from the* Rose *to the* Rhétoriqueurs (Ithaca, NY: Cornell University Press, 2011), pp. 76–7.

30. Armstrong and Kay, *Knowing Poetry*, p. 74.

31. Aristotle, *Poetics* 1461b, p. 2339. Vincent Descombes interprets this sentence as unveiling the secret of seduction through the use of language (*L'inconscient malgré lui*, p. 135).

32. David Hult, *Self-Fulfilling Prophecies: Readership and Authority in the First* Roman de la Rose (Cambridge: Cambridge University Press, 1986), p. 8.

33. "Le thème de ce préambule ressemble à un paradoxe: ce que l'auteur va dire est vrai, précisément parce qu'il s'agit d'un songe." Poirion, *Le Roman de la Rose*, p. 9. My translation.

34. Emmanuèle Baumgartner, "The Play of Temporalities; or, The Reported Dream of Guillaume de Lorris," in Brownlee and Huot, *Rethinking the Rose*, pp. 21–38 (p. 23). On the paradoxical temporality of the *Rose*, see also Hult, *Self-Fulfilling Prophecies*, pp. 136–74 and Heller-Roazen, *Fortune's Faces*, p. 42.

35. On the speech of the God of Love, see Nichols, "The Medieval 'Author'," pp. 86–9 and Heller-Roazen, *Fortune's Faces*, pp. 54–60.

36. See Émile Benveniste's classical account of personal pronouns in *Problèmes de linguistique générale*, vol. 1 (Paris: Gallimard, 1966), pp. 251–7, and, more recently, Catherine Kerbrat-Orecchioni, *L'énonciation* (Paris: Armand Colin, 2009), pp. 62–7.

37. See William Burgwinkle's introduction to his translation of *razos* in *Razos and Troubadour Songs* (New York: Garland, 1990), pp. xvii–xxxii; Michel Zink,

"Les *Razos* et l'idée de la poésie," in Rebecca Dixon and Finn E. Sinclair (eds.), *Poetry, Knowledge and Community in Late Medieval France* (Cambridge: D. S. Brewer, 2008), pp. 85–97.

38. Paul Zumthor has identified this "I" as a grammatical object in his foundational study *Essai de poétique médiévale* (Paris: Presses universitaires de France, 1972), p. 192, translated into English by Philip Bennett as *Toward a Medieval Poetics* (Minneapolis: University of Minnesota Press, 1992), p. 146. See also Sarah Kay's discussion of Zumthor's view of "the subject as either marginal or irrelevant to the lyric," in *Subjectivity in Troubadour Poetry* (Cambridge: Cambridge University Press, 1990), pp. 5–16.

39. "Guillaume de Lorris, who began the poem, is by medieval standards a boldly innovative poet; he assures us that his subject matter is new, yet he achieves his originality through a synthesis of conventional material that had been brought to a higher level of refinement by earlier poets working in a variety of separate forms." Winthrop Wetherbee, "The *Romance of the Rose* and Medieval Allegory," *European Writers* 1 (1983): 309–35 (p. 309). On the different genres Guillaume de Lorris appropriates and transforms, see Hult, *Self-Fulfilling Prophecies*, pp. 186–208.

40. See Matilda Bruckner, *Chrétien Continued: A Study of the Conte du Graal and its Verse Continuations*. Oxford: Oxford University Press, 2009.

41. Wetherbee, "The *Romance of the Rose* and Medieval Allegory," p. 316.

42. "En tant que prédication d'une qualité, l'attribution sera toujours, soit pléonastique, soit porteuse de contresens." Eric Hicks, "La Mise en roman des formes allégoriques: hypostase et récit chez Guillaume de Lorris," in Jean Dufournet (ed.), *Études sur le* Roman de la Rose *de Guillaume de Lorris* (Paris: Champion, 1984), pp. 53–81 (p. 76).

43. Heller-Roazen, *Fortune's Faces*, p. 62.

44. On the manuscripts of the *Rose*, see the *Roman de la Rose Digital Library*, realized by the Sheridan Library at Johns Hopkins University and the Bibliothèque nationale de France. http://romandelarose.org/.

45. Pasnau, *Theories of Cognition*, pp. 276–90.

46. On the designation of the "I" as "Lover" or "Author" and on his visual representations, see Hult, *Self-Fulfilling Prophecies*, pp. 74–89; Lori Walters, "Appendix: Author Portrait and Textual Demarcation in Manuscripts of the *Romance of the Rose*," in Brownlee and Huot, *Rethinking the Rose*, pp. 359–73.

47. Wetherbee, "The *Romance of the Rose* and Medieval Allegory," p. 334.

PART III FATHERS, SONS, AND FRIENDS

1. Regarding imagination as a mental faculty in medieval theories of the mind, see Giorgio Agamben, *Infancy and History*, pp. 15–28. See also my essay "Imagination," in Zrinka Stahuljak, et al., *Thinking Through Chrétien*, pp. 41–74.

2. See Bertrand Russell's distinction between knowledge by acquaintance and indirect knowledge in "On Denoting," p. 479.

7 ARISTOTLE OR THE FOUNDING SON

1. Kant famously presents logic not only as starting with Aristotle but also as ending with him. See preface to the second edition of *Critique of Pure Reason*, trans. N. Kemp Smith (New York: St. Martin's Press, 1929), p. 17. Among philosophers, logicians, and historians of philosophy who locate Aristotle at the origin of logic, see Werner Jaeger, *Aristotle: Fundamentals of the History of his Development*, trans. R. Robinson (Oxford: Clarendon Press, 1934), p. 370; I. M. Bochenski, *Ancient Formal Logic* (Amsterdam: North-Holland Publishing Company, 1957), pp. 8 and 17; J. L. Ackrill, *Aristotle the Philosopher* (Oxford: Oxford University Press, 1981), pp. 79–81; Lear, *Aristotle: The Desire to Understand*, p. 209; Robin Smith, "Logic," in J. Barnes (ed.), *The Cambridge Companion to Aristotle* (Cambridge: Cambridge University Press, 1995), p. 27; Blanché and Dubucs, *La Logique et son histoire*, p. 17.

2. I follow here Jaeger, *Aristotle*, p. 3 and Aubenque, *Le Problème de l'être*, pp. 71–93, but my emphasis is on the notion of succession and successors, and not on the relation between history and philosophy, or the problem of the constitution of a history of philosophy.

3. Zrinka Stahuljak, *Bloodless Genealogies* (Gainesville: University Press of Florida, 2005), pp. 30–1 and 11.

4. Fragments 40, 129, and 42, trans. Richard D. McKirahan, in *Philosophy before Socrates: An Introduction with Texts and Commentary* (Indianapolis, Ind.: Hackett, 1994), pp. 117–18.

5. See Jean-François Pradeau's comment in his edition: Héraclite, *Fragments (citations et témoignages)* (Paris: Flammarion, 2002), p. 275.

6. M. Heidegger, *What is Philosophy?*, trans. William Kluback and Jean T. Wilde (Plymouth: Vision Press, 1963), pp. 47–53.

7. These collections have disappeared except perhaps for one sentence. See Jaap Mansfeld, *Studies in the Historiography of Greek Philosophy* (Assen: Van Gorcum, 1990), pp. 84–96 and, by the same author, "Sources," in A. A. Long (ed.), *The Cambridge Companion to Early Greek Philosophy* (Cambridge: Cambridge University Press, 1999), pp. 26–8.

8. Pierre Hadot, *Qu'est-ce que la philosophie antique?* (Paris: Gallimard, 1995), p. 28.

9. Mansfeld, "Sources," p. 27.

10. Jan Ziolkowski remarks that the importance of authority in medieval culture "relates more than a little to the prominence of authority in Western Christian culture, which helps to explain why *authority* is not a headword in the *Oxford Classical Dictionary* but is one in the *Oxford Dictionary of the Christian Church*." Ziolkowski, "Cultures of Authority in the Long Twelfth Century," *Journal of English and Germanic Philology* 108.4 (2009): 421–48 (p. 424).

11. Some scholars consider Plato and Aristotle's overviews of other philosophers' opinions as doxographies, but this term (coined by Hermann Diels in 1879) is usually applied to works that are entirely dedicated to collecting and reviewing the opinions of various philosophers and schools on a specific subject.

Therefore, I will not use "doxography" for the reviews embedded in Plato and Aristotle's works. See Jaap Mansfeld, "Doxography of Ancient Philosophy," *The Stanford Encyclopedia of Philosophy* (2012 edn.), ed. Edward N. Zalta: http://plato.stanford.edu/archives/sum2012/entries/doxography-ancient/.

12. The parenthetical reference to Plato's works includes the "Stephanus numbers" (that is the page number and the letter of the section of that page in Henri Estienne's 1578 edition of Plato's work) and the page number of the English translation in *Plato's Complete Works*, ed. John M. Cooper (Indianapolis, Ind.: Hackett, 1997).

13. Isocrates, Speech 15: Antidosis (15. 268), in Isocrates, *Works,* trans. George Norlin and Laure van Hook, Loeb Classical Library, 3 vols. (New York: Putnam, 1928).

14. Mary M. McCabe, *Plato and his Predecessors: The Dramatisation of Reason* (Cambridge: Cambridge University Press, 2000), p. 10. J. Mansfeld also points out the fictional aspects of dialogues such as *Parmenides* (*Studies in the Historiography of Greek Philosophy*, pp. 66–8).

15. Pierre Hadot, *Éloge de Socrate* (Paris: Allia, 2002), p. 15. My translation.

16. Ibid., p. 12.

17. McCabe, *Plato and his Predecessors*, pp. 60–92.

18. The fragments of Aristotle's dialogues are edited and translated in *The Complete Works of Aristotle*, pp. 2389–426. For a list of titles of works attributed to Aristotle, see Diogenes Laertius, *Lives of Eminent Philosophers*, vol. I, pp. 465–71. The first nineteen titles are generally understood as representing dialogues. See Anton-Hermann Chroust's introduction to his edition of Aristotle, *Protrepticus: A Reconstruction* (Notre Dame, Ind.: University of Notre Dame Press, 1964), p. x.

19. David Ross, *Aristotle* (London: Routledge, 1995), p. 7.

20. John M. Cooper, "Introduction," in Plato, *Complete Works*, p. xiii.

21. On the difficulties of dating Plato's works, see ibid., pp. xii–xviii. On *Philebus*, see Cooper's introduction to its translation, ibid., pp. 398–9.

22. Ingemar Düring, *Aristotle's Protrepticus: An Attempt at Reconstruction* (Göteborg: Acta Universatis Gothoburgensis, 1961), p. 31.

23. Cicero, *Epistulae ad Atticum*, Book XIII, letter xix, para. 4. Latin text from the online full-text database: Library of Latin Texts, Series A (Turnhout: Brepols, 2013). My translation.

24. On the complexity of "one" and the interest of "monologic" discourses, see Sarah Kay, *The Place of Thought: The Complexity of One in Late Medieval French Didactic Poetry* (Philadelphia: University of Pennsylvania Press, 2007), pp. 3–4.

25. To give only one example: "Since we are seeking (*dzētoumen*, first person plural) this knowledge, it must be inquired (*an eiē skepteon*, impersonal) of what kind are the causes and the principals, the knowledge of which is wisdom" (*Metaphysics* I, 982a; p. 1553).

26. Strabo, *Geography* XIII, i, 54, cited by Jonathan Barnes, "Collecting Facts," in *Aristotle: A Very Short Introduction* (Oxford: Oxford University Press, 2000), p. 25.

27. Hadot, *Qu'est-ce que la philosophie?*, pp. 130–1.
28. For Jean-Paul Dumont this approach comes from the way Aristotle envisions dialectic, that is, as an investigation of the principles of knowledge – investigation whose materials are the various discourses on probable opinions. See his preface to *Les Présocratiques*, ed. J.-P. Dumont, D. Delattre, and J.-L. Poirier (Paris: Gallimard, Pléiade, 1988), p. xxii.
29. Suzanne Mansion, "Le Rôle de l'exposé et de la critique des philosophies antérieures chez Aristote," article originally published in 1961, reprinted in Mansion, *Études aristotéliciennes* (Louvain-la-Neuve: Éditions de l'Institut supérieur de philosophie, 1981), pp. 55–76 (p. 76).
30. Richard McKeon, in *The Basic Works of Aristotle* (New York: Random House, 1941), p. 219; in the 1984 Revised Oxford edition, the letters and roman numbers are suppressed.
31. Auguste Diès, in his edition and translation of *Parmenides*, states: "Aucune raison de voir dans ce dialogue un masque, même transparent. Platon pouvait très bien mettre un jeune Aristote dans son dialogue sans aucune allusion à l'Aristote qui reprendra plus tard, à son compte, les objections du *Parménide*." Plato [Platon], *Parménide*, ed. Auguste Diès (Paris: Les Belles Lettres, 1965), p. 8. Even in the form of denial, the coincidence cannot not be mentioned.
32. The passage (*Physics* I, 187a–188a) in which Aristotle compares different conceptions of the relation between unity and multiplicity attributed to Anaximander, Empedocles, Anaxagoras, and Democritus is difficult to understand and has puzzled editors and translators. See the copious footnotes in the Loeb edition (*Physics* I–IV, trans. P. H. Wicksteed and F. M. Cornford (Cambridge, Mass.: Harvard University Press, 1929), pp. 40–1) and compare the translation with McKeon, *Basic Works*, pp. 224–5 and the *Complete Works* in the Revised Oxford translation, pp. 319–20.
33. Jaeger, *Aristotle*, p. 374.
34. On Thales and ancient cosmogonies, see Richard D. McKirahan, *Philosophy before Socrates*, pp. 28–30.
35. The term "*theologoi*," qualifying Hesiod and his likes, is translated as "cosmologists" in the Loeb edition and as "mythologists" in the Revised Oxford translation. The latter makes more sense in this context.
36. The term *apodeixis*, translated as "proof," can also be translated as "demonstration."
37. For Glenn Most, Aristotle is the first to have made such a distinction between poets and philosophers. See G. W. Most, "The Poetics of Early Greek Philosophy," in A. A. Long (ed.), *The Cambridge Companion to Early Greek Philosophy*, pp. 332–3. J. Mansfeld also stresses the importance of this distinction in Aristotle's thought but notes that at times Aristotle accepts to put opinions of poets and philosophers on the same level (*Studies in the Historiography*, pp. 41–2).
38. Mansion, "Le Rôle de l'exposé," p. 63.
39. On leisure and knowledge, see Lear, *Desire to Understand*, p. 2.
40. On "first philosophy" in relation to knowledge, see ibid., pp. 247–8.

41. Herodotus, *The Histories*, 11, 109; trans. Aubrey de Sélincourt (1954), revised by John Marincola (1972) (London: Penguin, 2003), p. 136.
42. Herodotus tells three stories in which Thales helped his fellow citizens with his astronomical and practical knowledge (*Histories* 1, 74, 75; 170; p. 33, 34, 75); Plato, famously, portrays Thales as a goofy professor derided by a witty servant-girl (*Theaetetus*, 174a; p. 193).
43. McKirahan, *Philosophy before Socrates*, p. 27.
44. Several scholars have lamented the unfairness and biases of Aristotle toward earlier Greek philosophers. See John Burnet, *Early Greek Philosophy* (London: Adam and Charles Black, 1930 [1892]), pp. 31–2; Harold Cherniss, *Aristotle's Criticism of Presocratic Philosophy* (New York: Octagon Books, 1971 [1935]), pp. xiii–xiv, 14, and 352. More recently, W. K. C. Guthrie has reevaluated more positively Aristotle's contribution to the history of philosophy: "Aristotle as a Historian of Philosophy: Some Preliminaries," *Journal of Hellenic Studies* 77.1 (1957): 35–41, but his position has been criticized by J. G. Stevenson in "Aristotle as Historian of Philosophy," *Journal of Hellenic Studies* 94 (1974): 138–43.
45. A. A. Long, "The Scope of Early Philosophy," in Long, *The Cambridge Companion to Early Greek Philosophy*, pp. 1–21 (p. 8).
46. Sophocles, *Oedipus at Colonus*, l. 60, trans. Hugh Lloyd-Jones, Loeb Classical Library 21 (Cambridge, Mass.: Harvard University Press, 1994), pp. 420–1; Aeschylus, *Agamemnon*, l. 259, trans. Alan H. Sommerstein, Loeb Classical Library 146 (Cambridge, Mass.: Harvard University Press, 2008), pp. 30–1.
47. J. Mansfeld points out this passage about succession in "Sources," p. 32.
48. Ibid., p. 32.
49. It is of interest to note that the successors of Alexander the Great were also named *diadokhoi*.
50. Hadot, *Qu'est-ce que la philosophie antique?*, pp. 123–44; John Patrick Lynch, *Aristotle's School: A Study of a Greek Educational Institution* (Berkeley: University of California Press, 1972).
51. Long, "The Scope of Early Greek Philosophy," p. 8.
52. This designation was coined by Hermann Diels for the title of his edition *Die Fragmente der Vorsokratiker*, first published in 1903. See Long, "The Scope of Early Greek Philosophy," p. 5 and n. 10.
53. See Thomas Deman's comment on these passages: "Mais en même temps qu'il [Aristotle] souligne une influence, il disculpe Socrate de la théorie qui s'en est suivie: car lui ne séparait pas, et Aristote l'en approuve, l'universel des réalités sensibles particulières." *Le Témoignage d'Aristote sur Socrate* (Paris: Les Belles Lettres, 1942), p. 73.
54. Such as the "young Socrates" who is one of the protagonists of *Statesman*.
55. Lear, *Desire to Understand*, p. 286.
56. Lear recognizes that it is an extremely difficult book to understand (ibid., p. 273) and that other interpretations of Aristotle's "developing thought" on the nature of substance are as plausible as his (p. 266).
57. Ibid., pp. 269–70.

58. Ibid., p. 275. Lear's argument is based on his understanding of the Greek expression *tode ti* as a "this something" that is not necessarily an individual, but can refer to a species-form such as "human soul."

59. Stahuljak, *Bloodless Genealogies*, pp. 5–10.

60. "Ambivalence is a part of the essence of the relation to the father." *Moses and Monotheism*, in *The Standard Edition of the Complete Psychological Works of Sigmund Freud*, vol. 23, p. 134. "Our attitude to fathers and teachers is, after all, an ambivalent one since our reverence for them regularly conceals a component of hostile rebellion." "Address delivered in the Goethe House at Frankfurt," *The Goethe Prize* (1930), in *The Standard Edition of the Complete Psychological Works of Sigmund Freud*, vol. 21, p. 212.

61. See Louis Gernet, "Les Origines de la philosophie," an article first published in 1945, republished in *Anthropologie de la Grèce antique* (Paris: Maspéro, 1968), pp. 414–30.

62. Lear, *Desire to Understand*, p. 319.

63. Ibid., p. 320.

8 ABELARD OR THE FATHERLESS SON

1. Jean Jolivet describes Abelard as someone "who was spontaneously inclined to be opposed." *Arts du langage*, p. 342. For Catherine Brown, Abelard "constructs his identity as master in a fundamentally negative and exclusive movement." *Contrary Things*, p. 79. Michael Clanchy points out that Abelard's "fascination with contradiction exposed him to St Bernard's charge that he was altogether ambiguous: a dangerous split personality." *Abelard: A Medieval Life*, p. 18. Claire Nouvet stresses the animosity Abelard provoked in his contemporaries, particularly the monks: "For the monastics, Abelard had in particular the privilege to incarnate the arrogance and belligerence of dialectic" [Abélard aura notamment le privilège d'incarner pour les monacaux l'arrogance et la belligérance de la dialectique]. *Abélard et Héloïse: La passion de la maîtrise* (Villeneuve d'Asq: Presses universitaires du Septentrion, 2009), p. 14. My translation.

2. Marenbon, *The Philosophy of Peter Abelard*, pp. 332–9.

3. Sweeney, *Logic, Theology, and Poetry*, pp. 63–6.

4. See, for instance, the work of Claire Nouvet on Abelard as a master and his relations with his own masters. Nouvet studies only the autobiographical texts, leaving the philosophical ones to the specialists. *Abélard et Héloïse*, p. 23.

5. There are two references to Greco-Roman philosophers at the beginning of *Historia calamitatum*: "I began to travel about in several provinces disputing, like a true peripatetic philosopher" and "even Porphyry did not venture to settle it [the problem of differences between individuals of the same species] when he deals with universals in his *Isagoge*, but only mentioned it as a 'very serious difficulty'." *The Letters of Abelard and Heloise*, trans. Betty Radice, rev. M. T. Clanchy (London: Penguin, 2003), pp. 3 and 5. There is no explicit mention of Aristotle or Plato.

6. Abelard, *Dialectica*, p. 608.

7. Jolivet, *Arts du langage*, p. 178.
8. Marenbon, *The Philosophy of Peter Abelard*, pp. 38–9.
9. On the dating of these two works, see Mews, "On Dating the Works of Peter Abelard" and Marenbon, *The Philosophy of Peter Abelard*, pp. 40–3.
10. The logical canon consisted of Aristotle's *Categories* and *On Interpretation*, Porphyry's *Isagoge*, and four works by Boethius: *De topicis differentiis, De divisione, De syllogismo categorico, De syllogismo hypothetico* (Abelard, *Dialectica*, p. 146). This is the basis of what came to be called *logica vetus*, old logic, when a *logica nova*, a new logic, developed as the rest of Aristotle's *Organon* was made available to the Latin West. See Bernard Dod, "Aristoteles Latinus" and Martin Tweedale, "Abelard and the Culmination of the Old Logic," in N. Kretzmann, A. Kenny, and J. Pinborg (eds.), *The Cambridge History of Late Medieval Philosophy* (Cambridge: Cambridge University Press, 1982), pp. 45–79 and 143–57.
11. Jolivet, *Arts du langage*, pp. 176–7.
12. Abelard, *Dialectica*, p. 88. My translation. The disagreement is about the definition of relation and relatives (father/son, master/slave).
13. Michael Clanchy lists the different connotations of *Peripateticus Palatinus* "from the sublime to the ridiculous" (*Abelard*, p. 97).
14. In a letter to an unnamed opponent of dialectic, Abelard uses the same title for Aristotle, "the very prince of the Peripatetics," presented as the author of the *Sophistical Refutations*, and therefore as an exponent of the difference between dialectic and sophistry. *Letters of Peter Abelard, Beyond the Personal*, trans. Jan Ziolkowski (Washington, DC: The Catholic University Press, 2008), p. 181 (hereafter *Beyond the Personal*).
15. John Marenbon discusses this passage in "The Platonisms of Peter Abelard," *Aristotelian Logic, Platonism, and the Context of Early Medieval Philosophy in the West* (Aldershot: Ashgate, 2000), article xii: pp. 109–29 (p. 111).
16. Abelard, *Dialectica*, p. 146. On Abelard's brothers and nephews, see Clanchy, *Abelard*, pp. 137–8.
17. Eleonore Stump found his contribution to the theory of topics important and original. See *Dialectic and its Place in the Development of Medieval Logic* (Ithaca, NY: Cornell University Press, 1982), pp. 109 and 127–30. Christopher Martin claims "Abelard was the greatest logician between Aristotle and the Stoics in antiquity and William of Ockham and John Buridan in the fourteenth century." See "Logic," in Brower and Guilfoy, *The Cambridge Companion to Abelard*, p. 158. John Marenbon qualifies him a "highly proficient logician" (*The Philosophy of Peter Abelard*, p. 40). On Abelard and the arrival of the new logic, see Tweedale, "Abelard and the Culmination of the Old Logic" and Marenbon, *The Philosophy of Peter Abelard*, pp. 52–3.
18. Marenbon, "The Platonisms of Peter Abelard," p. 111. This article was first published in 1997. On Abelard and Plato, see also T. Gregory, "Abélard et Platon," in E. M. Buytaert (ed.), *Peter Abelard: Proceedings of the International Conference, Louvain, May 10–12, 1971* (Louvain: Leuven University Press, 1974), pp. 38–64; Jean Jolivet, "Non-Réalisme et platonisme chez Abélard: essai

d'interprétation," in *Abélard en son temps: colloque international, 14–19 mai 1979* (Paris: Les Belles Lettres, 1981), pp. 175–95; L. Moonan, "Abelard's Use of the *Timaeus*," *Archives d'histoire doctrinale et littéraire du moyen âge* 56 (1989): 7–90.

19. Marenbon, "The Platonisms of Peter Abelard," p. 128.

20. On the relative novelty of the term *theologia* in the early twelfth century, see Clanchy, *Abelard*, pp. 264–6.

21. On abstraction, fiction, and truth in Abelard's logic, see Sweeney, *Logic, Theology, and Poetry*, p. 70.

22. Abelard, *Theologia summi boni: Tractatus de unitate et trinitate divina*, ed. and [German] trans. Ursula Niggli (Hamburg: Felix Meiner, 1989) (hereafter: TSB), p. 30. The English translation is mine. Jean Jolivet published a French translation: *De l'unité et de la trinité divines (Theologia summi boni)* (Paris: Vrin, 2001).

23. *Confessions*, Book III, 5 and Book V, 14; trans. Henry Chadwick (Oxford: Oxford University Press, 1991), pp. 40 and 88.

24. Jean Jolivet, "Doctrines et figures de philosophes chez Abélard," in Rudolf Thomas, Jean Jolivet, D. E. Luscombe, and L. M. de Rijk (eds.), *Petrus Abaelardus, 1079–1142: Person, Werk und Wirkung*, Trierer Theologische Studien 38 (Trèves: Paulinus, 1980), pp. 103–20. On the tradition of reading and glossing the *Timaeus*, see K. Sarah-Jane Murray, *From Plato to Lancelot: A Preface to Chrétien de Troyes* (Syracuse, NY: Syracuse University Press, 2008), pp. 3–9.

25. On this passage, and Abelard's integretation of Plato in his theology, see Sweeney, *Logic, Theology, and Poetry*, pp. 82–3.

26. This would be a development of his effort to reconcile Aristotle and Plato's theories of the universals. For Alain de Libera, "Abelard's theory of the universals is one of the most original in the whole Middle Ages. It is also one of those that shows best the resonance of the disagreement between Plato and Aristotle on medieval thought." *La Querelle*, p. 148. My translation.

27. *Beyond the Personal*, p. 185. The Latin text is in Peter Abelard, *Letters IX–XIV: An Edition with an Introduction*, ed. Edmé Renno Smits (Groningen: Rijksuniversiteit te Groningen, 1983), p. 275.

28. On the dating, see Jan Ziolkowski's introduction to this letter in *Beyond the Personal*, p. 178.

29. See Clanchy, *Abelard*, pp. 81–3; Yukio Iwakuma, "Pierre Abélard et Guillaume de Champeaux dans les premières années du XIIᵉ siècle: une étude préliminaire," in Joël Biard (ed.), *Langage, sciences, philosophie au XIIᵉ siècle* (Paris: Vrin, 1996), pp. 93–123 (pp. 102–3); Marenbon, "Life," p. 34; Claire Nouvet, "Abélard ou l'hyperbole parricide," in Jean Jolivet and Henri Habrias (eds.), *Pierre Abélard: Colloque international de Nantes* (Rennes: Presses universitaires de Rennes, 2003), pp. 49–61 (p. 59); Jacques Verger, "De l'école d'Abélard aux premières universités," ibid., pp. 17–28 (pp. 23–4).

30. Jeffrey E. Brower, "Trinity," in Brower and Guilfoy, *The Cambridge Companion to Abelard*, pp. 223–57. For the reconstruction and chronology of the different versions, see Constant Mews, "Peter Abelard's *Theologia*

Christiana and *Theologia 'Scholarium'* Re-examined," *Recherches de théologie ancienne et médiévale* 52 (1985): 109–58.

31. For David Luscombe, the implicit and explicit references to Anselm are "the signs of an extensive and pervasive submission to some of Anselm's deepest thoughts." "St Anselm and Abelard," *Anselm Studies* 1 (1983): 207–29 (p. 218). Michael Clanchy suggests that Abelard's first admiration or at least favorable opinion toward Anselm turned into aggressive irony after the 1121 Council of Soissons. "Abelard's Mockery," *Journal of Ecclesiastical History* 41 (1990): 1–23 (pp. 14–19). See also David Luscombe's criticism of Clanchy's hypothesis in "St Anselm and Abelard," pp. 224–5.

32. These texts were gathered and commented on by François Picavet, first in an 1896 edition, reprinted in 1911: *Roscelin, philosophe et théologien, d'après la légende et d'après l'histoire* (Paris: F. Alcan, 1911). For a more recent assessment, see Mews, "St Anselm and Roscelin" and, by the same author, "Nominalism and Theology before Abaelard: New Light on Roscelin of Compiègne," *Reason and Belief in the Age of Roscelin and Abelard* (Aldershot: Ashgate, 2002), pp. 4–34.

33. Mews, "Nominalism and Theology before Abaelard," pp. 32–3.

34. I will continue to use the term "nominalist" here although it would be more correct to call Roscelin a "vocalist" since the term "*nominales*" does not appear until the middle of the twelfth century in oppositon to "*reales*" (realists), whereas the term "*vocales*" appears earlier. See Iwakuma, "*Vocales*, or Early Nominalists," pp. 37–40.

35. *Epistola Johannis ad Anselmum*, Latin text in Picavet, *Roscelin*, p. 113. All subsequent citations of the letters given in this book refer to "Picavet." English translations are mine.

36. *Epistola Anselmi ad Falconem* (Picavet, pp. 114–15). Sweeney remarks that this letter to Foulques "is at odds not just with his reply to his fellow monk, John, but with his attitude toward the student's objections in his three dialogues, toward Boso in *Cur Deus homo*, and toward Gaunilo." *Anselm*, p. 247.

37. Sweeney notes that "in *De incarnatione*, Anselm is doing exactly what he advised Fulco not to allow: discussing Roscelin's view." *Anselm*, p. 250.

38. *Epistolae de incarnatione Verbi prior recensio*, *Opera Omnia*, vol. 1, pp. 281–90 (p. 282). There is no translation of this earlier version in *Major Works*. The phrase "*a quodam clerico in Francia*" appears also on the later version addressed to the pope. See *Epistolae de incarnatione Verbi*, *Opera Omnia*, vol. 2, pp. 3–35 (p. 4); *Major Works*, p. 233.

39. Mews, "St Anselm and Roscelin," p. 64. *Epistolae de incarnatione Verbi prior recensio*, *Opera Omnia*, vol. 1, p. 282.

40. Cited by Mews in "St Anselm and Roscelin," p. 66. Sweeney attributes the change of tone in the letter to Foulques partly to "Anselm's new sense of his role as bishop." *Anselm*, p. 249.

41. Richard Southern describes Roscelin as a "rolling stone" who taught at Compiègne, Bayeux, Tours, Loches, in England, and Besançon. R. W. Southern, *Saint Anselm: A Portrait in a Landscape* (Cambridge: Cambridge University Press, 1990), pp. 175–6.

42. I push here further Sweeney's remark about Anselm's violent reaction: "it could also be because Roscelin, if not in his views then at least in his mode of questioning, is too close to Anselm rather than too far away." *Anselm*, p. 248.
43. The profession of faith goes on from p. 1 to p. 10 in *Opera Omnia*, from p. 233 to p. 238 in *Major Works*.
44. See Sweeney's presentation of this work (*Anselm*, pp. 277–9).
45. Picavet, p. 55; Clanchy, *Abelard*, p. 37 and 292–3; Marenbon, *The Philosophy of Peter Abelard*, pp. 8–9.
46. See his letter defending dialectic in *Beyond the Personal*, pp. 175–87 and his attacks against "pseudo-dialecticians" in his *Theologia summi boni* (Abelard, *Unité*, pp. 53–4 and 76–7).
47. Nouvet, *Abélard et Héloïse*, pp. 53–67.
48. Abelard, *Dialectica*, pp. 554–5. This passage is cited and translated in Eike-Henner W. Kluge, "Roscelin and the Medieval Problem of Universals," *Journal of the History of Philosophy* 14 (1976): 405–14 (p. 409). I give here Kluge's English translation, with a few modifications.
49. Mariateresa Fumagalli Beonio Brocchieri, *The Logic of Abelard*, trans. Simon Pleasance (New York: Humanities Press, 1970), p. 43 and Marenbon, "Life," pp. 27–32.
50. See Kluge, "Roscelin and the Medieval Problem of Universals"; Jean Jolivet, "Trois variations médiévales," p. 114; John Marenbon, "Life," pp. 31–2; Libera, *La Querelle*, pp. 142–6.
51. Picavet suggests that Abelard started because Roscelin had regained a preeminent position, and attacking dialecticians or "pseudodialecticians" would help him to strengthen his claims to be an orthodox theologian. Picavet, *Roscelin*, p. 58. For Marenbon, Roscelin might have started it when he heard about Abelard's teaching. Marenbon, *The Philosophy of Peter Abelard*, p. 57. See also Clanchy, *Abelard*, pp. 294–5 and Ziolkowski, *Beyond the Personal*, pp. 188–94.
52. Marenbon, *The Philosophy of Peter Abelard*, p. 54; Jean Jolivet, *La Théologie d'Abélard* (Paris: Éditions du Cerf, 1997), p. 26.
53. See Ziolkowski, *Beyond the Personal*, p. 196, n. 25.
54. Marenbon, *The Philosophy of Peter Abelard*, p. 57.
55. Translation from *Beyond the Personal*, p. 195.
56. Picavet, p. 129; *Beyond the Personal*, p. 96. Jan Ziolkowski remarks that, for Abelard, "praising the two men for their sanctity has the effect of putting him in good company" (p. 193).
57. Picavet, pp. 50–3.
58. This letter is given in Picavet, pp. 129–39.
59. Mews, "On Dating the Works of Peter Abelard," p. 127. Luscombe notes that "the three quotations from St Augustine's *De trinitate*, which Roscelin had produced in his letter to Abelard and which had not appeared in the condemned book, now appear in Book 5.38 of the *Theologia Christiana* and also in the early versions of the *Sic et Non*." Luscombe, "St. Anselm and Abelard," p. 210.
60. Libera, *La Querelle*, p. 145.
61. Mews, "Nominalism and Theology before Abaelard," VII: 9.

62. Ibid., VII: 12.
63. Claire Nouvet's reading of Abelard's vision of himself as Christ, while he was rather acting like a Cain toward his brothers, leads to such an interpretation. Nouvet, *Abélard et Héloïse*, p. 110. Brown arrives at a similar conclusion through her study of Abelard's use of contradiction as logical and pedagogical tool. She reads Roscelin's final invective, denying Abelard successively of the status and name of master, monk, and man, as a return to the sender: "[Roscelin] forces Abelard into the consequences of his own logic." *Contrary Things*, p. 78.
64. Constant Mews, "Philosophy and Theology 1100–1150: The Search for Harmony," *Reason and Belief in the Age of Roscelin and Abelard*, pp. 159–203 (p. 161).
65. Vincent Descombes states that in pre-modern societies "I declare my belonging to the group as I declare my religion, for the subject of religion is the group, not the individual," in contradistinction with modern societies, in which "I declare my personal faith as I declare my religious position." *Le Raisonnement de l'ours et autres essais de philosophie pratique* (Paris: Seuil, 2007), p. 332.
66. Nouvet, *Abélard et Héloïse*, pp. 95–6 and 104–16.
67. I borrow the idea of "fatherless sons" from Zrinka Stahuljak. She studies them in the context of late twelfth-century and thirteenth-century Arthurian romances, in which can be found "an unusual number of illegitimate sons, among whom Merlin the magician is the most prominent." *Bloodless Genealogies*, p. 79. These literary fictions reveal what philosophical phantasms obfuscate.

9 THE DIALECTICS OF FRIENDSHIP

1. Jean-Claude Fraisse, *Philia: La notion d'amitié dans la philosophie antique: Essai sur un problème perdu et retrouvé* (Paris: Vrin, 1974), pp. 162–3.
2. Jacques Derrida, *The Politics of Friendship*, trans. G. Collins (New York: Verso, 2005), p. 240; *Politiques de l'amitié* (Paris: Galilée, 1994), p. 269. The seminar was taught in 1988–9. The first published essay appeared as "The Politics of Friendship" in *Journal of Philosophy* 75.11 (1988): 632–45; a longer version appeared as "Politics of Friendship" in *American Imago* 50.3 (1993): 353–91. The book *Politiques de l'amitié* appeared in 1994, and its first translation into English in 1997.
3. Only *Lysis* focuses on *philia*, but Plato picks the problems addressed in *Lysis* again in *Symposium*, *Phaedrus*, and *Republic*. Fraisse, *Philia*, p. 127.
4. A. W. Price, *Love and Friendship in Plato and Aristotle* (Oxford: Clarendon Press, 1989), p. 159.
5. See for instance, John Boswell, *Christianity, Social Tolerance, and Homosexuality: Gay People in Western Europe from the Beginning of the Christian Era to the Fourteenth Century* (Chicago: University of Chicago Press, 1980). Boswell tends to subsume friendship in the broader affect of love, and does not study friendship in or for itself. For an opposed view on friendship and homosexuality, see Alan Bray, *The Friend* (Chicago: University of Chicago Press, 2003). However,

Boswell's thesis on the place of homosexuality in ancient and medieval cultures has provoked a renewed reflection on friendship. On this reflection, and the debate on Boswell's thesis among medievalists, see Damien Boquet, *L'ordre de l'affect au moyen âge: Autour de l'anthropologie affective d'Aelred de Rievaulx* (Caen: Publications du centre de recherches archéologiques et historiques médiévales, 2005), pp. 308–23.

6. Fraisse points out that, for Plato, if love is a powerful image of human endless quest and anxiety, the practice of friendship is an important aspect of the practice of philosophy, and Socratic dialogue functions as "une école d'amitié" [a school of friendship] (*Philia*, p. 127).

7. Demosthenes, *Against Medias, Androtion, Aristocrates, Timocrates, Aristogeiton*, trans. J. H. Vince, Loeb Classical Library (Cambridge, Mass.: Harvard University Press, 1935), XXIII, 56; pp. 249–51.

8. Demosthenes, XXIII, 122, p. 299. Both of these passages are cited and commented on in David Konstan, *Friendship in the Classical World* (Cambridge: Cambridge University Press, 1997), pp. 55–6. I use Konstan's translation for the second citation.

9. "'But what about when you come home to your mother, does she let you do whatever it takes to make you happy, like playing with her wool or her loom when she's weaving? She doesn't stop you from touching the blade or the comb or any of her other wool-working tools, does she?' 'Stop me?' he laughed. 'She would beat me if I laid a finger on them.'" *Lysis*, 208d; p. 692.

10. Fraisse, *Philia*, pp. 129–31.

11. For an assessment of Plato's complex views of the feminine, see Price, *Love and Friendship*, pp. 167–71.

12. On this move toward an anthropology of friendship, see Fraisse, *Philia*, pp. 193–4.

13. "Perfect friendship is the friendship of men who are good, and alike in virtue ... But it is natural that such friendship should be infrequent; for such men are rare." *Nicomachean Ethics* VIII, 1156B; p. 1827. *Complete Works* translates "*aretē*" as "excellence." I translate it as "virtue" in its Latin sense of excellence associated to manliness.

14. Barbara Cassin, "Aristotle with and against Kant," in Christina Howells (ed.), *French Women Philosophers: A Contemporary Reader* (London: Routledge, 2004), pp. 100–21 (p. 107). This essay translates a chapter of Cassin's book *Aristote et le logos: Contes de la phénoménologie ordinaire* (Paris: Presses universitaires de France, 1997).

15. See Price's comparison between Plato and Aristotle with regard to women's aptitudes (*Love and Friendship*, pp. 171–3).

16. Text and translation from Cicero, *De senectute, De amicitia, De divinatione*, trans. W. A. Falconer, Loeb Classical Library (Cambridge, Mass.: Harvard University Press, 1923).

17. Reginald Hyatte notes that the Christian writers John Cassian and Aelred of Rievaulx borrowed this superposition of *amicitia inter pares* and master-disciple friendship from Cicero and Seneca. See Reginald Hyatte, *The Arts of*

Friendship: The Idealization of Friendship in Medieval and Early Renaissance Literature (New York: Brill, 1994), p. 32.

18. Sandra Citroni Marchetti insists on the practical and realist aspects of Ciceronian friendship particularly in relation to politics, but, still, the ideal friendship between the *boni viri* Cicero describes in *De amicitia* imposes a certain tone and frame to the concept of friendship. See Sandra Citroni Marchetti, *Amicizia e potere: nelle lettere di Cicerone e nelle elegie ovidiane dall'esilio* (Florence: Università degli Studi di Firenze, 2000), pp. 6 and 31–6.

19. Laelius, rejecting the utilitarian concept of friendship, demonstrates its absurdity and "inhumanity" (*inhumanius*) by listing among its unwanted consequences that "little women" (*mulierculae*) would be better candidates for friendship than men, since they are more in need of defense and support (*De amicitia* xiii. 46; p. 157).

20. The habit of writing about friendship with reverence, decorum, and gloom persists until our time. See, for instance, the tone and mood of the citations used by Charles Stivale in his article "The Folds of Friendship: Derrida–Deleuze–Foucault," *Angelaki* 5.2 (2000): 3–15. On friendship and mourning in Montaigne, see Katherine Kong, *Lettering the Self in Medieval and Early Modern France* (Cambridge: D. S. Brewer, 2010), pp. 191–233.

21. Hyatte defines Cicero's *Laelius* "as a sort of secular hagiography" (*The Arts of Friendship*, p. 30).

22. Aelred de Rievaulx, *De spirituali amicitia, L'amitié spirituelle*, ed. J. Dubois (Paris: Éditions Charles Bayet, 1948), p. 4. English translation from *Aelred of Rievaulx: Spiritual Friendship*, trans. Mark Williams (Cranbury, NJ: Associated University Presses, 1994), p. 28.

23. Boquet describes Aelred's thought process as consisting in "*prendre appui sur cette tradition pour produire un discours spécifique, répondant à des interrogations propres*" [leaning on tradition to produce a specific discourse responding to his own questioning]. Boquet, *L'ordre de l'affect*, p. 281.

24. Ibid., pp. 282–3 and 329.

25. "La dialectique de l'amitié explique ainsi certaines tensions dans les écrits d'Aelred à propos des relations interindividuelles au cloître. En ce sens, l'amicitia carnalis, par exemple, possède un statut intrinsèquement ambigu dans la mesure où elle est traversée par la double polarisation de l'affectus carnalis, condamnable lorsqu'il aboutit à rendre l'homme esclave de ses passions charnelles, et tolérable lorsqu'il sert de base pour l'ascension vers la vertu. La cohérence du discours d'Aelred tient dans cette tension."Ibid., p. 321.

26. Cicero says: "*nisi in bonis amicitiam esse non posse.*" *De amicitia* iv. 16; p. 126.

27. In this case, Aelred's position toward women would be similar to Bernard de Clairvaux's position, as described by Jean Leclercq in his study *La Femme et les femmes dans l'œuvre de Saint Bernard* (Paris: Téqui, 1982). Leclercq is indeed biased in favor of one of the founding fathers of his order, but at the same time he convincingly demonstrates that the accusations of misogyny thrown against Bernard are not based on scholarly arguments, and that his works demonstrate a more nuanced and complex relationship with women and femininity than

basic clerical misogyny. Among twelfth-century clerical writers, he is the one who wrote the largest number of letters to women (p. 29), including two passionate letters to a certain Ermengarde, in which *caritas* sounds like *amor de lohn* (pp. 40–4).

28. According to Brian Patrick McGuire, Aelred developed his "emotional makeup" based on male friendship in the context of early Cistercians' strict avoidance of contact with women: "Like Bernard, he was not anti-woman, but a-woman. An all-male world made strong emotional and spiritual bonds among men natural, even desirable." *Friendship and Community: The Monastic Experience 350–1250* (Kalamazoo, Mich.: Cistercian Publications Inc., 1988), p. 332.

29. Boquet, *L'ordre de l'affect*, pp. 273–4.

30. Bernard de Clairvaux like Aelred "articulated . . . an affective spirituality whose expression of love and friendship, put in a religious key, encouraged personal repentance, contemplation and social reformation." Martha G. Newman, "Foundation and Twelfth Century," in Mette Birkedal Bruun (ed.), *The Cambridge Companion to the Cistercian Order*, Cambridge Companions Online (Cambridge: Cambridge University Press, 2012), pp. 25–37 (p. 31): http://dx.doi.org/10.1017/CCO9780511735899.004.

31. Jean Frappier, *Étude sur Yvain, ou Le chevalier au lion de Chrétien de Troyes* (Paris: Société d'édition d'enseignement supérieur, 1969), pp. 194–8. On the *Sic et Non*, see Marenbon, *The Philosophy of Peter Abelard*, pp. 61–3.

32. Frappier, *Étude sur Yvain*, p. 195. Clanchy, *Abelard: A Medieval Life*, pp. 90–1.

33. Frappier defines this passage as "a treatise of passions moderated by reason" [un traité des passions tempérées par la raison], *Étude sur Yvain*, p. 198. Tony Hunt interprets the opposition of friendship and enmity as representing two opposed conceptions of chivalry, one shallow and superficial, the other serious and responsible. "The Dialectic of Yvain," p. 298. For Leslie Topsfield, the fight between Yvain and Gauvain opposes selfish and selfless love, or *cupiditas* and *caritas*. *Chrétien de Troyes: A Study of the Arthurian Romances* (Cambridge: Cambridge University Press, 1981), pp. 202–3. For Eugene Vance, the use of dialectic in this passage signals a major transformation of vernacular narrative, evolving toward "far more ambitious intellectual constructions, as embodied, for example, in the *Roman de la Rose* and the *Divine Comedy*." *From Topic to Tale*, p. 26. For René Girard, the opposition between love and hate reveals the self-destructive effect of mimetic desire in chivalric culture and feudal society. "Love and Hate in Yvain," in Brigitte Cazelles and Charles Méla (eds.), *Modernité au moyen âge: Le défi du passé* (Geneva: Droz, 1990), pp. 249–62. For Per Nykrog, it is the fundamental opposition between superficial and real identity that is staged in the fight between Yvain and Gauvain, and presented as a subject of reflection in the digression. *Chrétien de Troyes: Romancier discutable* (Geneva: Droz, 1996), p. 176. Sarah Kay returns to love and hate as the most important pair of opposites in the passage and suggests that, by inviting us to think about this opposition, Chrétien shows us how difficult it is to distinguish between them. *Courtly Contradictions*, pp. 53–4.

34. Danièle James-Raoul, *Chrétien de Troyes: La griffe d'un style* (Paris: Champion, 2007), pp. 472–3.
35. D. Hult signals in his edition that several copyists garbled or abbreviated the passage (Chrétien, *Le Chevalier au lion*, p. 910).
36. *Amisté, amistage, amistance, amiableté* occur in Old French texts but are rarer than *amor* to qualify a bond between two men. They can also at times refer to love between man and woman. See Hyatte, *The Arts of Friendship*, p. 89.
37. Although one of the greatest medieval epic heroes, Guillaume d'Orange occasionally breaks the neck of people who provoke his anger. See, for instance, *Le Charroi de Nîmes*, ed. and trans. Claude Lachet (Paris: Gallimard, 1999), p. 102 (ll. 745–6).
38. Chivalric attitude toward one's opponent in combat shares certain features with chivalric attitudes toward one's comrades. In this ethical frame, perfect enemies can be imagined on the model of perfect friends. For instance, First World War airfighters both killed and honored their adversaries and were often compared to knights. See Allen J. Frantzen, *Bloody Good: Chivalry, Sacrifice, and the Great War* (Chicago: University of Chicago Press, 2004), p. 147.
39. See Mary Carruthers, *The Book of Memory* (Cambridge: Cambridge University Press, 1990), pp. 29, 38–9.
40. Boethius, *De topicis differentiis*, trans. Eleonore Stump (Ithaca, NY: Cornell University Press, 1978), 2.1188a, p. 51. This reference is given by Vance, *From Topic to Tale*, p. 27.
41. On the question of visibility and invisibility in this passage, see Hildegard Elisabeth Keller, "Making Sense of Invisibility in Courtly Epic and Legal Ritual," in S. G Nichols, A. Kablitz, and A. Calhoun (eds.), *Rethinking the Medieval Senses: Heritage, Fascinations, Frames* (Baltimore, Md.: The Johns Hopkins University Press, 2008), pp. 218–62.
42. Grace Armstrong, for instance, views the whole episode as signaling the "ineffectualness of the legal system to ensure the triumph of justice" and the rather comic ways Arthur assumes his role of dispensator of God's justice on earth as putting in doubt "his court's reputation for justice." Grace M. Armstrong, "Questions of Inheritance: *Le Chevalier au lion* and *La Queste del Saint Graal*," *Yale French Studies* 95 (1999): 171–92 (pp. 182 and 184). See also Karl D. Uitti on the way Chrétien uses the Arthurian background with "intellectual and comic detachment" to present courtliness as an ambiguous system of values. Uitti, "Le Chevalier au Lion (Yvain)," in D. Kelly (ed.), *The Romances of Chrétien de Troyes: A Symposium* (Lexington, Ky: French Forum, 1985), pp. 182–231 (pp. 210–12).
43. Renée Allen, "The Role of Women and their Homosocial Context in the *Chevalier au Lion*," *Romance Quarterly* 46 (1999): 141–54 (p. 150).
44. There is no known precedent for this character (Brian Woledge, *Commentaire sur Yvain*, 2 vols. (Geneva: Droz, 1988), vol. 2, p. 51). Philippe Walter associates this passage with several Irish stories, connecting a thorn, a ford, and a fight for sovereignty. The story of Cuchulainn's death associates a bush of thorn to the Morrigan's prophecy of the hero's death (*Canicule* (Paris: Société d'édition

d'enseignement supérieur, 1988), pp. 254–5). But in all these stories the thorn is a whitethorn (*aubépine*); the blackthorn (*épine noire*) in *Yvain* sounds like an anomaly.

45. Aristotle, *On Interpretation*, 19b–20b, pp. 30–2. See also Kay, *Courtly Contradictions*, pp. 13–15.

46. On the rehabilitation of the notion of changing in twelfth-century philosophy and literature, see Denyse Delcourt, *L'éthique du changement dans le roman français du XIIe siècle* (Geneva: Droz, 1990).

47. Twice the text insists on his absence: when Lunete needs a champion (ll. 3694–713), and when Gauvain's nephews and niece are threatened by a giant (ll. 3912–35). Gauvain has a good excuse: he is busy rescuing queen Guinevere, but still . . .

48. "O my friends, there is no friend" is an apostrophe attributed to Aristotle, and quoted by many authors through the centuries. Derrida quotes it in the French of Montaigne: "O mes amis, il n'y a nul amy" (*Politiques de l'amitié*, p. 12) and uses it as a paradoxical thread linking all his chapters. He also shows (convincingly) that the original text of Diogenes Laertius has most probably been mistranslated (*Politics*, pp. 208–14; *Politiques*, pp. 235–42).

CONCLUSION

1. Arthur Conan Doyle, "The Adventure of the Empty House," in *The Original Illustrated Sherlock Holmes* (New York: Castle Books, 1991), pp. 449–62 (p. 452).

2. Arthur Conan Doyle, "The Adventure of the Final Problem," ibid., pp. 327–39 (p. 339).

Bibliography

ANCIENT AND MEDIEVAL WORKS

Abelard. [Petrus Abaelardus]. *Dialectica*, ed. L. M. de Rijk (Assen: Van Gorcum, 1970).

"Glosses on Porphyry" [*Glossae super Porphyrium*], in *Five Texts on the Mediaeval Problem of Universals: Porphyry, Boethius, Abelard, Duns Scotus, Ockham*, ed. and trans. Paul Vincent Spade (Indianapolis, Ind.: Hackett, 1994).

Peter Abaelards philosophische Schriften: I. Die Logica "Ingredientibus": 1. Die Glossen zu Porphyrius, ed. Bernhard Geyer, *Beiträge zur Geschichte der Philosophie des Mittelalters*, 21 (Münster: Aschendorffschen Verlagsbuchhandlung, 1919).

Des Intellections, ed. and trans. Patrick Morin (Paris: Vrin, 1994).

Letters IX–XIV: An Edition with an Introduction, ed. Edmé Renno Smits (Groningen: Rijksuniversiteit te Groningen, 1983).

The Letters of Abelard and Heloise, trans. Betty Radice, rev. M. T. Clanchy (London: Penguin, 2003).

Letters of Peter Abelard, Beyond the Personal, trans. Jan Ziolkowski (Washington, DC: The Catholic University Press, 2008).

Theologia summi boni: Tractatus de unitate et trinitate divina, ed. and [German] trans. Ursula Niggli (Hamburg: Felix Meiner, 1989).

De l'unité et de la trinité divines (Theologia summi boni), trans. Jean Jolivet (Paris: Vrin, 2001).

The Aberdeen Bestiary. University of Aberdeen online resource: www.abdn.ac.uk/bestiary.

Ademar de Chabannes. "*Homo et Leo*" [The Man and the Lion], in Léopold Hervieux, *Les Fabulistes latins depuis le siècle d'Auguste jusqu'à la fin du moyen âge*, 5 vols., 2nd edn. (Paris: Firmin-Didot, 1893), vol. 2, pp. 150–1.

Aelred de Rievaulx. *De spiritali amicitia, L'amitié spirituelle*, ed. J. Dubois (Paris: Éditions Charles Bayet, 1948).

Aelred of Rievaulx: Spiritual Friendship, trans. Mark Williams (Cranbury, NJ: Associated University Presses, 1994).

Aeschylus. *Agamemnon*, trans. Alan H. Sommerstein, Loeb Classical Library 146 (Cambridge, Mass.: Harvard University Press, 2008).

Æsop's Fables, ed. and trans. Laura Gibbs (Oxford: Oxford University Press, 2002).

Anacreon. *Lyra graeca*, ed. J. M. Edmonds, 3 vols. (Cambridge, Mass.: Harvard University Press, 1922–8).

Anselm of Canterbury. *Opera Omnia*, ed. F. S. Schmitt, 6 vols. (Edinburgh: Thomas Nelson & Sons, Ltd., 1940–61). Online version, in InteLex Past Masters series (Charlottesville, Va.: InteLex, 2006).

   The Major Works of Anselm of Canterbury, ed. Brian Davies and G. R. Evans (Oxford: Oxford University Press, 1998). Online version, in InteLex Past Masters series (Charlottesville, Va.: InteLex, 2006).

   Cur Deus homo, in *Opera Omnia*, vol. 2, pp. 39–133; in *Major Works*, pp. 260–356.

   De grammatico, in *Opera Omnia*, vol. 1, pp. 145–168; in *Major Works*, pp. 123–50.

   De incarnatione Verbi, in *Opera Omnia*, vol. 2, pp. 3–36; in *Major Works*, pp. 233–60.

   Monologion, in *Opera Omnia*, vol. 1, pp. 1–87; in *Major Works*, pp. 5–81.

   Proslogion, in *Opera Omnia*, vol. 1, pp. 93–141; in *Major Works*, pp. 82–122.

   L'Œuvre d'Anselme de Cantorbéry, ed. Michel Corbin, 7 vols. (Paris: Éditions du Cerf, 1986).

   Proslogion. Suivi de sa réfutation par Gaunilon et de la réponse d'Anselme, trans. Bernard Pautrat (Paris: Flammarion, 1993).

Aristotle. *The Basic Works of Aristotle*, ed. Richard McKeon (New York: Random House, 1941).

   The Complete Works of Aristotle: The Revised Oxford Translation, ed. Jonathan Barnes, Bollingen Series, 71.2, 2 vols. (Princeton, NJ: Princeton University Press, 1984).

   Categories, in *The Complete Works of Aristotle*, vol. 1, pp. 3–24.

   Eudemian Ethics, in *The Complete Works of Aristotle*, vol. 2, pp. 1922–81.

   The History of Animals, in *The Complete Works of Aristotle*, vol. 1, pp. 774–994.

   On Interpretation, in *The Complete Works of Aristotle*, vol. 1, pp. 25–38.

   On Melissus, Xenophanes, and Gorgias, in *The Complete Works of Aristotle*, vol. 2, pp. 1539–51.

   Metaphysics, in *The Complete Works of Aristotle*, vol. 2, pp. 1552–728.

   Nicomachean Ethics, in *The Complete Works of Aristotle*, vol. 2, pp. 1729–867.

   Physics, in *The Complete Works of Aristotle*, vol. 1, pp. 315–446.

   Poetics, in *The Complete Works of Aristotle*, vol. 2, pp. 2316–40.

   Sophistical Refutations, in *The Complete Works of Aristotle*, vol. 1, pp. 278–314.

   On the Soul, in *The Complete Works of Aristotle*, vol. 1, pp. 641–92.

   Aristotle's Metaphysics, ed. W. D. Ross, 2 vols. (Oxford: Clarendon Press, 1953).

   Metaphysics, trans. Hugh Tredennick, 2 vols. (Cambridge, Mass.: Harvard University Press, 1933).

   Métaphysique, trans. J. Tricot, 2 vols. (Paris: Vrin, 1933).

   The Physics, trans. P. H. Wicksteed and F. M. Cornford, 2 vols. (Cambridge, Mass.: Harvard University Press, 1929).

Augustine. *Confessions: Introduction and Text*, ed. James J. O'Donnell, 3 vols. (Oxford: Clarendon Press, 1992).

   Confessions, trans. Henry Chadwick (Oxford: Oxford University Press, 1991).

De magistro, in Emmanuel Bermon, *La Signification et l'enseignement: texte latin, traduction française et commentaire du* De magistro *de Saint Augustin* (Paris: Vrin, 2007).

Bernard de Clairvaux. *Éloge de la nouvelle chevalerie*, in *Œuvres complètes*, ed. Pierre-Yves Emery, vol. 31 (Paris: Le Cerf, 1990).

Biblia sacra juxta vulgatam versionem (Stuttgart: Deutsche Bibelgesellschaft, 1983).

Boethius, *De topicis differentiis*, trans. Eleonore Stump (Ithaca, NY: Cornell University Press, 1978).

Le Charroi de Nîmes, ed. and trans. Claude Lachet (Paris: Gallimard, 1999).

Chrétien de Troyes. *Le Chevalier au lion (ou le Roman d'Yvain)*, ed. and trans. David F. Hult (Paris: Livre de Poche, 1994).

Cligès, ed. and trans. Charles Méla and Olivier Collet (Paris: Livre de Poche, 1994).

Cicero. *Epistulae ad Atticum*. Latin text from the online full-text database: Library of Texts, Series A (Brepols Publishers, 2013).

De senectute, De amicitia, De divinatione, trans. W. A. Falconer, Loeb Classical Library (Cambridge, Mass.: Harvard University Press, 1923).

Ctesias of Cnidus. *Ctesias: On India and Fragments of his Minor Works*, trans. Andrew Nichols (London: Bristol Classical Press, 2011).

[Ctésias de Cnide]. *La Perse, l'Inde, autres fragments*, ed. and trans. Dominique Lenfant (Paris: Les Belles Lettres, 2004).

Demosthenes. *Against Medias, Androtion, Aristocrates, Timocrates, Aristogeiton*, trans. J. H. Vince, Loeb Classical Library (Cambridge, Mass.: Harvard University Press, 1935).

Diogenes Laertius. *Lives of Eminent Philosophers*, trans. R. D. Hicks, Loeb Classical Library, 2 vols. (Cambridge, Mass.: Harvard University Press, 1972).

Epistola Johannis ad Anselmum, Epistola Anselmi ad Falconem, Epistola Roscelini ad Petrum Abelardum, in François Picavet, *Roscelin, philosophe et théologien, d'après la légende et d'après l'histoire* (Paris: Imprimerie Nationale, 1911).

Garlandus Compotista. *Dialectica*, ed. L. M. de Rijk (Assen: van Gorcum, 1959).

Guilhem de Peitieu. "Farai un vers de dreyt nien," in *Troubadour Lyrics: A Bilingual Anthology*, ed. and trans. Frede Jensen (New York: Peter Lang, 1998), p. 66.

Guillaume de Lorris and Jean de Meun. *Le Roman de la Rose*, ed. and trans. Armand Strubel (Paris: Livre de Poche, 1992).

The Romance of the Rose, ed. and trans. Charles Dahlberg (Princeton, NJ: Princeton University Press, 1971).

Le Roman de la Rose, ed. Ernest Langlois, Société des anciens textes français, 5 vols. (Paris: Champion, 1921).

Guillaume de Saint-Amour. [William of Saint-Amour]. *De periculis novissimorum temporum*, ed. G. Geltner, Dallas Medieval Texts and Translations 8 (Leuven: Peeters, 2008).

Heraclitus of Ephesus. Fragments 40, 129, and 42, ed. and trans. Richard McKirahan, in *Philosophy Before Socrates: An Introduction with Texts and Commentary* (Indianapolis, Ind.: Hackett, 1994), pp. 117–18.

Herodotus. *The Histories*, trans. Aubrey de Sélincourt (1954), rev. by John Marincola (1972) (London: Penguin, 2003).

Holy Bible, Douay-Rheims Version (Rockford, Ill.: TAN Books, 1989).

Isocrates. *Antidosis,* in *Works,* trans. George Norlin and Laure van Hook, Loeb Classical Library, 3 vols. (New York: Putnam, 1928), vol. 2, pp. 181–365.

Jaufré Rudel. "Non sap chanter qui so non di," in *The Songs of Jaufré Rudel,* ed. and trans. Rupert Pickens (Toronto: Pontifical Institute of Mediaeval Studies, 1978), p. 100.

John the Scot. [Johannes Scotus Erigena]. (*De divisione naturae* 4.5) *Periphyseon: On the Division of Nature,* trans. Myra L. Uhlfelder (Indianapolis, Ind.: Bobbs-Merrill, 1976).

King James Bible. The New Cambridge Paragraph Bible with the Apocrypha, King James Version, ed. David Norton (Cambridge: Cambridge University Press, 2005).

Le Livre des psaumes: Ancienne traduction française, ed. Francisque Michel (Paris: Imprimerie Nationale, 1876).

Marie de France. *Fables,* ed. and trans. Harriet Spiegel (Toronto: University of Toronto Press, 1994).

    Lais, ed. Laurence Harf-Lancner (Paris: Livre de Poche, 1990).

    The Lais of Marie de France, ed. and trans. Glyn Burgess and Keith Busby (Harmondsworth: Penguin, 1999).

The New English Translation of the Septuagint, ed. Albert Pietersma and Benjamin Wright, trans. Moises Silva (Oxford: Oxford University Press, 2009). Online: http://ccat.sas.upenn.edu/nets/.

Nigel de Longchamp. [or Nigel Wireker]. *A Mirror for Fools: The Book of Burnel the Ass,* trans. J. H. Mozley (Notre Dame, Ind.: University of Notre Dame Press, 1963).

Physiologus: The Greek and the Armenian Versions, with a Study of Translation Technique, ed. and trans. Gohar Muradyan (Leuven and Paris: Peeters, 2005).

Physiologus: A Medieval Book of Nature Lore, trans. Michael J. Curley (Chicago: University of Chicago Press, 2009).

Physiologus, Library of Latin Texts, Series A (Turnhout: Brepols, 2002–).

Plato. *Plato's Complete Works,* ed. John M. Cooper (Indianapolis, Ind.: Hackett, 1997).

    Lysis, in *Plato's Complete Works,* pp. 688–707.

    Parmenides, in *Plato's Complete Works,* pp. 359–97.

    Phaedrus, in *Plato's Complete Works,* pp. 506–56.

    Sophist, in *Plato's Complete Works,* pp. 235–93.

    Statesman, in *Plato's Complete Works,* pp. 294–358.

    Symposium, in *Plato's Complete Works,* pp. 457–505.

    Theaetetus, in *Plato's Complete Works,* pp. 157–236.

    [Platon]. *Parménide,* ed. Auguste Diès (Paris: Les Belles Lettres, 1965).

Pliny the Elder. [Pline l'Ancien]. *Histoire naturelle,* ed. and trans. A. Ernout (Paris: Les Belles Lettres, 1947 (book XI); 1952 (book VIII)).

Porphyry. *Introduction,* trans. Jonathan Barnes (Oxford: Clarendon Press, 2003).

    [Porphyre]. *Isagoge,* ed. and trans. Alain de Libera and Alain-Philippe Segonds (Paris: Vrin, 1998).

Rashi. *Rashi's Commentary on Psalms 1–89 (Books I–III)*, trans. Mayer I. Gruber (Atlanta Ga.: Scholars Press, 1998).

The Revised English Bible (Cambridge: Cambridge University Press, 1989).

Le Roman d'Eneas, ed. and trans. Aimé Petit (Paris: Livre de Poche, 1997).

Le Roman de Renart, ed. Jean Dufournet (Paris: Garnier-Flammarion, 1970).

Le Roman de Renart, ed. Naoyuki Fukumoto, Noboru Harano, and Satoru Suzuki (Paris: Livre de Poche, 2005).

Le Roman de Renart, ed. Armand Strubel, et al. (Paris: Gallimard, 1998).

Roman de la Rose Digital Library, realized by the Sheridan Library at The Johns Hopkins University and the Bibliothèque nationale de France. http://roman delarose.org.

The Septuagint with Apocrypha: Greek and English, trans. Sir Lancelot C. L. Brenton (London: Samuel Bagster & Sons, Ltd., 1851; repr. Peabody, Mass.: Hendrickson Publishers, 1986).

Sophocles. *Oedipus at Colonus*, trans. Hugh Lloyd-Jones, Loeb Classical Library 21 (Cambridge, Mass.: Harvard University Press, 1994).

Tanakh: A New Translation of the Holy Scriptures According to the Traditional Hebrew Text (Philadelphia, Pa.: The Jewish Publication Society, 1985).

Tertullian [Tertullien]. *Contre Marcion*, Book III, ed. and trans. René Braun, Sources Chrétiennes 399 (Paris: Éditions du Cerf, 1994).

Theodoret of Cyrus. *Commentary on the Psalms*, trans. Robert C. Hill, The Fathers of the Church, vols. 101–2 (Washington, DC: The Catholic University of America Press, 2000–1).

Thibaut de Champagne. "Chançon ferai car talent m'en est pris," in S. N. Rosenberg, H. Tischler, and M.-G. Grossel (eds.), *Chansons des trouvères* (Paris: Librairie générale française, 1995), p. 59.

Tyndale, William. *Tyndale's Old Testament*, ed. David Daniell (New Haven, Conn.: Yale University Press, 1992).

MODERN WORKS

Ackrill, J. L. *Aristotle the Philosopher* (Oxford: Oxford University Press, 1981).

Agamben, Giorgio. *Infancy and History: On the Destruction of Experience*, trans. Liz Heron (London: Verso, 2007).

Allen, Renée. "The Role of Women and their Homosocial Context in the *Chevalier au Lion*," *Romance Quarterly* 46 (1999): 141–54.

Armstrong, Adrian and Sarah Kay. *Knowing Poetry: Verse in Medieval France from the Rose to the Rhétoriqueurs* (Ithaca, NY: Cornell University Press, 2011).

Armstrong, Grace M. "Questions of Inheritance: *Le Chevalier au lion* and *La Queste del Saint Graal*," *Yale French Studies* 95 (1999): 171–92.

Aubenque, Pierre. *Le Problème de l'être chez Aristote* (Paris: Presses universitaires de France, 1972).

Auerbach, Erich. *Figura*, trans. Diane Meur (Paris: Macula, 2003).

Azzouni, Jody. *Talking about Nothing: Numbers, Hallucinations, and Fictions* (Oxford: Oxford University Press, 2010).

Barnes, Jonathan. *Aristotle: A Very Short Introduction* (Oxford: Oxford University Press, 2000).

(ed.) *The Cambridge Companion to Aristotle* (Cambridge: Cambridge University Press, 1995).

Truth, etc. Six Lectures on Ancient Logic (Oxford: Clarendon Press, 2007).

Barth, Karl. *Anselm: Fides Quaerens Intellectum: Anselm's Proof of the Existence of God in the Context of his Theological Scheme*, trans. I. W. Robertson (London: SCM Press, 1960).

Bartolomei, Maria Cristina. "Problemi concernenti l'opposizione e la contraddizione in Aristotele," *Verifiche* 10 (1981): 163–93.

Batany, Jean. *Scène et coulisses du* Roman de Renart (Paris: Société d'édition d'enseignement supérieur, 1989).

Baumgartner, Emmanuèle. "The Play of Temporalities; or, The Reported Dream of Guillaume de Lorris," in Kevin Brownlee and Sylvia Huot (eds.), *Rethinking the Romance of the Rose* (Philadelphia: University of Pennsylvania Press, 1992), pp. 21–38.

Baxter, Ron. *Bestiaries and their Users in the Middle Ages* (London: Sutton, 1998).

Bencivenga, Ermanno. *Logic and Other Nonsense: The Case of Anselm and his God* (Princeton, NJ: Princeton University Press, 1993).

Benson, Robert L., Giles Constable, and Carol D. Lanham (eds.), *Renaissance and Renewal in the Twelfth Century* (Cambridge, Mass.: Harvard University Press, 1991).

Benveniste, Émile. *Problèmes de linguistique générale*, vol. 1 (Paris: Gallimard, 1966).

Berti, Enrico. "A partire dalla logica aristotelica della non-contraddizione: Confronto con i paradigmi delle scienze clinico-psicologiche," in Maria Giordano (ed.), *Episteme e inconscio* (Lecce: Milella, 1990), pp. 3–23.

Studi Aristotelici (L'Aquila: L. U. Japadre, 1975).

Blanché, Robert and Jacques Dubucs. *La Logique et son histoire* (Paris: Armand Colin, 2002).

Bleuler, Eugen. "Vortrag über Ambivalenz," *Zentralblatt für Psychoanalyse* 1 (1910): 266.

Dementia praecox oder Gruppe der Schizophrenien (1911) (Tübingen: Edition Diskord, 1988).

Bloch, Howard. *The Anonymous Marie de France* (Chicago: University of Chicago Press, 2003).

Bochenski, I. M. *Ancient Formal Logic* (Amsterdam: North-Holland Publishing Company, 1957).

Bogdan, Radu J. *Predicative Minds: The Social Ontogeny of Propositional Thinking* (Cambridge, Mass.: MIT Press, 2009).

Boquet, Damien. *L'ordre de l'affect au moyen âge: Autour de l'anthropologie affective d'Aelred de Rievaulx* (Caen: Publications du centre de recherches archéologiques et historiques médiévales, 2005).

Boswell, John. *Christianity, Social Tolerance, and Homosexuality: Gay People in Western Europe from the Beginning of the Christian Era to the Fourteenth Century* (Chicago: University of Chicago Press, 1980).

Boureau, Alain. *L'Empire du livre: Pour une histoire du savoir scholastique (1200–1380)* (Paris: Les Belles Lettres, 2007).

Brandenburg, Hugo. "Einhorn," in *Reallexikon fur Antike und Christendum* 4 (1959), cols. 840–62.

Bray, Alan. *The Friend* (Chicago: University of Chicago Press, 2003).

Brecher, Robert. *Anselm's Argument: The Logic of Divine Existence* (Aldershot: Gower, 1985).

Brower, Jeffrey E. "Trinity," in Jeffrey E. Brower and Kevin Guilfoy (eds.), *The Cambridge Companion to Abelard* (Cambridge: Cambridge University Press, 2004), pp. 223–57.

Brower, Jeffrey E. and Kevin Guilfoy (eds.) *The Cambridge Companion to Abelard* (Cambridge: Cambridge University Press, 2004).

Brown, Catherine. *Contrary Things: Exegesis, Dialectic, and the Poetics of Didacticism* (Stanford, Calif.: Stanford University Press, 1998).

Brown, Dennis. *Vir Trilinguis: A Study in the Biblical Exegesis of Saint Jerome* (Kampen: Kok Pharos, 1992).

Brownlee, Kevin and Sylvia Huot (eds.) *Rethinking the Romance of the Rose: Text, Image, Reception* (Philadelphia: University of Pennsylvania Press, 1992).

Bruckner, Matilda Tomaryn. *Chrétien Continued: A Study of the Conte du Graal and its Verse Continuations* (Oxford: Oxford University Press, 2009).

"Mathematical Bodies and Fuzzy Logic in the Couplings of Troubadour Lyric," *Tenso* 14.1 (1999): 1–22.

Shaping Romance: Interpretation, Truth, and Closure in Twelfth-Century French Fictions (Philadelphia: University of Pennsylvania Press, 1993).

Burgwinkle, William. "Introduction," in *Razos and Troubadour Songs*, trans. W. Burgwinkle (New York: Garland, 1990), pp. i–lxi.

Burnet, John. *Early Greek Philosophy* (London: Adam and Charles Black, 1930 [1892]).

Cambridge Dictionary of Philosophy, ed. Robert Audi, 2nd edn. (Cambridge: Cambridge University Press, 1999).

Carnap, Rudolf. *Meaning and Necessity: A Study in Semantics and Modal Logic*, 2nd edn. (Chicago: University of Chicago Press, 1956).

Philosophy and Logical Syntax (London: Kegan Paul, 1934).

Carroll, Lewis. *Through the Looking Glass,* in *The Complete Works of Lewis Carroll* (New York: The Modern Library, 1936).

Carruthers, Mary. *The Book of Memory* (Cambridge: Cambridge University Press, 1990).

The Craft of Thought: Meditation, Rhetoric, and the Making of Images, 400–1200 (Cambridge: Cambridge University Press, 1998).

Cassin, Barbara. *Aristote et le logos: Contes de la phénoménologie ordinaire* (Paris: Presses universitaires de France, 1997).

"Aristotle with and against Kant," in Christina Howells (ed.), *French Women Philosophers: A Contemporary Reader* (London: Routledge, 2004), pp. 100–21.

Cherniss, Harold. *Aristotle's Criticism of Presocratic Philosophy* (New York: Octagon Books, 1971 [1935]).

Chierchia, Gennaro and Sally McConnell-Ginet. *Meaning and Grammar: An Introduction to Semantics*, 2nd edn. (Cambridge, Mass.: MIT Press, 2000).

Chroust, Anton-Hermann. "Introduction," in Aristotle, *Protrepticus: A Reconstruction* (Notre Dame, Ind.: University of Notre Dame Press, 1964).

Citroni Marchetti, Sandra. *Amicizia e potere: nelle lettere di Cicerone e nelle elegie ovidiane dall'esilio* (Florence: Università degli Studi di Firenze, 2000).

Clanchy, M. T. *Abelard: A Medieval Life* (Oxford: Blackwell, 1997).

"Abelard's Mockery," *Journal of Ecclesiastical History* 41 (1990): 1–23.

Clark, Willene B. *A Medieval Book of Beasts: The Second-Family Bestiary: Commentary, Art, Text and Translation* (Woodbridge: Boydell, 2006).

Colish, Marcia. *Medieval Foundations of the Western Intellectual Tradition 400–1400* (New Haven, Conn.: Yale University Press, 1997).

Contessa, Gabriele. "Who is Afraid of Imaginary Objects?," in Nicholas Griffin and Dale Jacquette (eds.), *Russell vs. Meinong: The Legacy of "On Denoting"* (London: Routledge, 2009), pp. 248–65.

Cooper, John M. "Introduction," in Plato, *Complete Works* (Indianapolis, Ind.: Hackett, 1997), pp. xii–xviii.

Copleston, Frederick Charles. *A History of Philosophy*, vol. 2. *Medieval Philosophy, Augustine to Scotus* (New York: Doubleday, 1950).

Dahlberg, Charles. "First Person and Personification in the *Roman de la Rose*: Amant and Danger," *Mediaevalia* 3 (1977): 37–58.

Dancy, R. M. *Sense and Contradiction: A Study in Aristotle* (Boston, Mass.: D. Reidel, 1975).

Danto, Arthur. *The Philosophical Disenfranchisement of Art* (New York: Columbia University Press, 2005).

Davies, Brian. "Anselm and the Ontological Argument," in Brian Davies and Brian Leftow (eds.), *The Cambridge Companion to Anselm of Canterbury* (Cambridge: Cambridge University Press, 2004), pp. 157–78.

Davies, Brian and Brian Leftow (eds.) *The Cambridge Companion to Anselm of Canterbury* (Cambridge: Cambridge University Press, 2004).

Delcourt, Denyse. *L'éthique du changement dans le roman français du XIIe siècle* (Geneva: Droz, 1990).

Deman, Thomas. *Le Témoignage d'Aristote sur Socrate* (Paris: Les Belles Lettres, 1942).

Derrida, Jacques. "The Politics of Friendship," *Journal of Philosophy* 75.11 (1988): 632–45.

"Politics of Friendship," in *American Imago* 50.3 (1993): 353–91.

The Politics of Friendship, trans. G. Collins (New York: Verso, 2005).

Politiques de l'amitié (Paris: Galilée, 1994).

Descombes, Vincent. *L'inconscient malgré lui* (Paris: Gallimard, 2004).

Le Raisonnement de l'ours et autres essais de philosophie pratique (Paris: Seuil, 2007).

Detienne, Marcel and Jean-Pierre Vernant. *Les Ruses de l'intelligence: la mêtis des Grecs* (Paris: Flammarion, 1974).

Dod, Bernard. "Aristoteles Latinus," in N. Kretzmann, A. Kenny, and J. Pinborg (eds.), *The Cambridge History of Late Medieval Philosophy*, pp. 45–79.

Dodds, E. R. *The Greeks and the Irrational* (Berkeley: University of California Press, 1951).

Donnellan, Keith. "Speaking of Nothing," *The Philosophical Review* 83.1 (1974): 2–31.

Dorival, Guy, Marguerite Harl, and Olivier Munnich. *La Bible grecque des Septante du judaïsme hellénistique au christianisme ancien* (Paris: Cerf/ Centre national de la recherche scientifique, 1988).

Doyle, Arthur Conan. *The Original Illustrated Sherlock Holmes*, reproduced from the original publication in *The Strand Magazine* (New York: Castle Books, 1991).

Ducrot, Oswald. *La Preuve et le dire* (Paris: Mame, 1974).

Dufeil, Michel-Marie. *Guillaume de Saint-Amour et la polémique universitaire parisienne 1250–1259* (Paris: Picard, 1972).

Dumont, Jean-Paul. "Préface," in *Les Présocratiques*, ed. J.-P. Dumont, D. Delattre, and J.-L. Poirier (Paris: Gallimard, Pléiade, 1988), pp. ix–xxv.

Düring, Ingemar. *Aristotle's Protrepticus: An Attempt at Reconstruction* (Göteborg: Acta Universatis Gothoburgensis, 1961).

Eco, Umberto. *The Name of the Rose*, trans. William Weaver (San Diego, Calif.: Harcourt Brace Jovanovich, 1983).

Einhorn, Jürgen W. *Spiritalis Unicornis: Das Einhorn als Bedeutungsträger in Literatur und Kunst des Mittelalters* (Munich: Fink, 1976).

Engels, L. "Abélard écrivain," in E. M. Buytaert (ed.), *Peter Abelard: Proceedings of the International Conference, Louvain, May 10–12, 1971* (Leuven and The Hague: Leuven University Press/Martinus Nijhoff, 1974), pp. 12–37.

Estin, Colette. *Les Psautiers de Jérôme à la lumière des traductions juives antérieures*, Collectanea Biblica Latina 15 (Rome: San Girolamo, 1984).

Evans, Gillian Rosemary. *Anselm* (Wilton: Morehouse, 1989).

"Anselm's Life, Works, and Immediate Influence," in Brian Davies and Brian Leftow (eds.), *The Cambridge Companion to Anselm of Canterbury* (Cambridge: Cambridge University Press, 2004), pp. 5–31.

Everett, Anthony and Thomas Hofweber (eds.) *Empty Names, Fictions, and the Puzzles of Non-Existence* (Stanford, Calif.: SCLI Publications, 2000).

Faderman, Avrom. "On Myth," in Anthony Everett and Thomas Hofweber (eds.), *Empty Names, Fictions, and the Puzzles of Non-Existence* (Stanford, Calif.: SCLI Publications, 2000), pp. 61–6.

Fleming, John V. "Jean de Meun and the Ancient Poets," in Kevin Brownlee and Sylvia Huot (eds.), *Rethinking the Romance of the Rose: Text, Image, Reception* (Philadelphia: University of Pennsylvania Press, 1992), pp. 81–97.

Reason and the Lover (Princeton, NJ: Princeton University Press, 1984).

Foulet, Alfred and Karl D. Uitti. "The Prologue to the *Lais* of Marie de France: A Reconsideration," *Romance Philology* 35 (1981): 242–9

Fraisse, Jean-Claude. *Philia: La notion d'amitié dans la philosophie antique: Essai sur un problème perdu et retrouvé* (Paris: Vrin, 1974).

Frantzen, Allen J. *Bloody Good: Chivalry, Sacrifice, and the Great War* (Chicago: University of Chicago Press, 2004).

Frappier, Jean. *Étude sur Yvain, ou Le chevalier au lion de Chrétien de Troyes* (Paris: Société d'édition d'enseignement supérieur, 1969).

Frege, Gottlob. "On *Sinn* and *Bedeutung*," in *The Frege Reader*, ed. Michael Beaney (Oxford: Blackwell, 1997), pp. 151–71.

Freud, Sigmund. *The Standard Edition of the Complete Psychological Works of Sigmund Freud*, ed. James Strachey, 24 vols. (London: Hogarth Press, 1957–74).

The Goethe Prize, in *The Standard Edition of the Complete Psychological Works of Sigmund Freud*, vol. 21, pp. 206–14.

Moses and Monotheism, in *The Standard Edition of the Complete Psychological Works of Sigmund Freud*, vol. 23, pp. 3–137.

New Introductory Lectures on Psychoanalysis, in *The Standard Edition of the Complete Psychological Works of Sigmund Freud*, vol. 22, pp. 3–182.

An Outline of Psychoanalysis, in *The Standard Edition of the Complete Psychological Works of Sigmund Freud*, vol. 23, pp. 141–207.

Fukumoto, Naoyuki, Noboru Harano, and Satoru Suzuki. "Les Manuscrits du *Roman de Renart*," in *Le Roman de Renart* (Paris: Livre de Poche, 2005), pp. 48–59.

Fumagalli Beonio Brocchieri, Mariateresa. *The Logic of Abelard*, trans. Simon Pleasance (New York: Humanities Press, 1970).

Geltner, G. "Introduction," in William of Saint-Amour, *De periculis novissimorum temporum*, Dallas Medieval Texts and Translations 8 (Leuven: Peeters, 2008), pp. 1–27.

George, Wilma and Brunsdon Yapp. *The Naming of the Beasts: Natural History in the Medieval Bestiary* (London: Duckworth, 1991).

Gernet, Louis. "Les Origines de la philosophie," in *Anthropologie de la Grèce antique* (Paris: Maspéro, 1968), pp. 414–30.

Gilson, Étienne. *La Philosophie au moyen âge*, 2 vols. (Paris: Payot, 1976).

Girard, René. "Love and Hate in Yvain," in Brigitte Cazelles and Charles Méla (eds.), *Modernité au moyen âge: Le défi du passé* (Geneva: Droz, 1990), pp. 249–62.

Goodman, Nelson. "About," *Mind* 70 (January 1961): 1–24.

Fact, Fiction, and Forecast, 4th edn. (Cambridge, Mass.: Harvard University Press, 1983 [1954]).

Gotfredsen, Lise. *The Unicorn*, trans. Anne Born (London: Harvill Press, 1999).

Gravestock, Pamela. "Did Imaginary Animals Exist?," in Debra Hassig (ed.), *The Mark of the Beast: The Medieval Bestiary in Art, Life, and Literature* (New York: Garland, 1999), pp. 119–35.

Greene, Virginie. "Imagination," in Zrinka Stahuljak, et al., *Thinking Through Chrétien de Troyes* (Cambridge: D. S. Brewer, 2011), pp. 41–74.

"Nothingness and Otherness in *L'Être et le Néant* or 'Pierre, Paul, Anny et les autres,'" *Journal of Romance Studies* 6.1–2 (2006): 143–53.

Gregory, T. "Abélard et Platon," in E. M. Buytaert (ed.), *Peter Abelard: Proceedings of the International Conference, Louvain, May 10–12, 1971* (Louvain: Leuven University Press, 1974), pp. 38–64.

Grice, Paul. *Studies in the Way of Words* (Cambridge, Mass.: Harvard University Press, 1989).

Guilfoy, Kevin. "Mind and Cognition," in Jeffrey E. Brower and Kevin Guilfoy (eds.), *The Cambridge Companion to Abelard* (Cambridge: Cambridge University Press, 2004), pp. 200–22.

Guthrie, W. K. C. "Aristotle as a Historian of Philosophy: Some Preliminaries," *Journal of Hellenic Studies* 77.1 (1957): 35–41.

Hadot, Pierre. *Éloge de la philosophie antique* (Paris: Allia, 2003).

Éloge de Socrate (Paris: Allia, 2002).

Philosophy as a Way of Life: Spiritual Exercises from Socrates to Foucault, ed. Arnold Davidson, trans. Michael Chase (Oxford: Blackwell, 1995).

Qu'est-ce que la philosophie antique? (Paris: Gallimard, 1995).

Hamblin, C. L. *Fallacies* (London: Methuen, 1970).

Haren, Michael. *Medieval Thought: The Western Intellectual Tradition from Antiquity to the Thirteenth Century*, 2nd edn. (Toronto: University of Toronto Press, 1992).

Haskins, Charles Homer. *The Renaissance of the Twelfth Century* (Cambridge, Mass.: Harvard University Press, 1927).

Hassig, Debra. *Medieval Bestiaries: Text, Image, Ideology* (Cambridge: Cambridge University Press, 1995).

(ed.), *The Mark of the Beast: The Medieval Bestiary in Art, Life, and Literature* (New York: Garland, 1999).

Hathaway, Nancy. *The Unicorn* (New York: Tess Press, 2005 [1980]).

Heidegger, Martin. *What is Philosophy?*, trans. William Kluback and Jean T. Wilde (Plymouth: Vision Press, 1963).

Heller-Roazen, Daniel. *Fortune's Faces: The* Roman de la Rose *and the Poetics of Contingency* (Baltimore, Md.: The Johns Hopkins University Press, 2003).

The Inner Touch: Archaeology of a Sensation (New York: Zone Books, 2007).

Henderson, Arnold Clayton. "Medieval Beasts and Modern Cages: The Making of Meaning in Fables and Bestiaries," *PMLA* 97.1 (January 1982): 40–9.

Hicks, Eric. "La Mise en roman des formes allégoriques: hypostase et récit chez Guillaume de Lorris," in Jean Dufournet (ed.), *Études sur le* Roman de la Rose *de Guillaume de Lorris* (Paris: Champion, 1984), pp. 53–81.

Horn, Laurence R. *A Natural History of Negation* (Stanford, Calif.: Center for the Study of Language and Information, Stanford University, 2001 [1989]).

Hult, David. *Self-Fulfilling Prophecies: Readership and Authority in the First* Roman de la Rose (Cambridge: Cambridge University Press, 1986).

Hunt, Tony. "Aristotle, Dialectic, and Courtly Literature," *Viator* 10 (1979): 95–129.

"The Dialectic of Yvain," *Modern Language Review* 72 (1977): 285–99.

"Glossing Marie de France," *Romanische Forschungen* 86 (1974): 396–418.

Husserl, Edmund. *Collected Works*, vol. 2, *General Introduction to a Pure Phenomenology*, trans. F. Kersten (The Hague: Martinus Nijhoff, 1982).

Hyatte, Reginald. *The Arts of Friendship: The Idealization of Friendship in Medieval and Early Renaissance Literature* (New York: Brill, 1994).

Iwakuma, Yukio. "Pierre Abélard et Guillaume de Champeaux dans les premières années du XIIe siècle: une étude préliminaire," in Joël Biard (ed.), *Langage, sciences, philosophie au XIIe siècle* (Paris: Vrin, 1996), pp. 93–123.

"*Vocales*, or Early Nominalists," *Traditio* 47 (1992): 37–111.

Jacquette, Dale. *Meinongian Logic: The Semantics of Existence and Nonexistence* (New York: Walter de Gruyter, 1996).

Jaeger, Stephen. *The Envy of Angels: Cathedral Schools and Social Ideals in Medieval Europe, 950–1200* (Philadelphia: University of Pennsylvania Press, 1994).

Jaeger, Werner. *Aristotle: Fundamentals of the History of his Development*, trans. R. Robinson (Oxford: Clarendon Press, 1934).

James-Raoul, Danièle. *Chrétien de Troyes: La griffe d'un style* (Paris: Champion, 2007).

Johnson, Harold J. "Three Ancient Meanings of Matter: Democritus, Plato, and Aristotle," *Journal of the History of Ideas* 28 (1967): 3–16.

Jolivet, Jean. "Trois variations médiévales sur l'universel et l'individu: Roscelin, Abélard et Gilbert de la Porrée," *Revue de métaphysique et de morale*, 97.1 (January–March 1992): 111–15.

Arts du langage et théologie chez Abélard, 2nd edn. (Paris: Vrin, 1982).

"Doctrines et figures de philosophes chez Abélard," in Rudolf Thomas, Jean Jolivet, D. E. Luscombe, and L. M. de Rijk (eds.), *Petrus Abaelardus, 1079–1142: Person, Werk und Wirkung*, Trierer Theologische Studien 38 (Trèves: Paulinus, 1980), pp. 103–20.

"Non-Réalisme et platonisme chez Abélard: essai d'interprétation," in *Abélard en son temps: colloque international, 14–19 mai 1979* (Paris: Les Belles Lettres, 1981), pp. 175–95.

La Théologie d'Abélard (Paris: Éditions du Cerf, 1997).

Jolivet, Jean and Henri Habrias (eds.) *Pierre Abélard: Colloque International de Nantes* (Rennes: Presses universitaires de Rennes, 2003).

Kant, Immanuel. *Critique of Pure Reason*, trans. N. Kemp Smith (New York: St. Martin's Press, 1929).

Kaplan, David. "Reading 'On Denoting' on its Centenary," *Mind* 114.456 (2005): 934–1003.

Kay, Sarah. *Courtly Contradictions: The Emergence of the Literary Object in the Twelfth Century* (Stanford, Calif.: Stanford University Press, 2001).

"Legible Skins: Animals and the Ethics of Medieval Reading," *Postmedieval* 2.1 (2011): 13–32.

The Place of Thought: The Complexity of One in Late Medieval French Didactic Poetry (Philadelphia: University of Pennsylvania Press, 2007).

The Romance of the Rose (London: Grant and Cutler, 1995).

Subjectivity in Troubadour Poetry (Cambridge: Cambridge University Press, 1990).

Kay, Sarah, Terence Cave, and Malcolm Bowie. *A Short History of French Literature* (Oxford: Oxford University Press, 2003).

Keller, Hildegard Elisabeth. "Making Sense of Invisibility in Courtly Epic and Legal Ritual," in S. G. Nichols, A. Kablitz, and A. Calhoun (eds.), *Rethinking the Medieval Senses: Heritage, Fascinations, Frames* (Baltimore, Md.: The Johns Hopkins University Press, 2008), pp. 218–62.

Kerbrat-Orecchioni, Catherine. *L'énonciation* (Paris: Armand Colin, 2009).

King, Peter. "Anselm's Philosophy of Language," in Brian Davies and Brian Leftow (eds.), *The Cambridge Companion to Anselm of Canterbury* (Cambridge: Cambridge University Press, 2004), pp. 84–110.

"Metaphysics," in Jeffrey E. Brower and Kevin Guilfoy (eds.), *The Cambridge Companion to Abelard* (Cambridge: Cambridge University Press, 2004), pp. 65–125.

Kinoshita, Sharon and Peggy McCracken. *Marie de France: A Critical Companion* (Cambridge: D. S. Brewer, 2012).

Kluge, Eike-Henner W. "Roscelin and the Medieval Problem of Universals," *Journal of the History of Philosophy* 14 (1976): 405–14.

Kong, Katherine. *Lettering the Self in Medieval and Early Modern France* (Cambridge: D. S. Brewer, 2010).

Konstan, David. *Friendship in the Classical World* (Cambridge: Cambridge University Press, 1997).

Koyré, Alexandre. *L'idée de Dieu dans la philosophie de St. Anselme* (Paris: Ernest Leroux, 1923).

Kretzmann, N., A. Kenny and J. Pinborg (eds.) *The Cambridge History of Late Medieval Philosophy* (Cambridge: Cambridge University Press, 1982).

Kripke, Saul. *Naming and Necessity*, 2nd edn. (Malden, Mass.: Blackwell, 1981).
"Outline of a Theory of Truth," *Journal of Philosophy* 72.19 (6 November 1975): 690–716.

Kurke, Leslie. *Aesopic Conversations: Popular Tradition, Cultural Dialogues, and the Invention of Greek Prose* (Princeton, NJ: Princeton University Press, 2011).

Lamarque, Peter. *The Philosophy of Literature* (Oxford: Blackwell, 2009).

Landes, Richard Allen. *Relics, Apocalypse, and the Deceits of History: Ademar of Chabannes, 989–1034* (Cambridge, Mass.: Harvard University Press, 1995).

Langlois, Ernest. *Origines et sources du* Roman de la Rose (Paris: E. Thorin, 1891).

Lavers, Chris. *The Natural History of Unicorns* (New York: HarperCollins, 2009).

Lear, Jonathan. *Aristotle: The Desire to Understand* (Cambridge: Cambridge University Press, 1988).

Leclercq, Jean. *La Femme et les femmes dans l'œuvre de Saint Bernard* (Paris: Téqui, 1982).

Léonas, Alexis. *L'aube des traducteurs: De l'hébreu au grec: traducteurs et lecteurs de la Bible des Septante (IIIᵉ s. av. J.-C.–IVᵉ s. apr. J.-C.)* (Paris: Éditions du Cerf, 2007).

Libera, Alain de. *La Philosophie médiévale*, 2nd edn. (Paris: Presses universitaires de France, 1995 [1993]).
La Querelle des universaux: De Platon à la fin du moyen âge (Paris: Seuil, 1996).

Logan, Ian. *Reading Anselm's* Proslogion*: The History of Anselm's Argument and its Significance Today* (Farnham: Ashgate, 2009).

Long, A. A. (ed.), *The Cambridge Companion to Early Greek Philosophy* (Cambridge: Cambridge University Press, 1999).
"The Scope of Early Philosophy," in A. A. Long (ed.), *The Cambridge Companion to Early Greek Philosophy* (Cambridge: Cambridge University Press, 1999), pp. 1–21.

Luscombe, David. "St Anselm and Abelard," *Anselm Studies* 1 (1983): 207–29.

Lynch, John Patrick. *Aristotle's School: A Study of a Greek Educational Institution* (Berkeley: University of California Press, 1972).

McCabe, Mary M. *Plato and his Predecessors: The Dramatisation of Reason* (Cambridge: Cambridge University Press, 2000).

McCord Adams, Marilyn. "Anselm on Faith and Reason," in Brian Davies and Brian Leftow (eds.), *The Cambridge Companion to Anselm of Canterbury* (Cambridge: Cambridge University Press: 2004), pp. 32–60.

McGrade, A. S. (ed.), *The Cambridge Companion to Medieval Philosophy* (Cambridge: Cambridge University Press, 2003).

McGuire, Brian Patrick. *Friendship and Community: The Monastic Experience 350–1250* (Kalamazoo, Mich.: Cistercian Publications Inc., 1988).

McKirahan, Richard D. *Philosophy before Socrates: An Introduction with Texts and Commentary* (Indianapolis, Ind.: Hackett, 1994).

Mann, Jill. "The Satiric Fiction of the *Ysengrimus,*" in Kenneth Varty (ed.), *Reynard the Fox: Social Engagement and Cultural Metamorphoses in the Beast Epic from the Middle Ages to the Present* (New York: Berghahn Books, 2000), pp. 1–15.

Mansfeld, Jaap. "Doxography of Ancient Philosophy," *The Stanford Encyclopedia of Philosophy* (2012 edn.), ed. Edward N. Zalta: http://plato.stanford.edu/archives/sum2012/entries/doxography-ancient/.

"Sources," in A. A. Long (ed.), *The Cambridge Companion to Early Greek Philosophy* (Cambridge: Cambridge University Press, 1999), pp. 26–8.

Studies in the Historiography of Greek Philosophy (Assen: Van Gorcum, 1990).

Mansion, Suzanne. "Le Rôle de l'exposé et de la critique des philosophies antérieures chez Aristote," *Études aristotéliciennes* (Louvain-la-Neuve: Éditions de l'Institut supérieur de philosophie, 1981), pp. 55–76.

Marenbon, John. "Anselm and the Early Medieval Aristotle," in *Aristotelian Logic, Platonism, and the Context of Early Medieval Philosophy in the West* (Aldershot: Ashgate, 2000), viii: pp. 1–19.

"Life, Milieu, and Intellectual Contexts," in Jeffrey E. Brower and Kevin Guilfoy (eds.), *The Cambridge Companion to Abelard* (Cambridge: Cambridge University Press, 2004), pp. 13–44.

The Philosophy of Peter Abelard (Cambridge: Cambridge University Press, 1997).

"The Platonisms of Peter Abelard," in *Aristotelian Logic, Platonism, and the Context of Early Medieval Philosophy in the West* (Aldershot: Ashgate, 2000), xii: 109–29.

Martin, Christopher. "Logic," in Jeffrey E. Brower and Kevin Guilfoy (eds.), *The Cambridge Companion to Abelard* (Cambridge: Cambridge University Press, 2004), pp. 158–99.

Megged, Matti. *The Animal that Never Was (In Search of the Unicorn)* (New York: Lumen Books, 1992).

Menn, Stephen. "Metaphysics: God and Being," in A. S. McGrade (ed.), *The Cambridge Companion to Medieval Philosophy* (Cambridge: Cambridge University Press, 2003), pp. 147–70.

Mews, Constant. "Nominalism and Theology before Abaelard: New Light on Roscelin of Compiègne," *Reason and Belief in the Age of Roscelin and Abelard* (Aldershot: Ashgate, 2002), 4–34.

"On Dating the Works of Peter Abelard," *Archives d'histoire doctrinale et littéraire du moyen âge* 52 (1985): 73–134.

"Peter Abelard's *Theologia Christiana* and *Theologia 'Scholarium'* Re-examined," *Recherches de théologie ancienne et médiévale* 52 (1985): 109–58.

"Philosophy and Theology 1100–1150: The Search for Harmony," *Reason and Belief in the Age of Roscelin and Abelard* (Aldershot: Ashgate, 2002), 159–203. Reprinted from Françoise Gasparri (ed.), *Le XIIe siècle: Mutations et renouveau en France dans la première moitié du XIIe siècle* (Paris: Le léopard d'or, 1994).

"St. Anselm and Roscelin: Some New Texts and their Implications," *Archives d'histoire doctrinale et littéraire du moyen âge* 58 (1991): 55–98.

Meyer-Bolzinger, Dominique. *La Méthode de Sherlock Holmes: De la clinique à la critique* (Paris: Campagne Première, 2012).

Mill, J. S. *System of Logic* (London: John W. Parker, 1843).

Minnis, Alastair. *Magister Amoris: The* Roman de la Rose *and Vernacular Hermeneutics* (Oxford: Oxford University Press, 2001).

Moonan, L. "Abelard's Use of the *Timaeus*," *Archives d'histoire doctrinale et littéraire du moyen âge* 56 (1989): 7–90.

Moreau, Joseph. *Pour ou contre l'insensé? Essai sur la preuve anselmienne* (Paris: Librairie philosophique J. Vrin, 1967).

Most, Glenn W. "The Poetics of Early Greek Philosophy," in A. A. Long (ed.), *The Cambridge Companion to Early Greek Philosophy* (Cambridge: Cambridge University Press, 1999), pp. 332–3.

Murat, Laure. *L'Homme qui se prenait pour Napoléon: pour une histoire politique de la folie* (Paris: Gallimard, 2011).

Murray, K. Sarah-Jane. *From Plato to Lancelot: A Preface to Chrétien de Troyes* (Syracuse, NY: Syracuse University Press, 2008).

Nagy, Gregory. *The Best of the Achaeans* (Baltimore, Md.: The Johns Hopkins University Press, 1979).

Neale, Stephen. "A Century Later," *Mind* 114.456 (October 2005): 809–71.

Newman, Martha G. "Foundation and Twelfth Century," in Mette Birkedal Bruun (ed.), *The Cambridge Companion to the Cistercian Order*, Cambridge Companions Online (Cambridge: Cambridge University Press, 2012), pp. 25–37.

Nichols, Stephen. "The Medieval 'Author': An Idea Whose Time Hadn't Come?," in Virginie Greene (ed.), *The Medieval Author in Medieval French Literature* (New York: Palgrave Macmillan, 2006), pp. 77–101.

Nouvet, Claire. *Abélard et Héloïse: La passion de la maîtrise* (Villeneuve d'Asq: Presses universitaires du Septentrion, 2009).

"Abélard ou l'hyperbole parricide," in Jean Jolivet et Henri Habrias (eds.), *Pierre Abélard: Colloque international de Nantes* (Rennes: Presses universitaires de Rennes, 2003), pp. 49–61.

Nykrog, Per. *Chrétien de Troyes: Romancier discutable* (Geneva: Droz, 1996).

d'Onofrio, Giulio. "Chi è l'Insipiens'? L'argomento di Anselmo e la dialettica dell'Alto Medioevo," *Archivio di Filosofia* 58 (1990): 95–109.

"La Dialectique anselmienne," in Coloman Viola and Frederick Van Fleteren (eds.), *Saint Anselm: A Thinker for Yesterday and Today*, Proceedings of the

International Anselm Conference, Paris, 2–4 July 1990 (Lewiston, Maine: Edwin Mellen Press, 2002), pp. 29–49.

Oppy, Graham. *Ontological Arguments and Beliefs in God* (Cambridge: Cambridge University Press, 1995).

Parsons, Terence. *Nonexistent Objects* (New Haven, Conn.: Yale University Press, 1980).

Pasnau, Robert. "Human Nature," in A. S. McGrade (ed.), *The Cambridge Companion to Medieval Philosophy* (Cambridge: Cambridge University Press, 2003), pp. 208–30.

Theories of Cognition in the Later Middle Ages (Cambridge: Cambridge University Press, 1997).

Pastoureau, Michel. *Les Armoiries: Typologie des sources du moyen âge occidental* 20 (Turnhout: Brepols, 1976).

Pastré, Jean-Marc. "Morals, Justice and Geopolitics in the *Reinhart Fuchs* of the Alsatian Heinrich der Glichezaere," in Kenneth Varty (ed.), *Reynard the Fox: Social Engagement and Cultural Metamorphoses in the Beast Epic from the Middle Ages to the Present* (New York: Berghahn Books, 2000), pp. 37–53.

Pautrat, Bernard. Preface and annexed texts, in Anselme de Cantorbéry, *Proslogion. Suivi de sa réfutation par Gaunilon et de la réponse d'Anselme*, trans. B. Pautrat (Paris: Flammarion, 1993), pp. 15–30, 111–44.

Picavet, François. *Roscelin, philosophe et théologien, d'après la légende et d'après l'histoire* (Paris: Imprimerie Nationale, 1896; repr. Paris: F. Alcan, 1911).

Poirion, Daniel. *Le Roman de la Rose* (Paris: Hatier, 1973).

Pradeau, Jean-François. "Introduction," in Héraclite, *Fragments (citations et témoignages)* (Paris: Flammarion, 2002).

Price, A. W. *Love and Friendship in Plato and Aristotle* (Oxford: Clarendon Press, 1989).

Putter, A. "Finding Time for Romance: Mediaeval Arthurian Literary History," *Medium Ævum* 63 (1994): 1–16.

Quine, W. V. O. "On What There Is," *Review of Metaphysics* 2.1 (1948); reprinted in Andrew B. Schoedinger (ed.), *The Problem of Universals* (London: Humanity Press, 1992), pp. 156–70.

Reilly, Diane J. "Bernard of Clairvaux and Christian Art," in Brian Patrick McGuire (ed.), *A Companion to Bernard of Clairvaux* (Boston, Mass.: Brill, 2011), pp. 279–304.

Rosier-Catach, Irène. *La Parole efficace: signe, rituel, sacré* (Paris: Seuil, 2004).

Ross, David. *Aristotle* (London: Routledge, 1995).

Rossitto, Cristina. "Opposizione e non contraddizione nella 'Metafisica' di Aristotele," in E. Berti, et al. (eds.), *La Contraddizione* (Rome: Città Nuova, 1977), pp. 43–69.

Routley, Richard. *Exploring Meinong's Jungle and Beyond: An Investigation of Noneism and the Theory of Items* (Canberra: Australian National University, 1980).

Russell, Bertrand. *Introduction to Mathematical Philosophy* (London: George Allen & Unwin, 1919).

"On Denoting," *Mind*, new series 14.4 (1905): 479–93.

Schaeffer, Jean-Marie. *Pourquoi la fiction?* (Paris: Seuil, 1999).

Schaper, J. L. W. "The Unicorn in the Messianic Imagery of the Greek Bible," *Journal of Theological Studies*, new series 45.1 (April 1994): 117–36.

Scheidegger, Jean. Le Roman de Renart *ou le texte de la dérision* (Geneva: Droz, 1989).

Schufreider, Gregory. *Confessions of a Rational Mystic* (West Lafayette, Ind.: Purdue University Press, 1994).

Searle, John R. *Speech Acts: An Essay in the Philosophy of Language* (Cambridge: Cambridge University Press, 1969).

Shepard, Odell. *The Lore of the Unicorn* (New York: Barnes & Noble, 1967).

Simpson, James R. *Animal Body, Literary Corpus: The Old French* Roman de Renart (Amsterdam: Rodopi, 1996).

Smith, Robin. "Logic," in J. Barnes (ed.), *The Cambridge Companion to Aristotle* (Cambridge: Cambridge University Press, 1995), p. 27.

Southern, R. W. *Saint Anselm: A Portrait in a Landscape* (Cambridge: Cambridge University Press, 1990).

Spade, Paul. *The Mediaeval Liar: A Catalogue of the* Insolubilia-*Literature* (Toronto: Pontifical Institute of Mediaeval Studies, 1975).

Spitzer, Leo. "The Prologue to the *Lais* of Marie de France and Medieval Poetics," *Modern Philology* 41 (1943): 96–102.

Stahuljak, Zrinka. "Adventures in Wonderland," in Zrinka Stahuljak, et al., *Thinking Through Chrétien de Troyes* (Cambridge: D. S. Brewer, 2011), pp. 75–109.

Bloodless Genealogies (Gainesville: University Press of Florida, 2005).

Stahuljak, Zrinka, Virginie Greene, Sarah Kay, Sharon Kinoshita, and Peggy McCracken. *Thinking Through Chrétien de Troyes* (Cambridge: D. S. Brewer, 2011).

Stakel, Susan. *False Roses: Structures of Duality and Deceit in Jean de Meun's* Roman de la Rose, Stanford French and Italian Studies 49 (Saratoga, Calif.: Anma Libri, 1991).

Steel, Karl. *How to Make a Human: Animals and Violence in the Middle Ages* (Columbus: The Ohio State University Press, 2011).

Stevenson, J. G. "Aristotle as Historian of Philosophy," *Journal of Hellenic Studies* 94 (1974): 138–43.

Stivale, Charles. "The Folds of Friendship: Derrida–Deleuze–Foucault," *Angelaki* 5.2 (2000): 3–15.

Strawson, P. F. "On Referring," *Mind* 59.235 (July 1950): 320–44.

Stump, Eleonore. *Dialectic and its Place in the Development of Medieval Logic* (Ithaca, NY: Cornell University Press, 1989).

Sweeney, Eileen. *Anselm of Canterbury and the Desire for the Word* (Washington, DC: Catholic University of America Press, 2012).

Logic, Theology, and Poetry in Boethius, Abelard, and Alan of Lille: Words in the Absence of Things (New York: Palgrave Macmillan, 2006).

Szittya, Penn R. *The Antifraternal Tradition in Medieval Literature* (Princeton, NJ: Princeton University Press, 1986).

Taylor, Kenneth. "Emptiness without Compromise: A Referentialist Semantic for Empty Names," in Anthony Everett and Thomas Hofweber (eds.), *Empty Names, Fictions, and the Puzzles of Non-Existence* (Stanford, Calif.: SCLI Publications, 2000), pp. 17–36.

Terry, Patricia. "Certainties of the Heart: The Poisoned Fruit Episode as a Unifying Example in *La Mort le Roi Artu*," *Romance Languages Annual* 1 (1990): 329–31.

Topsfield, L. T. *Chrétien de Troyes: A Study of the Arthurian Romances* (Cambridge: Cambridge University Press, 1981).

Tweedale, Martin. "Abailard and Non-Things," *Journal of the History of Philosophy* 5.4 (October 1967): 329–42.

"Abelard and the Culmination of the Old Logic," in N. Kretzmann, A. Kenny, and J. Pinborg (eds.), *The Cambridge History of Late Medieval Philosophy* (Cambridge: Cambridge University Press, 1982), pp. 143–57.

"Logic (i): From the Late Eleventh Century to the Time of Abelard," in Peter Dronke (ed.), *A History of Twelfth-Century Western Philosophy* (Cambridge: Cambridge University Press, 1988), pp. 196–226.

Uitti, Karl D. "Le Chevalier au Lion (Yvain)," in D. Kelly (ed.), *The Romances of Chrétien de Troyes: A Symposium* (Lexington, Ky.: French Forum, 1985), pp. 182–231.

Urbani Ulivi, Lucia. *La Psicologia di Abelardo e il "Tractatus de Intellectibus"* (Rome: Edizioni di Storia e Letteratura, 1976).

Vance, Eugene. *From Topic to Tale: Logic and Narrativity in the Middle Ages* (Minneapolis: University of Minnesota Press, 1987).

Vanni Rovighi, Sofia. "Intentionnel et universel chez Abélard," *Cahiers de la revue de théologie et de philosophie* 6 (1981): 21–30.

Varty, Kenneth (ed.), *Reynard the Fox: Social Engagement and Cultural Metamorphoses in the Beast Epic from the Middle Ages to the Present* (New York: Berghahn Books, 2000).

Vax, Louis. "Barbara, Celarent, Darii, Ferio, Baralipton," *Le Portique: Revue de philosophie et de sciences humaines* 7 (2001): 81–103.

Verger, Jacques. "De l'école d'Abélard aux premières universités," in Jean Jolivet and Henri Habrias (eds.), *Pierre Abélard: Colloque International de Nantes* (Rennes: Presses universitaires de Rennes, 2003), pp. 17–28.

Vitz, Evelyn Birge. "Inside/Outside: First Person Narrative in Guillaume de Lorris's *Roman de la Rose*," *Yale French Studies* 58 (1979): 148–64.

Wackers, Paul. "Medieval French and Dutch Renardian Epics: Between Literature and Society," in Kenneth Varty (ed.), *Reynard the Fox: Social Engagement and Cultural Metamorphoses in the Beast Epic from the Middle Ages to the Present* (New York: Berghahn Books, 2000), pp. 55–72.

Walter, Philippe. *Canicule* (Paris: Société d'édition d'enseignement supérieur, 1988).

Walters, Lori. "Appendix: Author Portrait and Textual Demarcation in Manuscripts of the *Romance of the Rose*," in Kevin Brownlee and Sylvia Huot (eds.), *Rethinking the* Romance of the Rose*: Text, Image, Reception* (Philadelphia: University of Pennsylvania Press, 1992), pp. 359–73.

Walton, Kenneth. *Mimesis as Make-Believe: On the Foundations of the Representational Arts* (Cambridge, Mass.: Harvard University Press, 1990).

Wesoly, Marian. "In margine al principio aristotelico di non contraddizione ed al problema della verità," *Eos: Commentarii Societatis Philologiae Polonorum* 70 (1982): 41–8.

Wetherbee, Winthrop. "Literary Works," in Jeffrey E. Brower and Kevin Guilfoy (eds.), *The Cambridge Companion to Abelard* (Cambridge: Cambridge University Press, 2004), pp. 45–64.

"The *Romance of the Rose* and Medieval Allegory," *European Writers* 1 (1983): 309–35.

Williams, Megan Hale. *The Monk and the Book: Jerome and the Making of Christian Scholarship* (Chicago: University of Chicago Press, 2006).

Woledge, Brian. *Commentaire sur Yvain*, 2 vols. (Geneva: Droz, 1988).

Woods, John. "Fictionality and the Logic of Relations," *Southern Journal of Philosophy* 7.1 (1969): 51–63.

The Logic of Fiction, Studies in Logic 23 (London: College Publications, 1974).

Zambon, Francesco. "*Figura bestialis:* Les fondements théoriques du bestiaire médiéval," in Gabriel Bianciotto and Michel Salvat (eds.), *Epopée animale, Fable, Fabliau: Actes du IVe Colloque de la Société Internationale Renardienne Evreux, 7–11 septembre 1981* (Paris: Presses universitaires de France, 1984), pp. 709–17.

Zink, Michel. *The Invention of Literary Subjectivity*, trans. David Sices (Baltimore, Md.: The Johns Hopkins University Press, 1999).

"Les *Razos* et l'idée de la poésie," in Rebecca Dixon and Finn E. Sinclair (eds.), *Poetry, Knowledge and Community in Late Medieval France* (Cambridge: D. S. Brewer, 2008), pp. 85–97.

La Subjectivité littéraire autour du siècle de Saint Louis (Paris: Presses universitaires de France, 1985).

Ziolkowski, Jan. "Cultures of Authority in the Long Twelfth Century," *Journal of English and Germanic Philology* 108.4 (2009): 421–48.

Talking Animals: Medieval Latin Beast Poetry 750–1150 (Philadelphia: University of Pennsylvania Press, 1993).

Zumthor, Paul. *Essai de poétique médiévale* (Paris: Presses universitaires de France, 1972).

Toward a medieval poetics, trans. Philip Bennett (Minneapolis: University of Minnesota Press, 1992).

Index

Abelard, 5, 8, 14, 16, 30, 39, 41, 52, 82, 86, 143, 144, 205, 211
  and Plato, 170
  Christian philosopher, 174, 179, 183
  cognitive theory, 31
  concept of status, 15, 17
  identification with Christ, 189
  imagination, 21
  logician, 8, 169
  mentions fictions, 18
  new Plato, 182
  ontology, 17, 20
  quarrel of the universals, 15, 30, 175, 180
  relation to literature, 17
  uncle, 168
Abelard, works
  De intellectibus, 14, 25, 31
  Dialectica, 166
  Glosses on Porphyry, 14, 18, 22, 25, 29, 166
  Historia calamitatum, 165, 166, 174, 183
  Logica, 166
  Sic et Non, 185, 206
  Theologia summi boni, 171, 173, 180
abstraction, 2, 5, 22, 24, 25, 29, 30, 31, 47, 51, 97, 119, 134, 139, 209, 219
absurdity, 18, 53, 78, 92, 196
Academy. *See* Plato
accident, 21, 22, 25, 65, 71, 73, 74, 198
Achilles, 14, 94
acquaintance, 55, 59, 60, 68, 73, 74, 86, 106, 121, 143, 175
Adam, 78, 79, 80
Ademar de Chabannes, 44, 45, 46, 47, 50
adstraction, 5, 24, 25, 27, 28, 31, 36, 39, 40, 47, 51, 52, 65, 71, 72, 104, 119, 139, 140, 209, 217, 219
Aelred of Rievaulx, 9, 144, 193, 201, 202, 203, 204, 205, 211, 215
Aeneid. *See* Eneas
Aesop, 14, 42, 43, 44, 71
affect, 2, 8, 9, 51, 52, 143, 144, 162, 163, 165, 179, 190, 193, 194, 201, 203, 209, 211, 212, 215, 218

Alcibiades, 149
Alcmaeon, 147
allegory, 7, 106, 118, 125, 135, 136, 137, 140, 169, 170, 171, 172, 206, 209
Allen, Renée, 213
ambiguity, 34, 49, 81, 96, 97, 113, 114, 121, 125, 137, 141, 201
ambivalence, 3, 6, 8, 9, 96, 97, 104, 111, 123, 125, 131, 141, 158, 162, 163, 179, 190, 191, 193, 211, 217, 218
Ambrose, 69, 185
Amphisbeton, 6, 7, 8, 89, 94, 95, 96, 97, 99, 100, 108, 109, 111, 112, 115, 118, 122, 123, 124, 125, 131, 135, 175, 179, 190, 218
Anacreon, 99
analytic philosophy, 2, 30, 51, 143
Anaxagoras, 95, 96, 97, 154
Anaximander, 153
Anaximenes of Miletus, 152
ancestor, 31, 85, 148, 149, 150, 152, 156, 166
Andreas Capellanus, 127
animal, 5, 22, 41, 217
  ancient treatises on, 6, 63, 64
  and humans, 40, 50, 74, 215
  as sign, 80
  character, 5, 14, 20, 30, 51, 76
  creation of, 78, 79, 80
  domestic, 39, 79
  genus, 35, 37
  horned, 64, 65
  human domination over, 37, 52, 80
  hunting, 70
  imaginary species, 6, 60, 61, 65
  in bestiary, 59, 61
  in exegesis, 68, 70
  in heraldry, 25
  in *Physiologus*, 69, 71
  individualized, 19, 41, 52
  irrational, 20
  literate, 36
  metaphor, 66

knowledge, 3, 55, 86, 101, 104, 108, 110, 133, 134, 146, 155, 157, 160, 169, 173, 191, 195, 218
Koyré, Alexandre, 108
Kripke, Saul, 5, 48, 51, 54, 59, 67, 72, 83, 119, 120, 139
Kurke, Leslie, 43

Lactantius, 185
Lady of the Fountain, 210
Lanfranc, 34, 106, 176
language, 17, 24, 40, 54, 57, 59, 82, 83, 89, 104, 132, 133, 180, 185, 189, 191
  and the Trinity, 186
  divine power of, 97
  formalized logical, 28
  imperfect tool, 97
  limit of, 124
  natural, 34, 57, 58, 59
Lear, Jonathan, 90, 91, 162, 163
Liar, 7, 45, 119, 135
liar paradox, 118, 119, 120, 121, 122, 218
Libera, Alain de, 15, 16, 31, 34, 185
lie, 122, 125
likeness, 127, 196, 197
lineage, 19, 46, 105, 106, 191, 192, 200, 213
lion, 5, 13, 20, 23, 24, 25, 26, 27, 28, 29, 44, 45, 46, 47, 48, 49, 50, 52, 61, 63, 64, 65, 71, 72, 215, 222, 225, 226, 261, 262, 266, 268, 273
literacy, 36, 38, 42, 69
literary criticism, 2, 3, 4, 67
literature, 3, 9, 14, 17, 18, 42, 76, 132, 219
logic, 89, 104, 106, 116, 173, 207, 209, 218
  and affect, 2, 143
  and fiction, 31, 82, 99, 190, 219
  and language, 190
  and literature, 3
  and mathematics, 55
  and mystic, 105
  and narrative, 1
  and philosophy, 174
  and the unconscious, 102
  applied to theological issues, 185
  corpus or canon, 16, 169
  definition, 2
  dominates clerical culture, 30
  foundation of, 6
  has no ontological implication, 33
  history of, 169
  love of, 1, 173
  medieval, 28
  modern, 28
  natural work of rational mind, 107
  revival of, 3, 31, 33, 106
  Socrates and, 159
  transmission of, 106

logicians, 1, 52, 59, 72, 82, 83, 168, 169, 171, 186
logos, 56, 97, 98, 102, 103, 146, 173, 174
Long, A. A., 158
love, 7, 131, 193, 194, 196, 206, 209, 218, 219
  as antithesis of reason, 128
  as folly, 126
  courtly, 128, 129, 132, 136, 209
  feudal and familial, 215
  of God, 202
  of one's enemies, 202
  sisterly, 214
Lover, 7, 118, 120, 140, 219
Lucan, 106
Lunete, 210, 215
Lyceum, 151, 157, 158

Macrobius, 172
madman, 6, 28, 90, 91, 95, 100, 101
madness, 26, 27, 97, 100, 125, 127, 131
Mahabharata, 70
Mansfeld, Jaap, 146, 157
Mansion, Suzanne, 151, 154
Marenbon, John, 165, 170, 181
Marie de France, 3, 5, 42, 43, 47, 51, 72, 82, 105, 133
masculine, 9, 49, 73, 196, 200, 204, 205, 216, 218
master, 8, 16, 24, 33, 34, 35, 40, 48, 51, 75, 81, 107, 123, 129, 133, 157, 158, 162, 163, 166, 167, 168, 169, 170, 174, 176, 179, 180, 187, 188, 189, 191, 198, 206
mathematics, 55
McCabe, Mary Margaret, 148, 149
McKirahan, Richard, 156
meaning, 5, 30, 46, 53, 66, 95, 99, 102, 103, 105, 124, 141
meditation, 31, 178, 218
Meinong, Alexius, 5, 54, 56, 57, 62, 68
melancholy, 166, 201, 217
Melissus, 147, 151, 153
Melusine, 84
memory, 31, 83, 106, 108, 143, 190, 200, 217
Mews, Constant, 186, 188
Mill, John Stuart, 54
mimesis, 6, 117
mind, 90, 98, 99, 102, 104, 107, 117, 128, 131, 139, 209, 219
modality, 117, 143
modernity, 191
monastic, 31, 106
monk, 31, 116, 123, 176, 177, 179, 188, 189, 193, 202, 203, 204
monokerōs, 64, 65, 66, 67, 69, 73
moral, 26, 30, 44, 46, 47, 50, 69, 75, 81, 95, 125, 194, 202
morality, 110, 184

possible, 60
real, 29, 82, 83, 90
things in the, 17, 21, 59, 98
wild, 28
writer, 1, 18, 129, 133, 150, 192, 207, 217

Xenophanes, 146, 148
Xenophon, 92

yale, 61
Ysengrimus, 76, 81
Ysengrin, 72, 76, 77, 81
Yvain, 27, 30, 50, 51, 65, 206

Zeno, 151, 152
Ziolkowski, Jan, 69, 76
zoocentrism, 52

CAMBRIDGE STUDIES IN MEDIEVAL LITERATURE